The
Most
Beautiful
Man in
Existence

# The Most Beautiful Man in Existence

*The Scandalous Life of*

*Alexander Lesassier*

## Lisa Rosner

PENN

*University of Pennsylvania Press*

*Philadelphia*

10 9 8 7 6 5 4 3 2 1

Published by

University of Pennsylvania Press

Philadelphia, Pennsylvania 19104-4011

Library of Congress Cataloging-in-Publication Data

Rosner, Lisa M.

   The most beautiful man in existence : the scandalous life of
Alexander Lesassier / Lisa Rosner.

     p.  cm.

   Includes bibliographical references (p.   ) and index.

   ISBN 0-8122-3486-3 (alk. paper)

   1. Hamilton, Alexander Lesassier, 1787–1839.  2. Physicians—Great
Britain—Biography.  3. Physicians—Scotland—Edinburgh—Biography.
4. Great Britain—Social life and customs—18th century.  5. Great
Britain—Social life and customs—19th century.  I. Title.

R489.H22R67  1999

610'.92—dc21

                                     98-48567

                                         CIP

Frontispiece: Sir William Allan, *Christmas Eve,* City of Aberdeen
Art Gallery and Museums Collections.

CONTENTS

List of Illustrations    *vii*

Preface: A Journal of Life    *ix*

1  Interest or Love    *1*

2  Born to Misfortune    *13*

3  Hot from Your Studies    *26*

4  This Despicable Rock    *40*

5  The Most Beautiful Man in Existence    *54*

6  Tinsel of Military Reputation    *72*

7  Soothing Hope of Speedy Promotion    *93*

8  Arrived at Wealth and Dignity    *108*

9  Thrown on the Wide World    *125*

10  Appearances Are of Essential Consequence    *141*

11  Consecutive Chain of Corroborative Evidence    *161*

12  Compare What I *Might* Have Been with What I *Am*    *180*

Epilogue: One Series of Hardships and Privations    *198*

A Note on Sources    *203*

Notes    *205*

Bibliography    *241*

Acknowledgments    *250*

Index    *251*

# ILLUSTRATIONS

Map of Portugal and Spain    74

*Illustrations follow page*    140

The title page of Alexander Lesassier's novel, published anonymously.

Alexander Hamilton.

James Hamilton.

Edinburgh medical school in 1815.

Isaac Cruikshank, *A Man Mid-Wife*, 1793.

Henry Heath, *Physic*, 1825.

George Cruikshank, *The Blue Devils*, 1823.

Engraving of the village doctor.

George Cruikshank, *The Examination of a Young Surgeon.*

Dress uniform of an officer in Lesassier's regiment, the 42nd Foot (the Black Watch).

The Serra d'Estrella mountain range in Portugal.

Depiction of the Battle of Salamanca.

Illustration from George James Guthrie's book on gunshot wounds.

Thomas Rowlandson, *Medical Dispatch, or Doctor Doubledose Killing Two Birds with One Stone.*

Illustrations from James Hamilton, *Collection of Engravings, Designed to Facilitate the Study of Midwifery,* 1798.

Fashionable new mothers in Edinburgh, ca. 1796.

Ladies and gentlemen of style promenading in Edinburgh.

Lesassier's "castle of a house" at 57 Northumberland Street.

Lady Louisa Kintore.

# A Journal of Life

I n 1833 Catherine Jane Hamilton, née Crokatt, returned from India to Edinburgh to seek a divorce from her husband, Alexander Lesassier Hamilton, M.D., then surgeon to the 41st Regiment. In Scotland a divorce could be obtained if the plaintiff could prove the defendant guilty of adultery, and it was the task of Catherine's solicitor, John Gibson, to obtain that proof. To assist Gibson, Catherine turned over to him a trunk containing her husband's personal papers, which he perused with close attention. Dr. Alexander Hamilton's agent tried in vain to retake possession of the trunk. Catherine won her suit, and then brought another action against her former husband, this time for aliment, or support, from the time she left him until the day the divorce was granted. Pending the outcome of this second legal action, the trunk was deposited in the library of the Royal College of Physicians of Edinburgh. Catherine won this suit, too, but took no steps to pick up the trunk. Alexander died in 1839 without ever returning from India. The trunk remained in the library of the Royal College, dutifully listed in its catalogue of manuscripts but otherwise untouched, until 1987, when the newly appointed archivist, Joy Pitman, was given the task of turning the mass of journals, rolled-up letters, and family papers into a properly catalogued collection. At that point the story of Alexander Lesassier (as I will refer to him for most of the book), which started in its most literal sense two hundred years earlier, was once again made available.

It is a remarkable story, told in fascinating detail: a passage from youth to maturity that is at the same time a window into the social history of Great Britain at the dawn of the modern era. It is not a conventional story of a Great Doctor, although some great doctors turn up in its pages; nor is it a unified narrative about early promise, continued industry, eventual success and perfect happiness in one's profession. Indeed, such a story would be anachronistic, for men of the early nineteenth century did not identify themselves wholly in terms of their occupations: confronted with the modern question "What do you do?" they would have been unable to give the modern brief answer. For Lesassier, the relevant question was not "What do you do?" but "Who are you?" He found his answers in novels, in his own sexuality, in social relations, and in warfare, as well as in his career of medicine. His journals, so carefully preserved in his trunk, were his great aids in this endeavor, and his process of self-construction, to use a modern literary term, continued throughout his life and was never entirely completed. "It is a work of very great labour and difficulty," as James Boswell noted, "to keep a journal of life, occupied in various pursuits, mingled with concomitant speculations and reflections," and we can see this work as the great unifying effort of Lesassier's life.

The result is a richly detailed portrait of Lesassier's life and times, that much more engrossing because it deals with so many matters long considered vital to the shaping of the modern world. Lesassier was born in 1787 in Scotland, at a time crucial to the formation of the distinctive national identity of Great Britain. It is significant that his first professional engagement was as assistant surgeon in the Peninsular War, for the Napoleonic Wars were themselves important in forging modern British identity. So, too, was the ever expanding British presence in India and Afghanistan, and the First Afghan War, during which Lesassier died in 1839, is one of many markers of the growth of British colonial power. In following his life, therefore, we are also tracing Great Britain's path to the British Empire, and if Lesassier's path takes us through Portugal and Edinburgh, so too did a nation's evolution.

There are other paths we can follow through history. Historians have debated the influences at work in the professionalization of medicine—the role of hospitals, medical schools, professional journals, and national licensing—as well as the way that professionalization has, in turn, influenced the conditions of medical education and practice. These discussions have usually assumed, rather than investigated, the personal characteristics of the practitioners involved. Whether professionalization is said to have started at the beginning of the eighteenth century or the end of the nineteenth—even whether the practitioners involved are male or female—all medical people are presented as "desirous of improvements in medicine," to borrow a phrase from a London medical student, all ready to adopt the medical persona as the distinctive stamp of their identity, all possessing both the ability and inclination to take proper advantage of the newly formed hospitals, medical schools, journals, and licenses. And yet if we take seriously, as we must, the idea that institutional structures lead to professionalization, we must also take seriously the idea that without those structures, professionalization cannot take place, or can take place only partially, or by fits and starts. As Alexander Lesassier's story reveals, a medical persona was not easily acquired; only some of the vast number of traits a young man might have could be molded to accommodate it; and the recalcitrance of the human personality to fit that mold must be factored into all subsequent histories of medical professionalization.

So too must the pervasiveness of romantic expression. Lesassier was not interested in the Romantic writers properly so called; there is no mention in his journals of Byron, Keats, or Shelley. He was, however, intensely interested in novels spanning the period from Fielding through Austen to Scott, and he actually wrote and published a romantic novel, *Edward Neville*. A penchant for reading oneself into romances, whether in books or on stage, has been traditionally ascribed to female readers and writers, but many men, too, longed to enliven the circumstances of their lives and turned to novels as naturally as we might turn to television. They also turned to the consumer culture that came to the forefront of social life after the Industrial Revolution. Historians have sometimes assumed that the proliferating shop windows and, later in the century, department stores, were aimed at women, but Lesassier's diaries remind us that men, too, could be enthusiastic consumers of the new material culture.

Yet if the story of Alexander Lesassier can be an illuminating guide to so many areas of human life, it can also be an exasperating tribute to the fact that historical actors are often completely unaware of what historians have labeled the main developments of their age, even those that affect them most directly. Historical biography is a dialogue between the life of its subject and his or her times. The generation to which Lesassier belonged came of age in the eighteenth century and had to adjust to the changing expectations in the nineteenth. Professional identity, nascent in 1780, was firmly established by 1840; the sexual mores of *Tom Jones* were under attack from the early Victorians; and though self-construction might take a lifetime it could not adapt, chameleon-like, to every change in social color. The first five chapters of this book trace the formation of Lesassier's character and prospects as a young gentleman on his way to making his fortune. The next three tell the story of his years as an army surgeon in the Peninsular War, where both his medical training and his personal characteristics contributed to his professional success. But success in one endeavor does not guarantee it in the next. The last four chapters in the book explore Lesassier's often rocky transition to civilian life. Marked by financial impropriety, racked with scandal, his years in private practice in Britain were also filled with the self-reflection that too often attends misfortune. For that reason, we may allow Lesassier the last word in his dialogue with his times.

History is also a dialogue between historian and documents. In the case of Lesassier's journals the dialogue necessarily becomes more vociferous than usual, as the historian is moved to correct, protest, and sometimes expostulate with Lesassier's own view of events. Although he was often an accurate reporter, his interpretations were frequently unreliable, since his own self-centered perspective colored all his judgments. The few times he succeeded in presenting an almost impartial judgment on himself, the tone of the journal is markedly different, as though some other, more perspicacious Lesassier were speaking. This discrepancy between Lesassier's experiences and perceptions occurs even when he is discussing events in his own life, an area where, if anywhere, his authority might be granted: when he bemoans misfortune, the reader is aware of modest success in Lesassier's life, and where he envisions triumph the reader holds her breath at the inevitable disaster. "That is good advice! Follow it!" she wants to write in the margins, or, falling into Lesassier's own idiom, "What inexecrable folly!" in response to some of his worse ideas. This dialogue has prevented the book from being what it first intended, a sober academic monograph on medical education and professionalization, with Lesassier's journals culled for good quotes and telling anecdotes. Instead, the dialogue has become the reason for the story, as I have delved deeper and deeper into Lesassier's world to find out the reason for a construction of a self that seemed so natural to Lesassier, but seems so profoundly, obviously wrong-headed to the modern world.

It must be admitted that the portrait of Lesassier presented in his journals and depicted in the following pages is not always pleasant. He was not an incompetent doctor, but neither was he an admirable one; he was in many respects a bad husband and irresponsible colleague; and though his personal and professional sins were quickly and thoroughly punished we may be as slow as his contemporaries to pardon them. But his faults are as revealing as his virtues, for both are indicative both of his times and his own life, and in any case a diary is unlikely to present a completely attractive picture, as Boswell's own diaries make clear. Young people of Lesassier's generation were taught to keep diaries as a moral exercise—"let me have the genuine sentiments of your hearts," said one teacher to her pupils—but what they and their preceptors were to do when the genuine sentiments conflicted with the ideal was never stated. Perhaps it is enough that both Benjamin Franklin and Edmund Gibbon show remorse for their own "errata," in Franklin's phrase, once they have come to realize that they have acted badly, and Lesassier, too, was often very sorry for his own ill conduct. A modern novelist, Patrick O'Brian, has disclaimed the need to provide the reader with "wholly virtuous, ever-victorious or necessarily immortal heroes," and surely a historian can be permitted the same license.

# CHAPTER 1

## Interest or Love

In an unnamed town sometime in the 1790s, poor Mrs. Neville lay dying. Her husband had preceded her to the grave by some months, leaving her destitute; six of her children had died long since. All that remained to her was her young son Edward, who, too young to understand his mother's condition and his own plight, begged her for a crust of bread, promising to share it with his faithful dog. Her devoted servant, Nelly, was by her side, and so was the equally loyal friend of her late husband, Mr. Melburne: to them she imparted the highlights of her family history, which went on for some pages and cost her last breath. She was a daughter of a noble and wealthy family who had cast her off when she married a mere army officer. Her husband, incensed at their treatment, had gone to quite incredible lengths to prevent them from tracing her, even getting her to promise never to tell her son of his connections, or any member of her family about her son. But her husband was now dead, and her poor child about to become an orphan; like Mrs. Blifil in *Tom Jones*, she had to confide Edward's true origins to someone who could assist him in the future. Yet though convention insisted that she demonstrate the strength of her maternal concern, it also dictated that her concern be thwarted, for if the hero was restored to his rightful position in society at once, he would undergo none of the trials and tribulations that made up the plot. Henry Fielding supplied the concern with the device of a deathbed confession, and the subterfuge that circumvented it with a letter purloined by the novel's villain. In the world of Edward Neville, though, the real villain was always Fate itself, and so in his case it is bad fortune that deprives the hero of his mother's last message. " 'Nelly!' she called, 'give me a little water—How faint—& breathless—this has made me—The—name—would—have—been—better,—but he—would—not—'. . . She feebly tried to swallow one other mouthful; but, in vain did she attempt to force the regurgitating fluid down . . . then, muttering low, she faintly moved her pallid lips, & sunk, for ever, down—outstretched in death."

We can blame this scene from the novel *Edward Neville* on *Tom Jones*. The two books are not comparable in literary quality, but novels like *Tom Jones*, *Pamela*, and *Clarissa* showed eighteenth-century readers that the lives of ordinary people could be fit subjects for a book, and inspired ordinary men and women to record the minutiae of their own lives in novelized form. In preparing to write *Edward Neville; or, The Memoirs of*

*an Orphan*, the author, Alexander Lesassier Hamilton, adhered to the ideal of a novel drawn from its author's life, sketching copious notes and plans, a table of fictional characters and their counterparts in real life, a chronology of historical incidents correlated with the ages of the hero and heroine, as though he were writing a research project rather than a piece of fiction. He had an abundance of first-hand material, for he had been writing the story of his life ever since he began a journal at the age of sixteen. Indeed, he had sources previous to that: his own memories, letters from his father, his parents' marriage certificates, a page from his mother's Bible.

And so even in the fictional Mrs. Neville's deathbed scene there is a kernel of hard fact. In Rochdale, in 1790, Christina Smith Hamilton Lesassier lay dying. She had been, if not cast out by her family, at least not rewarded for her choice of husband, and it is not unreasonable to think that her thoughts turned to the future of her young son, Alexander. Here, however, fact becomes more interesting than fiction, for instead of dying without revealing Alexander's family connections, she had carefully written the names and birth dates of her entire family in her Bible, including the particulars of her marriage three years before. The birth of her only child, Alexander, "September 12 1787 Afternoon 3.oclock," is the last event recorded in her own hand. It was left to someone else to complete the family record with the note "Christina Smith Le Sassier spouse of Peter Le Sassier, M:D: & mother of Alexander Le Sassier died in the town of Rochdale Lancashire on the 9th of Jan 1790 in the 20th year of her age, three months, & 20 days."

Christina's relatives were not noble, but their names were worth writing down, for she came from a distinguished medical family in the preeminently medical city of Edinburgh. She was born on 20 September 1769, the second child and eldest daughter of Alexander and Catherine Reid Hamilton. Her father was the founder of the family's medical fortunes, "toiling, for years, among the lower classes, without receiving any thing," but eventually building up an extensive practice. His membership in the College of Surgeons gave him access to the lucrative monopoly on surgery held by the College. His marriage to Catherine Reid, daughter of a prosperous merchant, advanced both his fortune and his interest, and in 1780 he was appointed Professor of Midwifery in the University of Edinburgh. Midwifery was a recent addition to the university curriculum, and the male midwife, like Dr. Slop in *Tristram Shandy*, was still a figure of derision in some circles, but Alexander Hamilton, blunt and energetic, author of the well-regarded *Treatise on Midwifery*, did much to make it respectable. By the 1790s he had become the most sought-after obstetrician in Edinburgh and the father of ten children.

It was a good family for a medical man, and so it must have appeared to Pierre Lesassier when he arrived at Edinburgh University to take courses in 1782. He was born in 1756 in St.-Crespin-aux-Bois, France, to Marie Anne Caucher and Pierre LeSassier, a surgeon. Toward the end of his life he would claim to be the illegitimate son of the Count de Rochepaliere, an officer of the Gardes de Corps, in which his putative father served as assistant surgeon during the Seven Years War. But Alexander later noted sadly, "My father's inexplicable mystery on the subject of his early life . . . renders it utterly vain to expect I should ever be able to arrive at a consistent, or even a credible, conclusion," and we must conclude that the story of noble paternity was as much a fiction as Mrs. Neville's death, with a similar kernel of fact: Pierre was born one month after his parents' marriage. He spent his early childhood with his maternal grandparents. His father returned to set up practice in Paris in 1762, and Pierre joined him, but "there was a coolness between my father and mother," Pierre later wrote, and she remained with her parents. Pierre himself received an excellent preliminary education, studying anatomy with Sabatier, botany with Jussieu, chemistry with Fourcroy, and natural history with Daubenton, all of them leading lights of the profession. He could have stayed in France and become one himself, or so he later claimed, but he found he "was perfectly disgusted with Paris and could foresee that there something was rotten in the kingdom of France (not in Danemark)." His travels were unusually extensive: between 1777 and 1780 he went to the Netherlands, then through France to Germany and Pavia, then to England, Ireland, and Wales, then to London, and back to France, to Strasbourg. From 1780 to 1782 he studied anatomy at Trinity College, Dublin; from 1782 to 1784 he studied in Edinburgh; in 1785 he returned to France to study surgery in Paris, and in 1786 he returned once again to Edinburgh. This is not quite the usual pattern of the medical Grand Tour. Pierre's travels have, indeed, an aimless quality about them, suggesting that Pierre was seeking not merely "medical improvement," to use the contemporary phrase, but rather a promising place to set up practice. Judging from his itinerary, he had in mind a flourishing university town, with opportunities for study and pleasure, and a good supply of paying patients.

But a good location was not enough by itself. As Jane Austen's contemporaries would have hastened to assert, a beginning medical practitioner without money or family must be in want of a wife. Pierre's own philosophy was "by all means to marry as soon as circumstances would permit—But not to chuse a wife entirely for either interest or love." As he later told his son, "Let there be affection . . . but there must also be either money or connections." Pierre Lesassier, thirty years old when he arrived in Edinburgh, may have felt he had found all three in Christina Hamilton, nearly seventeen in the summer of 1786. He might have met her when taking courses with her father two years before. He was one of dozens of students in Hamilton's lecture course seeking to acquire expertise in midwifery—an unrewarding branch of practice in itself, but useful in providing an entrée into more lucrative family practice. After completing the first course, though, Pierre went on to become a private pupil, "by which he had frequent opportunities," Alexander Hamilton wrote, "of witnessing along with me a great variety of extraordinary cases, & of performing delivery in many difficult & dangerous labors under my inspection, both in the Public Hospital & in private practice, which he did with the greatest success." Perhaps Alexander Hamilton invited his promising new pupil to dinner, where Pierre met Christina; or maybe Pierre took walks with her to Arthur's Seat or through the town, or called on her in the summer of 1786 when he returned from studying surgery in Paris to set up practice on his own.

We can only guess at Christina's side of the courtship, for we have no documents from her beyond her leaf from the Bible and her signature on the marriage certificate.

Her son, Alexander, had no memories of her and apparently never discussed her with his grandmother or aunts: his capsule description of Mrs. Neville, "Every thing that can render woman amiable," is a tribute to his mother's memory but not a delineation of her character. She was almost seventeen when she was married, a susceptible age; perhaps she simply fell in love with the handsome Frenchman, a newcomer to her family circle. But the young woman who recorded names and dates so carefully may have had more on her mind than romance. At the time of her marriage Christina had four sisters and three brothers, all but one younger than herself; another brother was born three months later, and still another after her death. As the oldest daughter, Christina would have been her mother's chief assistant in her many pregnancies. Perhaps when she went for walks during the long summer evenings in 1786, her oldest sister only twelve and her mother pregnant again, she thought more and more frequently of the advantages of starting her own household. And who knew how many more opportunities she would have? Professors' unmarried daughters could be found in every assembly in Edinburgh, in part because so much money was spent on their brothers' education that little remained for dowries. Christina's sisters had merely the very moderate sums of £1,200 for their portions, and besides her, only Isabella, the beauty of the family, would ever marry; the others remained at home with their mother.

Whether motivated by true love, or interest, or some combination of the two, Pierre and Christina were married in the fall. In *Edward Neville*, the hero's mother, "the eldest daughter of a titled family . . . runs away with [his] father," and the author's own mother did run away with his father to the nearby village of Musselburgh, where they were married on 1 September 1786. In Scotland, such marriages required neither parental consent nor a minister to be legally binding, and the border town of Gretna Green became notorious as the favored destination for eloping couples from England: "I am going to Gretna Green," wrote Lydia Bennet happily and unrepentantly when she ran away with Wickham in Austen's *Pride and Prejudice*. Mrs. Neville, like Lydia, did not repent her rash action, but unlike her "is never forgiven; & no communication maintained between her & any branch of her family." We don't know whether Christina Hamilton Lesassier repented, but she certainly must have been pardoned by her parents, for she and Pierre went through a second, more respectable ceremony in the Hamiltons' church, the New Episcopal Chapel in Edinburgh, on 11 October 1786. Christina herself seems to have regarded the second marriage in her family's church as the real one: it is the one she recorded in her Bible.

But Alexander and Catherine Hamilton must have disliked the match, or there would have been no need for the first marriage in Musselburgh. They may have had personal objections to Pierre. Handsome, perhaps charming, skillful, and well educated, he was also a foreigner with no money of his own, extravagant in his ideas, undisciplined, and in later life, at least, too fond of drink. They certainly would have had professional objections to him. A successful medical practice was a valuable piece of property, to be bought, sold, and passed on to their children. Like real property, a medical practice was seldom divided, but rather passed on to only one son, either the oldest or the most skillful. Other sons, even if educated as doctors, were established in practice elsewhere or joined the army or the East India Company. Unlike real property, medical practices were fragile things, requiring time and effort to build and maintain. It might take years to develop a practice capable of sustaining a gentlemanly style of life, and it might be ruined in an instant through no fault of the practitioner: by his premature death, by unlooked-for scandal, by the intrusion of a successful rival. Alexander Hamilton had brought up his eldest son, James, as his chosen successor; as capable as his father and far more polished, James's "natural & acquired abilities" were "astonishingly great—his suavity of manners unparalleled." But a later letter from Alexander indicates that his health "had for sometime before [the wedding] been precarious," and his next-oldest brother was only ten years old. If James were to die, there would be no one to sustain the practice and support the family in case of Alexander's own death. Perhaps James's illness had played a role in Pierre's wooing of Christina; Pierre may have counted on becoming heir apparent to the professorship; and Christina, too, may have dreamed of being a professor's wife. Maybe even Alexander had considered the possibility when he made Pierre his private pupil and later his son-in-law.

James Hamilton "entirely recovered his health," and if Pierre had been seen as a logical successor, all at once he went from being a useful insurance policy to an unwanted rival. He was determined to practice midwifery in Edinburgh, and had "the word Accoucheur"—a more genteel term than male midwife—engraved on the door. He also taught women midwifery, in direct competition with the Hamiltons' own midwifery course for women. The Hamiltons responded, Pierre later wrote, by tormenting Christina to prevail on him to settle elsewhere. "Their view was selfish and narrow, in the extreame, to give it no worse name," he said, "as there was room enough for the family practice." But the family practice, according to his new family, belonged first to Alexander and then to James Hamilton, "the idol of his aged father, the darling of his mother, and the hope of a large family and connections," and they were not disposed to yield. In May 1787, his wife pregnant, Pierre applied for admission to the Royal College of Surgeons of Edinburgh. Fellows of the College had a traditional monopoly over the practice of surgery within the old medieval boundaries of Edinburgh, and were among the most influential group of medical men in the city. As son-in-law of a fellow, Lesassier could have gained admittance for a reduced fee; among other privileges, this would have allowed him to give public lectures, becoming an even more direct competitor to the Hamiltons. The College refused his petition, stating that "it was objected, that as the petitioner is a Foreigner, and no evidence is produced of his being naturalized, he cannot be taken upon trials." The minutes do not say who, precisely, objected, but Alexander Hamilton was one of the College's officers. With this failed attempt, Pierre acquiesced. "A sacrifice must be made by somebody, for the peace of the whole family," he said, and he agreed to leave Edinburgh soon thereafter. Christina stayed behind, living in lodgings but almost certainly supported by her parents. Their son, Alexander, was born on 12 September 1787.

Pierre never forgave the Hamiltons for forcing him to leave a town where he felt certain he would have developed an extensive practice. "If I had married in any other family," he later told his son, "nobody in the world could have prevailed on me to leave . . . indeed nobody would ever have thought of it." Nor, it seems, did he ever thank them for their assistance. He claimed that moving to England had been his own idea— "I took a prompt resolution, and instantly the mail coach for York"—and that he, like Edward Neville's father, had fought his way through the world without any help from his wife's haughty family. But this is not true, for having won the main point, the Hamiltons were perfectly happy to help their daughter, son-in-law, and new grandson resettle in the prosperous town of Rochdale, near Manchester. A medical degree would be advantageous for Pierre, and though Alexander Hamilton could not procure him one from Edinburgh—Pierre had not taken sufficient courses to apply for graduation— he did arrange for Pierre to receive one from St. Andrews University, one of a number of eighteenth-century universities that awarded degrees based only on letters of reference from established practitioners and payment of a fee. The system was undoubtedly venal—the fees for medical degrees supported the university library—and when it was abolished in the 1820s only the most old-fashioned professors spoke up for it. But throughout the eighteenth century degrees from St. Andrews were viewed merely as another item to be disposed of by patronage, one within the province of medical professors and practitioners. In Pierre's case, Alexander Hamilton provided one of the letters of reference and his colleague Andrew Duncan, himself a St. Andrews graduate, supplied the other.

Duncan and the Hamiltons also provided Lesassier with letters of introduction to prominent practitioners near Rochdale. The Hamiltons' letter, in particular, is full of those smooth lies often found in letters of introduction when the truth would do the bearer no good. Pierre's reasons for moving—which had to be explained, of course, lest the recipient of the letter fear that it was due to Pierre's lack of skill—were put down to "the still contracted ideas of the people of this country, & the very great false delicacy with which the ladies of Scotland are, I had almost said, stigmatized." It was this delicacy, rather than the Hamiltons' successful corner on the obstetrical market, which prevented "any foreigner in finding his account in settling here." Lesassier's medical degree from St. Andrews is explained as a mere matter of expedience. "The people of Edinburgh," James Hamilton wrote, "even in cases which require medical assistance always, except at the last extremity, prefer surgeons to physicians"; for that reason, "Dr. Lesassier . . . did not choose to take a degree at this University, where his studies entitled him to it." It was with these letters, and with money advanced by Alexander Hamilton, that Pierre took his prompt resolution to go to Rochdale. Christina and Alexander joined him when Alexander was about a year old, in the fall of 1788. In January 1790 Christina was "seized with consumption" and died within a few days.

As a widower, Pierre could not be expected to care for his two-year-old son, who was sent back to Edinburgh to be looked after by his grandparents until he was old enough to go to school. As a young man, Alexander remembered almost nothing of this period beyond his great-aunt Campbell, "who behaved to me when a child, with infinite tenderness." James Hamilton called him "a sweet boy" in a letter sent with the young Alexander when he returned to his father at the age of five, a "dear little charge with whom we part very reluctantly." Alexander had lived for as long as he could remember in a big house with many servants, in an affectionate circle of grandparents, a great-aunt who could have been his own mother, and aunts and uncles young enough to be his brothers and sisters. Eighteenth-century novelists were not very interested in the sorrows of children forced to leave home—that had to wait for Charles Dickens and Charlotte Brontë—but Jane Austen, at least, spends a page or two with poor Fanny "crying on the attic stairs" in Mansfield Park, homesick for her family and beloved older brother. Yet what afflicted fictional children from Fanny Price to David Copperfield and beyond was their exile from the paradise of their real homes and parents to the horrors of schools or step-parents or orphanage or workhouse. Poor Alexander Lesassier at the age of five found that his real home and father lay outside the paradise of his early childhood and that he could never enter it again except as an occasional visitor. Perhaps Alexander, like Fanny, did his share of crying once back in his father's household, insisting that he wanted to go home, his tears only growing worse when it was explained to him that he *was* now home. He may have comforted himself with the thought that his father wasn't really his father, and that he had a different, much better home somewhere else. "How often I have sighed at the thought that nothing in this world could possibly confer on me the enviable privilege of noble blood; & yet, such, nevertheless, is actually my just & undoubted & inalienable right," he wrote many years later, an absurd conviction for a nonfictional adult but common enough among unhappy children in our day and perhaps in his as well. And in his own novel, the character of Mr. Melburne, based in large part on Pierre Lesassier, is only the hero's guardian, not his real father.

The home Alexander returned to at the age of five was very different from the big Edinburgh house he had left. We have no direct evidence of Lesassier's life at this time, but we can correlate, with caution, later comments from his journals with notes he wrote for *Edward Neville*, particularly a table listing each character and his or her real-life models. In the case of certain key figures, such as young Edward himself, Mr. Melburne, and Mr. Melburne's housekeeper, Dorothy, Lesassier wrote sketches, vivid and detailed, but lying outside the scope of the plot as it appeared in the manuscript and published versions. Those pertaining to the early life of the hero are written in the first person with no mention of Edward's, or any other, name. They are so heartfelt, so filled with precise description, that it is impossible not to see them, even if fictionalized, as containing a seed of Lesassier's own memories. There is certainly much within them that conforms to other, more reliable sources. And many later episodes in the novel can be documented to be based on a hard kernel of his own experience, as he perceived it.

These notes reveal no melodrama, nor do they suggest that Pierre Lesassier was a cruel stepfather or schoolmaster; indeed, he appears at least as fond of his son as convention required. But parents and children in even the wealthiest families often found, to put the matter bluntly, that they were competing for limited resources, for any money saved for the children was a check on present consumption. In the Lesassier household the resources were often very limited indeed. Pierre had moved to Manchester after his wife died, and though he was earning a living as a physician, it was not a genteel one. The elder Alexander and James Hamilton praised his "abilities and industrious attention to business" and his son his "professional zeal," but if we can make use of the portrait of Mr. Melburne, those fine qualities were unfortunately balanced by "irresolution and inconstancy of character." Building a practice required many years of hard work for little reward, and such perseverance was a challenge for Pierre. He also found it difficult to live within his means, and as for saving for the future, that was impossible. Pierre spent too much money on items he couldn't afford; from Lesassier's later journals, it is not hard to imagine him, like Mr. Melburne, spending "the best part of the money painfully collected for his rent, on a gold snuffbox." Indeed he frequently found himself perilously close to the border separating gentlemen from the lower classes. Despite his medical degree, he was not an elite practitioner: his patients and friends were not drawn from local gentry or manufacturing families but were instead local tradesmen, weavers, dyers, and joiners. Over time, Pierre's habits became less gentlemanly as well, and he grew "fond of smoking & getting tipsy." Anxious to be liked and reluctant to admit to insufficient funds, he stood surety for his friends' debts, once spending several days in Lancaster jail as a result. In *Edward Neville* the hero's father was ruined by a similar step, but George Eliot posed the economic dilemma of parenting more precisely when Caleb Garth in *Middlemarch* lost the money he had saved for his son's apprenticeship by guaranteeing his friend's loan.

Pierre Lesassier, then, lived in the world of genteel poverty, where money was always short and the great question was which shops would give credit; where fathers lost their fortunes, forcing sons to enlist as privates and daughters to go into service, "that uncertain, casual, precarious mode of existence," so feelingly described by William Hazlitt, "in which the temptation to spend remains after the means are exhausted, the want of money joined with the hope and possibility of getting it, the intermediate state of difficulty and suspense between the last guinea or shilling and the next that we may have the good luck to encounter." It was not a pleasant world in which to grow up. "I regret no past happy days," Alexander wrote after leaving home, "for I've had none."

The daily task of looking after the boy was left to Ann Collins, Pierre's housekeeper. Her fictional counterpart, Dorothy, is a dreadful woman, as vulgar and unpleasant as her author could make her: "Suspicious to excess, superstitious . . . ignorant & ridiculously illiterate, crafty, presumptuous, fond of tawdry finery—but meanly parsimonious—a consummate scold." Ann Collins was almost certainly Pierre's mistress, but the romantic novel of the 1820s did not allow such irregular relationships among its "good" characters. To preserve Mr. Melburne's respectability while remaining as true to life as he could, Alexander Lesassier had Dorothy trick her employer into marrying her, thus preserving his virtue though calling into question his sense. She dominates the first half of *Edward Neville*, much to the detriment of the plot and action, as Ann Collins must have dominated Alexander's early life. He was clearly jealous of her influence over his father, for the fictional Dorothy schemes to deprive her young charge of both his inheritance and his guardian's affection. He also resented having to obey a servant, and the sketches he wrote for his book include descriptions of the kind of mischief likely to aggravate a housekeeper: climbing on a patient's back to reach to the table to pilfer sugar, persuading "an old man to go with me to the pantry, & reach me down an apple pie," helping "children of a neighbour, in soaking up gravy of our roasting meat." Perhaps Ann Collins declared, like the fictional Dorothy, that she could not teach her charge anything, for he was sent to a school kept by a master in the next street. There he apparently "learned to read, it was true, & did not want for intelligence. . . . But, he was absolutely devoid of all application," and preferred to spend his time playing with his friends.

At the age of nine Alexander was enrolled in the Manchester Free School, which later acquired a great academic reputation, but which was chosen by Pierre, one suspects, primarily because it was free. If we can believe the notes from *Edward Neville*, Alexander continued to be devoid of all application and quickly became expert in avoiding his work. Scholars were required to translate Latin passages, but "what could be easier or more agreeable," he wrote, "than to be saved all the trouble of individual labor, by merely persuading another boy who was more diligent to teach you your lesson, or allow you to copy his exercise." There was no reason not to: students were never tested and were automatically promoted each year whether or not "their genius, application, & improvement deserved such a reward." In this way young Alexander moved up through the forms until he was twelve, making little progress in either Latin or Greek despite frequent flogging. "Idleness, & fighting, & pilfering alone, I acquire."

The childhood experiences revealed in the sketches resemble those of the most irascible of eighteenth-century heroes, Roderick Random and Perigrine Pickle, and Alexander's own character, too, was not unlike Roderick Random's. The "sweet boy" of James Hamilton's letter disappears once he arrived in Manchester, never to return: the sketches for the novel state, "I become sullen, capricious, obstinate, indolent, & liable to gusts of passion," and Alexander's own journals reveal similar traits. In *Roderick Random* a host of characters take it upon themselves to provide the hero with sage though unwanted advice, and in Alexander Lesassier's life that unenviable task fell to his uncle James Hamilton. "To a father any advice respecting the education of his son would be presumptuous," James Hamilton had written to Pierre Lesassier, "for every father must feel the necessity of instructing his son in the principles of religion, and the propriety of fitting him for social life by storing his mind with every useful branch of knowledge—and these are the two great objects of Instruction." But Pierre did nothing of the kind. The sketches portray a man who never went to church himself—"he always had urgent business, he said, or he was indisposed, or he durst not venture out in such weather, to afterwards sit in a cold Church with damp shoes"—but he "(absurdly) allows me," the sketches continue, "to attend indiscriminately, churches of all persuasions." Nor, apparently, did Pierre supervise Alexander's studies, for the hero's guardian follows the method "of utterly neglecting to personally see him go through his tasks." "I'm sure my father does not care a fig what becomes of me so that I never trouble him any more," Alexander later wrote bitterly in his journal, but it is only fair to Pierre to point out that educating Alexander would have proved an uphill battle for even a more conscientious father, for the sketches portray a young hero who could not "be prevailed upon to read, with attention, any work of instruction that would be likely to prove of the slightest ultimate advantage to him."

In October 1800, when Alexander was thirteen, Pierre decided to move to Paris, both with the hope of being able to live more cheaply and attract more patients, and to get away from Ann Collins, to whom he owed £140. She had him arrested while he and Alexander were in London on their way to France, and she was only mollified by Pierre's promise to pay her £63 immediately, take her with him to France, and pay her £10 per annum in future. Pierre did not prosper in Paris, either, and ten months later he returned to Manchester. Alexander never returned to school. His father arranged for him to have lessons in drawing and in foreign languages, but he was no more inclined to study, nor his father to insist, than before they had left, so that "in his french & italian, he was nearly as backward, as at his latin & greek."

At fourteen, Alexander was now a young gentleman, and his life improved the more . he was treated as one. He was taught to ride—as necessary a skill in his day as driving is in ours—and to fence by an emigré acquaintance of his father, once a member of Astley's Equestrian Circus. Though not especially accomplished in either, he took great pride in his skills, viewing them as essential evidence of his gentlemanly status in lieu of more material evidence—for Pierre's practice was as precarious as ever. He accompanied his father to the theater, entranced by operas like John O'Keefe's *Castle of Andalusia*, "all attention and amazement," like Edward Neville. As important as the play itself were the "splendid scenery, and gorgeous costume of the actors . . . [and] the blaze of fashion and beauty in the boxes." Alexander liked costumes, furnishings, and fashionable clothes; he was the perfect consumer in the fastest-growing consumer market in the world, or he would have been if only he had more money. "Lord!" he wrote when visiting London, the capital of that market, "If I had the treasures of Potosi"—the great silver mines of Peru—"I could spend them all in this amazing place. So much temptation on every side—such a profusion of everything that is valuable or useful that one is never wearied of gazing at the shops & admiring their contents. Besides which they are constantly putting you in mind of wants which otherwise would never have been called to mind." He liked beauty, too, in the form of young women, and pursued them in other public places besides the theater: in "gardens, race grounds & every place of amusement." He accompanied them to church, too, where his father's "absurd" permission took on a new, pleasing significance. "For a long time I frequent a Presbyterian meeting house," the sketches note with overwhelming circumstantial detail, "but Jane Berry is my reason. Then the Miss Rowbothams are my reasons for attending the Church of England; & in the Sunday evenings I would accompany my companions even to the Methodist Chapel to whisper & laugh with the Milliners Girls &c there."

But life was not a succession of Sundays; it was necessary to work in order to have a day of rest, and the older Alexander became, the greater the imperative that he prepare himself for some profession. This point was borne home when Professor Alexander Hamilton died in 1802. He left his grandson Alexander £200, held in trust for him by his uncle James with the stipulation that annual interest be paid until he was twenty-one. Pierre was left nothing beyond the stipulation that the "sums already advanced" to him were "not to be demanded from him," as long as he made no further claims on the estate. Perhaps Pierre had expected more for both himself and his son, for he had not saved any money to pay for Alexander's further education. This meant that the task of fitting him out for the world had somehow to be accomplished with the very limited sum of two hundred pounds. Edward Neville faced the same imperative as young Alexander, and the same dilemma, for he, too, had very limited means, and "In consequence of [his] disinclination, for every serious pursuit, Mr. Melburne felt completely uncertain what he should be able to make of him. . . . Although he could not bethink him . . . of any thing for which the fickle little gentleman seemed to be in the least adapted, still, as time was rapidly advancing, it was quite obvious that some decisive step ought to be taken without any further hesitation. After examining the subject in every possible light, it struck him, at last, that Edward might, perhaps, be induced to apply himself to Physic; though Mr Melburne greatly feared it would be too dry a study for his gay & thoughtless disposition."

To modern readers, used to the self-selecting rigors of premedical requirements and conditioned by over a century of biographies of physicians and scientists who demonstrated their passion for their subject at an early age, this sounds most peculiar: despite—or even because of—young Edward's or Alexander's "disinclination for every serious pursuit," his mentor felt he should become a physician. Complete lack of interest in any kind of study, let alone in science or medicine, would seem to us to be an obvious disqualification; it would have seemed so as well to the writers of medical-advice literature in Lesassier's own day, who cautioned against young men choosing to be physicians simply because "Dr. —— rides in a fine carriage, and receives a guinea for talking five minutes to a patient." A capacity for hard work and self-discipline had to override adolescent fancies: one of the most eminent medical men of the day, Sir James McGrigor, who was to figure prominently in Lesassier's life, might admit he chose to become an army surgeon in part because of the "splendid Highland uniform" of the 42nd Regiment, but that was after his professional zeal had been amply proven and rewarded. Above all a practitioner had to have "a love for his Profession" James Hamilton told Alexander, "without which he shall never shine in it."

This was sensible advice; but that did not keep it from being, in Alexander's case, simply irrelevant. For what, in fact, were his options? He had no money for the law, and positively no inclination for the church, the two professions that, with medicine, were the only acceptable ones for even a "fickle little gentleman"; apprenticing him to a trade, or a lawyer's clerk, or a merchant's counting house would have meant a lamentable loss of status, as well as, again, requiring more application than Alexander had ever shown. He was not a stupid boy, but in 1802 there were no obvious outlets for a young man of Lesassier's talents—an eye for detail and a facility for writing—any more than there had been thirty years earlier for an equally moody though more gifted adolescent, the poet Thomas Chatterton. Nor was it commonly accepted that earning money was supposed to be a means of self-expression, that how one earned one's bread should provide an outlet for individual abilities. One influential educator argued that young men should have no say in what they would become: the unlimited potential that modern educators like to see in modern teenagers all had to be channeled into the pathways appropriate to gender, rank, and fortune.

For some, then, medicine might be a calling, a vocation, a profession in the old meaning of public avowal of commitment, but for young men like Alexander Lesassier it was a business, selected because of personal contacts—in this case, his father and uncle—because of the comparatively low cost of medical education, and because of the youthful hope that it would "afterwards enable him" to live "in an elegant manner." The style of life that a physician could command was the focus of his ambitions, not heroic cures or scientific discoveries, still less the actual medical practice. If only he were to succeed, he wrote, "I would gradually furnish my house in an elegantly neat manner—The manservant . . . should be dressed well—I would have a compact surgery—A small library composed chiefly of reference books—I would pay all my debts . . . would purchase a handsome house. . . . Well then . . . I should want nothing in this sublunary world but an accomplished partner to share all my joys & griefs—A virtuous girl with an excellently cultivated mind & some beauty—would be the limits of my utmost wish—How I could look forward & see myself father of many children— These will shoot up in life, and succeed me who must sink into the silent tomb unincumbered with disease—& blessed by all who knew me." This was a mere daydream, he well knew, this "scene of uninterrupted success; but how all may vanish & like the baseless fabric of a vision leave not a wreck behind."

# CHAPTER 2

# Born to Misfortune

F rom this point in time our view of Alexander Lesassier shifts from distance to foreground, for he found a new friend, "One in whom we can confide our inmost thoughts, whilst we remain assured that they will never be revealed—One who is impartial and uninterested [he meant disinterested] and can listen to our anxieties & misfortunes and afford us consolation & in our perplexities direct us in that line of conduct the most eligible—One who may serve as a memorial of where we formerly have erred; by reviewing which, ourselves, or others may, in similar circumstances avoid those breakers on which we foundered." That friend was a journal, to whom he "trusted every thought" for the next thirty years. His journal was supposed to be completely private; indeed, he "commanded its secrecy." And yet his journals were, paradoxically, addressed to a public audience, the world, who would understand his description of incidents or of quarrels with his father for what they were: the early life of a young romantic hero. Commentators on romantic novels from Clara Reeve to the present have focused on young women readers, but no less an authority than Jane Austen informs us that young men, too, "read nearly as many as women": "I, myself," declared Henry Tilney in *Northanger Abbey*, "have read hundreds and hundreds." Young Edward Neville read the *Arabian Nights*, just like Lady Emily and Mary Douglas in Susan Ferrier's novel *Marriage*, and we may assume that novels formed a large portion of the books preferred by his author, "not always exactly those which would have been best adapted for his improvement." For novels, however engaging, were known to lead astray those young people thoughtless enough to mistake them for real life. A generation earlier, Samuel Johnson had warned that young men would not regard a novel's protagonist critically, as older readers did, but instead "fix their eyes upon him with closer attention, and hope, by observing his behavior and success, to regulate their own practice." "Where . . . in the name of wonder . . . did you pick up this unmeaning gibberish," Sir Edward asks his son in Austen's "Love and Friendship." "You have been studying Novels I suspect."

It was requisite to insert a description of the hero early in a novel, and since we have no portrait of young Alexander Lesassier himself we can borrow one of Edward Neville at about the same age: "His features, it is true, were not strictly regular; yet, his dark, expressive eyes, finely proportioned mouth, and beautiful teeth, together with his silky chestnut hair, and the ruddy tint of youth on his cheek,—heightened by every shade of emotion, that flitted across his susceptible and enthusiastic mind,—confirmed the pleasing impression, which his open and intelligent countenance had produced." He was inclined to prize his exquisite sensibility a little too highly, to pride himself on being "alive to impression from the winning efforts of kindness & affection, & enthusiastic in the gratitude & devoted attachment which they never failed to produce," while minimizing the "hasty impetuosity" that led to "his resentment of the remotest appearance of affront," and "aversions" to those around him "frequently almost without the shadow of a foundation"—aversions that, "once conceived . . . he never took any trouble to conceal."

With these traits, he was a hero better suited for a tragic ending than a happy one. "Some were certainly born for misfortune," a friend told him, and Lesassier was sure he was among them, that "the tricks of Fortune" might undo all his own efforts in an instant. His father's lack of success in the world seemed to prefigure his own, and heightened the ambivalent feelings perhaps natural to his age. Proud of his father's "aristocratic notions" and "manly figure and deportment," anxious to follow his advice, he was nonetheless led to "shed tears of pure vexation" at Pierre's weaknesses; as he got older and more critical, he shed tears of anger as well. "September 12th 1803 My birthday," began the first entry of his first notebook. "This day through the ill usage of my Father I resolved on leaving him: but am not yet certain what part of the world to move to." He was sixteen, and the question of what he was to make of himself could no longer be put off, but resources were as scarce as ever in the Lesassier household, and though he might dream of studying in Edinburgh, London, or Paris, debarring himself "of all pleasure but that of studying hard," he could do nothing without his father's consent and financial assistance. But "Such expense, such inconvenience," said Pierre during one of their quarrels, "to put myself to for an indolent Fellow, But like the Uncle of Gil Blas I'll give you a little money & never let me see your Face again," while Alexander, "almost choked with rage," retorted that "perhaps he would repent this," and went "upstairs to weep at the thought of such unnatural behavior from a father to an only son."

In a novel, he would have run off, or at least walked, to seek his fortune: Edward Neville, deprived of pecuniary support because of his guardian's scheming wife, set off on foot to join the army as a volunteer. In real life, however, the tension in the Lesassier household had to be resolved in a more mundane fashion: within two weeks of Alexander's birthday Pierre had arranged for his son's professional education by apprenticing him to Mr. Collier, "a Quaker and a respectable man," who practiced in Manchester as a surgeon and apothecary. The early nineteenth century was a great period of expansion in opportunities for medical education, and Great Britain was particularly blessed with excellent medical schools. Edinburgh was still the preeminent university-based center for medical education, "where every branch of science is regularly taught," and medical degrees conferred. In London, "the metropolis of the whole world for practical medicine," several hospitals had developed medical schools of their own, which, though they did not confer degrees, provided the same opportunities for study as many universities. The University of Glasgow had an up-and-coming medical school; Trinity College in Dublin was a well-known center for anatomy teaching; and of course, right across the channel were the incomparable opportunities of Paris hospitals and clinics.

And then there was apprenticeship, the most usual, the cheapest, and, according to enlightened medical opinion, the least useful form of medical education. Apprenticeship was supposed to teach a young man the rudiments of medicine, how to compound medicines, fold bandages, and the like; most important, it was supposed to introduce him to actual medical practice. After completing his indentures he would, presumably—for there was no test to guarantee his knowledge or skill—have learned enough to be able to set up in practice on his own. "Now on full conviction, I assert," wrote James Parkinson, an eminent London practitioner, "that of all the modes which could be devised for a medical and chirurgical education, this is the most absurd." "Apprentices," noted Andrew Duncan, Jr., professor at Edinburgh and son of the Andrew Duncan who had written so obliging a testimonial for Pierre Lesassier, "must spend a great deal more time on mere manual operations than is required for mastering them; . . . their leisure hours for study are cut up and frittered away by frequent calls for their occasional service; . . . and a single idle lad taints the whole shop." Young men would be better off studying Latin or Greek, or attending hospitals or lectures. If they must be apprenticed—for, medical writers conceded, not all young men could be trusted, at the age of sixteen, to benefit from more advanced forms of professional education—let them, at least, be apprenticed to a master who would "instruct them in the most perfect way," teaching them botany and pharmacy while they compounded medicines, anatomy and physiology while they folded bandages. We can imagine master and apprentice, hurrying from one patient to the next, employing their spare moments discoursing learnedly on the pathology and surgery of each case.

We expect advice literature to reflect the real world more closely than novels, for a novel can still give pleasure even if it strains credulity, while a guide to professional education that bore no relation to reality would have no use whatsoever. But advice literature is prescriptive, not descriptive; it can, like a novel, reflect the author's imaginary world rather than the world as it is; and of course it can have little impact if it is never read. There is no sign that Pierre, or Alexander or Collier, for that matter, made a point of consulting the extant literature when considering Alexander's future; enlightened medical opinion might have saved its breath as far as the Lesassier household was concerned. Pierre must have consulted James Hamilton, however, for Alexander's indenture was to last for five years and cost £100. Pierre had no such sum to spend on his son's education, and the money, therefore, had to come from Alexander's legacy. It amounted to half the money that he had been left by his grandfather, and he had no other money in the world. As Alexander's trustee, Hamilton had to give his consent, and it was to him as financial guarantor that the indentures were sent. Alexander himself was delighted to go to Collier's, "By which step I shall not only be out of my Father's reach but also save myself a world of trouble! for what would have become of me had I persisted [in his plans for leaving home] God only knows."

On 26 September 1803, young Lesassier, as we may now refer to him, moved into Collier's household, which consisted of Collier and his family, an older apprentice, Joseph Brown, and the servants. Apprentices ate with the family, and we may imagine Lesassier looking around attentively as he took his place at the table beside Brown, with whom he shared a room. It was not a scholarly household, nor was it a fashionable one; but Collier's "house which was furnished with every comfort" was a step up from Pierre's lodgings. Collier's own "figure was genteel & his manners those of the Gentleman." Lesassier did not pay much attention to Mrs. Collier, whose domestic duties sometimes included acting as peacemaker between her husband and his apprentices, but he may have noticed young Miss Collier, then thirteen; he certainly noticed Brown, "a very intelligent young man & . . . very independent in his opinions," who seemed to be in Collier's confidence. Lesassier and Brown became cronies, with the younger boy, perhaps, modeling himself on the older as they engaged in activities of the "boys-will-be-boys" variety: jointly pursuing a prostitute, "exquisitely formed . . . with a beautiful set of teeth," whom Lesassier succeeded in carrying off, and nearly burning down the house with the fireworks they kept in their room.

Collier was, in Lesassier's rather undiscerning view, "surrounded with practice," but it was mostly an apothecary's practice, and his apprentices' chief duties were to look after the shop, run errands, keep accounts, and take messages. Collier made little attempt to supervise his apprentices' professional studies, or to police their behavior in their free time, of which they seem to have had a surprisingly large amount: Collier may have needed Lesassier's £100 more than he needed assistance in the shop. He was "not strict at all," and Alexander, pleased to have so easygoing a master, "liked the situation extremely well." He liked it far less when Collier scolded him "over some mere trifling mistakes Brown and I made three days ago," for Lesassier resented criticism. The "harsh, though indirect," and entirely accurate assessment of Lady Caroline Grosvenor that Edward Neville's education had been sadly neglected led the young hero "most heartily to dislike her." Likewise, Lesassier's feelings about Collier changed: after what was undoubtedly a much harsher and more direct reproach, Collier went from "my respected Master" to "an infamous Rascal." Lesassier also resented the pecking order whereby he, as newcomer, had to do the more menial chores, including the "slavish task of carrying out all the medicines." Brown did not hesitate to pull rank as the senior apprentice, and "I wish he was gone with all my heart," Alexander wrote after six months at Collier's. "He is without doubt a most treacherous character. Interest seems to guide all his actions—His hastiness of temper renders him insupportable." He had his wish by the end of the year, as Brown left for further study at Edinburgh. Once the older boy had gone, Lesassier could take his place in Collier's affections: "I began to discover his character," he wrote, "& was as familiar with him as Brown had ever been." His position was enhanced by Collier's hiring "a little boy as an assistant" to carry the medicines and perform other chores. Now Lesassier had a subordinate of his own to whom he could delegate the more menial tasks—for his own experience of hierarchy did not lead him to behave any more democratically to those beneath him—"so that at present," having served one year of his indenture, he wrote, "I am very comfortable."

All his life Lesassier remained easily influenced by his immediate environment; he was ready to conform to expectations, if not always happy to do so. But expectations come in as many varieties as experience and can lead either toward or away from duty, or even towards or away from self-interest. The word *Influence*, according to the art historian Michael Baxandall, "is a curse . . . primarily because of its wrong-headed grammatical prejudice about who is the agent and who is the patient." If we make Lesassier the agent, rather than his environment, "the vocabulary," continues Baxandall, "is much richer and more attractively diversified: draw on, resort to, avail oneself of, appropriate from, have recourse to, adapt, misunderstand, refer to, pick up, take on, engage with, react to, quote, differentiate oneself from . . . everyone will be able to think of others." We may think of seventeen-year-old Alexander Lesassier picking his way among, drawing on, sometimes misunderstanding, the various acculturating ideas available in person or in print, ideas that shaped his own expectations and the expectations of those around him. This first step of his professional education was not marked with any inculcation of professional values: since Collier did not expect him to study, he made no attempt to do so; since he was allowed to spend a great deal of time with other young gentlemen, it was they, rather than his master, who shaped his behavior.

There was, of course, the expectation that he work hard and devote himself to Collier's "business with all the assiduity in my power." There were other, equally salutary expectations. He should not sleep with servants, or with any respectable woman, unless he intended to marry her. His affection, once given to a woman, should not be "a fickle one," nor should it be "so ardent as to consume itself," but instead be "a steady flame which I hope will last through life." He should learn from his friend Richard Jenoway, who had been unable to pursue a career in the law because of eye trouble but, instead of despairing, had purchased "a Lieutenant's Commission in the 3rd Lancashire militia," thus securing himself "an independency for life." "What perseverance he possesses," Lesassier wrote, "What difficulties he has overcome. I'll endeavor to imitate so great an example." He needed, more generally, to cultivate those virtues appropriate to the professional man, as Adam Smith so clearly described them: "The most perfect modesty and plainness, joined to as much negligence as is consistent with the respect due to the company . . . superior knowledge in his profession, and superior industry in the exercise of it. . . . Probity and prudence, generosity and frankness, must characterize his behavior upon all ordinary occasions."

But opposed to these were his own image of himself as a young gentleman, endowed with "natural pride, & chivalrous elevation of sentiment." Lesassier did not know any real noblemen; he imagined them—perhaps gleaning from his father's conversation, and from friends and novels—as people of privilege without responsibility, personified in Adam Smith's "young nobleman," whose "air, his manner, his deportment, all mark that elegant and graceful sense of his own superiority, which those who are born to inferior stations can hardly ever arrive at"; or in the novelist Susan Ferrier's Lord Lindore, whose "*nonchalance . . .* had nothing of rudeness in it, but seemed merely the result of high-bred ease." It was not an image that accorded well with his actual status as an apprentice, bound to serve his master faithfully in the old-fashioned legal form of the indenture, by work day and holiday. He compensated for this unaccountable lack of noblesse by spending as little time as possible thinking about his indentures, or his business. His duties were not particularly onerous, and we may suspect that he spent most of his time in Collier's shop, making up medicines when directed to do so for "the boy" to deliver, taking messages while Collier was out, but otherwise reading novels or forming "a scheme," like any young gentleman's, "of making a pedestrian tour through part of the French Netherlands . . . through France . . . part of Switzerland, Italy, and Spain" with his select friends.

He compensated as well by cultivating the trait he deemed most essential to a gentleman, independence—the trait that had attracted him to Brown, on whose behavior he perhaps began to model his own. "May independency of spirit ever meet with a proper reward," became his motto, and he attempted to live up to it during his first quarrel with his master. "Young men of open, generous dispositions," Henry Fielding told his readers, "are naturally inclined to gallantry"—sentiments which led Samuel Johnson to declare he scarcely knew "a more corrupt work"—and young Lesassier had an open, if not particularly generous disposition. He had probably read *Tom Jones*, and there is little doubt that he aspired to the hero's "obliging complacent behaviour to all women in general," manifested in his own case by going for a walk with Miss Collier. Collier demanded to know where his daughter had been; both she and Lesassier tried to lie about the incident; "Villain, seducer," Collier exclaimed, and ordered Lesassier out of the house. He left, but returned two days later, doing his work but refusing to beg his master's pardon and instead behaving "in as haughty a manner as possible." For nearly a month he dined in the kitchen, and for that month he and Collier barely spoke, but Mrs. Collier invited him to eat with the family again, and Collier "began by degrees," Lesassier said, "to soften his severity towards me." "This independent & spirited manner of acting, was & is of the utmost benefit to me," was his later analysis of the affair, but we might credit the intercession of Mrs. Collier and, perhaps, Collier's sense of humor, or at least proportion, for sharp-penned contemporaries were not slow to make fun of the assertion of independent spirit as a mark of high rank: in *Northanger Abbey* it is Miss Isabella Thorpe, trying to impress a high-born suitor, who claims, "My spirit you know, is pretty independent."

Lesassier thereafter stayed away from Miss Collier, whom he blamed for the incident, for Lesassier's conduct toward women was never distinguished by any "chivalrous elevation of sentiment" that we would recognize. Historians have noted the reform of men's manners effected by eighteenth-century ideas of civility and sensibility, but this should not obscure the fact that young men often behaved very badly indeed to young women, as Thomas Chatterton's response to a letter from an unknown girl makes clear.

The girl's letter begins: "I Send my Love to you and Tell you Thiss if you prove Constant I not miss but if you froun and Torn a way I Can make cart of batter Hay." Chatterton's response, entitled "The Letter Paraphras'd," begins, "My Loving Dear I send thee this / To tell thee that I want to piss / Pray let me speak the matter blunt / I want to stretch my narrow Cunt." He continues in a similar vein, which "To my ear and mind . . . speaks an implacably angry and outraged pride," wrote Chatterton's biographer E. H. W. Meyerstein. Lesassier was less obscene, but equally angry at Miss Collier. He had taken the walk, he wrote initially, "partly at her request" (later replacing the "partly" with "entirely"), and he was determined, he wrote with an injured air, to prevent "my master's daughter from taking any more liberties with me" by not speaking to her "any more than absolute necessity does require."

Lesassier disavowed all evil intent—"Every one that has heard of the business with his daughter thinks Collier was mad," he wrote—and we may believe him, for though his sexual activity flouted religious teachings it did not flout social convention. Young ladies—for so we may term a surgeon's daughter for now, though Lesassier later grew less democratic in his definition—were for romantic walks and perhaps the occasional chaste kiss. Other women—wives, widows, servants, "filles de joie"—were for other activities "unnecessary even to hint at." In fact, it did not take long for Lesassier to find a new "sweetheart," Ann Dean, one of the servants in the household and perhaps a reason why he was content to remain dining in the kitchen for so long. "Good heavens what risks I ran with her," he wrote, for if an apprentice "be imprudent enough to cohabit with his master's servant & he discover it he can oblige any such apprentice to board & lodge somewhere else at his own expense during the whole term of his apprenticeship," and "from a single heedless action," Lesassier wrote, "I might long repent." But "how could I resist the temptation. It was too powerful for anyone," for she was "ardently fond" of him, and "whenever I am certain that a girl is truly fond of me, I cannot resist fully returning her affection." Moreover, Ann Dean "possessed one of the most exquisitely delicate complexions I ever beheld & was in every point formed for voluptuousness." If only she had been "slenderer in her shape" he would have married her, he wrote later, but we should not believe him, for though she was the first servant to become his mistress she was far from the last. She was, however, the last that he referred to as "sweetheart": his definition for that word became less democratic as well.

After a year and a half at Collier's, he was "perfectly happy. . . . In fact I would not . . . change my situation with any young man in town." But we can see, underlying the journal, the seeds of conflict. There was no progression to apprenticeship: during his second year Lesassier did much the same sort of work that he had done during his first, and there was no mention of further study. All he had to look forward to were three more years of the same. The contrast must have been especially great after his best friend, Jenoway—whose own motto could be "May the honest heart ne'er know distress"—left town, and the young medical student Joseph Jordan became his closest companion. During the summer Jenoway had rented a one-room cottage, where the three young men "resorted in the morning & often in the evening—where sitting, watching the setting sun, we thought ourselves the happiest of mortals." The following January, Lesassier and Jordan proposed renting the cottage, which they called the summerhouse, for a new purpose, anatomical dissections, which "in Mr C.'s house was not only inconvenient, but also dangerous." This, the first mention of anatomical study in Lesassier's journal, is entirely in keeping with Jordan's interests, and so too was Lesassier's description of the one-room summerhouse as "a complete study for carrying on any experiment." For the first time Lesassier had a friend who was seriously interested in medicine, and this influence, too, had its effects.

Collier never liked the summerhouse, seeing it, rightly, as an attempt on Lesassier's part to remove himself from Collier's authority. "From the time Jordan & I took our garden," Lesassier wrote, "Collier was constantly suspicious & on the watch, lest I should convey provisions from his house to the garden." Jordan's first indenture had been to a practitioner much like Collier, and he had spent most of his time making pills and washing bottles. His mother, viewing this as a waste of time, found him a better master, who made him his assistant and allowed him to have unlimited access to the practice at the Manchester Infirmary. Perhaps Jordan expressed his opinion of his former indenture to Collier, for Collier—unable to predict that Joseph Jordan would grow up to be one of the most eminent of Manchester physicians and founder of the medical school—"took the first opportunity to quarrel with Mr. Jordan" and forbade him to come to the house "& thus I became deprived of my only companion."

No gentleman of spirit could refuse to bid "defiance to such slavery"; besides, Lesassier was enchanted with young Jordan, whose medical-student world of attending the infirmary to dress patients and going to classes but otherwise at liberty ("no fear of staying too long: no dread of an imperious master") seemed so far removed from his own. He "frequented the garden" all the more on account of Collier's prohibition: "One evening I . . . stayed out about 2 hours —Collier played the Devil with me—I retorted— & the shop was in an uproar. I demanded a separation." There was a fierce quarrel that unlike the previous ones was never resolved. "Thou'd better be cautious what thou are going to do Alexander," warned Collier, but "They best succeed who dare!!" wrote Lesassier. After uncertainty that lasted for the next few months—Would James Hamilton send Lesassier his indentures? Could Collier be compelled to repay part of the indenture fee? Could Lesassier keep it, rather than returning it to his uncle?—Lesassier decided to take the "bold decisive step" of leaving his master for good.

Breaking an indenture was a serious matter. A father's or guardian's consultation would have been useful, indeed essential, if Collier was to be taken to court, for Collier refused to refund any part of the money and Lesassier was too young to initiate any legal action. But Pierre had been arrested for debt; James Hamilton returned the indentures with only a "laconic letter"; and Lesassier was left to consult Jenoway, Jordan, and his own inclinations. He decided to simply leave: "The idea struck me that most surely my father would allow 5 shillings per week for keeping his books," he wrote, "That on this I could live & perhaps might borrow five guineas to go to the Infirmary with & so instead of spending nine months longer at Collier's I should be making rapid steps towards improvement." In order to make sure that nothing would interfere with this plan, "We considered that I had better leave Collier's before I told my Father lest he should refuse me his consent." With Jordan's help, he moved all his things from Collier's house to the summerhouse. "The seriousness of what I was about to do, together with our anxiety made me completely feverish," he wrote, "Going to leave an apprenticeship without anyone's consent without any visible means of subsistence." Fortunately, when he went to see his father and "informed him of what had happened He condoled with me & promised to allow me the five shillings per week which I required." With his father's consent and his uncle's tacit approval, Lesassier was free of his apprenticeship. "Nothing more seemed wanting to complete my joy," he wrote. He and Jordan moved into the summerhouse together. "At night we lighted an excellent fire, got some candles Ate bread and cheese & smoked our pipes—And here for the first times in our lives we could call ourselves masters None to oppose or to contradict our inclinations."

This arrangement lasted for about ten weeks. "The ardor I first had is not in the least abated," he wrote on 20 March, after two weeks.

> My father behaves very well, allowing me the five shillings regularly & taking the greatest pains to teach Mr. Jordan & me midwifery—My manner of living is well worth noting down. After Supper we uncoil a . . . bed which lies rolled up in a corner—Stretch it out on the floor & so make our bed In the morning about 6 we jump up & before putting any clothes on, we roll up the bed, cord it well & jam it into its corner—One of us then sweeps the carpet & places everything in its proper place—We then partly dress ourselves, clean our shoes, brush our clothes, wash & then finish dressing—We then study till ½ past 9 & go to breakfast—Mr. Jordan goes on home & I stop at a milk house & get 1d [1 pence] of Milk & 1d of bread—This constitutes my breakfast—I call on Mr. Jordan & we proceed to my Father's by 10 He lectures us till 11- I post his books, by the time I have finished, Mr. Jordan has dressed his patients at the Infirmary. We walk down to the garden on the road & buy a veal pie for 4d This I make my dinner of, the whole of the Afternoon we dedicate to Study—At 6 in the evening Mr. Jordan goes home to tea & returns at 7. We light a fire & bring the table with our papers near the fire. There we sit studying or examining each other till ½ past 9- I have generally a loaf & cheese or a black pudding, or a red herring & this with about a glass of mulled ale forms my supper—the bread &c costs me per night 3d—So that my day's expenses are 9d—There's economy—Now & then I get an invitation to dinner or tea So that I live.

It is a charming picture of two young industrious medical students: "Jordan on one side of the fire and I on the other, a table between us covered with books & pens & a blazing fire before us." Lesassier even managed to arrange to attend the Manchester Infirmary as pupil to a physician, Dr. Bardsley, "telling him that until a few months have passed," when he hoped to get some money back from Collier, "I could not give him the usual fee—he made no objections in the least & at 10 OClock I went to the Infirmary—Every advantage attends me." But the situation could not last. Pierre, erratic as ever, often refused to pay his son the promised five shillings per week; moreover, Lesassier complained, he "behaves to me & Mr. Jordan in the harshest manner—& I was informed by Miss [Ann] Collins that he had said I defrauded him of part of the money that I received for his accounts." In addition, Lesassier found "that absolutely I could not exist on 9d a day. I have got Miss Collins to let me dine at her house on credit," adding with a slightly defensive air, "Living in so very low a manner really prevented me from studying."

Lesassier also quarreled with Jordan: "How fickle are the Friendships of young men." Though Jordan and he had been close friends, their living together made them perhaps too close for comfort. Their breakup came in the course of a day's excursion. Lesassier took the arm of another friend while walking home; Jordan walked behind with his brother to make Lesassier jealous; each accused the other of neglect and "we ended," Lesassier wrote, "by mutually agreeing to part as soon as possible." The fact was, he noted in a reflective moment, "Both he & I were very proud & tenacious of our own opinions. Towards the close of our friendship we each suspected the other of great duplicity. Thence, many trifles were thought of in a serious manner." The result was, Lesassier wrote a month later, "We never take any more notice of each other when we meet than if we were utter strangers." This type of intense friendship, leading to an emotional break, was later to be condemned by Victorians who preferred a more "manly" reserve. But it was common among young men of Lesassier's day, along with weeping, sentimentality, dwelling on melancholic incidents, jealousy, and backbiting.

Lesassier and Jordan each moved back home, after more than a little haggling about the amount each owed for expenses of the summerhouse. The responses of their families may be considered to prefigure their future careers. Jordan continued his studies, and he later went on to attend lectures in London. Lesassier's father, in contrast, did nothing to provide his son with additional education. Instead, he believed that "the sooner a young man is established in practice the better," and encouraged his son to find a permanent situation. A position as apothecary to a dispensary in Stockport fell through; so did a position as assistant to a former friend, a country surgeon in Saddleworth. Finally, Pierre told Alexander that he had "a project by which I shall have it in my power to settle myself in the world": Alexander should settle in Rochdale and set up practice there, supplanting "an old gentleman, a Methodist preacher as well as MD, who is lately gone to Rochdale on account of the great need they are in of some medical practitioners." "The very town of all others that I esteem the most," wrote Lesassier in rapture, "So excellent an opportunity of settling for life—& what I so long have sighed after—With my father's approbation & assistance too . . ." How could he fail to succeed?

And yet it was perfectly foolish for Alexander to attempt to set himself up in practice; authors of medical-advice literature would have been aghast at an eighteen-year-old boy, whose education consisted merely of one and a half years of apprenticeship, pretending to be a medical practitioner. It should have been Pierre's task to advise him against it, but once again Pierre and Alexander were not getting along: though on 4 June Alexander wrote, "I am extremely comfortable & make no doubt but that I now may live with my father in a very happy manner." He wrote six days later, "Last night I was very much inclined to leave my Father entirely—His temper is so insupportable whenever he drinks more than necessary." Indeed, Pierre played his usual ambivalent part throughout the preparations for Alexander's new venture: telling him to make up a medicine chest without offering to pay for it, so that Alexander had to purchase all his supplies on credit; offering to introduce him to all his medical friends, but never actually accompanying him to Rochdale to do so; and promising to support him until he got into practice without specifying a precise amount. On 10 September 1805, four days after his eighteenth birthday and after a tremendous quarrel with his father, Alexander Lesassier set out for Rochdale.

Young Lesassier's behavior on arriving at the place he intended to set up practice would not have led writers of advice literature to reconsider their opinion. It was a commonplace that the gentry preferred their medical attendants to have the manners of gentlemen, and for that reason students were advised to cultivate "an easy obliging and attentive manner with a proper degree of skill" when setting up practice. Satirists claimed this manner was more important to the physician than education, skill, or experience, and Lesassier echoed this idea, so comforting in his present circumstances. "It was well known," he wrote, "the most shining abilities did not always ensure success—but frequently the reverse." Why should he not succeed, he wrote to reassure himself, "The town is large, populous, rich—My abilities are indifferently good—and I have the advantage of a father to direct my steps. Well then 'tis address I must think on—that grand point the influencer of the world's opinion." In Rochdale, he concentrated on social rather than professional skills to ingratiate himself with his preferred clients, the local gentry families. His father had told him, "Young medical practitioners do not show themselves enough. They ought . . . to frequent all places of public resort," and Alexander was punctilious in following advice that suited his own inclinations so well. He dressed as well as his limited means would allow, went to the Rochdale libraries to read the journals and be seen, went to church and lingered in the aisle so as to be invited to join the pew of "people of quality." He also took pains to meet the young ladies of the town, both for pleasure and in the hope that one would fall in love with him and rescue him from the need to practice. "We find," he wrote, "but few instances of a medical man gaining an affluent fortune unless he marry well—At Rochdale there are very many beautiful girls & with very fine fortunes too—& the best part is, that there are very few gentlemen. Besides they don't like marrying their own townsmen—I shall suit their inclination in that point to a hair but whether in other points also, must be seen."

Lesassier was right—a good marriage was the swiftest way for a medical man to secure a fortune—but his dreams of romance were a gender-reversed version of what a modern writer has called the Cinderella Complex and what we, considering his reading, might call the Aladdin Complex. He trusted his personal charms more than any of the sound advice from medical writers; he did not introduce himself to local practitioners or try to get an appointment at a local hospital or charity institution. Instead, he passed his time "as follows—About ½ past 7 in the morning I rise from bed—Breakfast by 9—Go to the Coffee Room & read the papers for half an hour Then walk about, to get myself known till 11- return home & study till dinner hour 1 o'clock—From 2 to 4 I study then walk or sleep till tea time ½ past 5—Walk from 7 till 8 o'clock & study &c till 11—Then once more to bed." How he would have loved "independancy," he wrote—of means, not just of spirit—"to attend all these assemblies to finish my education in dancing, music &c & to never want money or be obliged to toil hard for my living."

The result was that after a month he wrote, "I have had no patients yet—O Lord! O Lord!" Whatever satirists might say, the local gentry were not so gullible as to prefer manners above ability. Everywhere he went, Lesassier was asked about his education, and though Pierre had told him "that such questions were extremely impertinent & that any one who should make them would prove of little essential service to me," this was of no help dealing with them. One young gentleman, whom young Lesassier was extremely anxious to impress, "had heard I had taken my diploma as MD at Edinburgh—Here was a disappointment for him. Then followed questions of where I studied &c." Of course, any young practitioner who had received an extensive education would have been delighted to have the opportunity to discuss it, but "Zounds thought I what a devil of a hobble—Here damme I shall be found out—I must tell some cursed lies which probably may be discovered to be such. . . . If unfortunately I be detected I hope my manners & abilities will soften the blow. . . . It's scarcely to be imagined what questions I had to answer—what a strain of refined politeness to keep up—& how necessary to wear on my face a constant placid smile." We may suspect that it was not very convincing, even to Lesassier himself, for the slightest appearance of coolness on the part of his new acquaintance led him to fear that his lies had been found out. With no income from practice, and without his father's promised support—for Pierre was as reluctant as ever to make his promised payments—Lesassier found himself sitting in church and planning "to obtain a quantity of the *Laurus Cerassus* & give it to my druggist in Manchester & get him to distill it in the most careful manner & as strong as possible—Alleging that I wish to may some experiments on it—I shall then make trial of the effects of this most powerful poison on some animal. . . . Then I would defy all the tricks of fortune. . . . Indeed it is distracting to reflect that in the numberless ups & downs of life I have already had—no undertaking of importance ever succeeded with me."

He was rescued from this dire fate by his uncle. Lesassier had written to him to ask for an advance upon the interest due him from his inheritance, a total of £15 for the three years remaining until he reached twenty-one and could claim the total. Though James Hamilton sent £10, he was afraid, he wrote back, "that I was too deficient in point of medical knowledge to fill my present undertaking." James Hamilton's "anxiety had been greatly excited on hearing that several pregnant women had engaged me—not knowing that I had any acquaintance with midwifery." Actuated perhaps by concern for the family reputation as well as for Lesassier, he sent a friend, Mr. Hewit, to speak to Lesassier about his future plans. Would it not be best for Lesassier to go to Edinburgh to study for a year? asked Mr. Hewit. "Such a plan would fulfill my utmost wish," Lesassier replied, but he had no money. Had he not "expressed a wish to his Uncle to enter the Army" at one point? Yes, Lesassier said, "but that scheme like many others had failed from want of money—Well but returned he the Navy requires no capital—this I granted but explained that my motives for not entering the Navy were founded on the little profit to be gained and the poor plight ones character is in when one wishes to settle in the world." At that point the conversation ended, with Lesassier and James Hamilton, through Mr. Hewit, conveying their mutual regard. As a result of that conversation, James Hamilton sent a letter with a proposal: that Lesassier abandon practice in Rochdale at that time, and come to Edinburgh where James Hamilton would advance him the money from his inheritance to attend medical lectures. He even sent Lesassier ("Bravo! Bravissimo!") an additional £10. After only a brief consideration—"This piece of news does not overjoy me so much as it would have done at first," he wrote, "I have formed friends, am acquainted with the place & should very soon get in to practice"—Lesassier accepted wholeheartedly: "Oh but when I reflect on the advantages which will arise from it I am quite overjoyed I can finish my education completely—Oh dear it's delightful."

Lesassier once again packed up his belongings, "my library—pictures—clothes &c," and prepared to leave for Edinburgh. Among his belongings were some books and a desk purchased from Collier's auction, for Collier had sold everything and left town the year before. He was leaving, Lesassier heard, to go to Leyden and "there be dubbed Doctor—Oh vanity vanity how powerful thou art." But it was a major undertaking for him to leave a town where he had been in practice for twelve years. "Such events do not often take place thence they should be examined in a deliberate manner & So fulfill one grand object of a note book—that at a future period by reviewing these data & reflections on the follies of others I may be able to correct my own." The reason, he thought, was that Collier had formed a connection "with a woman who bore him several children though his legitimate wife and child were living—Here we may date the commencement of his misfortunes. . . . How evident it is where he failed with the same that has caused the ruins of many besides him—I mean improper connections with women." The thought stayed with him, and he returned to it again when he received a letter from Ann Dean after Collier's household broke up, a letter he tore up and never answered: "Young men should avoid connections with women, as they would destruction."

# CHAPTER 3

# Hot from Your Studies

On 3 November 1805, Alexander Lesassier set out on the two-day journey to "Edinburgh my native place" for medical improvement, sitting up with the coachman to catch his first view of the city, the moon shining "with a most vivid splendor" and "the entrance to town . . . beautiful just like going through a garden." His arrival was a kind of homecoming. He was greeted warmly by his uncle, who "ran forwards & got hold of my hand—& said he was very happy to see me." His grandmother "ran to me & embraced me repeatedly & wept very much"; his three aunts, Jean, Margaret, and Isabella—the latter only five years older than he—"embraced me in turns." He also met his great-aunt Campbell ("the lady who behaved to me when a child, with infinite tenderness—She received me with open arms & appears overwhelmed with joy") and her children, his half cousins Mary and Archibald. We can only guess how Mr. Hewit had described Lesassier to his uncle—a pleasant, well-spoken lad, perhaps, who needed further instruction and a steadying influence, and would derive benefit from both. Now that he had met his nephew, James Hamilton invited him to live in his house as a member of the family, a proposal that "was so different from what I expected," Lesassier wrote, "that I was both amazed & delighted. . . . Besides the advantages which I should derive from living with him, of seeing a great deal of company, I should also avoid a great expense as lodgings in this town, I understand are very dear." Indeed they were: six months lodging in Edinburgh would easily have eaten up Lesassier's funds; moreover, James Hamilton may have felt that having him under his own roof would be a "great incentive to exertion, and a powerful preventive of idleness," of the sort recommended by medical reformers. His offer was, therefore, both practical and generous.

"Who could ever suppose that I should return to Edinburgh & see all those I have so often spoken about," Lesassier wrote, for whom it was a professional as well as a personal revelation: for the first time he saw how a successful medical man could live. The Hamiltons had done well to put their faith in James Hamilton, for the heir to the jealously guarded professorship and practice had prospered. At thirty-nine he was "a little man . . . with a neat brown wig like natural hair & his face was very expressive—but appeared old." He had become the sole professor of midwifery three years earlier, on his father's death, and was proud of the fact that he reworked and updated his lectures every year. He also directed the Edinburgh Lying-In Hospital—providing free deliveries for indigent women—as a teaching hospital for both male and female midwifery students. His quarrels with his professional colleagues were remarkable even in Edinburgh, where such quarrels were both frequent and public, but his patients adored him and he, like his father, was the most sought-after obstetrician in Edinburgh, "one of the liveliest men I was ever near," Lesassier noted, "never in an ill humor—and always in motion—like quicksilver never still—at the same time he is the Man of Science & the complete gentleman." Like his father, he had married a local merchant's daughter rather than a medical man's—"a fat plain looking woman with however a very open cheerful countenance . . . very agreeable and an excellent housewife," rather than a "fine dashing lady." He had four daughters and one son, Joseph, who was six at the time of Lesassier's visit. James Hamilton lived in a fine house on Nicolson Square, "a very beautiful one of white stone"; he had a country house, "a sweet retired spot about three quarters of a mile from Edinburgh," and owned additional property in the area; drove through the elegant streets of Edinburgh "in his carriage—which was a very pretty one"; and counted among his patients the Earl of Mar, giving his nephew "a great idea of my Uncle's professional connections."

Manchester, Pierre, Collier, even his own ideals of a gentleman gave way before such a shining example of professional success: Lesassier was happy to model himself anew on his uncle, "the sprightly agreeable companion the benevolent, sincere friend the finished gentleman." Lesassier, too, could be a sprightly agreeable companion when he was happy, "the merriest by far . . . of all the merry Grigs I ever knew," according to a later admirer; under his uncle's influence the indolent, indigent little gentleman became a model of cheerful studiousness and fiscal responsibility. He had to pay for lectures in advance, and though they cost only £18 James Hamilton "advanced me £25 unasked." Lesassier imagined it a kind of "trial of my steadiness," to see what he would do with the money, and therefore "I gave him a stamp-receipt, one day after dinner. . . . As he could consider it a mark of reflection." "Hoot man," said Hamilton, "there was no occasion for this—& he seemed much pleased." Unlike Collier, James Hamilton made it plain to Lesassier what he expected of him. "That I should not by any means stay out late with any of my friends but always be in to supper," and "I have made a rule," Lesassier wrote, perhaps thinking of his father as well as his uncle, "to never drink wine after dinner, or spirits after supper, & never to go out at night except on business & never to stay out to supper—so that if a steady & studious conduct will gain the esteem of my Uncle I surely must possess it."

Lesassier was assisted in this good resolution by the university courses themselves. Lesassier had never been a particularly studious boy, but the medical school at Edinburgh was organized to turn not particularly studious boys into scholars, at least for the time they were there. Edinburgh University had led the way in many of the innovations in medical education of the age: facilities such as an anatomical theater, a botanical garden, a chemical laboratory, a hospital for clinical lectures, opportunities for anatomical dissection, surgery, and midwifery. By 1805 William Cullen, Joseph Black, Alexander Monro secundus—the brightest academic stars of the previous age—had died, but younger, if dimmer luminaries,—Thomas Charles Hope, James Gregory—had taken their place, and in northern Britain, at least, Edinburgh remained "the first medical school in the empire."

What mattered as much as the courses in encouraging study was the structure of the medical school. Professors were expected to be masters of their subject, and to present a comprehensive view of it. Each course was offered at a separate hour, with a bell that rang to mark the end of one lecture and the beginning of the next. Most students found themselves following a strict schedule, with hours outside of lecture allocated to visiting patients in the Royal Infirmary, copying lectures, or doing additional reading. "This week has been spent very industriously indeed," Lesassier wrote soon after the term started. "On Tuesday last I began attending the Professors' lectures & have not had a moments leisure since—I rise in the morning at 8, finish breakfast, & get seated in Dr. Gregory's Class room by 9—from 10 to 11—I hear Dr. Hope on Chemistry—from 11 to 12—Dr. Barclay on Anatomy—Then from 12 till 1 I attend the Infirmary. From 1 till 2 the famous Dr. Monro [Alexander Monro tertius]—from 2 to 3 I go home & take a basin of soup—from 3 till 4 o'clock my uncle's lectures on Midwifery—then from 4 to 5 dinner from 5 till ½ past 6 studying & reviewing what I've heard during the day—Tea over by a little past 7 & I go to the Infirmary . . . quarter past 9 supper & to bed by ½ past 10." He was far from objecting, for study under these circumstances was very different from the tedium of grammar school. "I enjoy every comfort that I can wish for here," he wrote, "The fire in my room is always lighted by the time dinner is over & my table & a candle set ready—In the morning before I get up the Servant brushes my Coat & cleans my shoes—How is it possible to live in a more agreeable manner?" Leisure for study itself became a kind of luxury, for which the busy practitioner might sigh in vain, a point made indirectly to Lesassier by his uncle, who—in contrast to his father—"will not allow me to assist him in any shape whatever, requiring of me nothing but application to my studies." For the first time in his life Lesassier lived like a gentleman, dressing well, with money advanced by his uncle, going to church in a carriage, and writing his journals in a warm, well-furnished room. For the first time, too, he had a sense of purpose: the university environment worked its magic, and Lesassier found that "by constantly attending lectures during the day till 4 o'clock in the afternoon & then dining the time appears much shorter than it formerly did." And for the first time since he had planned to be a medical man he could look forward to professional success, which had formerly been "a mere dream-especially when I recalled to mind the numerous struggles which I had had with my hard fortune—ever since I left the Grammar School." And all this was owing to James Hamilton: "What can be more nobly generous than my uncle's behaviour towards me—Supporting me in his own family, & advancing money for my education—What should I have been but for his assistance! A mere ignorant country quack—& hereafter I can rank with the highest of them—Oh! delightful thought."

But could he? Alas for Lesassier, though he was more industrious he was no more knowledgeable about the structure of his chosen profession. Edinburgh students might crowd together into the anatomy theater or spend their days in rigorous schedules, but they did not all follow similar courses of study or have similar expectations for the future. Only the wealthiest could afford to pay the £500 or so necessary for three years of study leading to graduation; the majority attended, like Lesassier, for only one year, cramming in as much anatomy, chemistry, and pathology as they could. The former returned home to establish practices among the gentry who were their neighbors; the latter contented themselves with much more modest practices, "forming a smoky trio," Lesassier was later to write bitterly, in a country village "with the curate & the exciseman." In other words, Edinburgh students tended to return to the same income bracket from which they had come. Lesassier did not have the money to join the elite band of graduates; indeed, he did not fully realize that the graduates formed an elite, and though James Hamilton could have enlightened him on the subject he may have preferred not to bring it up at all.

For though there is no doubt that James Hamilton wanted to do right by his nephew, his view of doing right was strictly demarcated by birth and kinship. The terms of Alexander Hamilton's will enjoined him to act as tutor and curator to Alexander Lesassier, as well as to James Hamilton's own siblings; so did his own inclination. But he did so according to strict rules of precedence, in which brothers came before sisters and sons before sister's sons. His youngest brother, Henry Parr Hamilton, was an excellent scholar, educated fashionably and expensively at Cambridge University, and became a well-known mathematician. Even his brother John, with no obvious talent to match Henry's, was treated with great liberality. Sent out to India as a cadet in the East India Service, he "led a dissipated life . . . spent £500 and to crown the business, he quarreled with his superior officer—threw up his commission & returned home pennyless," whereupon James, "though greatly enraged," bought him an ensigncy in the 93d Regiment and sent him out again, no doubt with stern warnings about behaving himself in the future, warnings that may not have been without their dire effects. In contrast, he refused to help when his sister Isabella's husband faced a financial crisis, though "a sister, in distress," she said, "one might suppose, had claims, upon him which were imperious, yet he cruelly left me, to struggle, alone." "He ought not to have deserted me," she said, indignantly, but Isabella had her portion, James might have answered, and he could not support her family as well as his own.

He might have used similar arguments with his mother, still "very young looking" and "as active as her son," to persuade her to give up the fine house in Nicolson Square and move instead to a house in Stockbridge, then on the very outskirts of town. She was entitled by both her prenuptial contract and her husband's will to remain in the house until her death, but no doubt James pointed out to her the necessity for the professor and his household to remain close to the university and his patients; Catherine Reid Hamilton had become a kind of dowager professor, and the house in Stockbridge now became her dowager house. She may have acquiesced easily for the sake of her beloved James, but Isabella, at least, grumbled at "his unnatural conduct, to his own mother & sisters," which exiled them beyond the New Town to a far-from-fashionable part of the city. The money for Lesassier's education came from his legacy; he only had £100 left, and James Hamilton had neither the power nor wish to change the narrowness of his nephew's fortunes. What was within his power, what was, indeed, his obligation as both an uncle and the custodian of Lesassier's funds, was to help Lesassier spend his legacy to some purpose by applying it to his education instead of frittering it away on his ill-fated Rochdale venture. Men had acquired an independence with less, and there was every reason to hope that Lesassier could do the same. That men had also acquired a much greater fortune with more—that Hamilton himself owed his greater fortune in large part to his having started with much, much more—was beside the point.

Lesassier had as yet no inkling that he was being treated as a mere nephew, not a privileged son, as a collateral relation of less concern to the family than the main branch, and his gratitude for the "paternal conduct of my dear uncle" knew no bounds. "How generously how tenderly he had behaved to me," he wrote, "there is nothing—no absolutely nothing that I would not do for him—at the very expense of my existence. I could not say more." He was less satisfied with the generosity of his other relations. "My father said before I left Manchester," he wrote, "that I should be overpowered with presents— that I should have a gold watch immediately—but this alas! so far, is all fudge—My grandmother aunts &c can invite me to dinner once in a week & can caress me with compliments but the devil of any thing more do they give." He carefully noted the presents he did receive and—mercenary wretch, we might say—their value: from his aunt Isabella, "a Scotch Pebble" (these agates were highly prized by collectors of trinkets) "with the initials of my name on it—worth perhaps ten or twelve shillings!"; from his uncle John, briefly home after having disgraced himself in India, a "present of 12 views of India which he brought over with him & a flageolet. The engravings are at least worth five guineas!"; and, from his grandmother on New Year's Day, "the first present that I've received this year . . . on coming away she put a couple of guineas into my hand."

By the beginning of January Lesassier's exemplary studiousness was beginning to pall: "My life passes along in a most uniform manner," he wrote, and he had little to put in his notebook; even some misfortune would have been welcome. "May we not imagine," he wrote, "that misfortunes are sent us to obviate that dreadful sameness which must otherwise mark the whole tenour of our tedious lives. . . . This however is undeniable that every one enjoys an almost proportionate share of happiness—altogether depending on the acuteness of his feelings—happiness is imaginary—For if we are greatly afflicted at the ills of life so in turn we become greatly exhilarated at their reverse—Whilst others endowed with more apathy of mind though they meet misfortune with phlegmatic sullenness yet to counterbalance this felicity makes no impression on them." He would have agreed with the melancholic Henry Seymour in the novel *Death's a Friend*, who declares to his correspondent, "You condemn the impetuosity, the madness as you term it of my passions, and affections. I glory in it, and more than equally despise your cool, philosophic, calm indifference. I was born to feel every sensation in the most violent extreme; and tho' I suffer at this time, agonies, which your constitution keeps you exempt from, and ignorant of the force of, I would rather be their eternal victim, than be only capable of lukewarm emotions." Such sentiments had become cliché, and Lesassier could have acquired them from any of a dozen sources. It is tempting, though, to believe that he might have had *Death's a Friend* in mind, for the specific emotion that agitates Henry Seymour in the opening letter of the novel is caused by incest: he has fallen in love with a young lady who turns out to be the illegitimate daughter of his brother, and though they cannot be united he cannot suppress his guilty passion for her. In the winter of 1806 Lesassier found himself in a similar situation, for he had fallen in love with his Aunt Isabella.

Isabella was, from the first, Lesassier's special friend. "A fine lovely blonde" and "a romantic creature," he wrote on first meeting her. She gave him "the first present I have received from any of my relations" and, in a gesture of affection in keeping with Lesassier's concern for the value of his presents, said she would remember him in her will. "Egad!" he wrote, "I've need to be remembered in that way by some body or other," and it was all the better that it be from "the most lovely young lady I ever set my eyes on. . . . I could readily be up to my eyes in love with her only it would be rather out of the way to fall in love with one's aunt." Out of the way it may have been, but Isabella and her younger brother John already doted rather too strongly on each other. "I never before saw so much affection between a brother & his sister," Lesassier noted, though we cannot tell whether he considered what Herman Melville would call "the ambiguities" inherent in that affection, and Lesassier, two years younger than John, was said to "much resemble" him. "Poor fellow he has been unlucky too!" Lesassier wrote when they met, "though he is very giddy . . . yet he is possessed of an excellent heart." Perhaps Lesassier was aware that an incestuous passion in a novel demanded at least the attempted death of its unfortunate harborer, for when the unfortunate John later "blew his brains out . . . after a life of thoughtlessness & dissipation," Lesassier assumed that "It could have been no one but Isabella's lovely self who was the innocent cause of John's horrid suicide."

Lesassier saw Isabella every Saturday when he dined with his grandmother, and as the days grew longer, they took walks on Thursday evenings, occasionally conversing, "but oftener walking in silence responsively sighing," pressing each other's arms as closely as they dared. "Alas how blessed I should be with such a girl as she is—But heaven has ordained it otherwise!!" he wrote. "We must not attempt to combat with prejudice," Isabella said much later, "when . . . growing with one strength—and, which no arguments of ours, however powerful can overcome—it is a subject that must not be commented upon—I lament it but duty tells me to submit to its decrees." To mask the clandestine romance, Lesassier referred to her as "dear Laura" in his journals. The fact of their love being doomed gave it an added charm, for on one walk near the end of term, "the moon shone out with all its splendor," Lesassier wrote, "& rendered the scene doubly pleasant but very melancholy for I chanced to touch a tender key—& my poor Laura burst into tears & continued sobbing almost the whole way—I was reminding her that she would never again see me on a Saturday & walk in the evening as we have done so regularly for six months—the thought pierced her soul with anguish &

thus she paid a tender tribute to our unfortunate affection." Lesassier did not remain faithful to her, but his "ever Dear Laura"—his image of Isabella, perhaps, rather than Isabella herself—was never entirely dislodged from his heart. The same might be said for Isabella: she married Thomas Hodgeson of the East India Company within twelve months, but years later she still assured Lesassier "that there is no person, that holds, so strong a hold, on my affection as yourself. . . . Never, for one moment, doubt my constancy."

At the end of January, James Hamilton had a long discussion with Lesassier about his future. The "best plan," he said, was for Lesassier "to obtain a medical situation in the Army." He would have to first serve as hospital mate, "then be Assistant Surgeon and lastly Surgeon," and he was "pleased to say," Lesassier wrote proudly, "that he did not doubt in the least but that by my exertions & industry I should soon make rapid progress in the Army." Besides, James Hamilton promised, he would use his own influence, particularly with the Earl of Mar, to have Lesassier promoted to surgeon quickly. Lesassier was delighted with the idea, for "besides being a most respectable life," he wrote, "I should live famously, be always with gentlemen & in twenty years retire with a considerable half pay." A small consideration was Pierre's consent, but Lesassier was sure this would raise no difficulties, since, as Pierre put it in his letter a week later, "he agrees to any plan that my dear uncle may think fit to propose."

As the end of term grew near, James Hamilton started to mobilize his connections so that Lesassier would "have the place ready to pop into by May at which time the Classes finish." He wrote to his friend John Thomson, recently appointed Regius Professor of Military Surgery, "requesting Mr. T. would have the complaisance to employ his interest for a situation for me in the Army, as Dr. H. said he considered me fully qualified for it. There was a compliment." He also introduced Lesassier to George Bell, a prominent surgeon, who "had promised to procure me an Hospital mateship," and gave him a letter of introduction to Dr. Shapter, Inspector of Hospitals in Edinburgh. Dr. Shapter "was excessively polite," but told Lesassier "that I ought by all means to go instantly to London—because several young men had applied already to him—& the most likely way to obtain a situation speedily must be by being before hand with the young fellows from the Classes."

That meant leaving before classes ended, for once they were over "great numbers of young men will be flocking to London for situations." Indeed, it meant leaving immediately, for before obtaining a position Lesassier had to pass two examinations, and he only had four days to get to London in time for the first examination in May. He took an affecting farewell from his relatives, including Isabella, with whom he "went to the door . . . stopped—grasped her hand—looked once more at her lovely face—embraced her & hurried away," leaving a "pathetic" letter for her to read before she went to bed; meanwhile, James Hamilton attended to practical matters, procuring a formal certificate "of my having attended the Classes here" and handing Lesassier his indentures. James Hamilton took Lesassier to the mail coach at three in the afternoon of 27 April 1806. Lesassier "then thanked my Uncle though very abruptly for his kindness shook his hand," said goodbye to his cousin who had come to see him off, and set off in the mail coach for London. He reflected "how happily I had spent the last five months of my life—And that now I was about to leave all behind never perhaps to revisit my native town again—to ever see those I hold the dearest in the world—I also thought on the paternal conduct of my dear uncle . . . how generously how tenderly he had behaved to me—Alas! I can never repay him!" But his main concern was his immediate future, and in anticipation of his "approaching trials in London," he set off, like many a Scots lad before him, on the high road to London to seek his fortune.

Lesassier arrived in London at 5 A.M. on Wednesday, 30 April, "heartily tired . . . after travelling 400 miles without stopping." He immediately "went to bed being resolved to sleep until 9," and though exhausted from the trip he had too much on his mind to sleep well. The next few days, he knew, would determine his fate. Much lay beyond his control: whether he was appointed to a position in Britain, the Continent, the West Indies, or India, or whether "from dread of the reported peace taking place," there would no longer be positions available. But the most worrisome matter lay entirely in his own hands. To receive any appointment, he had to pass two oral examinations, one administered by the Army Medical Board and the other by the College of Surgeons of London. The medical board examination decided whether a candidate should be given an appointment, while the College of Surgeons gave a much more rigorous test to determine what position he was qualified for. "You are hot from your studies," James Hamilton had told him, "and I have no doubt of your passing your trials." "Good God if I should be rejected?" Lesassier wrote, "What would become of me—I should die from despair," for passing at Surgeon's Hall was an absolute prerequisite to any military medical position.

Prior to 1800, the examinations had been a mere formality, with the reputation of caprice or interest, but the Napoleonic Wars had produced a demand for better-educated practitioners and positions in the medical service had been reformed to attract them. The lowest rank of medical practitioner, hospital mate, now had a commission, ranking with an ensign, the lowest rank of commissioned officer. His commission gave him that coveted privilege, a small pension when not on active service. The usual next step in the medical hierarchy was regimental assistant surgeon, who ranked with a lieutenant, and was entitled to half-pay when not on active service. The step after that was regimental surgeon, ranking with captain, and also entitled to half-pay.

In practice, the medical chain of command, pay, perquisites, and status was quite a bit more complicated than the stated ranks implied, but for now, Lesassier was not concerned with complexities. The usual first appointment was a hospital mateship, but it was possible to be appointed assistant surgeon right away if the examinations went well, and Lesassier, like other candidates, had set his heart on the higher position. How he was to achieve this, he did not know, for there were no clear-cut requirements for the level of education and experience required for each appointment. Indeed, the whole process of examination and appointment was shrouded in mystery, at least for the candidates themselves, and the medical board retained the reputation for caprice:

Lesassier heard that the inspector general could "create a young man Hospital mate one week—the next—Assistant Surgeon—& then Surgeon all in succession." Since these rapid promotions were clearly not based on additional study or experience, he concluded that "advancement then must depend on interest." Indeed, the process appeared so mysterious to candidates that they came to London armed with letters of introduction from anyone—medical professors, family connections, and high-ranking officers—who might help them in the business of securing their future.

Lesassier's first few days in London were both busy and frustrating. When he woke up on Wednesday he set out to the medical board, the administrative office of the army medical service, to obtain the hoped-for appointment. From this office, Francis Knight, the inspector general of hospitals, Thomas Keate, the surgeon general, and Lucas Pepys, the physician general, regulated the examination, appointment, promotion, and pay of army medical officers. Lesassier had a letter of introduction to present to Knight, but on arriving at the medical board office when it opened at 11:00 he was told Knight would not be in until 12:30. This was his first experience of dealing with a public office, so he duly left and "lounged about for an hour but this appeared an age to me." On returning promptly at 12:30, he found that Knight still had not appeared, and in fact did not come in all afternoon. The office was a meeting point for candidates and junior medical officers in town to take examinations or receive appointments, a clearing house of gossip and rumor. Lesassier recognized one of the other candidates, "an old schoolfellow—a John Harrison who had been an apprentice at the Manchester Infirmary and then had gone as Assistant Surgeon into a Militia Regiment—He was called into the office & soon returned into the waiting room to tell us with a long face that he was appointed Hospital Mate in the West Indies."

In addition to milling about, Lesassier also found out some hard information: the examinations for the medical board were held only on the first and third Thursday of each month, and candidates had to sign up for the examination the day before. That meant he had to sign up at once in order to be eligible for the exam the next day, or else wait for two weeks. Since he had to be examined by the medical board before he could be examined at Surgeon's Hall, postponing one test would mean postponing the other.

He hit the first stage of the process intended to weed out unsuitable candidates when he tried to put his name down for the medical board exam. Knight's clerk, Mr. Reed, asked "if I had any certificates of having attended lectures or of my medical education. I replied I had not attended any hospitals in London—but had gotten tickets of lectures that I attended during a winter at Edinburgh—These he looked at. I told him I had been an apprentice in Manchester. He wished to look at the indentures." James Hamilton had told him he could "pull out my indentures & most likely they will never look at the date," but the first question Reed asked was "How long did I serve?" "About a year & a half," Lesassier replied, "because my master left town & my father would not allow me to follow him"—a barefaced lie, of course, but a very smooth one, probably suggested by his uncle. Where else had he studied? Reed wanted to know; the Manchester Infirmary a few months, replied Lesassier, and when pressed for more evidence of medical education, "Sir! my father is a physician, and I've studied under him my whole life." "Oh—Oh—very well," Reed responded, and told Lesassier to return the next day, bringing his lecture tickets and indentures with him. He also took and read Lesassier's letter of introduction to Knight, and Lesassier left, "heartily tired."

The next day he returned to the Army Medical Board at noon, when the office opened for business, to find "about ten young men to be examined." He was called for his exam at about 3:30. His examiners "began," he wrote, "by enquiring minutely where I had studied—& appeared astonished that I had studied so short a time in a regular manner, as they enquired the exact time I had been an apprentice." The examination itself consisted of questions on measles, smallpox, and cholera, common infectious diseases. Lesassier admitted that he was questioned "more minutely than I had expected." Still, he "got through it," and received the letter certifying that he had passed his first hurdle.

The next step was the examination at Surgeon's Hall. The College of Surgeons issued several diplomas: either a general diploma for the army, indicating that the candidate was competent for any position found for him, or a diploma for a specific position, such as a hospital mateship, indicating that the candidate was competent only for that position. The general diploma was much more prestigious and valuable, because it allowed promotion to any position in the surgical staff. Lesassier duly picked up his letter from the War Office the next day, took it to Surgeon's Hall, and received a ticket for his examination, set at 6:30 P.M. In the afternoon, disaster struck: like David Balfour in Robert Louis Stevenson's novel, he realized his pocketbook was stolen. It contained not only all of his personal papers, but also the examination tickets, lecture tickets, and indentures he needed for the evening's examination. Though devastated at his misfortune, Lesassier showed commendable presence of mind. Without his ticket, he knew, he could not take the examination; without proof of his medical education, he might be rejected. He therefore raced back to the College of Surgeons and was able to get another ticket, and ran back to the medical board and got a letter saying that he had already presented the necessary proofs of his medical education.

Losing a pocketbook was almost a diversion compared to waiting for his examination. He and an Edinburgh acquaintance, Alexander Macpherson, in London for the same purpose, "sat in the greatest anxiety till half past six—and then went to learn our doom." There were thirty men waiting, "all much agitated." Lesassier was not called until 8:15 P.M. Candidates went into the room in batches of six or seven. They were confronted by thirteen examiners, six on either side of the president, sitting around a table covered with a green cloth. Each candidate was assigned to an examiner, and "during the short moment of arranging the young men I uttered a prayer that I might be sent to a mild examiner," Lesassier wrote, but "Fate had otherways ordered this." His examiner was David Dundas, one of the most influential of the London surgeons. Dundas began by asking questions about Lesassier's education, and he, too, was surprised that Lesassier had studied for so short a period of time. "These were very unfavorable symptoms for poor me," was Lesassier's accurate prognosis. "Because I expected that he would be more minute with me on this account."

And so he was. Dundas started with the skeleton: "The bones of the Cranium," he began, "How joined—names of sutures—bones of the face." And here, Lesassier had to admit, "I was rather confused." "Number of vertebra," Dundas went on, "processes— what bone supports the tibia—What supports the astragalus—Which lies next to the astragalus anteriorly—& which to the cuboids laterally." But Lesassier was "at a stand," for "These last were unexpected & I could not for my life recall the situations & names of these bones." Nor were the muscles and blood vessels any easier: "What muscles are inserted into the patella? The branches of the arch of the aorta? of the aorta in the thorax? Of the same vessel in the abdomen? The contents of the abdomen? The origin of the thoracic duct? Its course & termination?" And then on to physiology: "How is chyle taken from the food? Describe the circulation? The course & division of the carotid artery? The branches of the external carotid?" And "here," Lesassier "missed too." Finally Dundas came to surgery, the branch Lesassier was most deficient in. "Definition and minute treatment of compound fractures? Where the inflammation continues the treatment? What is the most desirable event in compound fractures? Treatment if gangrene supervenes? When sphacelus? The best parts of the limb in case of amputation? Describe all the steps of amputation of the leg? Define hernia? What are its species? Where is hernia commonly formed? The symptoms of strangulation? The means to relieve this? These failing—Describe the steps of the operation for inguinal hernia?" And here, Lesassier wailed, "He made me tell him the parts I should cut through the direction & the instruments I should use." "The favorable prognoses," Dundas went on, inexorably, "After the operation? The peculiar diagnosis of hernia? How distinguished from variocele, circocele, and hydrocele? Define hydrocele? How treated & the various means that have been recommended for this & the best of these? Congenital hernia what & how formed? Symptoms of compression of the brain"—and here, Lesassier noted, "in answering I forgot vomiting," one of the most obvious symptoms—"How would you discover depression? How would treat it? Go through the steps of the operation for the trepan? What parts of the skull would you deem improper to apply the trepan over? What are the muscles of the abdomen? What vessels are taken up in amputation of the leg?"

The examination lasted an hour. "I answered all these numerous and collateral questions with facility," Lesassier wrote, but his examiner obviously thought otherwise, and he was told that he "had not anatomical knowledge enough for anything but a Hospital Mate." This verdict "struck me cold with amazement," he wrote, and "I certainly deserved more." But Dundas was implacable, and Lesassier was told "this was often done & that I must study and pass some future period," any time after six months.

"Good God! my fate is decided!" Lesassier wrote, "it is cruel and undeserved! Am I always to be unfortunate in every important undertaking? . . . After all the lonely, anxious hours that I have spent in study to be thus treated!" In fact his fate was not particularly cruel, as Dundas pointed out to him: Lesassier had, after all, been given an appointment. The goal of the reforms had been to attract better-educated men, and, as Lesassier noted accurately, his examiners "thought it absolutely impossible that I could understand any thing from such short studies." Lesassier might prefer his own quick wit and gentlemanly manners to Macpherson, who "has received a tolerably fair education yet he appears excessively dull and stupid. However this is merely from his manners being somewhat rude." But Macpherson had attended medical classes at Edinburgh for three years, completed a surgical apprenticeship with a fellow of the Royal College of Surgeons of Edinburgh, and obtained a diploma from the college after an examination very much like that at Surgeon's Hall; he was rewarded for his extensive education with a surgeon's diploma. The failures Lesassier noted made his relative lack of education even more prominent. Another Edinburgh acquaintance, Richmond Robert Stubbs, had been rejected outright when he was examined for a position in the East India Company. When Lesassier saw him, he was attending lectures in London before trying again; he eventually succeeded and was appointed assistant surgeon in the East India Company in 1808. The most poignant cases Lesassier noted were of two men who "were rejected on examination—though they had been in the army for many years because they had no certificates of the classes they had attended—So that poor fellows they must be forced to attend lectures and hospitals over again." One can imagine, then, Dundas's train of thought during Lesassier's examination: your father is a physician, and your uncle a famous one—you've studied for a year, and remember a fair amount of what you were taught—the army needs hospital mates—very well, you'll do.

Lesassier spent a disconsolate few days waiting for the papers to come through, homesick and dejected over what he considered his hard fate. But on 7 May—one week after arriving in London—he received his warrant appointing him hospital mate as of 6 May with a pay of six shillings and sixpence per day. He was thrilled to receive what he regarded as an enormous sum, the first money he had ever earned in his life. "I am now handsomely independent of any one," he wrote, "& may with care not only keep up appearances & live like a gentleman but may also save money." If sent abroad, he would be entitled to seven-and-sixpence per day, and lodgings, "a devilish pretty sum let me tell you," and two shillings per day in case of peace, "so that I think I may say I am secure from starvation." No longer the poor relation, he had crossed the line to independence, finally achieving the essential feature of a gentleman.

His rather tempered pleasure at his new position turned to unmixed glee, though, when he found out that in one respect he had gotten the better of his examiners: strictly speaking, he shouldn't have been allowed even to take the examination, since the minimum age for all appointments was twenty-one. Another Edinburgh student had learned this the hard way; he had been asked his age at the medical board, and on replying truthfully that he was eighteen, had been told "that the orders of the War-office were positively to not examine any person who was not more than 21." "I have been a thousand times more fortunate than either I dreamed of or deserved," was Lesassier's exclamation when he wrote this, for he, too, was only eighteen. He had no thought, of course, of going to the medical board and confessing his true age. Nor should it surprise us that none of his Edinburgh referees—neither James Hamilton, John Thomson, nor George Bell—had seen any reason to mention the age requirement to Lesassier, though concern over the age of Edinburgh students presenting themselves at Surgeons' Hall had been the subject of at least one official letter from the War Office to the Edinburgh College of Surgeons. James Hamilton had mentioned "the illiberal antipathy" the medical board had against Edinburgh-trained practitioners; perhaps he and his colleagues took this as a license to ignore War Office regulations where it proved inconvenient; or perhaps illiberal attention to minutiae like age hardly weighed in the balance against the grand object of securing a position for a deserving relative.

Lesassier was delighted: in his personal contest with the medical board, he had bested them in at least one particular. "Wiseacres that you are! my face has cheated you—has fairly & completely humbugged you all—Bravissimo! . . . Ah! ah! ah! I shall laugh at this for twenty years to come." Instead of bemoaning his fate for receiving only a hospital mate's diploma, he "should have gone down on my bare knees—& thanked my kind stars for my good fortune—in obtaining such a situation two years & a half before I had a title to it." His father sent congratulations, "delighted at my having got forwards so rapidly," and Isabella sent a keepsake, "a gold pencil—a most superb one indeed," together with "a copy of verses on our affection—very prettily written—indeed they put me to the blush for I cannot compose any thing of the kind." Good fortune smiled upon him once more: he received a letter from James Hamilton "condoling with me on the injustice of my sentence at the College—and saying that my *Pocket-book is found,*" and had been returned to him. "Who the devil! would have imagined after my losing it in this town . . . that I should hear from a place 400 miles distant that it was found."

Was Hamilton disingenuous to call the college decision unjust? Whether or not he knew of the age requirement, he surely knew that barely one year of classes was a very limited education for a medical man, even in the army. The Army Medical Board had made it quite clear to Lesassier that he had not studied long enough for a full diploma, and it probably was clear to Hamilton and his associates as well. They were all medical professors, who had seen many, many young men depart their classes for opportunities in London. Why, then, had Hamilton sent his nephew on his way with such inflated expectations? Why did he send him on his way so soon? Could he not have supported Lesassier through one or two more years of study, asks the reader accustomed to the generosity of Jane Austen's kindhearted fathers? Or at least warned him that the world might be less eager to embrace him than he was to embrace the world?

Perhaps the best answer comes from Lesassier himself, for however much we may rejoice at our hero's improved prospects in the world, we cannot help sighing for the one opportunity that he let slip through his fingers. When Lesassier first arrived in London, Inspector General Knight offered him the "particular favor" of a medical cadetship, explicitly in consideration of his letter of introduction from James Hamilton. Cadetships were new positions, designed to recruit and retain better-educated practitioners for the army. Medical cadets had to attend lectures and the London hospitals for six months at their own expense, but were then admitted as hospital mates right away, without being examined at Surgeon's Hall. They then attended classes another six months while drawing their pay, a portion of which was deducted to pay for the classes and other expenses. At the end of twelve months they had to take and pass the examination at Surgeon's Hall, with the promise of rapid promotion. The only obligation was that medical cadets had to agree to stay in the army for seven years.

"This is most undoubtedly an excellent plan," Lesassier wrote, and indeed it was. Cadets had the incentive of being paid for attending part of their classes, and of having their date of commission start six months prior to their actual duty—an important consideration for seniority—together with the expectation of rapid promotion. The army had seven years' service from well-qualified men. It was also an offer finely attuned to fulfill a patronage obligation to his uncle, for what could be more suitable for a professor's nephew than an opportunity for further study, and study that was obviously tied to future advancement? This was patronage as Addison had defined it a hundred years earlier, "where there is power and obligation" on the part of the patron, and "merit and expectation" on the part of the recipient. Lesassier's first instinct was to say that he must consult with his uncle, and he might have been better off if he had. On his own in London, the prospect of additional study was much less attractive than it might have seemed under his uncle's roof in Edinburgh; besides, he "wished so much to get all over" in one day. A major difficulty was the initial six months' study in London, and Lesassier refused the offer, claiming he was unable to face asking his uncle to support him, for "after his beneficence to me . . . he would have a poor opinion of my gratitude." Or perhaps James Hamilton might have agreed to the plan, recognizing that Knight's "particular favor," like most forms of patronage, carried with it the obligation of acceptance if there were to be future favors. The medical cadetship that year went to another Edinburgh student, David MacLagan, who perhaps had letters from John Thomson and George Bell as well. He had completed an apprenticeship with a fellow of the Royal College of Surgeons of Edinburgh and received an M.D. from Edinburgh University in 1804; the opportunity for further study in London for a year with a guaranteed appointment in the army was too good to pass by.

Lesassier never recognized that Knight's offer was a missed opportunity, much less that he had been offered, and had overlooked, tangible evidence of his uncle's ability to assist him in his career. He was, in fact, disappointed in his uncle, whose patronage he thought of as a magic spell to propel him farther than he could have gone on his own merits. Instead, "my having taken a letter of introduction to the Inspector General has not advanced my affairs a single step," he complained, "for I was the last on the Hospital Mate list & I did not obtain my warrant till my turn came . . . so that all my expectations from influence were vain." Still, he would not give up hope "that interest may do wonders in my favor" thereafter, "in advancing me to an Assistant Surgeoncy & afterwards to a Surgeoncy." After all, did he not owe his present fortunate circumstances entirely to his uncle? "Well I'll not waste my paper in diffuse expressions," he wrote, but "gratitude shall continue to the last gasp of my existence."

# CHAPTER 4

## This Despicable Rock

H is warrant received, Alexander Lesassier's immediate future was assured: he was now a military man with a gorgeous new uniform, "scarlet coat—with black velvet collar—epaulet of gold on black velvet—A cocked hat with black feathers—& blue pantaloons & boots—regulation sword and black waist belt." Lesassier had never been so well dressed in his life; "Zounds," he wrote with satisfaction, "how fine I shall look with my grand sword." The only question was where he would be posted, for that was "completely uncertain." "Choose wherever I go," he wrote cheerfully, now that the dreaded examinations were past, "I shall find some peculiar convenience in it." It might be England, and if so he could study and retake the examination in six months; it might be Sicily, where Lesassier would find himself "in the most exquisite climate under the sun. I shall live cheaply and deliciously—I shall save a great deal of money—and see much surgical practice." When would he find out? Surely, Lesassier thought, "as my pay is going on they will not keep me idle very long," but day after day passed without his receiving marching orders, and one hospital mate warned that he had been kept waiting two months in London for his own marching orders. For the first time he was living a "nobly idle life"—"receiving a handsome pay & not doing any thing for it"—but he was too keyed up to enjoy it. "Oh! it's dreadful having nothing to engage one's time with." In fact it took ten days for the War Office to send him word to hold himself in instant readiness, and another week for his marching orders to arrive. He was to go to Portsmouth to embark for Gibraltar ("of all the places in the world this I least expected to go to"). He spent from midnight to 3 A.M. writing Isabella his farewell letter, and he wrote other farewell letters as well, to his uncle, to friends, and to Jenoway—finally returning the £1 he had borrowed years before. And at 5 A.M. Sunday morning, Lesassier and Macpherson—by now described as "a devilish good fellow," though "not the brightest I ever saw—the Army will rub the Scotch rust from him no fear" set off on the coach to Portsmouth. They had just missed two ships bound for the Mediterranean, and no one knew exactly when others would arrive, so the newly appointed mates were told to find lodgings for an indefinite period, and "call often and enquire." Lesassier's first tour of duty thus began with logistical problems: how to get to Portsmouth, and then to Gibraltar, and how and when to purchase the necessary equipment and food for the journey. It is not too much to say that logistical problems—how to get himself, and later, his patients, from one place to the next, how to arrange food, lodging, and supplies, and how to find the money to pay for this—were to dominate his experience of the army, as they already dominated War Office business.

In 1806 the British army was fighting in Italy; there were garrisons to maintain in India, the Mediterranean, the West Indies, and North America. So extensive a military presence required enormous organization of men and supplies. Soldiers had to be recruited and dispatched to their garrisons; officers had to be commissioned and sent to their regiments, and medical staff had to be transported from whatever place of origin to whatever garrison, regiment, or hospital required their services. Not all the movement was outward from Britain, for men might be sent home on disability, officers could get leaves of absence, and entire battalions or regiments had to be moved around as they were needed. Movement of men also required movement of food, for all were entitled to certain rations which varied according to rank and location, as well as other supplies, including weapons, certainly, but also bedding, cooking utensils, and other necessities, again varying according to location. And it required movement of money, so that officers and men, lodgings and food, weapons and equipment could be paid for on a regular basis.

For the War Office, the movement of men was comparatively simple. The navy provided transports to move men, and purveyors to move supplies; both types of ships were sent in fleets protected by British men-of-war. Enlisted men were recruited and transported under the guard of an officer, usually an ensign, for they were not trusted to make their way on their own. But officers, including medical officers like hospital mates, were merely given orders and permission to board an available transport, advanced their pay, sometimes issued travel money and told where to report. How they got there was their own concern. For hospital mates like Lesassier, this freedom was hardly a favor. From the privileged position of professor's nephew, he was relegated to a cog in the War Office machine, and a low-ranking cog at that. He had too little money to travel in any kind of style, for though his salary might make him independent of his father and uncle, it did not allow him to live according to his idea of a gentleman. Between the expenses of his examination and his gorgeous new uniform, he had used up the £30 his uncle had advanced; that is, he had, as an eighteen-year-old, used up the inheritance he would receive at twenty-one. When he received his orders, he also received his pay from May 6, amounting to just over £6, but most of that went to settling the final bill for his lodgings. He would not have had more than a pound or two if the army had not advanced him three months' pay, plus an additional £3 travel money, so that he had a total of about £40 with which to travel to Gibraltar and live for three months. Of course, any money he spent on the trip lessened the money available in Gibraltar. "Live always within your income," James Hamilton had told him, "and you will ever be independent—If you exceed it you will suffer the fate of many—ruin," but after three weeks in the army Lesassier was already drawing on his future pay. It did not bode well for his financial future.

To save money, Lesassier and Macpherson agreed to take a room in Portsmouth for eighteen pence per day, though they had to share a bed. They also teamed up with two other hospital mates bound for Gibraltar—Ryan and Flanagan—to share the expenses of the trip. The army, in its munificence, provided hospital mates with two-thirds of a seaman's allowance of beef, biscuit, and rum, but no one was expected to survive the trip without additional supplies, and the four men pooled their resources to provide a stock of food: eggs, bread, butter, milk, brandy, biscuits, gingerbread, ham, tea, and sugar, and eating and drinking utensils, a tea kettle, and a pan. Their initial idea was to board their transport as soon as it arrived, for Portsmouth inns were ruinously expensive. But the master and crew "looked remarkably cool upon us," Lesassier wrote, and refused to put themselves out for mere hospital mates. They asked for and were given a candle, but no candlestick, "so we used a bottle." They had a kettle, but "no body would either fill it with water, or take it to the kitchen fire," and they could not light a fire in their own cabin. Their rations, they found, were given out twice a week, not daily. They first tipped the cook to prepare their food; then, finding that the cook was supposed to prepare them without being tipped, took their money back. The result was that the cook, aware that he was much more important to the journey than four hospital mates, refused to prepare their dinner, and they ended up tipping him after all. They were given bedding, but "Oh Lord! Oh Lord! what beds they were. A thin, narrow short mattress . . . a thin single blanket . . . and a pillow—that I could . . . have put into my breast pocket." They complained to the staff surgeon in Portsmouth, Mr. Courtney, "one of the most gentlemanly affable men in Office," but "there was no redress to be procured against the scoundrel." Courtney had to tell them, "all masters of Transports resembled each other & we must bear it patiently."

Courtney was more helpful in another matter, the procuring of a servant, a serious problem for hospital mates. Lesassier, while living with Jordan in the summerhouse, had done his own cooking and cleaning, but now that he was a gentleman with an officer's commission such menial tasks were very much beneath his dignity. The provision of a soldier servant was a perquisite of military officers, but hospital mates, by a quirk of army regulations, were not entitled to one. The problem could have been easily solved: a soldier on his way to Gibraltar could act as their servant on the trip, but the general at Portsmouth "refused point blank" to assign any of his soldiers to the four mates. Courtney, however, referred the matter to the inspector of hospitals, Mr. Joeburn, who gave them a letter to a personal friend, a colonel stationed on the Isle of Wight. Lesassier and Macpherson spent a day delivering the letter to the colonel who graciously assigned a soldier to act as their servant. In this small matter we can see the interplay of professional allegiance—Courtney and Joeburn assisting their junior officers—and personal connections, with a private letter to a colonel succeeding where a formal request to a general failed. "Here was an illustrious model for the copying of all men in office," wrote Lesassier, who made it clear that he felt the army ought to trouble itself more on his behalf. "Can any person, endowed with common sense—conceive, that a haughty, pompous behaviour, to inferiors, can either ensure respect for their rank or admiration of their abilities." He did not record how the four hospital mates treated their servant. Regrettably from their point of view, the servant came aboard officially under the authority of a higher-ranking regimental officer, Captain Romilly, which was "somewhat degrading," Lesassier thought. But at least he had someone to cook his eggs and look after his bedding. And the medical staff had scored a point against military regulations.

The ship weighed anchor on Saturday, 14 June, at 9:30 A.M., "and our little fleet, consisting of twelve Victuallers, & transports, convoyed by the Chiffonne, frigate of 30 Guns, got under sail." The trip took two weeks. It was Lesassier's first long sea voyage, and he was sick for the first few days, though he had time to note that the "Sea, when my sickness permitted me to look at it, exhibited the most sublime scene—Such an immense body of water boiling & foaming into hills of snow." He spent most of the time "chiefly on deck in reading some novel or other; for to study was absolutely impossible." Most of the entertainment, though, came from human rather than natural elements. The four hospital mates had been prevailed upon by Mrs. Geddes—an elderly gentlewoman, they thought—to allow her, her granddaughter, another young woman, and "a parrot—a kitten a dog" to share their cabin. Greenhorns that they were, they had assumed that she must be well born and well connected from the way she spoke of "Brigadier General Evely, her friend," but found out, once under way, that they had inconvenienced themselves for a mere midwife. "But of course according to her own account," wrote Lesassier, "one of the most respectable of her profession—Especially insofar that she never was tipsy in the whole course of her practice. . . . We nevertheless frequently observed her tippling our rum—and almost every day she got drunk." In revenge for having been duped, or perhaps out of sheer bad temper, Ryan and Captain Romilly, "concerted that to throw her dog into the Sea, with a rope round its neck, & then to shoot at it with pistols, would be a most excellent sport." Lesassier did not like Mrs. Geddes any more than his associates, but he was fond of dogs, and managed to rescue this one before his associates actually started shooting. Ryan did succeed in throwing the dog overboard later in the trip, claiming "it had dirtied his bed."

By 1 P.M. on 28 June the ship neared Gibraltar, and Lesassier stood on the deck looking through his telescope. This was his first glimpse of the garrison where he was to be stationed for the next eighteen months. "In coming up the Straits," he wrote, "you would not suppose that Gibraltar differed at all from the mountains on every side. It forms the farthest wing of land, that encloses a bay of about six miles deep & six broad—The remaining part of the semicircle is formed of a ridge of mountains being the Spanish coast. . . . The Rock itself is peculiar in rising abruptly on the side towards Spain, from a plain of sand of some extent. . . . Though the whole of the foot of the Rock is covered with buildings yet the town itself is merely about three quarters of a mile long & its breadth—little more than three or four hundred yards."

In this small space was enclosed the principal British garrison for controlling access to the Mediterranean. Its peculiar geography, and heavy fortifications, made it virtually impregnable, but also made it notoriously claustrophobic for the officers stationed on it. When the border was closed during war with Spain in 1803, "the situation of officers," wrote one of them, Thomas Walsh, "is very melancholy; cooped up in a prison, from which it is impossible to stir," and William Dent, an army surgeon stationed in Gibraltar in 1810, couldn't wait to get off "this despicable rock." In 1806, when Lesassier arrived, the garrison was at peace and reasonably healthy, but even in winter, "during the flowering season of the orange & lemon trees," when "every breeze that blows comes laden with perfume," Lesassier found it "impossible to overcome my aversion to this execrable place. I am not singular in my dislike. Every one with whom I have conversed expresses a similar detestation of being cooped up." The inhabitants of the town were not any happier about the garrison's presence than the army. As Lesassier later noted, "The civilian inhabitants of our Garrison, from being so completely under submission to a military Government, detest most cordially every one that wears a uniform."

Lesassier's own description of the inhabitants, written a few days after his arrival, shows the prejudice that prompted the townspeople's detestation. The town itself, he wrote, "is a most irregularly built place consisting of one long, narrow street, composed of dirty, paltry shops, & streets running from this in various directions." How poorly it must have compared to the glittering streets of London, or the symmetrical squares and crescents of Edinburgh's New Town! It was crowded, too: "It was computed, that the inhabitants of this garrison amounted to 20,000. . . . But certainly never in so small a compass, was ever assembled so motley a crew as the people of various nations that are seen in these streets." Spanish, rather than English, was the main language, and Lesassier eventually learned to make his way in it. "These Spaniards," he continued, "are of course shopkeepers—& merchants. Amongst them there are some very elegant Spanish girls—They are not at all remarkable for beauty of face . . . But they all possess elegant figures. Being generally tall and slender—But this is greatly improved by the exceedingly tasteful manner in which they dress." In contrast, he wrote, echoing a common British prejudice, "the men are a most filthy looking set."

He had a keen, if equally insular eye for the other nationalities in Gibraltar. "The Moors are very numerous & fill up the meanest offices—As porters—of which there are immense numbers—cobblers—fruit sellers &c—They are of a very brown complexion, but have regular enough features—their hair is cut entirely off & they wear a small red cap—They have a kind of close jacket, & loose, blue linen drawers—Their legs are bare & they have in general, a kind of morocco leather slippers—These men are seen everywhere, squatting down, like apes, in groups at the sides of streets; or carrying enormous weights on poles."

There were also Spanish Jews "dressed in a very curious manner—Their hair cut short also black caps—ear rings sometimes—A brown, or black waistcoat with a sash round their waist—A short black cloth Mantle—& loose white trousers & slippers but without stockings—They also wear beards—though short. The higher orders are dressed much more superbly—but in the same style." In contrast were the English Jews, who "dress in our fashion." Spanish peasants came into town as well. "Most of their dress consists of leather with an endless number of little buttons and hooks to it. With enormous hats—the crown scarcely visible, & the brim a foot or more broad." Lesassier was most partial to the "The Genoese, & Moors of Rank who dress pretty much alike. In the Turkish manner with Turbans."

The group he found most distasteful were the Greek traders. "They are all remarkably muscular men," he wrote, "very dark complexioned—with monstrous mustachios & beard—Their hair hangs in an immense bush round their heads. . . . Their dress very much resembles that of the Moors—A small conical cap—half covering the top of the head—A tight kind of a jacket—with loose blue drawers, their monstrous legs bare—& slippers on their feet." He refused to believe that men so "gaunt & villainess" could be anything other than a degeneration from the Greeks of the classical age, whom he perhaps imagined tall and fair. "These fellows," he continued, "likewise speak Greek but like them time has changed it into a most barbarous, from a most polished language," though we may wonder how Lesassier knew this, since he did not read or speak classical Greek himself. The only group Lesassier did not describe was the one to which he belonged, the throngs of British officers, dressed in their woolen regimentals, crowding the streets,—"the numerous red-coated puppies sauntering about," as Lesassier later referred to them—or "whole bands of soldiers and sailors," according to Walsh, "literally lying in the streets in the most degrading state of inebriety."

If the topography of Gibraltar fell short of Lesassier's imagination, so did his reception on arrival. He had expected to report at once to the deputy inspector, Abraham Bolton, no doubt to be welcomed with open arms, given a glass of wine, and furnished with comfortable lodgings—where he could "repose my bruised limbs, in a fine soft bed!" Instead, he and the other three hospital mates tried three times to find Bolton at home, but didn't succeed until the next day; in the interim they made the unpleasant discovery that inns were crowded and dirty, and that even wine and coffee, which they expected to be cheap and delicious, were expensive and bad. In fact, they subsequently learned, almost anything they wanted to buy, from food to equipment, was very expensive on Gibraltar, both because much of it had to be imported and because local merchants knew they had a captive population in the garrison community.

They were not cheered up when they finally did reach the deputy inspector, who invited them to breakfast "as graciously as his nature admitted." Bolton had been an army medical officer for many years and had a decided knack for making himself comfortable on foreign service. Many, many hospital mates had passed through his department—the preceding set on Gibraltar, Lesassier was told, had behaved so badly that they had to be sent home—and though he tried to save them from their own follies the effort made him appear, according to Lesassier, "a very sulky fellow." He had found quarters for three of the mates on Gibraltar, he told the four men. The fourth was to go to Sicily as assistant surgeon to a regiment stationed there.

Since all four had already decided that Gibraltar was "an execrable place," they all "snatched with avidity" at the chance to leave. But Bolton chose Macpherson because he had a letter of introduction. "This partiality"—for Lesassier refused to believe that Macpherson could deserve to be appointed instead of him—"enraged us all very much—But we could no way remedy it—so put up though very sulkily with it." To add insult to injury, though the remaining three men were given quarters, they had to buy their own bedding. "This was a severe stroke indeed—because, we might much more cheaply have brought it with us from England; & at the same time have slept more comfortably during the voyage." Lesassier had, in fact, heard a rumor in London that he would have to buy his bedding in Gibraltar, but had discounted it, not wanting to spend the money then. He was still not entitled to a servant, another cause for irritation. Pity the poor hospital mates, wrote William Fergusson, an army medical officer of many years' standing, "thrown into a strange army, where they have neither place, nor home, nor experience, nor knowledge how to guide themselves, without even being allowed a servant that could speak their language." And to cap it off, Lesassier discovered that his initial idea of returning to London to retake the examination in six months had to be abandoned: leave of absence from the garrison was granted only after eighteen months.

Why the mates had been sent out to Gibraltar at all was a mystery Lesassier never solved, for as Bolton said at once, "there was but little for us to do." There was no general hospital at Gibraltar to employ hospital mates on a regular basis; instead, each regiment had its own small regimental hospital in a private house, under the care of the regimental surgeon. Since there was no fighting at Gibraltar at that point, the only medical or surgical cases were those associated with a peacetime army: infectious diseases, the occasional accident, and venereal disease. Bolton used hospital mates as a kind of medical temporary service, to fill up any vacancy or carry out any vaguely medical task. Lesassier's first assignment was to assist "the Apothecary to the Forces, an infernally stupid fellow, in drawing up returns of the stores &c in his possession." He was furious at "this degrading duty," considering it "a most infamous thing; to convert us gentlemen of the Medical Staff, into Apothecary's Clerks." Was it for this that he had spent his inheritance on his education? As the summer wore on, any ambition for study or seeing practice had dried up in the simmering heat, "the weather creating such a lassitude that it is impossible to do anything." When finally given a more interesting assignment, surgeon to the hospital for the Royal Barrack Artificers, he complained even more: "The hospital the sick are put in is the most miserable hovel imaginable," he wrote, and he had "to act not only as surgeon, but apothecary, purveyor, & overseer—if my fourth office may be so termed namely to see that every part of the Hospital be cleaned properly—that no cobwebs be seen &c &c . . . besides all this . . . the trouble of attending the officers & their families if they choose to call me in." It was merely a way of getting extra work out of him with "no perquisites, no advantages. . . . Not even the opportunity of entering a mess."

It was common for hospital mates to resent their low status: one surgeon called the title "cacophonous to the last degree" and "a barbarism of the middle ages," and it was replaced in 1808 with the less offensive "hospital assistant." The status carried with it certain dangers, too. Two hospital mates on their way to their first appointment were dismissed from the service in 1810 for what amounted to a shipboard fight with two other young officers, not unlike the one between Lesassier and Ryan over Mrs. Geddes's dog. But the two other officers in this case were an ensign and lieutenant, the hospital mates' superior officers, and the mates were therefore found guilty of "highly mutinous, scandalous, and infamous conduct . . . in breach of the Articles of War." Though Lesassier was never confronted with that kind of difficulty, he spent much of his time on Gibraltar "constantly reflecting & brooding on my examination. Cursing my own hard fate & envying everyone who had passed. Ashamed whenever I was questioned why I was so long an Hospital Mate and alarmed lest the true cause be detected." He longed to behave as he had done with Collier, to declare that his own good behavior was contingent on obtaining good treatment, to demand that he be treated as befit a gentleman and not "imposed on & ill treated by every coxcomb in office."

Like most hospital mates, Lesassier managed, encouraged by his uncle's promise of "his best endeavours if I behave myself with prudence." His room turned out to have a view of a garden; his temporary position at the hospital had the perquisite of a hospital orderly to wait on him; and once he bought bedding and acquired the furniture the army allotted him he was reasonably comfortable. He and his companions worked out various schemes for eating, involving creative juggling with their allotted rations, for they found that they could keep some and sell the rest, using the money to purchase other food. They diverted themselves with the chief amusement of British officers, excursions into Spain. They attended a bullfight, a much tamer affair than Lesassier had been led to expect by his image of the "days of chivalry"; they visited the little town of San Roque, "charmingly situated on a hill & commanding an enchanting prospect," with houses "built of either brick or stone, stuccoed, & white washed," in which "wooden shutters supply the place of glass" and "windows commonly have iron plated balconies in front." Like nearly all other officers, they visited the English inn La Fonda de la Catalan, run by a widow, her son, and daughter, and where—in the small world of the British empire—Lesassier encountered "the eldest son of Mr. Mosman of Nicolson Square Edinburgh, my uncle's next door neighbor . . . most nobly drunk."

Lesassier, rather less typically, also joined the "extensive & tolerably select" circulating library kept up for officers at the garrison, reading, among other things, Gibbon's *Decline and Fall of the Roman Empire*, which inspired both his rapturous delight at the "*immortal work*" and his sincere, if "preposterous wish" to "renew my childhood, and have the guidance with my present judgement, of a second education." He picked up enough Spanish to make his way around town and into the countryside, and acquired a Spanish maidservant, Maria de Garcia Vaissa, whose "relations agreed that she should serve me on my own terms." She was sixteen, "much handsomer than the lower order of Spaniards are in general," "tolerably intelligent & docile," and extremely poor, for Lesassier had to pay "more than seventeen guineas" to dress her in a respectable manner. It did not take long for her to become his mistress; "After being at so much trouble & expense in procuring this girl of mine," he wrote, "I concluded that at all events I might console my self by possessing in her an excellent companion." He was fond of her, "from the willing attention she has ever paid to all my little wants—from her untutored artlessness of behavior—from her apparent attachment to me—& still more from her friendless orphanlike situation. . . . Besides," he wrote, warming to his subject, "I also am an isolated being in this part of the world—no single friend—or acquaintance that can feel the slightest solicitude for any possible event that may happen to me. . . . How dear then to me must that person be—who without dissimulation, can participate in all my joys—& all my griefs:—And when this consoler proves to be a pretty female he that can feel surprised at my attachment to her must be dead to every sensation of humanity." This was rhetorical flourish, for he later complained of the "tedium & difficulty attended in explaining myself in a foreign language," and he soon found another reason to complain, for he caught gonorrhea, puzzled, as men were to be for many years to come, how such a thing was possible, since "the girl herself has not the slightest symptom of such a complaint. There can exist no mistake in the matter as I have examined her with the utmost attention."

After eight months on Gibraltar, then, Lesassier had set up housekeeping like a poor-man's independent gentleman—a poor-man's deputy inspector, let us say—complete with apartment, hospital orderly to act as errand boy, and servant/mistress. After ten weeks, however, an opportunity arose that turned his attention away from Maria. Lesassier had seen from the first that of all the positions on Gibraltar, by far the best was the appointment to a vacant assistant surgeoncy to a regiment, for "the medical staff of regiments is," as William Fergusson put it, "on the whole, very good; its officers have a defined position in the army; they are under the protection of a corps, enjoying the benefits of its mess in the best society"—and, he might have added, the benefits of a servant. Macpherson, who had started out with a temporary appointment in Sicily, was given the permanent appointment in three months. Flanagan also was appointed temporary assistant surgeon to a regiment in Gibraltar. Lesassier had been badgering Bolton for months to appoint him to a vacant assistant surgeoncy as well, and at the end of April 1807, Bolton finally assigned Lesassier to the position of temporary assistant surgeon in the First Battalion of the 42nd Regiment, the famous Black Watch. Of course Maria had to go, for his new position carried with it, finally, the perquisite of a soldier servant, and "Poor Maria," Lesassier wrote, "the look thou gavest me when closing the door after thee for the last time cut me to the heart." He then drew a line across the page, and, taking a mental deep breath, turned his attention to his new regiment.

The Black Watch at this point was part of the Gibraltar garrison, and Lesassier was delighted to be part of it, for "This regiment is so highly celebrated, the dress is so brilliant & the officers such gentlemanly Men." His social life improved markedly, for Lieutenant Colonel James Stirling had a daughter, Joanna, "a young lady of about 20," Lesassier wrote. "Her face is not handsome but her person is extremely elegant—The trifling gift of beauty is however totally overlooked after a short acquaintance with the aimiable Miss Joanna Stirling—Her cultivated mind rank her amidst the foremost of her sex." Lesassier saw her in company with other young ladies and other, equally admiring officers, on walks, as part of a party going to a ball, on picnics, or with family, with whom, Lesassier wrote, "I am on such intimate terms that I generally visit them twice a week—& am frequently invited to tea &c." Although he never saw her alone, he was sure they were in love: alas, a doomed love, which added to his enjoyment. She married the paymaster, John Home, a few months after Lesassier joined the regiment, but, he wrote, "I shall never forget the look Miss S. gave me when I went to wish her joy—it was in itself a volume."

His appointment to the 42nd was beneficial in more lasting ways: it gave him an incentive for taking an interest in medical matters. The regimental surgeon, John Erly, was on a leave of absence, which left the assistant surgeon Daniel McLean as his superior officer, "and unluckily for my comfort he is a damned stiff fellow—So that I am under the necessity of doing all the disagreeable duty," for the army was much worse than apprenticeship when it came to a hierarchical division of labor. The two men got on well, however, and within a few months the "damned stiff fellow" had become "my colleague McLean," the first medical man Lesassier ever referred to as a colleague.

Deputy Inspector Bolton, too, changed from an obstacle to a medical colleague, as he became an ally in Lesassier's efforts to obtain a permanent appointment with the 42nd. Lesassier had originally hoped that his temporary appointment would be made permanent, but "Until I get home & pass my examination," he wrote, "it is needless to expect any promotion." In the meantime, another young assistant surgeon, Alexander Mc-Lachlan, was duly sent out from England in October to fill the vacant position. But there was another possibility, as Bolton pointed out to Lesassier. The 42nd Regiment had two battalions, and the second was recruiting in England. Each was entitled to two assistant surgeons, but one of the assistant surgeons in the second battalion had recently died, while McLachlan, who had just filled the vacant position in Gibraltar, had been the second. That meant that there were two vacancies in the second battalion, and if Lesassier could be appointed before anyone else, he would become the senior assistant surgeon of that battalion. Bolton advised him "to write immediately to the Surgeon-General, Thomas Keate, requesting the vacant situation & likewise to obtain of Lt. Colonel Stirling a letter of recommendation." This he did, and the paymaster of the regiment—soon to marry Miss Stirling—agreed to forward the letters privately, so that Lesassier didn't have to wait for a packet boat. Even regarding little things like the mail, it was an advantage to belong to a regiment.

This possibility made it essential that Lesassier return to London and retake his examination, and Bolton gave "his word that I should go home as soon as possible." Colonel Stirling informed Lesassier that he had indeed written in his behalf. That left him "to look after two grand objects—studying hard & saving money" to pay for his passage home. The first of the two went well. Lesassier was reasonably optimistic that he might pass his examination on his next try, for "Having had previous experience of their examination I am prepared on what subjects to study. . . . I am studying from morning to night." In case he was rejected, he would try again in six months after attending lectures in London "and surely the devil will be in it if I miss both times." His studying proceeded "very much to my satisfaction. In the course of a few days' severe application to my profession, I have recovered all I lost, & have gained more than I ever knew." He fretted, though, that he might be too late, for he heard that another two men had applied for the vacant position. They were turned down, though he didn't know why, so he continued to hope. He also wrote to his uncle for help in obtaining the position, who wrote back that he "has employed considerable interest."

He was not as successful in his second great object, saving money. He left the officers' mess after two months, because it was too expensive, and he was very proud of himself for not succumbing to temptation and buying the uniform of the 42nd Regiment until he obtained a permanent appointment, for "what young man can quietly resist the fascination of two rich gold epaulets & a superbly laced jacket." Even so, six shillings a day didn't go very far, and when in November 1807 he settled his accounts, hoping to go home by Christmas, he found "to my utter consternation that with all my care I have spent my full pay—Curse it! what a damned fellow I am! What's still worse I don't know how it's spent—Zounds it turns me mad to think that now the time for my going home is so very near at hand, & I incapable of laying by money to carry me thither."

He was kept on tenterhooks about being able to go home until the last minute. In October Bolton had told him he could go at Christmas, when Bolton intended to send invalids home. In November, Bolton said he probably couldn't, "because he had written home for four Hospital Mates & consequently it would be very ridiculous to send me home who am in fact the only "*disposable mate on the Rock*" as he was pleased to elegantly express himself—Damn & blast such a beggarly title!" But on 28 November word came that a convoy was approaching, and on 1 December Bolton was cautiously hopeful that Lesassier could get leave of absence. On 2 December, Bolton told him definitely no, but on 28 December Lesassier was amazed to receive an order from Bolton to be prepared to leave immediately for England.

Once again Lesassier had to make preparations to leave at a moment's notice. He spent the next few days rushing around packing and saying goodbye to his friends and associates. These included Captain Fraser, "a veteran, worthy officer" who "agreeably surprised me by saying that in case I should want money, he had a trifle"—twelve guineas—"at my disposal"; it also included his lovely daughter, who on hearing he was leaving, "said nothing but gave me a look which expressed volumes." To raise more money, Lesassier arranged an auction to sell everything he did not want to take. Everything he owned, he lamented, nearly in tears, was "thus thrown away for merely £17." He particularly regretted his superb ass, purchased in Spain and possessing "amazing strength & spirit. . . . It was of a light ash color & had small delicate limbs." Perhaps he felt "suffocated with grief," as he did later about a favorite mule: "I shall never forget the last look it gave me."

Lesassier was determined that his voyage home "would be the very reverse of my last; and that I should enjoy every comfort which such accommodation could afford." He was no longer the eager boy he once had been, and, he wrote, "my conception of things was now quite the reverse of what it was when I entered the Army. *Then*, I felt a pleasure in saving others as much trouble as possible by contributing every exertion in my power to render them happy—It was the illusion of an hour. I found that such conduct on my part procured me neither the permanent respect or esteem of others. So I altered my behavior." One of his fellow passengers, an ensign, was still new enough that he "retained my former manners, & was by no means averse to cater & purchase every thing necessary for the voyage." They met before the trip to plan their stock, and "all was arranged—or in other words, I agreed that he should take upon himself the whole trouble." He took no trouble about his medical assignment on the way home either, looking after 113 invalids, together with medical stores sent on board by Bolton. Bolton "advised me in a friendly manner to be extremely careful to note down every article of either medicines or stores that might be delivered to my Patients so that the issues might accurately correspond with the remains." It was good advice, but Lesassier didn't take it. "The Invalids," he found, "were affected merely with ulcers," which was fortunate for him and them, since he was very seasick "for the first nine or ten days of being at sea." Even afterward he preferred to devote his attention to a shipboard affair with Kitty, wife of a soldier garrisoned in Gibraltar, whose "manners had been so engaging that I could not think of parting with her for ever without experiencing the acutest regret." He turned over the care of his invalids to one of the men, "a soldier who having formerly been an *orderly* in an hospital understood the mechanical part of surgery & pharmacy. So I had very little to do." The soldier did look after the men, but also made off with "more than half of the stores," and Lesassier had an anxious hour or so when he had to submit the records to an official examination. But the officials merely "lengthened their important faces—looked at each other & then shrugged up their shoulders" and requested him "to sit down & write a letter of explanation to the Surgeon General: & I was then allowed to retire to my infinite delight."

By 15 February Lesassier was in London, determined that his stay there, like his voyage, should be the "very reverse" of his last. He found a comfortable and agreeable lodging house, a tailor who would give him new clothes on credit, and, attired in "a beautiful blue great coat with covered buttons, blue velvet collar & lapels & lined with black silk," he was, he wrote, "really so distinguished that I hardly recognized my old friend the Hospital Mate." His next task was to go in search of his two months' back pay. At first he hit the bureaucratic snag that he could not receive his pay unless he had an official certificate stating that he had not already been paid in Gibraltar. After an afternoon spent running from one army office to another, he found out that he could not get such a certificate until the Gibraltar pay receipts were in, which would not be for another two months. By now, Lesassier had developed a certain ingenuity in dealing with such problems. He persuaded the paymaster general's office to give him a certificate stating that all Gibraltar staff were paid every three months in arrears, so he could not have received his pay before leaving. This strategy worked, and he received two months' back pay of £24 to add to his stock. He even disbursed some patronage of his own: unexpectedly meeting his former fellow apprentice Joseph Brown, now a hospital mate, Lesassier "forgot all our former enmity . . . & . . . wrote a memorial to the Surgeon General, to procure him an Assistant Surgeoncy." Brown received the appointment a few weeks later, and Lesassier was happy to take the credit: "for the comforts he now enjoys he may thank me."

His examination also turned out to be the reverse of his previous experience. Instead of being penalized for not having studied long enough, Lesassier was rewarded for his experience, finding "that my having been so long in the Army may be of the utmost advantage to me as the Clerk at Surgeon's Hall took a particular note of it." He had the same examiner, Dundas, and was asked the same questions, thus demonstrating at once the value of a journal "if it be kept with diligence, accuracy, & precision"; the only difference was "that this time his anatomical questions were more difficult & numerous & his Surgical ones more simple & fewer." He was especially pleased that he was questioned carefully on the arterial system, a topic he had, he wrote, "at my finger ends." During his anatomical questions, "to every answer Dundas rejoined 'very well Sir' 'very well indeed Sir'—That was pleasing!"

The whole examination only lasted about half an hour, "most likely," as he noted, "from my answering with such facility. Indeed I was very well prepared." And his preparation was crowned with success, for he was now "entitled to a diploma whenever I choose . . . Lord! how enraptured I felt when my examination was over. I could have danced about the room." He had a right to be so pleased. By determination to be promoted from the detestable rank of hospital mate, he had succeeded in, first, obtaining the appointment as temporary assistant surgeon, then in getting leave of absence to retake the examination. By hard study, he had answered all questions with such facility that he was awarded the diploma without needing to attend more lectures. Dundas, too, had a right to be pleased, as did the medical board and the College of Surgeons, at the wisdom of their regulations. A promising but poorly educated young man had spent eighteen months getting acclimated to life in the Army Medical Service where his lack of knowledge could do little harm. He had returned older, more confident, and much better versed in anatomy and surgery. If Dundas remembered Lesassier at all, his "very well indeed Sir" may have referred to the part his original decision had played in Lesassier's improvement as much as to the answers.

Lesassier packed away his books and burned his examination papers: "Enough of dry anatomy & still drier examinations," he wrote, "I have done with you forever!" He was now free to turn his attention to obtaining the permanent appointment to the 42nd Regiment that he wanted so much. Here, too, his efforts were crowned with success. When he went to the medical board to ask about the vacant assistant surgeoncy, he was told that the 42nd had three assistant surgeons already between the two battalions, and though they were entitled to four, "that it was a rare case indeed where they could allow a regiment its full complement of Assistant Surgeons, as medical gentlemen were not to be procured." "This amazed me beyond expression," Lesassier wrote, because he only knew of two, and he asked to hear their names. When he heard them, he realized that there had been a mistake: a Mr. McDermid was listed as the third assistant, but Lesassier knew that he had left the 42nd to join another regiment. The clerk checked the War Office book "when to their utter amazement they found that I was correct & that their own book was wrong." Their mistake explained why the two previous applicants had not been appointed to the position. It had nothing to do with Colonel Stirling's recommendation of Lesassier, or any other kind of influence, but rather a clerical error.

"Thus by the most singular mistake possible," Lesassier wrote—and, we might add, his persistence in pursuing the matter despite setbacks—he obtained the position of senior assistant surgeon in the second battalion of the 42nd Regiment. "O dear! how delighted I feel to be appointed at last to a regiment I am so fond of—One that must inevitably soon be sent on service—that has distinguished itself so nobly." But what was most on his mind at once was his new uniform, the uniform he had coveted, but refrained from purchasing, while on Gibraltar, the superb Highland uniform: "A jacket—single breasted—with ten ribs of gold lace in front. . . . Blue collar with a stripe of gold & a button on each side—Blue cuffs with four stripes of gold & buttons. The edge from the edge of one lap to the other bordered with gold, blue, & white—The laps turned back with white & a brilliant star. Four buttons in a row on each side behind with gold button holes—Two massive gold Epaulets with a star on each. White, or blue pantaloons embroidered & half boots. And a superb Highland bonnet with pendant ostrich feathers. Together with the Highland claymore if I choose to wear it. There's a noble uniform. . . . If my father could but see me in such a dress"—his first mention of his father in many months—"how he would exult." He considered paying him a visit, but a letter from a friend informed him that Pierre had become involved in some new scandal, and now that Lesassier had become so supremely fortunate himself he would risk no taint from his past.

His new appointment was posted a week later. It was finally official, he wrote, "So at last I am an Assistant Surgeon & have forever done with all the inconveniences & disgrace of an Hospital Mate." His uncle wrote, "extremely delighted" with his success in passing his examination—"his letter . . . by far the most affectionate he ever wrote," for James Hamilton liked success. Firmly in possession of his new appointment and back pay, Lesassier mused on the changes that had taken place since his return from France six years ago: "My views were at that time uncertain & obscure. I was completely dependent on my father. I was possessed of no profession, whereby to earn my livelihood—& was at the same time irresolute as to what steps I should follow. But now, how great was the contrast. Totally independent of every one—& holding an honorable rank in society, I could gaze with delight, on the surrounding scenery; & pronounce myself perfectly happy."

# CHAPTER 5

# The Most Beautiful Man in Existence

On 24 March 1808, after five weeks in London, Lesassier boarded the packet boat bound for Aberdeen to join his regiment at Fort George. "Fare thee well great city!" he wrote, "I have by the Divine Providence met with such good fortune that I never before enjoyed such happiness. Completely my own master, I rose when I liked—read—walked—went to the theatre or played many an hour with one of the pretty maids at the house where I always dine." He left behind three young women, private milliners, "handsome and well-informed," and also a small debt to his landlady's brother, and larger ones to both his personal and regimental tailors. His trip was replete with the adventures incidental to even the most routine sea voyage. The bowsprit of their ship became entangled in another ship's rigging as they left Wapping, and they almost lost the tide. Snow and bad weather forced them to put into Harwich, and "two fathoms three quarters was the cry. . . . Then two fathoms & a half Then two fathoms." "Zounds," exclaimed Lesassier to William Forbes, a young assistant surgeon returning home to his family in Aberdeen, "didn't you tell me that this is what our vessel draws?" and at that moment, "with a violent, thundering shock," the ship struck a sand bank. They soon got free, but their adventures were not over, for two miles from Aberdeen, while the young men stood at the stern looking up at the broad expanse of sail, and exulting at the ship's speeding along, the main halyard broke, the rigging crashed, and the ship rolled, according to Lesassier's watch, at a rate of sixty times per minute. They were rescued by an Aberdeen smack that towed them safely into harbor. Lesassier still had one hundred miles to go to get to Fort George, and no money to travel there. Seeing an officer dressed in the uniform of the 42nd, he hesitantly asked to borrow £5; Captain Davidson, remembering his own days as a young officer, obliged, and by 13 April Lesassier had arrived in Fort George, £56 10s. in debt, but having now officially joined his regiment.

The fifteen months that Lesassier spent with the 42nd Regiment in England were probably the happiest of his life. As a handsome young officer in a gorgeous uniform, he was made much of, for Britain, in contrast to Gibraltar, often gave "the preference to a military society." For the first time in his life, he had both leisure and opportunity for social life; he had leisure, too, for indulging his interests in reading, in long romantic walks, and in writing. He lived, in fact, as much like an independent gentleman as he would ever manage, drawing his pay with very little work, since there were very few calls on his medical or surgical skills. There was, in fact, little incentive for Lesassier to concentrate on medicine, for once again the army had taken him "hot from his studies" and then left him to his own devices. The only medical duties he mentioned during his time in Britain was the occasional attendance on a sick soldier, and recruiting missions where he had to spend, he wrote, "from 10 in the forenoon until 5 p.m. . . . a close prisoner in a disagreeable barrack room examining the volunteers for various regiments," on one occasion "178 of those vagabonds" in three days.

Therein lay the danger. Contemporaries had harsh words for the intellectual level of young officers, "a set of idle superficial young men," according to Mary Wollstonecraft, "whose only occupation is gallantry, and whose polished manners render vice more dangerous, by concealing its deformity under gay ornamental drapery." More light-hearted, Susan Ferrier lumped them together with other young men in possessing "a species of humility rather to be admired in those who, feeling themselves destitute of mental qualifications, trust to the abilities of their tailor and hairdresser for gaining them the good-will of the world." This was hardly a society in which industry and learning flourished. Indeed, James McGrigor wrote, an army medical man "labours under one disadvantage of no mean importance," the lack of incentives to study. "The army is officered by gentlemen of anything but a studious turn of mind," he noted.

> There is more of gaiety, and perhaps of giddiness, or thoughtlessness, among them, than among any other class. Unless in time of war, their duties on entering the service are slight, and amusement is too often their principal occupation. A great many of them being well born, and all of them gentlemen, they do not look with much respect to a profession which requires study and close attention, or what they term plodding and drudgery. In fact, not a small portion of them have betaken themselves to the army from their distaste to study, and some of them from unsteadiness. . . . They have viewed with envy the seemingly easy, gentlemanly life of some officer in the army, who happened to have no other object than riding out after the morning parade, or sauntering about a town, ogling and coquetting with the fair who admired his dress and equipments, and who was an object of notice at concerts, theatre, and evening parties.

This "nobly idle" life could not fail to attract the young medical officers, so much more enticing than studying "dry anatomy" or writing up case histories. "Unless the medical man, just come from the schools, possesses a good share of steadiness," McGrigor went on, "he is very apt, on joining a corps, to be captivated with all this, and to fall into the idle habits and pursuits of those around him; and if he be of good figure and engaging manner, the danger is greatly increased. He reads less and less every day, makes his hospital duty as light as he can, stops but a short time with his patients, and is in haste to join his brother officers in their plans of amusement for passing the day."

There was, in other words, an ongoing tension between qualities expected of an officer and a gentleman and those which would lead to professional improvement.

McGrigor possessed more steadiness than most: as a young surgeon, he, like Lesassier, filled notebook after notebook, but with accounts of his patients rather than of his own life. But he, too, had experienced this tension, and his attempts to avoid drinking too much at dinner—without being thought of as a prig—by being called away, nightly, to urgent cases at the hospital, became a standing, if good-natured, joke with the other officers. Lesassier had, perhaps, less than his share of steadiness; he was certainly of "good figure and engaging manner." "My dear *graceful* friend," wrote his shipboard companion, Forbes, "the ladies of Aberdeen will not soon forget the genteel the all accomplished Mr. Lesassier"—he had always been susceptible to peer pressure, and the image of himself as a gentleman was far dearer to his heart than professional study or mores could ever be. Small wonder, then, that he quickly became "tainted with the indolently luxurious manners of a military life," and paid as little attention to medicine as possible. When James Hamilton wrote proposing he study French and Latin, and intimating he might make Lesassier his assistant, Lesassier was more dismayed than pleased. "If it had been proposed to me previous to my entering the Army," he wrote, "no proposal would have been received with so much rapture. But now I have so far imbibed the genuine spirit of a modern soldier that after the shortest stay in any place I pant with eagerness for other countries—& that I have become habituated to receive money with the mere exertion of applying for it I am little solicitous of any change."

There was more to this than youthful thoughtlessness, however; the army itself did little to encourage esprit de corps among medical officers, or—until McGrigor became director of the medical service in 1815—inducements for further study. As an officer, a surgeon was part of the military hierarchy, subordinate to the captain of the regiment or the colonel of a brigade: as a young surgeon, McGrigor had brought upon his head the wrath of his commanding officer by attending patients in the hospital rather than appearing on parade. Medical men, like purveyors, were often merely tolerated as useful but inconsequential to the main business of the army, because they didn't fight, and only with much effort could McGrigor prevail upon the Duke of Wellington to mention the medical staff in his public dispatches: "Very well, I will add something about the doctors," Wellington said, the first time "the medical officers . . . had been publicly acknowledged, in the same manner, as those of the military officers." And Lesassier was furious when he found army medical men were not entitled to wear gold epaulets, thus "tearing from us the only test our dress afforded of our being Commissioned Officers."

Ever sensitive to rank and status, Lesassier initially gravitated toward his nonmedical colleagues. The Second Battalion of the 42nd, Lesassier noted when he arrived at Fort George, consisted of 729 men, and his mess of 16 officers. The commanding officer, Major Maccara, had already received letters from James Hamilton and Lesassier's cousin, Mrs. Major Campbell. He repaid Captain Davidson his £5 as soon he was issued his salary; he had paid back Captain Fraser, too, by September; in contrast, he did not get around to repaying his tailors until 1814. Lesassier was more apt to refer to himself as a subaltern than an assistant surgeon, to speak feelingly of the hazards of a soldier's life, and when he wrote of having a "settled profession," he meant his profession as an officer.

But there were forces pulling him back toward medicine: the tension was a genuine one, not to be easily resolved. No one bothered to send letters to Lesassier's immediate superior, the surgeon Swinton McLeod, whom Lesassier described as "a little stiff gentleman possessing none of that *suaviter in modo* which so highly ingratiates a stranger in one's good opinion. It's true, he is not a pompous puppy as some surgeons with whom I've been acquainted—It's as well that he is not; such a character would meet with an awkward reception from *me*." But the "little stiff gentleman," who remained surgeon to the 42nd until 1829, was consistently generous to Lesassier, refusing to accept any money for the three weeks Lesassier breakfasted with him at Fort George, and lending him a horse for a recruiting expedition. Lesassier was not quite as dissipated as some of his "puppyish brethren"; his passion for reading, which made the local library his first stop in any town in which he was stationed, set him apart. Over the course of his career he received most help and guidance from medical officers, though he did not always appreciate it, and his Edinburgh education, too, gave him a common bond with other medical officers, including McLeod. His inseparable companion in the 42nd became William Lindsay, a former medical student at Edinburgh who gave up his profession in disgust when he could get an appointment only as hospital mate rather than assistant surgeon. He joined the 42nd as ensign, and his companionship, Lesassier wrote, "enables me to pass away some of the tedium of a military life in sensible conversation." Lesassier's personal Edinburgh connections also helped to remind him that his own profession was medicine, not soldiering. James Hamilton's letter, which complimented him on his "uniform steadiness of conduct," had its intended effect, for Lesassier and Lindsay decided to study both Latin and French for one hour per day. As usual when Lesassier applied himself, he did very well, and he wrote that he "must sincerely thank my dear uncle for his kindness in stimulating me on to a plan of study which," he added—for "we are evermost pleased with . . . our own opinion"—"I have often had in contemplation."

The regiment remained in Fort George only for three weeks, for at the beginning of May it received orders to march for Glasgow, there to embark for Ireland. Lesassier was not at all sorry to leave this "barren country," where he had been thoroughly bored, though he had arranged to be sent books from the library in Aberdeen, "the greatest boast of this remote town . . . supplied with all the useful magazines; & London newspapers . . . and containing a circulating Library containing 60,000 volumes including all new works." The battalion was split up into six divisions with Lesassier and McLeod assigned to different divisions. Lesassier left Fort George on 3 May. His particular companion for the trip was a friend from Gibraltar, Lieutenant Duncan Stewart. Stewart, who commanded the division, was, Lesassier wrote, "equally poor with myself"; their joint goal for "this pedestrian excursion," in addition to leading the men and saving money, was to see the countryside, for Lesassier found that, barren as the Highlands might be, there was much that was both picturesque and sublime.

Lesassier had become a picturesque traveler. The word *picturesque* had a specific meaning in Lesassier's day: "A picturesque landscape" according to one historian, "called forth in the mind's eye a sublime romantic subject . . . varied and broken surfaces and the dramatic use of chiaroscuro." Its chief delineator was William Gilpin, author of numerous books describing his travels through England and Scotland in search of "beauty of every kind, which either art, or nature can produce," but most especially picturesque views. In Gilpin's view the picturesque was active, not passive; it did not really exist without a viewer; and the traveler had to go out into nature seeking it. For "as many travel without any end at all," Gilpin wrote, "amusing themselves without being able to give a reason why they are amused, we offer an end, which may possibly engage some vacant minds; and may indeed afford a rational amusement to such as travel for more important purposes." Jane Austen satirized his views in *Northanger Abbey*, where after much discussion of "fore-grounds, distances, and second distances—side-screens and perspectives—light and shades," Catherine Morland "voluntarily rejected the whole city of Bath, as unworthy to make part of a landscape." But his books inspired a multitude of young men and women, including Lesassier, with a desire for "the pen of a *Gilpin* to impress on a stranger a proper conception of the innumerable beauties to be observed."

The tone of the journals shifted as Lesassier moved through a different moment of self-creation: he was now a travel writer rather than a novelist. He kept careful account of his travels, in the ever popular guidebook style of his day, mentioning sights, antiquities, bridges, inns, distances between towns. He did his best to be accurate, asking for local information and checking distances against maps or milestones marked on the road. On his march through the Highlands, Lesassier and Lieutenant Stewart generally tried to rise early and order the drum roll to marshal troops and be on their way by 5 A.M. or so, but the troops they marshaled appear to have delayed as long as they could, so that they seldom left before 6. Even so, they often marched the required twelve or fifteen miles by midmorning, allowing plenty of time for the officers to go sightseeing. Their route led them by Cawdor castle, "famous," Lesassier wrote, "for the murder of Duncan—a King of Scotland." They marched south to Granton, where the local doctor, his wife, and friends entertained the officers with eating, drinking, and dancing all night, followed by a walk through the village at dawn. "It was the merriest evening I ever passed," Lesassier wrote, particularly impressed by the stamina of the young ladies—"Such hardiness would astound our lowland countrywomen"—especially on the march the next day, when he was so tired, he wrote, "that at every step I thought my blistered feet & aching limbs would fail me." He grew less happy on the march as they went through the Cairngorm Mountains in a cold driving rain, but by the time they approached Blair Atholl they were "superior to such trifles" as bad weather. The road near the old garrison of Ruthven "became extremely picturesque. It leads through a small wood of brush. Through the trees you see the land (confined by hills on every side) in the highest state of culture." So was the view from a bridge near Drummochter: "Down a deep rocky ravine, the river rushes foaming—& falls with great violence in several cascades." It was a commonplace that Highland views, like the Highlanders themselves, were barbarous and rude: "Sometimes we were so closed in by high, black hills that it was impossible to extricate ourselves." Such barbarousness, once tamed, became extremely pleasing, as Lesassier found on the Killicrankie pass, where, he wrote, though "surrounded & hemmed in by huge mountains rising abruptly on every side . . . our jaded eyes rest in pleasure on the green foliage . . . The landscape was ever varying, every interesting. Can I say more than that the high cultivation of England was joined to the rude majestic scenery of the Highlands?" Gilpin's own description of the pass of Killicrankie is more extensive, but his print precisely illustrates Lesassier's huge mountains and green foliage. Perhaps Lesassier, like Catherine Morland, had so imbibed Gilpin's precepts as to see landscape with Gilpin's eyes; or perhaps the brand new edition of the *Observations on the Highlands of Scotland* had arrived in the Aberdeen library in time for Lesassier to consult it before leaving for Fort George.

However majestic the scenery, Lesassier's heart obviously warmed the closer he got to real towns. "Our present inn puts us in mind that we have entered a civilized country," he wrote when they arrived in Dunkeld, where he especially admired the newly constructed "Gothic" bridge with seven arches, and the "sublime" waterfall, "a cataract foaming below, at a dizzying depth." In Perth, which they reached the next day, he wrote, "Indeed I was never in any provincial town which attracted me so much." Perhaps this was because of the numbers of "handsome girls," but perhaps also it was because they "once again enjoyed the novel sight of a stage coach." Perth, too, had a lending library and a theatre, which Lesassier attended, receiving "more amusement . . . than I have for many years past." Lesassier's taste in living areas was definitely urban; not for him the secluded country cottage, or even estate: "In a large town," he wrote, "I am ever more at my ease than in a small place. Every want can be satisfied. There I can read the newest publications—I can now and then amuse myself at the theatre—I can pursue every study."

From Perth, Lesassier's division went to Sterling, which he duly described, but after that point the diary entries become sketchy notes. He may have been traveling by horse by now, for he mentions that one of the young officers, Lord Berridale, came to ask for his medical advice, offered to lend him money, which Lesassier refused, then offered him his horse to ride to Glasgow. We may suspect the offer was less a favor than a contrivance on Lord Berridale's part to have his horse transported to Glasgow, but Lesassier never did. Clearly thrilled to have a titled friend—he had never before been in a position to ride a lord's horse—he accepted the offer even though he expected it to add five shillings a day to his expenses. Lesassier became ill as they approached Glasgow, and a rough passage across the Irish Sea did nothing to make him feel better, but he was happy to arrive on 7 June in Armagh, "a poor looking ill-built place" with, however, "an extensive & select library . . . of 80,000 Volumes . . . open gratis to readers from 11 till 2 o'clock P.M." His cousin Mrs. Major Campbell had again written on his behalf, and more unexpectedly, the newly married wife of his old friend Jenoway turned up in Armagh and introduced him to "some very agreeable society." In addition, a well-to-do local doctor named Atkinson made a point of welcoming officers to his house, the better to marry off his ten daughters, Lesassier thought at first, but later decided it might well be disinterested hospitality. Within a week of his arrival, he wrote, "Armagh contents me very completely."

At this point in his military life Lesassier began a new, personal campaign, one fraught with important consequences for his heart and his purse: the search for a wife. This was not the first time he had considered marrying. In Manchester, at the age of sixteen and seventeen, his thoughts had turned to marriage whenever he became fond of a woman: in addition to his maidservant sweetheart Ann Dean, he had thought of proposing to a Miss Harrison whom he had courted over a period of seven weeks. Since then he had become more discriminating, and more mercenary. Three years earlier he would have thought his seven shillings per day a handsome independence, but by now he knew how easy they were to spend. He was happy to find he could live within his salary, but he still had debts to pay, and "alas!" he wrote, "when once one becomes involved in debt it requires a very hard struggle to get free again." He had learned in Gibraltar—for it must have been a frequent topic of conversation there as elsewhere in the army—the difference between officers who had to live on their pay and those who did not. He attributed the paymaster's successful courtship of Miss Stirling to his £150 per annum; and he considered proposing to the daughter of the innkeeper at San Roque on the assumption that she had a large dowry; "if I obtained this treasure," he wrote, "& a pretty Spaniard with it, I purposed behaving with respect to his Majesty's service, in a most independent manner." It was, it seemed to him now as it had in Rochdale, only through marriage that he could obtain additional income to clear his debts and achieve true independence—not for him "the Luxury of living in every Distress that Poverty can inflict, with the object of his tenderest Affection"—and Armagh might be his last chance, for Lord Blantyre, lieutenant colonel of the 42nd, was set on ensuring that the regiment be sent on active service.

Of course, no maidservant could be considered suitable in his present circumstances, and even well-off shopkeeper's daughters were "seulement des Bourgeoise," only bourgeois. What he needed was a young lady, preferably young and beautiful, for then he could fall in love with her for herself rather than for her fortune. Love might not conquer all, but Lesassier certainly assumed that it obviated any further discussion of his motives. And if his love was reciprocated—as he assumed it would be, for never had he "failed in my attempts at gaining any lady's affections . . . or known the pang of disappointed love"—there should be no further objections to the match. William Hazlitt asked in an essay why the heroes of romantic novels are insipid. "Because it is taken for granted that they must be amiable and interesting" was his answer. "To put it to the proof, to give illustrations of it, would be to throw a doubt upon the question." If the hero himself "indeed seemed to entertain a doubt upon the subject, the spell of his fascination would be broken, and the author would be obliged to . . . make him do something to deserve the good opinion that might be entertained of him." The heroes of novels did not have to try to be clever, handsome, good, or talented, because the beautiful and wealthy heroine would fall in love with them anyway. "They have only to show themselves to ensure conquest," Hazlitt said. Lesassier, in this sense if no other, was every inch a hero.

Lesassier, then, at twenty-one, was an insufferable coxcomb, but he was also handsome and charming, and he set out to captivate Miss Alicia Irwin, who lived four miles away but was in town visiting her aunt, a friend of Lesassier's cousin Mrs. Major Campbell. She was "the only young lady in this part of the country who has the good opinion of all who know her," Lesassier wrote, an important consideration, for he could not think of associating himself with a lady who would not reflect well on him before his brother officers. She was seventeen, "handsome & accomplished," and he promptly fell in love with her. His first mention of Alicia Irwin betokens only mild enjoyment. He met her in September, but spoke to her for the first time at a "grand party" given by her aunt in the beginning of October. He was, he wrote, "perfectly captivated with Alicia the first evening I was in her company & she has secured my fetters still further in my second interview with her at the ball yesterday—So it may be fully believed that I enjoyed yesterday evening extremely."

By the next entry, a week later, the affair was heating up. "Last night," he wrote, "I spent a far more delightful evening than I ever did before. I was at a select party. . . . My dear Alicia was there. . . . My whole time was occupied in the dear girl's company. She was remarkably playful with me & ceremony was totally laid aside." His enjoyment of the dear girl's company was enhanced by external circumstances. The setting—an elaborate party—was Lesassier's vision of a genteel life, and it was a select party: only one other officer from his regiment had been invited. He took this as his opportunity to carry out a more or less conscious plan, to make Alicia fall in love with him in as short a time as possible. He did this by trying to break down the barriers of formal conversation and heighten the emotional and sexual intensity as much as possible—in a word, by flirting.

Other people's flirting often appears more comic than romantic: "I wish your heart were independent," says Captain Tilney to Isabella Thorpe, in a continuation of the conversation mentioned earlier. "That would be enough for me."

"My heart, indeed! What can you have to do with hearts? You men have none of you any hearts."

"If we have not hearts, we have eyes; and they give us torment enough."

"Do they? I am sorry for it; I am sorry they find anything so disagreeable in me. I will look another way. I hope this pleases you" (turning her back on him); "I hope your eyes are not tormented now."

"Never more so: for the edge of a blooming cheek is still in view—at once too much and too little."

Next to that we may place the following excerpt from Assistant Surgeon Lesassier and Miss Alicia Irwin:

"I fear you have not gotten rid of your cold yet," said Lesassier.

"O yes I have," replied Alicia.

"Why then do you still wear that patch?"

"O because I think it looks conceited & I like being thought conceited."

From the first their conversation was dominated by possessions in a way that may shock the sensibilities of those used to the more restrained materialism of novels. "I sat by her side at supper," Lesassier wrote one evening, "& added a zest to her conversation by quarreling with her on various pretexts in order that I might enjoy the pleasure of begging her pardon." The pretext in question was Alicia's ring, which Lesassier wanted, for she "frequently gave me hopes that I should obtain it & then disappointed me." Lesassier, never chivalrous, refused to let her have the upper hand: "pretended to quarrel with her & on rising to return home coldly bade her goodnight. Scarcely had I gotten out of the room when I heard the little wretch crying out in a plaintive voice 'O what shall I do!'" Lesassier himself was much affected: "Since last night," he wrote, "I have found myself utterly incapable of applying to any of my usual pursuits. I am perpetually thinking of her & at the same time regret the immense distance that separates us. . . . Before we again meet she may have forgotten that such a person is in existence. How mortifying the thought." By now he was, he decided, in love with her: "Never since the days of my love for Laura"—that is, Isabella—"have I felt myself so completely unhinged as now—I had falsely imagined that my heart was for ever steeled against such another impression. . . . But now I find my error."

For now, Alicia remained in possession of her ring, but Lesassier returned to the attack at a crowded supper-party the following week. Why had she not given him the ring when he asked for it? "How could you refuse me such a trifle? Really you are very ill natured!"

"How could I give it you?" she replied, "For to tell the truth it is not mine."

"Not your own!? Indeed then you could not with propriety have given it away."

"But now," Alicia asked, "were it your own & given you by a valued friend would you give it away?"

"To *you* I would," he replied, "though it were the most valuable thing I possess."

But "Mr. Lesassier," she protested, "if I had given you the ring you teased me so much about, what could you have thought of me. After so slight an acquaintance it would have been contrary to all rules of propriety & decorum. I'm sure you did not expect that I would give it to you although you were so earnest in begging it."

"Indeed *though* I did," he responded, for "How could it have been so very improper a step when it is impossible that any person but myself could have known it."

"Ah! Mr. Lesassier the impropriety of an action does not depend on its being made public. It is on what we ourselves feel—I have always been accounted too giddy but surely that step would have given sanction to such a character."

"But surely Ma'am," perhaps leaning a little close, "intimacy of acquaintance must be estimated otherwise than by the number of times two persons meet—Nothing is more usual than to be in the company of those for ages with whom strictly speaking we are not intimately acquainted—This depends on our not thinking about them. But where we are interested, our frequent thoughts upon the same person must rapidly advance our acquaintance although we should have been little in each other's company. If you estimate the degree of my intimacy with you by the frequency with which we have met, I have no chance of *ever* being except on the most formal footing with you. For there is no likelihood of our regiment remaining in this town long enough for me to see you often." He spoke "in so mournful a manner that she seemed to regret what she had said."

"But how does what you have been telling me, refer to our acquaintance?" she asked.
"Thus Ma'am because I am most highly interested in you—"

"Indeed Sir (bowing)," and affecting to misunderstand him, "I am extremely obliged to you for both your good wishes & good opinion—"

"Good heaven!" he exclaimed, "how can you misunderstand a meaning so plainly expressed—However as this party must soon break up, I am determined rather to be rude than that we should part as much strangers to each other as ever—well then, permit me to say that when I stated to you how highly I was interested in you, I made use of the *poorest possible words* to express myself, & I beg of you to take the meaning in its *most unlimited sense*."

Who could resist so eloquent a protestation of affection? Not Alicia, who refused to answer, though there is little doubt that she was pleased: possession of a ring had devolved into a more intimate form of possession. Her refusal to answer in turn pleased Lesassier, for it meant they had gone beyond formal drawing-room conversation. "What has so suddenly made you thus gloomy," he asked. "You were wont to have inexhaustible topics for conversation but now—they are all gone—This is most unaccountable." But he had no difficulty in accounting for it, and happily walked her home to her aunt, with "the delightful sensation of her arm leaning on mine—At parting I took the liberty of pressing her hand in mine."

He saw her again the next day for a brief period. She was walking on the mall with her sister Eliza and a friend. Again, she and Lesassier had a tug-of-war over an article in her possession, this time keys. "When I met her," he wrote, "she had two small keys in her hand—I begged to carry them—She told me that one of them was the key of her jewels—At parting, having forgotten to give her keys back she called to me—I returned & made an apology & was offering them when her companions told me not to give them to her—I followed their advice & ran away Every now & then turning round laughing & kissing my hand to her & calling out 'Adieu'—She lingered awhile looking after me expecting that I would return. But I soon lost sight of her." Another possession produced another quarrel and reconciliation: Lesassier "had . . . been at considerable pains to plait a hair ribbon for her keys purposing to enjoy her astonishment at my gallantry," but was so annoyed at her coming in late to a party "although she knew I was to be there, that I most completely neglected her." He was "hurt that Alicia should appear thus indifferent to me"; again, not for him the unswerving devotion to *la belle dame sans merci*: he wanted to know, and for others to know, that his efforts were appreciated. He repented the next day, and called on them to make "ample amends for my former behaviour & was freer with her . . . than I had ever been before. We were as playful as possible together." They again played their game of possessions and possession. "I begged to know from her," Lesassier wrote,

> if she had noticed the bow I had fastened her keys with. She asserted that she had not; but with such an arch look that I could not but suspect that she was joking.
> I told her that now, she was aware of the circumstance, I begged to know how she

meant to act: for if she accepted it such a step would allow me scope for an unlimited conclusion in my own favor. However she would not decide either to keep it or throw it away—The same afternoon I jokingly told her that her gloves were extremely shabby: upon which she desired me to buy her another pair— This I did & presented them to her yesterday. She accepted them but soon reprobated what she called her impropriety of conduct in making thus free with a stranger. Nevertheless, she kept them, [saying] sweetly. . . . No, I will not part with these gloves!—but whenever I look on them, I shall think on the giver!

With these proofs of Alicia's affections and interest, if we may be allowed a deliberate pun, Lesassier may have felt he had, so to speak, hooked his fish. "Scandal," he wrote, "now attacks me open mouthed. The public have no mercy on me—They *will* have us married in spite of ourselves." At a Halloween party at Dr. Atkinson's, the guests played a game called "burning nuts" to discover who would be married. "Two hazel nuts previously dried, are named after a lady & a gentleman & being placed together on the first bar of the fire grate are set fire to. If they both burn together the meaning is obvious & vice versa." Alicia was not there, but nonetheless she and Lesassier "were the first *burnt*." Lesassier had no objection to the rumors, or to the idea. "I must say," he wrote, "that *if*, I were to obtain an increase of pay to 10 shillings per day, as is now confidently asserted, & *if* Alicia had without any doubt, or uncertainty £2,000, as report states, why then *if* she had no objections we might perhaps become *inseparable*."

The results of the game had not been propitious: instead of burning together, he and Alicia's nuts blew up and flew away separately, his with a "loud explosion." This was an ominous sign, Lesassier felt, and he was sure it was confirmed by events later that night. After the party he decided to spend the night with "a kind friend of mine," Betty, a servant in the house he lodged in. He obviously had no sense that he was being unfaithful to Alicia, nor that there was anything improper or ungentlemanly in listening to a story Betty told of Alicia's former attachment to a young ensign, Eeston. Eeston had lodged there when his regiment was in town, a few months before. According to Betty, "Eeston was distractedly fond of Alicia. She returned his affection. They were always together. . . . Alicia was ever in town & if she was at home in the country Eeston was with her. As a proof of her excessive love for him, Betty related to me that, once he had strained his ankle Alicia was in such agonies that she, her sister & Aunt came to see him. Alicia was distracted. She went down on her knees & rubbed his ankle herself. He would have prevented her & she was heard repeatedly to say 'O! my dear Eeston, I *will* rub it for you.' "

There were several points in this story that upset Lesassier. The first was that he had a rival: "whilst I had fondly imagined she did not look on me with an unfavorable eye, her thoughts & heart were far, far, from me." According to the story, Eeston must have been a favored rival, for he had been at Alicia's home, while Lesassier had never been invited there. Moreover, according to Betty, Alicia "had loaded Eeston with favors," while Lesassier had not even been able to extract the cherished ring from her; indeed, he had given her presents but had received nothing in return. He resolved to bring up the subject to her as soon as possible, which turned out to be the next day, when he met her with her sister and aunt.

He started off, once again, with the subject of presents. "I begged a keepsake from her in return for my gloves," he wrote, "which she refused me." "This stung me to the quick"; hadn't she given keepsakes to Eeston? He responded with some rapid insults, "Well Ma'am I'll repeat what I have often said to you that you are very ill natured," and "I shall never think on you without an unpleasant reflection." He then got to the point, the topic of Eeston. "I may as well hint to you," he told her, "that I am acquainted with secrets of yours which were I to tell them you, you would think I had employed enchantment to become a partaker of them." Which ones? she wanted to know, but it was only by slow, torturous degrees that he let on, while "piercingly eyeing her" that it concerned "a *certain serious accident* that happened to a *dear* friend of yours—in which you displayed so much *tender anxiety* & *solicitude*." Alicia was furious: "Mr. Lesassier, you thought, that by telling me of this, you would make me blush, & be ashamed of myself; but allow me, to say, that I neither blush, nor am ashamed of what I then did— & must tell you that were *you* in such a situation, I *would not do* as much for *you*."

This sudden thrust, Lesassier wrote, "shocked me so much I scarcely knew where I stood. I felt a sudden sickness, & an indescribable sensation coming over me. Alicia had her complexion of a lively red. Her eyes flashed fire—I knew not what to say." An apology might, perhaps, have been in order but Lesassier had no intention of humbling himself: "In a fit of rage I made the most awful & tremendous vow never to be reconciled to her unless she makes me an apology." Instead he assumed that Alicia was simply speaking the truth, that she would not do for him what she did for Eeston, and that she therefore did "not feel any sensation for me but that of indifference." The two young lovers spent the next week ostentatiously ignoring each other. Lesassier "felt a most pungent sensation at my heart at this hauteur," he wrote, "& with the utmost difficulty concealed my feelings. . . . I was convinced that now I had forever lost her acquaintance. . . . An oppressive weight seemed threatening to suffocate me—My face burned with an hectic blush of the deepest hue—All our officers observed my gloom at dinner—I could neither speak nor eat." Alicia, too, was affected, and when he called at her aunt's house she entered the room late, deliberately dramatic, "Her complexion, was very pale—Her eyes were swollen—& red—& traces of tears were seen on her cheek. She attempted to wear a smile on her pensive face." "Never had I seen her look so interesting," Lesassier wrote, but he was worried. His foolish quarrel had come too soon, before he had quite reeled in his fish, and he might have lost Alicia and her purported £2,000: this "was not acting like an able General."

Alicia's aunt helped to reconcile the two. Once again they sat side by side at supper. "A free & ample explanation took place. We were both so very stiff that I dreaded our separating again as we had met—but when I frankly confessed to her the vow I had made & the conditions, she affably apologized to me first & then—all went smoothly on—We became completely reconciled—& I kissed her hand to seal the agreement."

But Lesassier's time was running out: the regiment was ordered to Newry in early November, though he managed to stay in Armagh until the twenty-fifth "in charge of a few sick." If he were to truly secure Alicia's affections, he had to act quickly, else their "love will vanish into air—When distance separates us—when time has intervened—& new objects present themselves, we shall think no more of each other."

In lieu of a more decisive step, Lesassier tried to persuade Alicia to correspond with him secretly, arguing "against her ideas of the impropriety of such a step—that there could not exist any possible impropriety in the matter unless she considered my situation in life too far beneath her." Alicia stood firm, despite all his entreaties: "Her Father had ever behaved with so much tenderness & affection towards her," she told him, "that she could not think of concealing such a circumstance." Edward Neville, as eloquent in love as his author, tried to persuade the fair Emily to a secret correspondence by informing her "I should think almost no sacrifice—within the bounds of innocence and honour—too great for a lady to make to the man she truly loves." But both Alicia and Emily stood firm. Alicia was not such a giddy girl as she liked to consider herself: her behavior with Lesassier and Eeston, if the story was true, showed that she might allow her sensibility to push her behavior to the limits of propriety, but she would not enter into a correspondence that would permanently endanger her reputation. Her determination forced Lesassier to the next step. He had not, perhaps, really intended to propose marriage yet, but as the conversation turned from a secret correspondence to obtaining her father's consent the question of his intentions naturally arose. The only way such a correspondence could with propriety be maintained was if Lesassier was accepted as a worthy suitor for Alicia. Thus asking for permission to write was a prelude to a proposal, and involved the wounding risk of rejection. Neither one wished to take that risk. Alicia said, according to Lesassier, "If my own feelings were to be sacrificed & that would effect our wishes I would not hesitate a moment." But she did hesitate. Lesassier had stated his circumstances honestly: his lack of private fortune, his expectations of promotion, but no money from his uncle, and she may have had second thoughts about his suitability as a husband. She told Lesassier that "her father would not pay so much attention to the state of his circumstances, as to whether she could be happy with one of so recent an acquaintance—whether in short, she could love a person, whom she had known so short a time," and she herself may have wondered, now that the regiment had left and the season was ending, whether this really was true love after all.

Lesassier tried to extract from her precisely what her fortune would be, to estimate, we might say, whether the expected return would be worth the risk of rejection. He told her he could not write to his uncle to ask his permission "unless I could state to him what fortune she possesses," "a very delicate subject." She told him "that she could form no idea as to what fortune her father intended to give her." Nor could her aunt, as she "had never heard the subject mentioned—However as Mr. Irwin loved his daughters better than his two sons something handsome might be expected with it." Eventually Lesassier hit upon a rather complex plan: rather than visiting Alicia's father, he would write a letter to Alicia at home under the pretext of wishing her a happy return, but also ask for her and her father's permission to visit her. If he consented, matters could go from there. It seems to have satisfied Alicia, for she told him that "if the business should fail of success I [Lesassier] could not possibly blame myself & that the sacrifice I had made of my feelings in the whole affair was a more convincing proof to her of my affection than the most eloquent language."

The end of the affair in fact came very quickly. On Wednesday Lesassier sent the letter, and on Sunday, 20 November, Alicia left town. He wrote that he "took leave of her in a very foreboding, gloomy style & presaging that we should never meet again." Characteristically, their parting was dominated by presents: Lesassier complained, "Contrary to her promise she did not leave me the hair-ribbon which I looked for— However she requested to her Aunt to inform me that on Tuesday next she will send me either that or some other bagatelle." The following Tuesday, when Lesassier went to call on Alicia's aunt, "her features struck me as peculiarly melancholy. . . . After a while I begged to know if Alicia had remembered to send me the little keepsake she had promised upon which she gave me a packet containing a long lock of Alicia's beautiful hair & a heart of gold with "souvenir" engraved on it & containing a small lock of hair. These were unaccompanied with any letter from her. Still it struck me that something unforeseen had happened. . . . I pressed her to inform me—At length she burst into tears, & sobbing told me, that I should too soon learn my misfortune."

Mr. Irwin had been very angry to hear that matters had gone so far without his being informed, and had flatly refused the match. "He insists on my relinquishing all further ideas of the business," Lesassier wrote, and not wishing to "trifle with my feelings . . . was decisive—Then he goes on to assert in proof that his decision against me was not owing to any report that had reached him but that I must have a very low opinion of his understanding were he to engage his daughter to one whose affairs there was no probability of his hearing any thing of but from myself besides which that he did not consider my situation as a proper one for the comfortably managing of a family." For those reasons, he "requests me to *relinquish every idea of the business.*"

"I was agitated by a conflagration of contending passions," Lesassier wrote, "Wounded pride—grief—love—alternately struggled for the sway. Grief at last over-came every other sensation." Alicia's aunt, who perhaps was more involved in her young niece's romances than she would admit, "was more affected that I should have imagined it possible. She seemed peculiarly anxious to know, if I would remain con-stant to Alicia—Whether or not if Mr. Irwin would not consent to our present union, I should still persevere in my affection until the sun of better days shall shine upon me." Lesassier was honest, if not gallant: "I told her that were it in the nature of things here below that affection should remain for ever in all the glowing fervor of its first existence then indeed I could promise fidelity—but that alas! our whole mind & all its connected chain of passions were daily undergoing the most material changes—& that from every one's experience no person can place any reliance on his firmest resolutions." Alicia's aunt "appeared much hurt at these unfortunate truths. . . . Often & often she wished I had never known her family—which, I sorrowfully joined in."

Alicia herself eventually wrote, and her letter was brought to Lesassier by her aunt's footman just as he was getting into the coach to join his regiment in Newry. "With great trepidation I broke open the seal—It was a short letter & in a strain of resigned melancholy She deplored her distressing situation to be under the necessity of writing in such an affair—expressed her gratitude for my affection—hoped I would not blame her in the affair from submitting to her father's commands—trusted that change of scene together with my own good understanding would give me fortitude to submit to this disappointment—& ended with assuring me, ere she bade me farewell, that my happiness in life would be the greatest source of delight to her." Perhaps her aunt had told Alicia of Lesassier's response to her request for constancy, for, her letter concluded, "if I should eradicate my present affection & form another attachment she fervently prays I may meet the return I merit." It is tempting, but probably incorrect, to impute to her any irony.

Lesassier did not forgive Alicia for giving in, and even, according to Mr. Irwin's letter, agreeing to her father's objections to him. "Whichsoever way I regard her conduct it lessens her effectually in my estimation. If she accede to her father's observations merely from fear, not daring to advance a single argument in favor of one who loved as I did—She evinced a degree of tame submission which in any other I would term meanness—On the other hand if really she do not return my affection & agreed with the truth of her father's strictures on me—merely because as uninterested—it was immaterial to her in what manner the business might be decided—then have I less reason than ever to regret the issue of this affair." In a fitting end to an affair dominated by material objects, Alicia's aunt and Lesassier exchanged keepsakes: "I gave her a pearl ring—before she had offered me anything and I was very much gratified to find that she was about to send me a packet—On returning home I opened this & found an affectionate letter accompanied with a superb ring of a most beautiful emerald set with brilliants—Of course I was much flattered by this valuable proof of her regard."

"The spell is broke," Lesassier wrote at the end of November. "Perhaps—nay it is more than probable that I shall never truly love any one as I have loved Alicia," but in December, the regiment moved on to Dublin, and by March he had met Ella D., later Ella Anderton, a woman who lived up to his most romantic expectations. She was eighteen years old, originally from Liverpool, and had been married for two years to the captain of a merchantman. "She lived with him merely five weeks," she told Lesassier, "when he went on a voyage & did not return during a year. After three or four weeks he again left her." She was visiting her aunt and uncle in Dublin, and she and a cousin seem to have often gone to the parade grounds, where she first saw Lesassier. Passionate, emotional, and rather lower than he in station, she fell in love with him at first sight with an intensity that surprised even him. "She was young, gay, & highly susceptible of impression," he wrote, "while at the same time, the splendor of my dress—& the romantic celebrity of my Regiment, completed the delusion." Ever afterward she thought of him as "Alexander of the Highland watch," "the *most* beautiful man in existence."

It was some time before she could find a way to introduce herself to him, but one day after their regiment was on parade, she and her cousin walked along with him. "Ella wore a veil," Lesassier wrote, "I knew not if she were handsome—but . . . I continued to walk with them—E's conversation was too familiar & I considered her to be a fille de joy." The next time they met, she did not wear her veil, and "My astonishment was inexpressibly great," he wrote, to find her "young and beautiful." This time, her conversation was "reserved yet most fascinatingly affectionate," and he concluded that though she might not be a prostitute, she had probably been seduced and was looking for another protector. With that in mind, he "persuaded her to come & see me in my barracks" the next night, 26 March. Instead of the expected woman of easy virtue, however, he found that he had on his hands a respectably married woman who, "By one of those strange revolutions which love effects in the human breast," he wrote, had become "violently attached to me—She had long known me by sight but chance had never given her an opportunity of becoming acquainted with me until that Field day before mentioned Her fond heart panted to secure our casual knowledge of each other; & so intent was she in pursuing this object that she unwarily overlooked that line of conduct toward me which alone was proper to obtain what she so anxiously wished for. However her real character gradually developed itself to me & I could not withhold my affection from the dear girl." She became his mistress, perhaps two nights later; "She bade me note down Tuesday March 28th 1809!!!" Lesassier wrote, and Ella herself later "retraced the night when we returned from the theatre—you said alas poor Ella how much I regret that I have not the least thing to offer you for supper—when at the same time you had got a fine large dish of jelly &c &c for me how heartily we laughed when it appeared on the table." He had never met "with any circumstance so romantic," he wrote, "That a beautiful, accomplished, woman of scarcely eighteen, & of affluent circumstance, should throw herself into my arms, is an affair bordering too much on the improbable to meet with credit—A multitude of facts press themselves on me as uncontrovertible proofs of all her actions being the result of pure affection *for me*. This is would be madness to doubt—Hence my astonishment at my own good fortune."

Ella, for her part, regarded Lesassier as the love of her life, and the days they spent together in Dublin as "that blessed period—when I was the sole beloved of the *most beautiful man in existence*—the tone of whose voice *never* yet for a moment left my ear." Seventeen years later the mere sight of the 42nd Regiment was enough to send her into a frenzy of emotion. She wrote to her "*still*" dear Alexander how she "went out to meet this dear regiment—the sight of this regiment caused *such* painful feeling in my heart that I was scarcely able to *walk home*. Ah can I ever forget the time when my Alexander was the *flower* of this *regiment*—and I the happiest of the happy." On a trip to Dublin, on "a fine moonlit night I went to the Royal Barrack and stood looking at your *former* room for more than an hour with a bitter heart and many a sad sigh. . . . Ah! said I there is the room where I spent the happiest days of my life with my Alexander." Lesassier had been afraid that one of his brother officers had designs on her, having "lately discovered him guilty of deep dissimulation," but, Ella wrote, "how was it possible" that she could "*even bear* the thought of an old—ignorant plain being like him—while *you* smiled upon me *you* who was at that period one of the most truly beautiful accomplished—and fascinating beings in existence."

Despite the intensity of the affair, they actually had very little time together. On April 6, two weeks after they met, Ella had to return to Liverpool to await her husband. Their leave-taking was as emotional as either could wish. Lesassier saw her on board the packet to Liverpool: "After confiding her to the steward's care," he wrote, "& seeing that she was every way comfortable I tore myself away from the poor weeping girl." She arrived safely, and sent him "a present of delicious mocha coffee. This was very attentive as she knew how fond I am of it." Ella had no objection to a clandestine correspondence, and the two had worked out a system for Lesassier to send letters to the post office so her husband would not find out, but Ella forgot the system by the time she arrived home, and kept going to the steward of the packet to see if any letters had come for her. By the time they had found out the mistake, Lesassier wrote, "she had sickened with anxious expectation & had been some days confined to bed—It would be impossible to convey in the most glowing language an adequate conception of the sensations I experienced in reading this agonizing letter." He was distressed, certainly, but it also gave him a certain satisfaction to harrow up his feelings. "Alas!" he wrote, "what melancholy proof poor Ella is of the power of love. Her affection has impaired her health so much that little or no hopes are entertained by her friends of her life—Till a few days ago she had gotten only one letter from me during a long period of ten weeks—This apparent neglect on my part pressed with such dreadful ravages on her constitution that I greatly dread she is undeceived too late—Her passions are most unfortunately too strong—How strangely she has been hurried away by the impetuous torrent of her affection—even from the first hour we met—Nothing half so romantic in any novel will be met with. And should the little story of our love at a future period be related it would at once be rejected as the fictitious productions of a disordered imagination." However, Ella did not, in fact, die of love, not even when she heard he was to be sent overseas. For the first time, Lesassier's love affair did not end when he went away, largely because of Ella's "continued perseverance in the same impassioned line of conduct," and letters to and from her remained his main source of emotional sustenance throughout his time on foreign service.

However satisfactory a lover Ella might be, though, she was obviously unsuitable for a wife, and would therefore be of no use in providing for his future. Fortunately, Lesassier still had his profession, whether defined as an officer or as a medical man. Thanks to his uncle's encouragement, he had continued his studies, and when he heard his regiment was to be stationed in Dublin, he even considered attending medical lectures there, since military officers were admitted free. The army itself also provided encouragement, for now that Britain was at war it had discovered a need for medical men. "Do you mean to be an Inspector General or the village doctor?" his friend Jenoway had written him in August, when Lesassier was stationed in Armagh. Definitely the former, Lesassier replied. "Few things should induce me to leave the army," he mused on 6 May 1809, three years to the day since he had entered the service, "for by persevering in it I am assured of an handsome independence whereas in private life a thousand fortuitous events may at the close of life reduce one to indigence."

Lesassier had other indications that the war provided increasing opportunities for medical men. His friend Lindsay, fed up with being an ensign, decided on Lesassier's advice to resume his medical career. He passed his examination at Surgeon's Hall right away, and was appointed senior assistant surgeon in the 73rd Regiment. His own battalion got its second assistant surgeon, Donald McPherson, making four for the whole regiment, instead of the three the War Office had thought was sufficient a year earlier. McPherson, like Lindsay, passed at Surgeon's Hall on the first try, a little to Lesassier's disappointment, but only a little, for he liked McPherson, "a worthy—well-informed companion," and he also liked having a colleague he outranked, or, as he put it, "a sharer of my duty."

All these new opportunities were in preparation for one purpose: to get the battalion on the field. On 13 June 1809 he wrote, "Officers are rejoining us every instant from all quarters," for the 42nd received its marching orders for the Cove of Cork. There was no time for the dilatory fourteen miles per day they had made on their march through the Highlands: the regiment covered the last twenty-five miles to the ships in a single long march that started at midnight on 21 June and ended at 11 A.M. In an hour they were on board the three transports, together with three other regiments, and prepared to embark, "for God knows where!" Lesassier wrote, in despair at leaving his dearest Ella. Now that Britain was at war, all destinations were official secrets, but unofficial rumor had it, accurately, that they were bound for "Portugal, the present conspicuous scene of British valor."

# CHAPTER 6

# Tinsel of Military Reputation

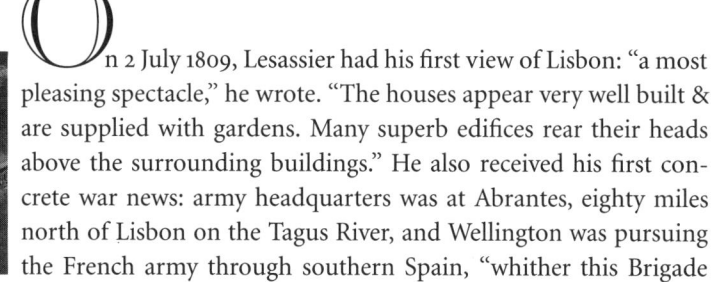

On 2 July 1809, Lesassier had his first view of Lisbon: "a most pleasing spectacle," he wrote. "The houses appear very well built & are supplied with gardens. Many superb edifices rear their heads above the surrounding buildings." He also received his first concrete war news: army headquarters was at Abrantes, eighty miles north of Lisbon on the Tagus River, and Wellington was pursuing the French army through southern Spain, "whither this Brigade must hasten with all possible dispatch." The 42nd, and the rest of their brigade, had in fact arrived just too late to take part in the bloody and hard-won fight of Talavera, where 5,363 men—25 percent of the British army present—were killed, missing, or wounded. "There are five thousand of these poor fellows," Lesassier heard, "& only a few medical officers to take charge of them all." Indeed, he heard, "such is the scarcity of medical officers" that all who could be spared from any quarter were hastily "sent off to Talavera . . . with medicines," a fitting introduction to Lesassier's next five years of medical service on the Iberian Peninsula, which would be spent almost entirely in transit.

The Peninsular War began in 1808 when Napoleon, wanting to compel Portugal to accede to the French blockade on British ports and to place his brother on the throne of Spain, invaded both countries. The Portuguese royal family fled to Brazil, while the Spanish king and heir became involuntary guests of the French in Paris. Napoleon had counted on the Spanish, especially, rising against their ancien régime nobility and accepting King Joseph as a liberator. Instead, there was armed revolt against Joseph, and the Spanish called on Britain for help. The British agreed to aid the Spanish, to contain Napoleon, and to protect their Portuguese shipping and ports, important not only for trade but for guarding access to the Mediterranean. It was Arthur Wellesley, Duke of Wellington after Talavera, together with Lord Castlereagh, British secretary of war, who worked out the military strategy that governed the British effort. Spain was considered indefensible because of its size and ready access from France; moreover, the aftermath of Talavera showed that an army in Spain could not be adequately supplied. But if the British army could hold on to Portugal—even, as events were to show, if they were confined to little more than the outskirts of Lisbon—they could be supplied by the British navy, and continue to fight.

This strategy implied a long war, rather than a series of quick and easy victories. "The

Spanish Ulcer," Napoleon called the Peninsular War: a long-running sore that drained men and equipment from his other fields of operations. For the British, it was also a complex war, based on a series of interlocking parts: the British army, of course, but also the British navy, necessary for supplies; the Portuguese army, reorganized by Marshal William Carr Beresford according to British principles and with British officers; the Spanish army; the Portuguese and Spanish militia, the guerrillos, who not only harassed the French but captured many of the French dispatches that allowed the Allied Army, as it came to be called, to work out the size, position, and strength of the Enemy. Within the army itself two more of the interlocking parts functioned: the commissary department, which was responsible for the mechanics of moving men, arms, and food out from the depots in Portugal along supply lines to the ever-moving war front, and the medical department, responsible for healing the sick, dressing the wounded, and moving them back from the front to hospital stations along those same supply lines.

When Lesassier's regiment officially landed on 4 July 1809, Lesassier's first experience of army life on active service began. He was instantly miserable. Instead of the comfortable lodgings he had been used to, his regiment was encamped on an open field. In fact, he quickly learned, all forms of comfort were allotted according to military rank. Tents were one example of this: the regiment was divided into companies, with four tents allotted to each company, but each captain was allocated his own private tent, while two subalterns had to share a single tent. Far from being able to live like a gentleman, Lesassier wrote,

> Every privation—every petty misery, have I endured since our encampment here. For two successive days, I procured nothing to eat, but a casual, & precarious morcel from those of my brother officers who had accidently been more provident than myself. And to send for anything from town was impossible as our servants were prevented from leaving the camp—At length I & a few others established a species of mess. We are each of us allowed—as well as the Private soldiers—a pound of Beef & the same quantity of bread per day. On this we live—As to our tents they afford a pleasant enough retreat during this scorching season of the year but must be perfect sieves during the rains—We sleep on the ground which almost moves with insects of various kinds—Serpents are very numerous—although I am ignorant whether or not they be venomous— But the ants are by far the most tormenting. Nothing is free from their attacks. They are found every where. Hence a conception may be formed of our uncomfortable life.

Within two weeks Lesassier thought he had found the solution. His "old friend Bolton" was now deputy inspector of hospitals at Lisbon, comfortably established with a good quarter and a pretty Portuguese mistress. Through him, Lesassier was temporarily detached from his regiment and assigned to the hospital at Belem on the outskirts of

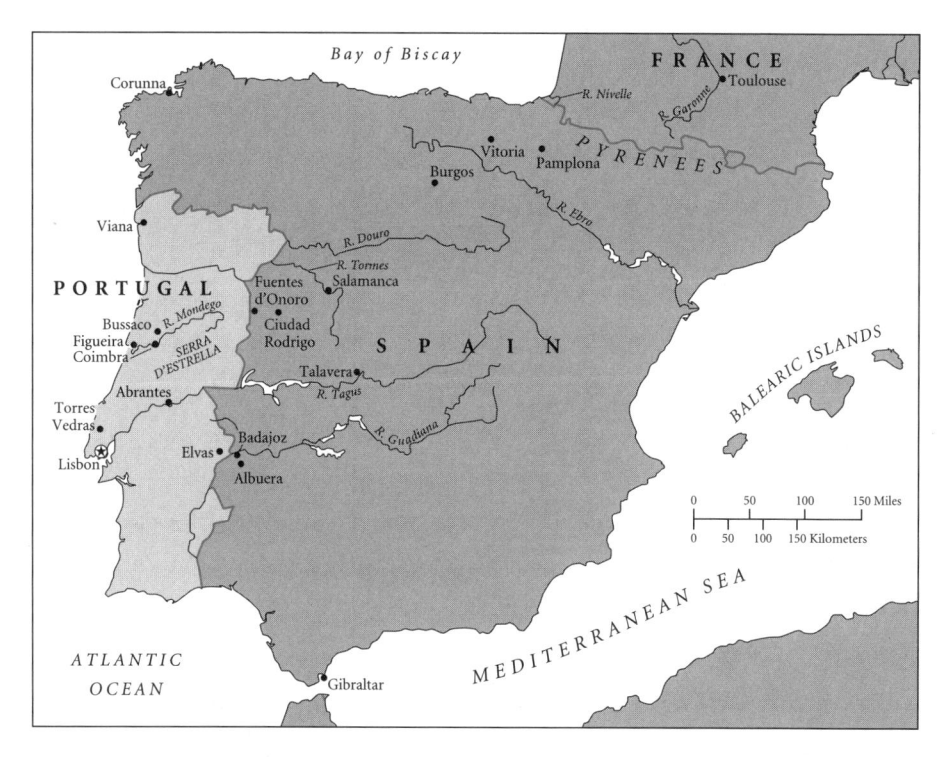

Map of Spain and Portugal

Lisbon, intended "for the reception of all the sick that may be left at Lisbon by Regiments marching up the country. It forms part of a small barrack intended for the reception of all detachments from the British Army in Portugal. Another barrack in Belem accomodates the cavalry." Erly, the surgeon from the 1st Battalion of the 42nd, had been appointed to the hospital a few months previously, but had gone home sick. "To what most singular vicissitudes are we all subject," Lesassier wrote. "When I heard in Dublin that Erly was doing this duty how could I suppose that I should shortly fill the same office?"

It was not very gallant of Lesassier to leave his regiment as soon as they arrived on foreign soil, but then the first part of his stay on the Peninsula was marked by ungallant behavior. It was not only that he wished for "relief from the harassing duties of a camp": for Lesassier, the essential feature of a gentleman was independence, and as subaltern he was anything but independent of the "galling shackles" of military authority, what he termed the "increasing severities of that tyrant," the lieutenant colonel of the regiment, Lord Blantyre. In his appointment to the Lisbon hospitals, in contrast, his "present situation is beyond every thing serene & agreeable—I have very little to do & have no one to answer from my practice to. In fact excepting that it is of far greater extent & consequence my present situation most exactly resembles that to which I was appointed in Gibraltar namely the Barrack Corps." But that "greater extent & conse-quence" made a great deal of difference. Lesassier had complained in Gibraltar of having so much work with so little authority; now, with his higher rank, and the regimental perquisite of a servant, he could enjoy hospital medicine. And Lisbon was a far more enjoyable station than Gibraltar, for he could enjoy promenading the streets, dispensing charity to beggars, joining the circulating library, attending the opera, "a most magnificent building almost entirely composed of dove colored marble," and sleeping with one of the opera singers, "a most lovely girl."

Detaching an assistant surgeon from his regiment was common practice, but one that created much ill feeling between medical and military staff, for it brought the duties of the medical man into direct conflict with the duties of an officer. The British medical service, with its division between regimental and general staff, was rather a hodgepodge of personnel attached to existing army institutions than a well-constructed institution, and reformers sighed in vain for the "flying ambulances"—the forerunner of modern MASH units—implemented by Napoleon's surgeon general, Baron Dominique Jean Larrey. At the most elementary level, the need for medical services arose because soldiers and officers became sick and wounded when on campaign, and, if they did not die, had to be returned to active service. Out of this need had come the regimental medical staff, since the regiment was the basic organizing unit of the army. Each regiment of more than seven hundred men had a surgeon, with two assistant surgeons, who were responsible for the ordinary care of the soldiers and officers. All medicine and supplies were issued at the regimental level, and, according to the army medical officer and writer John Hennen, "the first and peculiar care of the medical officer, on com-mencing a campaign, should be carefully and minutely to examine his Medical and Purveyor's stores." Routine care for the regiment might consist of setting fractures, treating venereal disease and the itch, dressing powder burns or flog wounds, treating cuts from runaway horses, prescribing emetics for cases of food poisoning, and diag-nosing measles.

Wounds might take weeks or months to heal; illness, too, lingered on for weeks or months, and in the meantime the regiments had to continue with the campaign. To fill the need of caring for the sick while the regiment carried on, general hospitals were set up in safe locations to the rear of the army. Since they were not attached to any regiment, they were staffed with the general medical staff: physicians to the forces, staff surgeons (also called surgeons to the forces, to distinguish them from regimental surgeons), and the much-despised hospital mates, by 1809 officially called hospital assistants but still at the bottom of every hierarchy. There were never enough medical men at the general hospitals, and the shortage was exacerbated by the general preju-dice against mates—"apothecaries' boys," declared one soldier, "who, having studied a session or two were thrust into the Army as a huge dissecting room, free to mangle with impunity." In the field, in the meantime, either the regiment had many sick or wounded, or it didn't; in the former case, the surgeon and his assistants might be overwhelmed with work, but in the latter, they would have nothing to do. It seemed a sensible solution to an administrative problem, then, to assign "disposable" assistant surgeons to general hospitals as long as they were not needed in the field.

It seemed highly sensible to assistant surgeons, too, and not only because of the delights of Lisbon. Medical work was not allocated democratically, on the field or in general hospitals. In regiments, the surgeon organized medical tasks. For the period during and just after a battle, medicine came before military rank: surgeons and their assistants worked together in doing amputations, bandaging, and applying poultices; or the most experienced surgeon dealt with the most serious cases, leaving the more routine to the assistants. On other occasions, though, the surgeon could, and did, delegate the most unpleasant chores to the assistants. "The surgeon goes round the wards, writes the prescriptions, and gives the book over to the assistant," according to one anonymous commentator, "with orders to make up the medicines, dress the sores, apply the bandages, make up the accounts, in short, all the drudgery, and then walks away to pursue his amusements, or if he has any private patients, visits them." In a general hospital, in contrast, the assistant surgeon nicely filled the niche between the hospital assistants, who could be assigned all the medical drudgery, and the staff surgeons, who could act in a supervisory capacity. He could stay in one place and be comfortably quartered, while seeing a variety of practice: "Thinks I to myself," wrote surgeon Walter Henry while assigned to the hospital station in Coimbra, "this is mighty pleasant campaigning." He lived, in other words, like a modern civilian doctor with a hospital appointment, drawing a salary for attending the sick. There was, in 1809, no other medical position like it, in military or civil life.

Moreover, hospital stations carried with them another important advantage: contact with high-ranking medical men, and for that reason, Lesassier noted, "my present duty will form a far more powerful claim for future promotion than any I could be engaged in." It is not too much to say that all Lesassier's success in the army was due to his persistence in remaining at hospital stations. So, too, were most of his reprimands. Military staff from Wellington on down disliked the detachment of assistant surgeons from their regiments, and Lord Blantyre had no intention of allowing his assistant surgeon to amuse himself in Lisbon while the regiment marched toward Spain. So Lesassier had to march away from the hospital at Belem, where, he complained, "some hundreds of sick were daily expected—notwithstanding which there was not a single disposable medical officer to replace me in a duty of such consequence." In the meantime, Lesassier had found that his new Lisbon mistress had given him venereal disease. He considered reporting himself sick, reflecting "with horror, that either, I must expose my constitution to irreparable injury, by enduring the utmost severities, of both weather, & situation, or be assured that secret calumny would ascribe my remaining in Lisbon to the worst of motives." The former seemed the lesser of the two evils, and he left Lisbon with the rest of the 42nd, having purchased, with his fellow assistant surgeon McPherson, "a small though very strong ass at 20 dollars & on this we shall carry our trunks or rather small portmanteaus."

Lesassier's regiment was transported up the Tagus on boats as far as possible, then marched the rest of the way to Abrantes, arriving 30 July. Lesassier was still an avid pursuer of the picturesque, and Abrantes, he noted, was "an irregular town seated on the right bank of the Tagus. . . . It is built on the top of an abrupt hill & its situation is extremely commanding. . . . The sides of this hill are covered with naturally planted olive trees as is likewise the whole neighbouring country." Lesassier also described the castle with its distinctive "bastions of a long elliptical figure," situated "on an eminence which rises above the Town," from which the windings of the Tagus "form a most picturesque sight." Lesassier promptly reported himself sick and remained in town after his regiment marched away. "My time hangs heavy on my hands," he wrote, but he amused himself with "three fine *Portuguesas*" who lived opposite him and who may have inspired him to begin learning Portuguese. He was not left alone to amuse himself for long, however, because of the continuing shortage of medical men: "I myself although unwell am forced to take charge of two Hospitals!!" But a few days afterward he was given another charge, one "equally pleasing as it was unexpected": to convey the sick of his two hospitals down the water to Lisbon. Later he would consider transporting the sick a most disagreeable task, but this time he was happy to be returning to Lisbon so soon. "I could not expect to recover my health in a sufficiently short space of time to enable me to join my Regiment & see any actual service," he wrote, "& surely I should feel a thousand times happier in Lisbon than in this petty miserable place."

Transporting the sick was, by and large, one of the most hated tasks of the war. Medical treatment during the war is best understood if it is remembered that a soldier was an instrument for fighting a war that involved rapid movements for the army. A sick or wounded soldier was a useless instrument, and therefore had ideally to be quickly cured and returned to his regiment, or, only slightly less ideally, quickly transported out of the army's way so as not to impede its movements and his own recovery. The pressing military need to move on was not in the best interests of the patient. It was, however, a fact of military life, and the administrative issue was how to do it most efficiently and humanely. Wellington's comments about his soldiers called down upon his own head the accusation of inhumanity—he shocked one cavalry general by talking about "*expending* such and such Battalions in such and such affairs, as you would talk about expending so much shot and powder"—but he was an efficient deployer of his military instruments and the "proper care of the wounded was," as the historian John Keegan put it, "a matter of morality."

The sick were usually sent in bullock carts under the command of a junior officer, with one or more medical attendants. Officers and men alike hated "the eternal screeching of the ungreased wheels of the Portuguese bullock carts," the long exposure to the weather in uncovered wagons, the lurching over rocky roads, the difficulty of obtaining shelter at night or provisions for a protracted journey. "I dread a removal of the sick to Lisbon," Wellington wrote, "the last cost us many men, and they must go on bullock carts: the next will cost us more in consequence of bad weather." The trip was bad enough for the merely feverish; for the wounded, with no means to alleviate their pain, or for those seriously ill with dysentery, it was a nightmare. "So great was the suffering of the wounded after one retreat," according to surgeon James Elkington, "that some of them requested to be shot, rather than continue the horrible journey to Lisbon." Lesassier was fortunate on this trip in being able to use the Tagus. At the appointed hour—3 A.M.—he was at his hospital, and "after infinite labor I assembled the Men & marched them down to the river a distance of about a mile & quarter. There we found another body of invalids from some other hospitals under the charge of an Assistant Surgeon." But no boats were ready, and when the inspector of hospitals who had ordered the transport was sent for, he had no explanation, because "the business had been entirely left to the storekeeper." The storekeeper was duly sent for, but "when found could give no account of the matter until his deputy arrived. At length with much & laborious perseverance of inquiry it appeared that the poor wretched Portuguese whose boats were pressed were kept days & days in suspense without a farthing of wages & that as the poor creatures were dying with hunger they had run away & hid themselves—so there were our boats & the half of them without sailors. . . . Much was said," he continued, "by our Inspector about roguery & negligence—& reporting the whole business—& then he embarked all the patients into eight boats—& then went about his business no doubt perfectly convinced of the successful issue of his well directed exertions!" Lesassier and the commanding officer of the detachment decided that unless they themselves did something they might remain there "until dooms day." They therefore "instantly ordered a guard to follow us & without ceremony pressed a sufficient number of men from other boats to man our own"; at 1 P.M. "our little flotilla of eight boats" finally set off.

Once in Belem, the officers disembarked the sick men. Lesassier waited on Bolton, who was happy to see him and assigned him to one of the hospitals. Lesassier was pleased to do so, and to recover his health and enjoy himself in Lisbon. He was well by the end of the week, and he heroically refrained from courting infection again by revisiting his former mistress. He remained in Lisbon this time for just under three weeks, long enough to receive news of his promotion: the promotion of one of the more senior assistant surgeons, McLean, his colleague in Gibraltar, made him the second assistant of the 42nd, entitled to serve in the First Battalion. The news temporarily reconciled him to his regiment, for on 4 September he received the order to join the 42nd in a village near the border town of Elvas—"esteemed the most important Fortress in Portugal"—with equanimity, remarking only that he was pleased to have an opportunity to visit his "fair friends" in Abrantes on the way.

The 42nd, and the rest of the army, stayed near Elvas in villages along the Guadiana River until December. Wellington chose the position for strategic reasons: it was in Portugal, so he could obtain supplies for his starving army, but close enough to the Spanish border to keep the Spanish, and the French, from thinking he was leaving Spain open to attack. But malaria, endemic in the region, spread throughout the army. "No sooner am I comfortably situated than some event occurs to derange all my plans," Lesassier complained on 24 September, for the increasing sickness of the men meant that he and McPherson had to take turns conducting them from camp to the general hospital at Elvas: "It will prove a disagreeable infernal duty." A week later, he was ordered to remain at Elvas, "Graces à Dieu." He found himself "perfectly eaten up with *ennui* in this cursedly dull town—as I have very few companions & no books," but being attached to a hospital was still better than being encamped with the regiment, "seeing that we are not very likely to meet with any other description of service except that of marching far & faring ill." He also heard news of old friends, for both William Lindsay, his companion in Armagh, and Joseph Brown, his erstwhile fellow apprentice, were now stationed in the Peninsula.

What did Lesassier's "duty" consist of? It is no use trying to find out from his journal: medical men on the Peninsular campaign, Lesassier included, devoted their diaries not to medicine but to war news, scenery, insular British opinions of the Portuguese and Spanish, and, inevitably but maddeningly, to endless descriptions of billets, good or bad. We know, for example, that surgeon Charles Boutflower's "experience, during the Peninsular war, was very great," for the eminent surgeon and anatomist George James Guthrie included some of Boutflower's cases, including dissections—and it surely shows great dedication to carry out dissections under the conditions of a campaign hospital—in his later writings on the surgery of the war. But Boutflower's own journal for the war never mentions the practice of medicine, and it is only because Boutflower fell ill and had trouble finding a billet in Lisbon that we learn he was even acquainted with "a most particular friend in the Person of a Mr. Guthrie," let alone that he consulted with him professionally. James McGrigor, the director of the Army Medical Service on the Peninsula for the second half of the war, based sections of his *Autobiography* from the journals he kept while there, but even he gives much less information on military medicine than we would like: of his arduous medical activities during the siege of Burgos, for example, he wrote only that "The wounded were numerous, we were without adequate hospital accommodation, and the cases were of the severest character," while interrupting the narrative to tell us of his billet, in a "miserable quarter, in a poor dilapidated house in the suburb." Some medical men, notably Guthrie, McGrigor, and John Hennen, wrote accounts of medicine in the Peninsula after the war, and a few officers and soldiers wrote about their own or their friends' illnesses and wounds. It is to them we must turn to find out just what kind of work Lesassier's position entailed.

The main diseases for which a soldier might be sent to a general hospital were malaria, dysentery, and, toward the end of the war, infectious gangrene. Bloodletting was used for any kind of inflammation, or, as we would say, fever from systemic infection, including fever that developed after amputation. So was purging, to keep the stomach open. It was axiomatic that serious infectious diseases required strong remedies, what one writer called "that active and decided practice by which acute diseases are often arrested in their progress at the beginning, and by which, in the military service, the soldier is at once restored to health and his duty." Treatment included "the use of calomel, of antimony, and of the stronger purgatives, and . . . of every active remedy," a "free and liberal use of the lancet," and the "cold bath in fever." It is tempting to see this rough treatment as a strategy to keep malingerers out of the hospital, if not a "kill or cure" treatment intended to minimize the expense to the army of caring for a sick soldier who was no good on the field, a paraphrase of Scrooge's comment "if they be like to die, they should do it, and save public money." Indeed, Lesassier noted at the hospital at Elvas, "This day our number of sick here amounts to 950. Since the first establishment of the hospitals here . . . 900 men have died. Out of this great proportion 500 died before they had been in hospital 24 hours."

But medical men expected these remedies to restore the soldier to health, and they had enough faith in this kind of treatment to use it on themselves. Surgeon Walter Henry used the cold bath, supplemented by several dozen leeches applied to the head, to cure himself of malaria, and Lesassier, wet through with rain and fearful of a relapse for the same complaint, wrote that he "threw off all my clothes—sponged myself head to foot with cold water; then used violent friction with a rough towel." Indeed, at least one soldier, Corporal Costello, approved of this method, noting that "the manner of cure adopted by our doctors" in one epidemic "principally consisted in throwing cold water from canteens or mess kettles as often as possible over the bodies of the patients; this in many cases was effectual, and I think cured me." Heroic medications, on the other hand, found little favor with the patients on which they were used: Private Gunn of the 42nd delayed seeing his regimental surgeon as long as he could because he "very much disliked doctors' drugs."

Sickness continued to increase in Lesassier's regiment, and on 14 November he was ordered back to the 42nd, because the surgeon Swinton McLeod had to come to Elvas to regain his health. They were now quartered in the village of Lobon, and, Lesassier wrote, "I here joined McPherson in his billet & mess & assisted him in most unpleasant duty. Our hospital is crowded with 100 sick, an enormous proportion for so weak a regiment." Regimental hospitals were only equipped to care for approximately sixty patients, and with all regiments in the same state, there was chronic shortage of medicines and clean bedding. The crowded conditions facilitated the spread of disease, as all medical men understood, though they did not understand the mechanism whereby it was spread. When Dr. James Franck, the inspector of hospitals for the Peninsular Army, visited, he "ordered the greatest part of our sick," to be sent to the general hospital. But only four carts were available, and so the sick had to be sent on in stages, Lesassier and McPherson conveying them in batches to the first stage, where they had to be removed from one set of carts and packed onto another before continuing to the general hospital.

Back in Lobon, Lesassier complained it was an "ill built small irregular place . . . of about 2000 inhabitants—The houses . . . not being stuccoed & white washed as Portuguese houses are . . . present a most miserable appearance. The people of this small place appear to be poor & wretched." But, he complained a week later, "Even this obscure village had its attractions & I am hurried away. My Billet was one of the best in town & I had formed some most agreeable connections when my evil stars would have it that I must be chosen for one of the most disagreeable of all possible duties," detached duty with another regiment. Surgeon John Wylde of the 24th had fallen sick with "Intermittent Fever," probably malaria. Lesassier was therefore ordered to take Wylde's place "notwithstanding that I am acting Surgeon to our regiment" in McLeod's absence and had only just returned from "the unpleasant task of conducting four wagons full of sick this morning. . . . Such is the wretched situation of an unfortunate Assistant Surgeon on foreign service. I am perfectly conscious that no sooner shall I find myself comfortably situated with the 24th Regiment than I shall be hurried back again."

In fact he did find himself comfortable with the 24th. "The officers," he wrote, "are a very genteel set of men." The commanding officer, was a "mild affable gentleman . . . indeed all that a commanding officer ought to be—My billet is the best in the regiment—and I have *two* servants—As a grand desideratum one of them is a professed cook." So content was he that he "contrived to get the surgeon of the 24th to Elvas for the recovery of his health—& that the chance of my being ordered back to the 42nd may be diminished." He was quite right, though, that he would not long remain undisturbed. Wellington had decided to send the army into cantonments in northern Portugal, and on 7 December the 24th, and Lesassier with it, was ordered to march first to Lobon, and then to Elvas. As acting surgeon, he was in charge of moving the sick, and "Having plenty of leisure previous to our march," he wrote, "I arranged all the complicated business of moving an hospital to my wish." The trip itself "was become unpleasant & difficult beyond conception being absolutely forced to act as a carter—for without my own unwearied personal exertions the mule cars would never arrive at their destination." But having arrived at Elvas, and "delivered up my sick to the General Hospital," he transferred his unwearied personal exertions to the task of getting himself removed from the 24th and detached to the hospital, forcing Surgeon Wylde to return to his regiment. "Wylde was in an agony of rage," he wrote, unrepentant, "& stated officially . . . that he was unfit to do the duty of his regiment. Luckily nothing availed & here am I once more in Elvas. My billet is most excellent & the people of the house are very civil—We are all bustle & confusion here sick in hundreds are pouring in upon us." By the end of December there were, he noted, "nearly 5000."

Lesassier spent his first Christmas on the Peninsula, then, in the comfortable situation of a hospital station, accompanied by congenial medical colleagues. He had been assigned the task of caterer for Christmas dinner; perhaps his ability to provide for his own comfort had been remarked by his associates. And "I may venture to say," he wrote, "that our dinner was most excellent—for exclusive of the two national dishes of roast beef & plum pudding we had a great diversity of luxuries besides Madeira & Port wines." "Now cease awhile, the deafening din of war," began the poem he wrote for the occasion:

> The trumpet's clangor; & the cannon's roar
> May idly waste their direful sounds afar;
> And near this festive spot be heard no more.
> The present moment, we will call our own;
> Nor e'en our miseries, on a foreign land, bemoan.

Altho' we distant from our native Country roam,
And think with many a heaving sigh of home;
Yet nought but smiles & mirth this time be fit,
As rous'd by humor, or inspired by wit;
For, many a . . . year may fall away,
Ere thus again, we spend our Christmas day.

Back at his regiment, assistant surgeon McPherson had fallen ill and gone to Lisbon. That left the regiment without an assistant surgeon, and on 30 December Lesassier was ordered to rejoin the 42nd. On the way he was ordered to take medical charge of conveying some convalescents to Coimbra; "So I may lay my account with having abundant annoyance," he complained. The trip was marked by the not very edifying spectacle of the officers racing each other for the most comfortable billets. Lesassier began it by always leaving early in the morning before the convalescents in order to reach their next halting station and secure a good billet for himself and the other surgeon. One of the other officers tried to do the same, but few could compete with Lesassier in pursuit of his own comfort. On 18 January 1810, the party reached Coimbra, "celebrated for its University," Lesassier duly noted, where "medical students attend their professors gratis." Like Lisbon, Coimbra was a main hospital station, and Lesassier managed to rid himself of the convalescents, this time making use of an order to rejoin his regiment. "This," he wrote, "I pretend prevents me from losing a moment although I have no intention of hurrying myself." Accompanied by several officers from the 42nd who had been convalescing in Coimbra, he finally rejoined his regiment in the village of Mangualdé in the Serra d'Estrella, the mountains of northwest Portugal, on 24 January, after having been apart from it for almost two months. He was pleased with Mangualdé, containing "about 200 families," he wrote. "A stranger will be surprised at the great number of excellent houses & shops that this place contains—All the houses have glass windows & are neatly whitewashed. In fact it is one of the very best villages in Portugal. The greatest ornament of Mangualdé is a large sumptuous Chateau." On arrival, however, he promptly became very ill: "How sudden, how most strange has been this attack," he wrote when well over it "I who through the whole campaign have enjoyed such uninterrupted good health: who braved with impunity disease in every shape so often & so long in Elvas!"

Lesassier spent the next six months with his regiment quartered in one or another of the villages around the Serra d'Estrella. Aside from occasionally conveying the sick to a general hospital, he had almost nothing to do, for though his division was put on alert in June, no action took place until mid-August. He amused himself with picturesque descriptions of the countryside, such as the "wild & majestic scenery" from the village of Santiago: "The Ravine down which the road runs to the Mondego River is dreadfully steep & at least 900 feet above the River. A very light & simple bridge of three arches here crosses the Mondego. . . . Below rushes the Mondego between abrupt & projecting rocks & falling into frequent cascades with great violence whilst its high & craggy banks assume a thousand fantastick shapes & are ornamented with an immense variety of Trees & shrubs amongst which the red, grey, & purple heath have conspicuous appearance." Nor, he wrote, could he remember having "beheld a sweeter little valley than that which surrounds the village of Muscatella. The neighboring heights were cloaked with young oak & all the adjacent land richly ornamented with all the luxuriant verdure of spring." He had acquired a Portuguese servant, Manoel, to look after his animals, by now consisting of several mules and a horse; he also acquired a dog, Capitano, who became his constant companion. His journals became even more self-consciously the adventures of a young hero, as he made a point of including the descriptive titles common to novels at the top of each page: "We march 12 miles," "My unequaled misery," "The Enemy's movements," "An unmerited insult," "And the steps I took."

The 42nd was in the mountains of northern Portugal, not for their picturesque beauty but because they were considered a safe place for the retraining of the army, with ready lines of retreat, if necessary, to Coimbra and even Lisbon. Those lines of retreat now became necessary for both Portuguese and British armies, as Marshal André Massena, commander of the French Army of Portugal, advanced toward the border. The 42nd, under arms, began to fall back; in the meantime, Lesassier found that he had been "poxed" once again. He consulted with surgeon McLeod, who advised him "to conceal the whole until the first detachment of sick marches & then go with it & when arrived at my destination report myself sick." He followed this advice when ordered to transport the sick of the 24th regiment towards the hospital station at Farinha Poudre, near Coimbra, "of course highly pleased at thus having a plea for leaving my regiment without reporting myself sick & particularly as the guard was again in motion." At Farinha Poudre he "instantly gave up the charge of our sick and . . . reported myself sick to the senior medical officer." The next day he traveled to Coimbra with 250 sick men.

Strikingly unaware of the significance of the army's movements west and south, Lesassier had hoped to be allowed to stay undisturbed in Coimbra. Instead, the principal medical officer, Dr. Cabbell, insisted that he convey the sick to transports on the coast, where they would be conveyed to Lisbon. Lesassier tried to plead illness, for he was attacked with intermittent fever—probably malaria—"in so violent a manner that I wrote to Cabbell, stating the *absolute* impossibility of my leaving Coimbra on the following morning." Cabbell came in person to expostulate and, perhaps, even to try to explain matters. The French were advancing and would almost certainly try to take Coimbra; any sick men remaining in the hospital would be taken prisoner and lost to the army; all those who could travel had to be conveyed down to the comparative safety of Lisbon as soon as possible. There was a shortage of medical officers, and assigning one to transport the sick would keep him absent for several days. Under those circumstances no assistant surgeon was going to be allowed to stay in bed if he could be put to good use, "& at length," Lesassier wrote, "I consented to try."

On 30 August Lesassier reluctantly conveyed his sick to the "pretty town" of Figueira, "a place of most fashionable resort during the bathing season," he wrote, "and the houses are chiefly new or have at least that appearance." He had assumed he would be able to travel with them to Lisbon, and had directed one of his servants to take his animals and most of the luggage there by land. But again his comfort had to be sacrificed to the war effort, for "To my astonishment," he wrote, he was ordered back again to Coimbra. "In vain did I represent my peculiar situation that I was sent to Lisbon more to recover my health than to do any duty. I might have saved myself this trouble for nothing would do but back I must go." On returning to Coimbra he was ordered once more to take a detachment of sick to Figueira, and this time he was allowed to accompany them to Lisbon. This was on 4 September 1810. By 17 September Wellington was sending instructions to "order all your sick away from Coimbra . . . and send people down to be in readiness to remove or destroy your ammunition and other stores there without loss of time," and on 4 October the French entered Coimbra. The British army and many of the inhabitants had retreated previously, and under Dr. Cabbell's administration all but 400 of the sick had been transported and the hospital broken up. The French were driven out of the city by the Portuguese militia a few days later, leaving their own hospitals, "indeed a most masterly action," Lesassier wrote when he heard of it, with no recognition that their fate could have been his. Massena continued to move south, but by that time the Allied Armies were entrenched behind the lines of Torres Vedras, a series of encampments which later became famous for their decisive role in securing Allied victory.

But Lesassier could neither read the future nor anticipate Wellington's strategy, and he approved of the retreat, for "as every step we take in retreating approaches us toward our native country so in proportion is the satisfaction I feel on the occasion." This was the second year that Wellington had been forced to retreat, and Lesassier was sure, like many others in the army, that the retreat was prelude to as precipitous a withdrawal as Sir John Moore's two years earlier. "Everything in Lisbon is in a state of forwardness to prepare for the worst," Lesassier wrote. "All the sick which are deemed incapable of walking are on board of hospital ships." Lesassier more than half hoped that the worst would happen, for he was a sad croaker, as the expression went, someone who was sure that the French would win, and that soon the British must be driven into the sea as they had been at Corunna. "A certain great man at his table laughs at the idea of Massena attacking *his* lines," he wrote, repeating common army gossip about Wellington, "asserting that the whole force of French could not drive him from his fortified position. This may be termed a most ridiculous boast as assuredly it is the first time one heard of an *impregnable position*." Wellington had his own answer to comments like these. "It is impossible that many officers of the army can have a knowlege of facts to enable them to form opinions of the probable events of the campaign," he wrote in *General Orders;* they should therefore do their duty and not spread idle nonsense. Yet as a modern historian has pointed out, the widespread pessimism about British prospects was in part due to Wellington's habit of providing even his closest associates with very little information about his plans. His own quartermaster general, Sir George Murray, had views similar to Lesassier's, for he had no better information on Wellington's strategy "than that which any general officer in the Peninsula might have obtained." And the most prevalent opinion, noted Surgeon Charles Boutflower in the winter of 1810, "is that the Enemy will make every effort to concentrate such an overwhelming force by the ensuing spring, as shall render all resistance on our part unavailing. Unquestionably the majority of the officers of this army would hail any circumstance that should compel us to quit the Peninsula without absolute disgrace."

Lesassier remained in Lisbon that winter recovering from yet another bout of venereal disease—"Ah! that eternal perdition may fall upon false faithless perfidious woman!" he wrote, "Thrice have I trusted to Portuguese beauty & thrice have I been severly punished for my credulity. How supremely unfortunate I am"—and doing duty in the Lisbon hospitals, where there were nearly seven thousand sick under Bolton's charge. But Lieutenant Colonel Blantyre, "that haughty tyrannical scoundrel," wanted him back, and Lesassier received "a most peremptory order to leave Lisbon within twelve hours." He "instantly waited on my old friend Bolton & explained to him how improper it would be for me who was affected with a dangerous disease to expose myself to all the hardships of both situation & weather which I must of necessity suffer were I with our Army at present. Bolton coincided with me in this & sent me to a Staff Surgeon a *friend of his*," for his examination. Lesassier was able to get one month's leave of absence and used it to perfect his traveling arrangements to ensure his greater comfort on the march or in camp. "I have been busied ever since I arrived in Lisbon in reducing the experience of my eight months' campaign into practice," he wrote. The method he had come up with was to use two light, strong baskets to carry both his clothing and his food and utensils, instead of a portmanteau for the former and a basket for the latter. These baskets, "two feet long & one foot broad," united the "two important properties of *great space & little weight*." One, intended for clothes, "is covered with canvass—The other is painted the same color but uncovered. The ties fasten down with padlocks which pass thro' two rings that are attached one of them to the lid the other to the body of the baskets." These baskets had several additional advantages besides being light. "Although made of wicker work," they were "so strong as to admit of being used as seats." Two similar baskets were also much easier to balance than a basket and a portmanteau. The final advantage, ease of arrangement on the pack animal, was one Lesassier was especially proud of, for it cost him "more thought than all the other desiderata. . . . My present method is as follows. As two straps would not at all events be required for each basket to keep down the lid the sole addition to these straps is that of two short straps without buckles to one basket & with buckles to the other. So that all that is required is to buckle these four short straps at proper distances & placing the baskets' bottoms on the packsaddle." Lesassier indeed found on his trip back to join his regiment that his new arrangements worked very well: he reflected happily "that I shall now join my Regiment more amply provided with every necessary nay every luxury than either any Subaltern or any Captain in the Regiment."

For Lesassier's concern with comfort was above all a concern with status. There was nothing unusual in British officers trying to reduce the hardships of war by bringing with them as many accoutrements of civilization as they could. Robert Ballard Long, as a well-off young cavalry officer on his first command in 1793, went campaigning with "marquee and tent, cot and case, hair-mattress, bolster, pillow, sheets, blankets, counterpane, bedside carpet and floor-cloth, stool, table, and a round tent for his servant." Before the battle of Albuera, he asked his family to send him "ankle-boots, watches, dressing-gowns, and books . . . cheeses, tongues, portable soups, a supply of good tea, and other appropriate seasonings." The difference is that, for Long, these luxuries were the benefits of wealth and high rank; for Lesassier, as much comfort as he could muster became the substitute for them. He was a low-ranking officer in a service considered subsidiary to the main business of the war; his almost obsessive concern, not just with his comforts, but with the comforts that he had and others did not, became his compensation for that low rank. If I cannot convince you that I am a gentleman by my position in the army, he might as well have said to his brother officers, I will convince you by living more like a gentleman of rank than you are capable of doing.

Such a statement, explicit or implied, was not calculated to make him friends when he finally rejoined his regiment. Lesassier saw nothing wrong in his constant attempts to remain in hospital stations: avoiding the discomforts of camp life "cannot be deemed blameable & more especially when we consider that the absence of a medical officer from his regiment must entail on him much extra duty—I myself have ever had ten times as much duty to perform whilst away from my regiment than whilst with it." For that reason, he wrote, he "need fear but little from the insinuations of my brother officers when I return to them." But the war had finally caught up to the 42nd: they had been under fire at the battle of Bussaco, though their part of the line had not engaged the French, and the destruction wreaked by the fighting, Allied retreat, and French advance was clear to see. Just north of the lines the towns were anything but picturesque. "The French were here," Lesassier wrote of Alhandra as he passed by on his way to join the 42nd, "& the whole town is nearly deserted. The doors & windows of almost every house are gone & many of the houses filled with human excrement. Hardly an inhabitant could be seen." Vila Franca, a mile and a half further, was even worse. "This town which I before stated as being the prettiest little town I had seen I could not now recognize. The whole place deserted of its inhabitants, its streets choked up with filth." They could not get a billet, "as those that are not filled up with Spanish soldiers are either unroofed or filled with human ordure." Near Castanheira Lesassier found only "the ruins of a gentleman's house. . . . Two or three of the villagers had returned to this village." Of Vila Nova he wrote, "This once lovely place now exhibits a scene of ruins & of desolation." And near Cartaxo, which "has been a pretty town," he wrote, "A rising ground here affords a very fine view. Farm houses & gentlemen's country seats are seen in every direction But alas! how gloomy the reflection of that dreary solitude alone that reigns within their walls. I observed several human bodies lying by the roadside unburied affording a dreadful feast to the dogs that every where in this neighborhood roam about without a master." Once arrived at his regiment, Lesassier found his division "under arms every morning before day-break," and he himself arranged "to provide against a sudden alarm during the night a wax taper & apparatus for striking a light are placed beside me."

Under these conditions, the Belemites—"those regular skulkers," who spent their time "sauntering about the Belem depots in Lisbon, while their regiments are in advance"—were cordially disliked. "And pray where, in God's name, have you been for the last two years?" one noncommissioned officer was greeted on finally returning to his regiment. "The company has seen a little fighting during that period"—and the *General Orders* for the fall of 1810 contain a stream of reprimands to officers for failing to return to their regiments as expeditiously as possible. Lesassier was fortunate to still retain the good opinion of surgeon McLeod, who had written "condoling with me on the *shattered state of my health*," and recommending "me not to leave Lisbon until I be completely strong," in a letter in which we, though not Lesassier, might detect some irony. Few other officers were likely to share McLeod's good opinion; nor would they have shared Lesassier's own satisfaction in his three months in Lisbon, where "more comfort has been my share than has fallen to the lot of almost any officer in our army."

By this time, the "utmost disgust & detestation" that Lesassier had acquired for his battalion may have been heartily returned, for at the end of February 1811, Lesassier became involved in a quarrel with another young officer, Lieutenant White. The two men had been playing flute in White's tent, and White later missed some writing paper and accused Lesassier of being the thief. This was a dueling matter, for though duels were, strictly speaking, against regulations, hot-headed young officers fought them anyway over more trivial matters than writing paper. Lesassier managed to obtain an apology from White, and wrote a letter of explanation to the other officers in the regiment to make sure that they approved his behavior in accepting it. The affair made him dislike his regiment all the more, though, and when Marshal Massena ordered the French army to retreat in March Lesassier jumped at the opportunity to leave his regiment to do duty at the newly reopened hospitals in Coimbra.

Professionally, this detached duty was very fruitful. The previous year he had heard about medical appointments in the Portuguese army and had forwarded an application for one to Dr. Franck, the inspector of hospitals. "I am ignorant of the advantages that in detail may attend this situation," he wrote, but he was sure that both the rank and chances of promotion were greater than his own position. But Franck replied that he had "neither communication with, nor control over, the Portuguese Medical Staff," and when Lesassier applied personally to Marshal William Carr Beresford he was told, "most politely . . . that the granting of my request was not in Beresford's power . . . and besides that only twelve were allowed & that that number was already appointed." One of these was David MacLagan, the Edinburgh M.D. who had accepted the medical cadetship that Lesassier had turned down. His new position meant that having joined the service at the same time as Lesassier, he now outranked him by a considerable amount, evidence of lost opportunity of which Lesassier, mercifully, was unaware.

Now, comfortably stationed at Coimbra, "its numerous churches, convents, & palaces, towering above each other with the grandest disorder—whilst the eye swept with delight along the picturesque background framed by the mountain of Bussaco & the more distant Serra d'Estrella," Lesassier learned more about the Portuguese medical service from a new friend, Dr. Andrew Halliday, one of the first surgeons appointed to the Portuguese staff. Halliday was an Edinburgh M.D., pleased to have the opportunity to write to James Hamilton about his nephew's "uniformly correct conduct" and to act as Lesassier's introduction to William Fergusson, another Edinburgh man, currently head of the medical department of the Portuguese army. Perhaps it was the desire to make a good impression that led Lesassier to conduct himself so carefully, since it was also at Coimbra that Lesassier received the first official commendation on his medical competence since he had arrived on the Peninsula. He had been acting in the capacity of a staff surgeon, that is, as supervisor of a division of the hospital, and during one inspection, he wrote, "very flattering expressions were made use of by that most severe man Deputy Inspector Tegart . . . who minutely inspected my Division; & publicly told me, that my Division was the cleanest & most correct of all the hospitals, adding 'Indeed I have made that general observation on you'—I certainly felt very highly gratified by this honorable distinction."

Lesassier had been supervising hospital wards ever since Gibraltar, and his professional experience was paying off. So too were his distaste for dirt, disorder, and irregular behavior, coupled with the minute attention he was accustomed to paying his personal environment. "Some men," he later wrote in a statement that can be taken as both his personal and professional philosophy, "if hazard should place them in a cheerless, uncomfortable situation, make themselves still more unhappy—under the idea of inuring themselves to hardships!" To accommodate oneself to events, he went on, "is certainly a good maxim—but I should not content myself merely, by tamely & sluggishly submitting, without a struggle, to all the disagreeable consequences of accident & event. I would endeavor to take advantage of, & improve on every possible means of smoothing away the rugged aspects of my situation." He was later to become a martinet as a hospital administrator and we may suspect that even at this stage he delegated the most unpleasant chores while insisting that they be promptly attended to by his subordinates. But cleanliness and order were the chief weapons the medical service had against disease and despair; in deploying them Lesassier was obeying service objectives as well as his own inclinations; and he copied into his journal Tegart's letter expressing his "best thanks. . . .for his zeal, & attention while doing duty in this hospital."

On the Spanish border, Lord Blantyre was less gratified by this distinction. On 3 and 5 May, his brigade had been involved in the battle of Fuentes d'Onoro. The 42nd had gallantly repulsed a cavalry attack, and Blantyre himself was cited in Wellington's dispatch and later awarded a medal for the battle. This was the first real fighting the Second Battalion of the 42nd had done, and it did Lesassier no honor to be absent from it. The number of wounded in the 42nd, two men on 3 May and twenty-three on 5 May, had probably not been greater than surgeon McLeod and assistant surgeon McPherson could handle. But their regiment was brigaded with the 79th, which had, with the 71st, defended the village of Fuentes for eight hours on 5 May, with nine officers and 126 men wounded. To make matters worse, Lesassier's colleague at Coimbra was assistant surgeon David Perston of the 79th. He, too, had been allowed to remain away from his regiment, kept on as a courtesy to the sick officers, "as there is no disposable Staff Surgeon here, & the officers"—who stayed not in hospitals, but in private billets— "dislike being attended by any of the Hospital Mates." Perston, like Lesassier, had already shown a distinct inclination to stay away from his regiment; with both of them gone, Blantyre's brigade was severely shorthanded. The whole division suffered from a lack of medical staff: Lieutenant William Grattan of the 88th, arriving at the hospital established for the reception of the wounded after Fuentes d'Onoro, was shocked at the "frightful appearance" of men still awaiting surgery. "They had been wounded on the 5th and this was the 7th," he wrote, "their limbs were swollen to an enormous size, and the smell from gunshot wounds was dreadful." And where in all this, we can image Blantyre asking grimly, is assistant surgeon Lesassier?

Blantyre, "highly enraged," wrote to Inspector of Hospitals Franck for an explanation. Franck, always sensitive to criticism, by 1811 was worn out by the administrative task of directing medical care throughout the Peninsula with too few resources. He had to staff his hospitals and provide medical attendance for sick officers—apt to be difficult patients, for, John Hennen later wrote, though "much is to be conceded to the peevishness of sickness, and much to the habits of command in which officers have been educated . . . I have heard the medical officers reprobated in the most insulting terms for non-attendance at specific hours"—and assistant surgeons were his main resource. He responded to Lord Blantyre, according to Lesassier, "that he had several times ordered me to join—all which orders I had evaded." "Inconsistent, & capricious fool," Lesassier called him, but Franck could have returned the compliment, for Lesassier's predicament had been made worse by his own imprudence and bad timing. He waited on Franck for an explanation. "Our interview was, as might be expected a very unpleasant one. . . . He accused me of attempting on all occasions to absent myself from my regiment. I not only allowed this to be correct but likewise added that I intended leaving my regiment." Strictly speaking, Lesassier belonged to the First Battalion of the 42nd, not the Second, but he could not leave the Second until his replacement arrived. And Lesassier heard that "the skulking rascal our junior assistant," though ordered to Portugal, "has nevertheless obtained leave of absence for two months under the idea that the First Battalion will be sent here before the expiration of that period," as successful a strategy for evading the rigors of active service as Lesassier himself ever devised. Lesassier asked Franck to send him home anyway, but Franck was "pleased to warmly express his resentment at my having applied to go home. He *wisely* conceived it dishonorable in me to wish to leave the country when my regiment was in the field."

"I thank Heaven!" Lesassier wrote, "that those whom God has blest with reason, will not think as the profound doctor does," but the officers of his brigade certainly did, for the affair with White came up again. Word had gone out in the brigade that one of the 42nd's officers had been called a thief, but had not had the courage to issue a challenge at such an insult; White himself informed Lesassier that he, White, was to be sent out of the regiment, and Lesassier was to be sent to Coventry, that is, treated as greatly disgraced. None of this made him anxious to rejoin his regiment at the end of June, when the hospitals at Coimbra were broken up: "after a long & tedious march to meet the officers as though I met my executioners is indeed galling."

The campaign of 1811 was decisive in driving the French out of Portugal, but aside from a few days at the end of September, the 42nd was never close to another battle. Lesassier managed to make his excuses to both Blantyre and his brother officers. He was still a disposable assistant surgeon likely to be tapped for official duties: in August he was assigned the task of setting up a detachment hospital, the "most unpleasant of all unpleasant duties," at Niza, "the dullest, & most melancholy quarter I was ever doomed to pine away in." Soldiers away from their regiment—even in a hospital—were one of the chief administrative headaches of the army, for all officers took it for granted that soldiers, released from discipline, would run off, get drunk, commit atrocities, or never be seen again. Being sick or wounded was almost the only legitimate way a soldier could be absent from his regiment, and to ensure that he did not take advantage of it, the surgeon in charge of a hospital had a host of administrative duties, designed to make hospitals into a medical version of barracks, complete with sentries and noncommissioned officers, especially enjoined to be careful "to prevent liquor . . . from being carried into the hospital . . . nor are they to allow any Patient to go out (to the Necessary excepted)" without the permission of the surgeon. In setting up the hospital, Lesassier had to keep track of all soldiers admitted, and make sure their regimental surgeons were informed, because nine pence per day was stopped from soldiers' pay for their medical attendance, and regimental surgeons were responsible for filling out monthly returns for their sick. He also had to fill out tickets, in triplicate, indicating each soldier's name and how many of his "necessaries," such as clothing, blankets, arms, and accoutrements, he had come in with, checking off each of the twenty-five separate items and having each ticket countersigned by one commissioned officer. The necessaries themselves were to be placed in storage, and the soldier would have to present them, and his ticket, to his commanding officer when he was discharged from the hospital, to make sure he had not sold his blanket for drink. Lesassier also had to draw up preliminary medical records, including names, ages, diseases, diet, and treatment. Finally, he had to select a noncommissioned officer, with the "approbation of the Commanding Officer," to supervise the patients; that done, we may assume, Lesassier retired to his billet to write up his notes.

He passed his time with further erotic adventures during that long hot summer. "An incomplete adventure," was the heading he gave the page describing the day he met Rita, "a pretty little brunette," who lived next door to the house where he was quartered. "She was sitting beside me in the evening—& our hearts beat in voluptuous unison. I was fondly anticipating the most rapturous enjoyment when at an unlucky moment her guardian returned home. Appearances were so strongly against her, that the ferocious wretch treated poor Rita, with the utmost brutality." A modern hero would have prevented him, but Lesassier, never gallant, "durst not interfere from an apprehension of disturbing the neighborhood." He was, however, "seized with the strange whim of begging her to accompany me"; prudence argued against it, but when he was ordered back to her village to look after some sick soldiers, he considered it, "in my usual superstitious way, as a kind of fatality:—& that it was destined that I should ultimately succeed in my attempts in carrying away my young friend."

He did succeed, by enacting a scene from popular ballads and disguising Rita as a boy. He employed "a hair dresser of the Guards, to cut her hair in the same manner as my own was. She had now the appearance of a smart English boy." She lived with Lesassier as his servant, waiting at table and doing his washing. In ballads like "Mary Ambree" or "The Valiant Virgin," the heroine dresses as a boy to follow her true love to war, and modern historians have pointed out the feminist implications of this theme, but it is clear that Lesassier's motive for re-creating this fiction was his own sexual enjoyment. He lay down rules for Rita: in front of his mess companions, the other officers, "she was to act as a servant," but "in private, I should endeavor to make her amends for so much restraint." His own idea of how to "make her amends" was through his own affection and sexual prowess, but it soon became apparent that Rita felt this was not quite enough. "I must confess," Lesassier wrote, "that my patience was perpetually put to the severest test on account of Rita's continued forwardness & petulence in the presence of strangers. I was in constant dread of such conduct leading to a discovery of her sex." There were frequent "petty quarrels," and soon both Lesassier and Rita were heartily tired of each other. Lesassier's Portuguese servant, Manoel, began to make advances to Rita, an additional source of anger and jealousy for Lesassier.

The affair came to an abrupt end after three weeks. Rita had spent the day "in washing, & making every thing around me, as comfortable as possible," and when Lesassier went off to dinner, she asked him for the keys to his baskets, those panniers of which he was so proud, saying "that she had something more to wash." It was excellent psychology, for Lesassier handed her the keys without a second thought, and left, only to find her gone in his return. Her parents had come for her, he later found out, accompanied by two men hired to guard her in case he should offer any opposition. "So, she left me," he wrote, relieved at so effective an end to the affair, and he proceeded to harrow up his feelings in his usual way by dwelling sorrowfully on his own harshness, which, he imagined, had led her to "this desperate step." His pleasant melancholy was abruptly replaced by indignation, however, when he found that Rita "had robbed me of a set of gold buttons; that cost me between five & six guineas!! That a young creature of scarcely sixteen, after receiving from me such repeated proofs of the tenderest friendship, should reward me with an act of such atrocious black ingratitude, is equally horrible, & shocking to humanity," he went on, once again warming to his subject once he had pen in hand. "She voluntarily flew to my arms for protection—she came to me, arrayed in all the winning attractions, of youth, & innocence. In me, she ever found the most solicitous protection & the sincerest friendship. And how did she repay me?" It did not occur to him that he had promised to make amends to her without providing any tangible recompense, that she had acted as his servant, making everything around him as comfortable as possible, without pay, that she had provided precisely the same proofs of the tenderest friendship as Lesassier without receiving any of the presents that Lesassier thought his own due from women; that, in sum, she might have felt she deserved the gold buttons. Of course it could not occur to him, for he was too self-centered to try to see matters from her point of view: Rita was an incidental character in his own life story, and he lacked the imaginative sympathy that would have suggested to him that she might be the heroine of her own. And yet, though he did not understand her, he was an excellent reporter. The portrait he gives us of Rita is very vivid; a sensuous, high-spirited girl with her own sense of justice, for "what added trebly to the mortification," Lesassier wrote, was that Rita took only his gold buttons from the panniers, not the five dollars lying next to them, "because she knew, that *the money belonged to my Portuguese Servant.*" A perfidious mistress was tolerable, not at all uncommon in novels, but a mistress perfidious to him while behaving honorably to his servant was beyond his comprehension: "The thought almost drives me to madness."

Rita's departure left him with little to keep up his spirits beyond the hope of going home. "Thus Alas! patience is my only resource," Lesassier wrote, and as the fall wore on, it looked as though his patience would be rewarded. Always the weaker of the two battalions, the second had only had 391 men at the Battle of Bussaco in September 1810; by 31 May 1811, Lesassier described them, with sarcasm, as "*the formidable force* of 250 bayonets"; by November, it seemed likely they might go home in the spring. Lesassier asked surgeon McLeod once again for help—this time for a leave of absence—and McLeod "interested himself for me to such a degree that he conducted the whole affair himself," perhaps thinking he would have more success if Lesassier kept out of it. On 26 November *General Orders* announced that "Assistant Surgeon Lesassier, 42d Regiment," was given leave to "proceed to England to join the 1st Battalion"; on 2 December Lord Blantyre signed his orders. Overwhelmed by a "burst of rapture . . . at such unlooked for good fortune," Lesassier started for Lisbon. By early January he was back in London and obtained a formal leave of absence from the medical board, much disgusted with life in active service. "What have I or any other medical officer to do with the tinsel of military reputation?" he wrote, in words that can serve as the fitting end to his first tour of duty in the Peninsula. "Are *we* likewise gaining laurels—who 'ne'er unsheathed a sword'! Do *we* assist in winning battles—or does victory crown *us* with praise?"

CHAPTER 7

# Soothing Hope of Speedy Promotion

Lesassier spent his three months' leave with Ella, much of it in Manchester to make sure no rumors of their affair could reach her husband. He had not been the least bit faithful: in addition to Rita and the three Portuguese women from whom he thought he had caught venereal disease, there were a host of others whose names he had written down on the back cover of one of the journals, keeping track of them as he kept track of each town or village he passed through. None of this made a difference to him or to Ella. He had left her "a gay—giddy—thoughtless girl—eager in the pursuit of every transitory pleasure; & as susceptible as wax of every impression," but found her not only "in every acquirement, singularly improved," but also much more beautiful: "Like a rose, whose lovely petals had voluptuously expanded beneath the ardent rays of a midday sun, but whose blooming beauties had closed again, after a refreshing shower; & now displayed more vivid color & diffused around a sweeter fragrance than before." He knew she had faults, for they sometimes "mutually lost their good humor," but he magnanimously conceded that he, too, had his failings, and in any case his "adored Ella . . . was less shaded by the foibles of her sex than any other woman whom he had ever met with." She was still as passionately in love with him as ever and willing to do anything for him, including paying his debts. "This is affection to some purpose," he wrote, making explicit his view of the connection between affection and compensation, "This is not feigned—Hers is the language of the heart." Indeed, with that "bewitching delicacy so peculiar to herself," she offered to pay for all Lesassier's expenses during his stay in Britain, considering it, she told him, not "as liberality on her part"—for liberality, from a mistress, would be demeaning—"but as an act of duty—looking upon me as the only real master both of her heart, & of all that she possesses." It was as well that she said so, for though he did not want to ask her help directly, he would "mentally have taxed her with a cruel degree of levity" if she had done nothing. Her offer increased his affection for her and led him to extend his own financial metaphors to new heights: "O God!" he wrote, "how I tremble lest accident should rob me of such a brilliant gem. I watch around her, with the agitated anxiety, that a miser would display over his countless hordes of wealth."

Lesassier may not have been aware that his discussion with Ella echoed traditional ballads like "The Trooper and Maid," in which a soldier cheerfully takes everything the maiden has to offer and then rides off, promising, in one version, to marry her "when cockle-shells turn silver bells." But his visit to his father while in Manchester came straight out of the ballad tradition of a young soldier, returning from the wars, testing his sweetheart's affection by pretending he is a stranger. It had not been easy for Lesassier to return to Manchester, "a place where so large a portion of my life had been passed; & which had been the scene of so many disastrous events." Not "one single pleasing sensation" did he experience as his coach jolted over the well-known streets: instead "each successive recollection brought only increasing disgust; & I should have sickened at the long, & gloomy perspective of abhorred remembrance," if it were not for the presence of his beautiful and adoring Ella to remind him how far he had come from his younger self. He delayed visiting Pierre for some time, for he did not know his address and had to get it from Ann Collins, now respectably married to one of her lodgers but still an unwelcome reminder of his childhood. Pierre was home, Lesassier wrote, and "I was introduced to him, as an officer who had lately arrived from Portugal, & had seen his son." It was a strange, romantic whim to appear before his father in this way—no one else in Manchester had had the slightest difficulty in recognizing him despite his six-year absence—and it is hard to believe Lesassier when he wrote that his own father did not know him, "but enquired with all that fascinating suavity of manners so peculiar to him," what news his visitor could give him of his son. Lesassier, perhaps with Pierre's tacit complicity, appears to be enacting his own private version of the ballad's final verse; "My heart was so full, as I gazed at the venerable author of my being," he wrote, "that I could not keep up the deception but sprang into his arms, falteringly exclaiming 'Do you not know me, my *dear father?*'" To Lesassier's surprise as well as pleasure, Pierre was "most elegantly dressed, & most genteely lodged"; he spent the afternoon there and called several times afterwards, and he left Manchester on better terms with his father and his own past than he had been for many years.

The campaign of 1812 in the Peninsula began in January with the successful, though bloody sieges of Ciudad Rodrigo and, in March, Badajoz. For Lesassier it began on 30 March 1812, when he was ordered to rejoin his regiment, now the First Battalion of the 42nd. On 20 April 1812, they landed in Portugal, Lesassier noting that the regiment, drawn up in parade in Lisbon's Praça do Commercio "was a grand sight." The next day was fair day, and he purchased "a handsome saddle horse & a baggage beast." One of his friends, going home with the Second Battalion, gave him the invaluable present of a tent, large enough for three men. Thus, he wrote, he "was amply prepared to encounter all the well known difficulties of this harassing service. I was admirably mounted; & my baggage comprised within it, every necessary, & many luxuries, that could serve to smooth the rugged track over which my destiny was again about to lead me. Thus circumstanced, I had less to dread, than the greatest part of my brother officers." The 42nd, and Lesassier with it, left Lisbon on 8 May to join the First Division, in Spain. They arrived in time for Lesassier to retrieve his horse from his old Armagh friend William Lindsay, now assistant surgeon to the 36th, and to join the advance against Marshal August Marmont that pushed the French army back toward Salamanca.

The tone of Lesassier's journals changed from the previous campaign. He had joined a victorious army this time, and one that was now on the offensive: we hear no more of the British being pushed into the sea. More experienced, he now realized that it would be a long campaign, and he had prepared for it. His new tent could be "pitched in a few minutes, & afforded the most delicious shelter during the worst heat of the day—& an ample protection from the heavy dews of the night." Within it, he could, for at least part of the day, pretend to be an independent gentleman in retirement from the bustle of the world. "This retired spot," he wrote at one camp, "is formed by an amphitheatre of hills, which gave it a romantic appearance," and he took care to make his "tent as a agreeable a retreat as possible, by covering the ground with my horse cloth, which formed a handsome carpet; & converting my baskets at the upper end of my tent, into a large table; which when covered with my English green cloth, had really an elegant appearance. It was always my first care, to have my little pavilion arranged in the most finished manner, & my books piled on my table; after which, I could at leisure refresh myself, by changing my dress, while our breakfast was preparing." In this one area, at least, he could be superior to his higher-ranking associates: "my tent was envied by all, & of course, *I* was execrated, for being in possession of those comforts, which others looked up to, & sighed for in vain."

His professional expectations were most important in shaping his attitude. The surgeon of the First Battalion, John Erly, had used his time in Britain to obtain an M.D. from St. Andrews University, and in June 1812 he was appointed physician to the forces. Erly's promotion left the First Battalion temporarily without a surgeon. As the senior assistant surgeon, Lesassier hoped he might be appointed to the surgeoncy, and he appealed to James Hamilton's much-vaunted interest, sure that "the slightest exertion on Dr. H's part" would have secured it. Hamilton had boasted of his interest in military circles to his nephew, and assured his nephew that he "should scarcely complete three years in the Army, ere he should obtain a surgeoncy"—but now, James Hamilton wrote back, he had no influence with the medical board, and feared that Lesassier might not be able to get the position because he was not "the senior Assistant Surgeon in the Army." Hamilton was right, as usual; all promotions were governed by strict seniority within the medical service, and Lesassier was not appointed to the surgeoncy of the 42nd. Instead, the position was taken by Alexander McLachlan, who had previously superseded him in the assistant surgeoncy when the 42nd was stationed in Gibraltar. Lesassier, as might be expected, was not mollified by his uncle's prescience. Patronage, in his view, was still a special dispensation from the requirements of seniority and merit that beset other medical men. Of course he was not the senior assistant surgeon: "if I were I should claim my advancement, as a right," and not need to ask his uncle's assistance. It was precisely because he was not in line for the position that he required patronage to place him ahead of his brother officers.

Hamilton had probably not meant to mislead his nephew. In the late 1790s, as the medical service expanded, assistant surgeons commonly were promoted to surgeon within three years. John Erly, for example, had served three years as assistant surgeon of the 42nd before being promoted to surgeon. Hamilton may have had every expectation that would happen to Lesassier and was not averse to taking credit for it. But by 1812 the service was fully staffed, and promotions came much more slowly. Some few openings occurred because of a surgeon becoming a physician, like Erly; fewer still because of retirements, for what surgeon would retire and give up full pay in the middle of an active campaign? The majority of openings came about because of deaths in service, a reminder that military medical men had no immunity from the diseases that afflicted their patients. Lesassier should have been aware that the pace of promotions had slowed considerably in the preceding ten years, but he did not apply that knowledge to himself. To have done so would have reduced him to a mere bit player in the "many scenes" of life, returned him to his former status of one of the many born to misfortune rather than one of the few chosen to succeed. He preferred instead to ignore both the external circumstances that affected his individual condition and the real limits of his uncle's power. His low rank then became no more than the temporary setback of a novel's hero, produced by the temporary victory of the novel's villain, a position increasingly assumed by James Hamilton. For Lesassier remained convinced that Hamilton could have had him promoted, if only he had chosen to do so, and he never forgave Hamilton for this "shallow pretext for abandoning my welfare."

Many observers, including Wellington, complained of the practice of the medical board of filling vacancies with newcomers according to seniority across the whole medical service, rather than promoting up from within the regiment or even from within the Peninsula: "It would be but justice," Wellington argued, "to promote those on the spot, who are performing the duty." Not doing so was bad for morale, for those who felt themselves most entitled to the vacancy ended up having to assume it on a temporary basis, only to relinquish it, and their higher rank, when their new superior medical officer arrived. This is precisely what happened to Lesassier, for in the spring of 1812 the successful candidate for the surgeoncy, McLachlan, was surgeon of the 71st with the Second Division, and he could not leave the regiment to accept his new position. Lesassier therefore became acting surgeon, with all the responsibilities but few of the perquisites of the position. Despite his "supreme mortification," he consoled himself with the thought that his promotion might come more quickly from the professional contacts he had made than from the ordinary process of seniority. He had kept in contact with William Fergusson regarding a surgeoncy in the Portuguese service; Fergusson, though "most anxious," Lesassier said, "to serve me . . . really had not the patronage of the situation, that I wanted." He did, however, say he had written a letter to the new director of the medical service in the Peninsula, James McGrigor.

We have already encountered James McGrigor's pronouncements on young army surgeons, and it is as a reformer of the conditions under which they worked that his path finally crossed Lesassier's. McGrigor was one of the administrative heroes of the Peninsular War, whose improvements in the medical arrangements for the army were credited as saving Wellington the equivalent of a division of fighting troops for the later campaigns. Formally, McGrigor was under the command of the Army Medical Board, a civilian department which reported directly to Parliament, not the commander of the forces. But McGrigor, an experienced army medical man, had seen at once that the key to effective administration was close cooperation with Wellington. He became part of Wellington's staff at headquarters, keeping close watch on the movements of each division, ready at a moment's notice to allocate available medical men where needed. He would have liked to organize mobile medical units—complete with surgeons, wagons, stretchers, and bearers—similar to those used by the French, but he could never persuade Wellington to approve them. He did, however, persuade him to approve the use of regimental and brigade hospitals as temporary stations, to halt the costly, inefficient flow of men and wagons to the general hospitals and back. Regimental medical staff, under McGrigor, were rousted from general hospitals to staff the regimental and brigade hospitals with no excuses allowed for not obeying orders instantly. Indeed, "all Medical Officers," in McGrigor's acerbic statement, "who are not equal to duty of every kind & at all times in this country, are to hold themselves in readiness to be embarked for England." Hospital assistants alone were to make up the junior staff of the general hospitals, with experienced staff surgeons to supervise them, as McGrigor "found, that the complaint . . . that the care of the sick in General Hospitals was confided to Hospital Mates & Assistant Surgeons has not been entirely groundless." And to stave off future complaints from officers and men in hospital and on the field, staff surgeons everywhere were to instruct their subordinates in medicine, surgery, and hospital administration.

Under McGrigor, the worst administrative mistakes were avoided. Never again were two assistant surgeons from the same brigade left in general hospitals while their regiments were under fire, the situation that had sparked Lord Blantyre's wrath against Lesassier after the Battle of Fuentes d'Onoro. Delinquent officers like Lesassier's old friend Lindsay, who "has hardly done an hour's duty with his regiment, for the two years he has been in this country," McGrigor reported grimly, were granted sick leave to England and speedily replaced. Not even McGrigor, though, could do anything about the fact that professional recognition came more readily to medical staff in general hospitals than in regiments, for it was there that medical contacts were made. His own long-standing interest in the nature of infectious diseases led him to take painstaking notes on the progress of disease in the major hospital stations, and it is from those notes that he wrote his later sketch of the medicine of the Peninsular War; the men he singled out for special recognition were those at general, not regimental hospitals. John Erly was one of those singled out, and it is indicative of the way the system worked that he should be thus rewarded for his three years on a staff appointment, rather than for his fifteen years in regimental service.

Lesassier called on McGrigor at headquarters soon after the army crossed into Spain in early June. He was received, Lesassier wrote, "in the most affable manner"—James McGrigor, too, had studied at Edinburgh—and "He assured me that Inspector Fergusson's letter of recommendation had prepossessed Dr. McGrigor exceedingly in my favor: and although there was no vacancy at present, he would embrace the earliest opportunity of serving me." McGrigor disliked the personal applications for promotion with which he was inundated soon after his arrival on the Peninsula—each applicant received the chilly reply that his "claim for promotion will be considered conformably with those of other meritorious officers in this service"—and took steps to require that all applications be forwarded through staff surgeons and other medical officers under whom the applicant had served. He was not interested in letters from civilian patrons, and though he adhered to the rules of seniority within the service the "material points" of any recommendation were "zeal and attention to duty, medical talent, and education." Lesassier therefore acted astutely in getting a letter from Fergusson: paradoxically, his efforts to remain in the Coimbra hospitals, rather than rejoin his regiment, had once again reaped professional rewards. Lesassier made one more effort by writing to Deputy Inspector Tegart, another astute move, for Tegart, like Fergusson, stood high in McGrigor's favor. With that effort, and McGrigor's assurance that he would serve him at the earliest opportunity, Lesassier had to rest content.

Hope of promotion, and recognition that it would depend upon his good behavior, made Lesassier much more careful on this campaign. He had become ill in May, probably with an intermittent fever. "To a person, whose health was in so critically a delicate situation," he wrote, "an exposure to all the deadly effects of baneful moisture, was truly shocking." Two years earlier, the merest hint of illness had led him to report himself sick and stay behind; this time, in contrast, "to report myself sick, I felt impossible to do; without drawing on me all the fatal consequences, that the bitterest malignance of malevolence could wreak on my devoted head. As I was induced to encourage the soothing hope of speedy promotion, so I resolved to run no risks of darkening the fairness of my prospects, by any piece of inconsiderate folly."

This was prudent, especially since his new commanding officer was no more willing than the last had been to let him get away with neglect of his duty. Lesassier had looked forward to being under his "old friend" from Gibraltar, Colonel Stirling, assuming that he would "be treated like a gentleman & be permitted to exercise that independence for which I so long have sighed." But "Daddy" Stirling, as he was known to his men, was a different man on campaign from the amiable host of Miss Joanna Stirling's admirers and insisted that his officers do their duty on and off the field. Lesassier had begun the campaign by taking mess with two other officers, who also shared his tent. In addition to practical and social advantages, this meant that he rode near the front of the regiment, and thus was able to avoid the delays and shortage of forage that afflicted those riding in the rear. Stirling "severely scolded" him for continuing to do this even after he became acting surgeon: Lesassier's place was in the rear, with the regimental hospital. Fear of another scolding kept him from visiting the "renowned fortress" of Ciudad Rodrigo with his two friends when they passed it the next day: "my present responsible duties, & delicate situation with regard to my Commanding Officer—prevented me from quitting the encampment." He heard from his friends that the town was "very much destroyed," and the inconvenience of traveling in the rear was ameliorated by his taking mess with the quartermaster, who kindly helped Lesassier eke out his own meager supplies of tea, sugar, and money. Nothing could soothe his anger at Stirling, who became "the old brute" in his journal for presuming to give him orders, but this time his anger did not keep him from carrying out those orders. Stirling, for his part, acquired a medal and two clasps in the Peninsula, ending the war as a major general.

Even fear of Stirling's reprimand and desire for promotion could not make Lesassier perfectly attentive to orders. While on campaign, orders to march immediately meant just that: neither officers or men were supposed to delay, even if they were in the middle of dinner. But Lesassier had learned that in the confusion, no one would notice if he delayed to eat his food or pack his belongings: "Dinner ready when ordered away+ Dined however," reads one entry. He also routinely ignored the order to send baggage and pack animals to the rear, designed to make sure the brigades could execute their movements unencumbered, because it would mean a later delay in setting up his little pavilion and eating breakfast. There was also the chance that, in the rear, the baggage might fall into French hands and be lost forever. He had a close call near the town of Olmeda, when he and his mess companion "determined to steal away and visit this place." They left their column and rode off to the town, but as Lesassier wrote, "I had nearly involved myself in an awkward adventure on this occasion, for Lord Wellington had had his headquarters in this town during the preceding night; & I narrowly avoided being seen by him." He risked a court-martial and he knew it, for Wellington had no sense of humor about officers that acted as though they were on a pleasure trip, but in this, as on other instances of insubordination, Lesassier was lucky enough to avoid detection.

As Wellington's army approached Salamanca, General Marmont ordered the French to retreat from the town, but he left eight hundred men in three strong forts overlooking the Tormes, from which Lesassier's regiment could hear "an occasional firing of both cannon & musketry," when they approached Salamanca on 17 June. Wellington entered the city with a small escort, set his Sixth Division to work setting up batteries to besiege the forts, and positioned the rest, including Lesassier's regiment, in the hills to the north and east. This was Lesassier's first close contact with the enemy after two and a half years on the Peninsula. He never had a chance to write up his rough notes, which, from the rapid juxtaposition of ideas, have a narrative power his more elaborate descriptions lack. On either 17 or 18 June he visited the city: "narrow+houses antique+many of wood+but most splendid square with medals of kings+and superb Gothic cathedral & other colleges+People affect greatest joy to see us+Crowded with inhabitants+Plenty of shops+Pretty women." The French had left a "fortified convent & 2 forts garrisoned with 1000 men," whose firing impeded Lesassier's sightseeing, "I could not enter any street commanded by these as many lookers on have been wounded &c+narrow escape from a shot striking cathedral."

In the meantime batteries had been set up by the British to attack the French forts. On 19 June Lesassier went into town again, accompanied by Stewart, his fellow assistant surgeon. He later described in *Edward Neville* the town "crowded with Officers of various Regiments, amusing themselves with sauntering about the streets." "Much exposed to bullets," he noted at the time, "+ . . . Salamanca singularly destroyed considering . . . +The Cathedral 300 feet long+Architecture resembles Westminster but much lighter & more beautiful+All the churches &c built of a species of close grained sandstone at distance like marble but of so durable a texture that smallest sculptured ornaments uninjured by time." Ever the assiduous consumer, he noted, too, "my torturing situation at passing shops with such piquant odors & without money to purchase a single luxury," a sensation which remained with him years later when he wrote about Edward Neville, whose walks through town "afforded him infinitely less gratification, than otherwise he would have derived from them, if his extreme want of money had not prevented him from indulging in many a little comfort which he saw displayed temptingly in the shop windows."

For the next week he remained out of town with his regiment, under arms because a battle with Marmont was daily expected. On 20 June "The rear of our regiment although on brow of little hill exceedingly exposed to shot+I do not know how I escaped"; on 26 June "I went about 7½ o'clock inside of Battery+Excessive danger that I ran." The forts surrendered on 27 June, and Wellington and Marmont spent the next month maneuvering around each other, each looking for a favorable opportunity for a battle. Lesassier's activities consisted of looking after the sick of his regiment in the regimental hospital, constantly moving to new quarters as the armies marched north and east, then south and west back toward Salamanca. The battle came on 22 July, after "a truly awful night," according to Lesassier and many other observers, with so much thunder and lightning that his horses, and some of the cavalry's, ran off and had to be caught. During the battle itself, the First Division, including the 42nd Regiment, were stationed on a hill to the north of the main action "where we remained until about 6 in evening," Lesassier wrote, "galled however by occasional round shot." It was his first experience of battle, and he remained riveted, watching "in the coolest manner with my telescope rested on the two medicine panniers and an impressive sight it was—I was so intent on the scene before me that I forgot my own danger as balls were flying every now & then over my head." It was the grandest theater he had ever experienced: the "perpetual roar" of the "Enemy's guns . . . the march of our columns along the valley— raked through & through with round shot & men knocked down in terrific manner . . . a *brilliant overwhelming, sublime* spectacle was the whole battle+The attack on centre hill & finally taking with horrid carnage." Toward evening, his division was involved in an ineffectual pursuit of a portion of the French army: "I narrowly escaped having my head carried off by a 9 pound shot Had I not providentially thrown myself on the ground I should have been dashed to atoms." As his brigade continued to advance, he stayed behind "with instruments to operate in a safe situation," but when no action occurred he rode on to join his brigade. "Firing did not cease entirely until 9 at night," he wrote. "It was as clear a moonlight as ever I beheld+Our victory was splendid & decisive." It was Wellington's first clear victory in a battle, rather than a siege, "regarded," as John Keegan has said, "by those who like to write about battles in such language as his 'masterpiece.'"

The battle at Salamanca had been the ultimate sublime landscape, but it was the last that Lesassier had time to describe in such language, for now it was the 42nd's turn to be deployed, and he had to abandon his role of picturesque traveler for that of medical officer. Following Salamanca, Wellington marched south and retook Madrid. Lesassier's brigade, with Colonel Stirling at its head, marched later, and rejoined the main army only after Wellington had decided he could not hold Madrid, and retreated. On 19 September the army arrived outside of Burgos, held by the French and heavily fortified. The main garrison was in what had once been the medieval castle, greatly strengthened and extended to include a redoubt, or hornwork, on the nearby hill of San Miguel.

"That same evening," Lesassier wrote, "it was determined that our regiment, supported by Pack's Brigade, should attack the Redoubt." There were two parts to this attack. The first was a false attack on the rear of the redoubt, as a diversion. The second, the main attack, was to be a direct assault: the 42nd would provide cover and set up ladders, which Pack's brigade would use to scale the walls. As the historian Charles Oman has described, "The storm succeeded, but with vast and unnecessary loss of life, and not in the way which Wellington had intended. It was bright moonlight, and the firing party, when coming up over the crest, were at once detected by the French, who opened a very heavy fire upon them. The Highlanders [that is, the 42nd] . . . remained for a quarter of an hour, entirely exposed and suffering terribly." "For, you may believe," as Private Gunn of the 42nd put it, "it is not boys' play to be going up a scaling ladder and a nimble Frenchman disputing your right to be there." To continue with Oman: "Having lost half their numbers they finally dispersed, but not till after the main attack had failed. . . . The advanced parties duly laid their ladders: they were found somewhat short, and after wavering for some minutes Pack's men retired, suffering heavily." The attack was only successful because the scaling party acted as a diversion from the attack on the rear, which drove the French from the hill of San Miguel to the main part of the castle.

"The Redoubt stormed & taken in a most gallant manner at 9 at night of the 19th," was Lesassier's comment, "+My incessant labor from that very hour." Stirling's brigade had been chosen for the assault because it was one of the strongest, having seen no action during the campaign so far. That ended with the assault on Burgos, in which two officers and thirty-three men were killed, while five officers and 164 men were wounded. As acting surgeon, Lesassier was therefore responsible for 169 wounded men. Surgeon George James Guthrie later described his own first battle, where two hundred men were wounded "and most of these men were lying in a line of two hundred yards extent; they were all known to me by name as well as by person: the conflict was soon over, and the difference of expression in begging for assistance, or expressing their sense of suffering, will never be obliterated from my memory." Distressing as this must have been for him, Guthrie was at least already an experienced surgeon; for Lesassier, who after three years in the Peninsula had never treated wounds fresh from the battlefield, it must have been far worse. If there were "splinters of bone or shell, bits of cloth, dirt, &c" in their wounds, he would have had to pick them away; if there were "sharp pieces of bone sticking out" of compound fractures, he would have had to "saw them off, and then apply the many-headed bandage and proper splints, cushioned off by tow or rags." He probably also had bayonet wounds to treat, "rare in the Peninsula," according to Guthrie, because "opposing regiments, when formed in line, and charging with fixed bayonets, never meet . . . and this for the very best possible reason, that one side turns around and runs away as soon as the other comes close enough to do mischief." But the men of the 42nd had no place to run away when scaling the horn-work, and according to one account, "every man who reached the top of a ladder was instantly bayoneted, and in his fall he knocked down several others." To treat those who survived, "after cleaning away the blood and filth," Lesassier would have had to "lay the lips of the wound neatly together with straps, or, if necessary and practicable, with ligatures, and support the part with a bandage"; for "a deep thrust," he would have had to "lay a compress along its course, and bind it up moderately tight." If the intestines hung from the wound, he would have had to "replace them, and close the orifice with ligatures and straps"; if they themselves were cut, he would have had to "secure them to its lips by a few close stitches." All this had to be done at once, for "Military surgeons," according to Guthrie, "endeavour to have all their operations performed within the first twenty-four, or at most forty-eight hours after the injury."

The needs of the military, as well as the needs of the patient, dictated speed. The seriously wounded had to be removed to the rear as soon as possible, an important reason why amputation continued to be the main technique of military medicine. Surgeon Walter Henry tersely described treatment after a major battle as "collecting, dressing, amputating and packing the wounded into spring wagons." There was controversy during and after the war about whether unnecessary amputations were performed, for, according to John Hennen, "It is a very prevalent idea among the uninformed private soldiers, and some of the junior officers, that the surgeons, 'lop off,' as their phrase is, limbs by cart-loads, to save trouble." Certainly the most pungent image of wartime surgery was of surgeons, "stripped to their shirts and bloody," and stacks of "arms and legs, flung here and there without distinction, and the ground . . . dyed with blood." But amputation on or near the field of battle, "with as little delay as possible," according to Hennen, was the safest form of treatment for anything other than a simple incised wound, certainly any case where the bone was shattered, the joint seriously injured, or the "soft parts" so badly damaged that there was "no hope of the circulation and other functions being carried on." In all of them, delay would only worsen the condition, and so would transport, for, wrote Guthrie, "I had officers and soldiers . . . for forty-eight hours together travelling almost constantly in waggons, immediately after amputation, without any bad consequences; but I have seen the most dreadful ones ensue after the removal of persons with shattered bones, and more especially where the injury had existed some hours." Once amputation was decided on, and the patient agreed to it—the patient's assent or refusal is as present in the medical literature as any description of his pain is absent—speed in performing the operation was a necessary part of the treatment, to lessen pain and shock and reduce loss of blood.

There were other, less heroic surgical techniques. "If the ball has passed through the fleshy part of the arm, thigh, or buttock," Hennen wrote, "we do no more than sponge the part clean, place a small bit of folded lint on each orifice, which we retain by two cross slips of adhesive plaster, and lay over, at most, two or three turns of a roller." If a ball was still in the body, and easily accessible, "we cut upon and extract it at once; and we should lay it down, as a rule not to be deviated from, to extract on the spot every extraneous body that we possibly can." Otherwise it became much harder to extract, as one wounded officer named Harry Smith found when a ball was extracted from an ankle wound after some months had passed. "It was five minutes, most painful indeed, before it was extracted. The ball was jagged, and the tendinous fibres had been so grown into it, it was half dissected and half torn out with most excruciating torture for a moment, the forceps breaking which had hold of the ball." Smith was comparatively fortunate in the position of the wound, for it was not always possible to extract the ball or other foreign bodies. Hennen advised the surgeon not to promise "a certain extraction, however urgent the patient may be," unless he were quite sure he could do it, "for as nothing is more cheering than presenting him with the ball, so nothing is more disheartening, or tends more to shake his confidence in his medical attendants, than a disappointment under these circumstances." "Under these circumstances": Hennen's phrase, together with Smith's description, are useful reminders that in military medicine, as in all other medicine of the period, the patient was an active participant during his own operation, unless he fainted or died.

Lesassier had little education or experience in surgery—Tegart's commendation had been for hospital administration, not operative technique—and both Hennen and Guthrie give examples of the kind of mistakes beginning surgeons could make. Without much knowledge or skill in anatomy, an incision to remove a ball could become a dangerous wound. Even a ball that could be "felt at the distance of an inch, or even half an inch below the skin" might be hard to extract, "for all that seems to be required is, that a simple incision be made down to the surface of it, when it will slip out, which is not always found to be the case," either because "the young surgeon . . . makes his incision too small, and cannot at all times oppose sufficient resistance to prevent the ball from retreating before the effort he makes for its expulsion forwards," or because it "also requires to be cleared from the surrounding cellular substance to a greater extent than might at first be imagined." Hennen cautioned all surgeons to be sure to tie all large exposed arteries, whether bleeding or not, for "from a neglect of this rule," he wrote, "many lives have been lost." And a mistake "which," Guthrie said, "I have frequently seen in the first operations of gentlemen entering into the service," was leaving too little skin after an amputation to cover the stump, with the result that the bone was exposed for "one or two inches," in which case the stump, even if healed, "will still be very conical, tender, and always obnoxious to injury."

There is reason to think that in this, his first experience of battlefield medicine, Lesassier may not have risen to the occasion, for he noted his "anxiety at insinuations of my not doing my duty. Which being repeated by acting staff surgeon on October 4th, I challenged him." The most likely result is that it was explained to him that challenging one's superior officer to a duel was contrary to the Articles of War and could get him court-martialed. He went to visit Burgos during a parley on 23 September, a conspicuously bad time for a surgeon with a hospital full of wounded men to be sightseeing. Perhaps, too, it angered the other assistant surgeon, Stewart, who must have been left with the sick and wounded while Lesassier was away. Or perhaps Lesassier was overwhelmed, like the surgeon mentioned by Walter Henry who "became so nervous that although half through his amputation of a poor fellow's thigh, he dropped the knife, and another hand was obliged to complete the operation." Perhaps he took time to have his dinner prepared or sleep in his comfortable tent while there were wounded to be dressed. Or he may have been as conscientious as he could be, but there were too many wounded for him to treat them promptly: even as dedicated a surgeon as Guthrie was accused of neglecting the sick when the pace of his operations could not keep up with the number of wounded. In any case, Lesassier wrote, "from that period began a degree of toil & confusion & distress to me that I could have formed no conception of— & which almost overcame me with disgust—aversion—& detestation of the army & all connected with it." And the wounded kept coming, though not in such numbers: fourteen in the next two days, another thirty-one in the following weeks.

The siege of Burgos was unsuccessful and Wellington, disappointed, had to withdraw his troops toward Portugal on 19 October, "and if it was not a retreat," Private Gunn later wrote, "I do not know what to call it." Under James McGrigor's administration, those wounded who were able to be moved had been evacuated over the course of the siege, but even so Lesassier had "a thousand perplexing difficulties & managements respecting the sick." There is a gap in Lesassier's otherwise full diaries between 19 October and 15 December 1812. They thus do not mention the dreadful retreat of 15–18 November, when the arrangements for food and quarters broke down, and men, marching through the mud and rain, went for three days without being issued rations. Dysentery was very prevalent among the divisions, including the First, that "had been employed at the siege of Burgos, where the men were frequently for 24 hours up to their middle in water in the trenches, sleeping frequently in the open air, or in tents on ground which was moist or quite wet . . . ; and it may easily be conceived, in what state cases of dysentery must have arrived, after having sustained a journey in extent from four to twenty days, conveyed chiefly in bullock cars or on the backs of mules, sometimes under incessant rain for several days together." They had other miseries to endure as well, for Guthrie later noted that "the removal of the wounded" provided a clear, if gruesome, case for the superiority of early amputation to trying to save the limb: "the amputations having recovered in a very fair proportion, whilst a very severe loss followed the attempt of saving such doubtful cases of injury as were not considered proper for amputation."

By 15 December, the 42nd, now in the Sixth Division, was cantoned in the Serra d'Estrella, where they remained until May. At some point, Lesassier was detached from his regiment and assigned to a brigade hospital in a nearby village. Perhaps it was that hospital that Major General Edward Pakenham came to inspect when he took over temporary command of the Sixth Division in January 1813. On arriving at the hospital, according to Private Gunn, he immediately "asked for the doctor. He was told none of them was come yet. 'What,' says His Lordship, 'do you mean to say that one of them does not attend here all night? Send for your head doctor immediately.' The doctors made their appearance and so did the Colonel. The General addressing the Colonel said, 'I am surprised you do not command your doctors attend to their duty and have one here all night.'" The "head doctor," in Gunn's account, defended himself by saying "he left instructions with the hospital sergeant what medicine to give, but if a change of medicine was required he was to send for us." Formally he was within his rights, for medical-board regulations did not include any provision for medical staff being on call at all times. Instead, they were to visit the sick twice a day and to come when called by the orderlies. But it seemed obvious to general officers that a doctor, not a sergeant, should be on call all night—Wellington insisted upon "the Officers of the Medical department," not just orderlies, "being at all times in the wards of the hospitals"—and Pakenham responded to the head doctor's excuse with a sarcastic "Oh, and it is very likely you would come." Pakenham also inspected the room with the "worst cases," and found it to be up an outside stair, and obviously neglected, with "two poor fellows . . . laying there on a pallet of straw unconscious, and some snow on the floor." He ordered that a fireplace be built, that men who could be moved be "shifted from place to place for the benefit of change of air," and that one of the medical men be in constant attendance. Gunn gave the credit to "our good and kind General Lord Pakenham" for he and his fellow soldiers "regaining our health to perform our duties again in the next campaign," not to any of the doctors. Pakenham agreed, writing home of "the trouble I have had . . . particularly with the Highlanders. . . . They however get better." It is tempting to suppose that Lesassier was one of the doctors present, and that he was subsequently ordered to find quarters where he could remain on call all night: it would explain his later being able to ward off being turned out of his billet by "obstinately persisting in General Pakenham's having granted me the privilege of not being interfered with."

The long period of rest allowed the men of the 42nd, and of almost all of the rest of the army, to recover their health in time for the fresh campaign: by 1 March, Pakenham wrote with evident satisfaction, "My people are much better, and I shall be able to give over my charge in high order or take a good turn out of them." The winter of 1812–1813 had been a costly one for Napoleon. His Russian campaign had ended in a miserable retreat. In the Peninsula, the Spanish guerrillos encouraged by the allied victories of 1812 and their own hard-won experience, had proved impossible for even Napoleon's best generals to subdue. Wellingon's plan was to take advantage of this by bringing his entire army around to bear on the western flank of the French army, concentrated in the region between Salamanca and Burgos. From there, he wrote, "our next operation will depend on circumstances. I do not know whether I am now stronger than the enemy. . . . But of this I am very certain, that I shall never be stronger through the campaign, or more efficient, than I am now: and the enemy will never be weaker." According to Oman, he already had in mind the shape the campaign would assume: a rapid push of the French army over the Spanish border into the Pyrenees.

The success of the campaign depended on rapid deployment of the army. Marching orders went out to divisions between 13 and 16 May 1813, and on 14 May Lesassier wrote to the staff surgeon to find out what he should do next. He received the answer at 11 P.M. that the division was on the march and he should rejoin his regiment. Arrangements had been made to facilitate mobility of the army and make it possible to set up and move camp as quickly and efficiently as possible. Regimental hospitals were fully equipped, and for the first time Wellington allowed the use of portable field hospitals made of wood, which could be set up and dismantled as quickly as necessary without having to depend on available buildings. Spring wagons, too, were attached to each brigade to make it easier to transport the sick and wounded. Arrangements were also made to improve conditions on the march, as Lesassier, with his keen eye for the comforts of life, noted. "The men," he wrote, "were now for the first time furnished with tents. Every company having three—which were carried by the former camp kettle mules. The old heavy iron kettles were replaced by light ones—carried by the men themselves. Every one of these kettles was intended for six men. This improvement was incalculably great & many lives would thus be preserved." The tents and light tin kettles meant soldiers could be comparatively comfortable even if no other shelter was available; it also made it possible to set up and break camp more rapidly and simplified cooking and commissary arrangements. The new arrangements, long rest, and perhaps anticipation of success had its effect, for Private Gunn noted that on the "second day's march, we were surprised at ourselves."

The general enthusiasm for the new venture seems to have spread even to Lesassier, who for the first time sounded pleased to be on campaign. He had not neglected his own comforts, again putting his experience of previous campaigns to use in preparation for this one. He had enlarged and improved his tent and purchased "an excellent stock of tea" and other items. Indeed, he wrote, his arrangements while encamped in his tent, "assuredly were enviable. The ground being first covered with an oilskin—over which was a new & brilliant colored horse rug—my horse cloth lying at the upper end, edging the baskets, that, covered with a green cloth, formed an elegant table—My little camp chair—made of leather—& my saddle—camp bed, cloak &c &c placed round the side of the tent, completed the singular uniformity & pleasing appearance of the whole." Even the expectation of a campaign in the heat of a Spanish summer did not bother him, "as there was a simple mode of cooling the tent—by fastening a blanket to the top of the tent & then extending it so as to leave a space of ½ yards between the blanket & the tent. Air is an imperfect conductor of heat thus this method of mine proved sufficient to reduce the temperature not less than 10 degrees Fahrenheit."

As usual, Lesassier had to console himself with his enjoying "many advantages that others did not," as a compensation for his low military status, for "my situation was still, unfortunately, the same vile one as it had been for so many years," that is, assistant surgeon. His first professional task of the new campaign, therefore, was to take charge of a "new & a degrading duty . . . a duty of all others the most unpleasant," conducting the "sick-cars of the brigade." This was, as he noted, a new duty: for the first time brigades were allotted a cart for transporting the slightly ill, who were expected to recover en route. Prior to this campaign, they either would have had to march, or be left behind. This, like other innovations in medical administration, was McGrigor's doing. Not only was it successful in returning sick soldiers to duty as quickly as possible, it also cut down on the manpower drain created by sending noncommissioned officers, subalterns, and assistant surgeons with each detachment of the sick to hospitals in the rear of the army.

Lesassier saw "our great man" McGrigor on 3 June, almost a year since the last time, when he had received the disappointing news of not being promoted to the surgeoncy of the 42nd. "I rode up to McGrigor," Lesassier wrote, "& he received me cordially—shaking me by the hand. He doubtlessly fancied I should attack him regarding my promotion. He deceived himself. I did not even hint at it." It was just as well that he showed such tact, for his promotion came very soon, effective as of 3 June, the very day he saw McGrigor: he was promoted to brevet staff surgeon to the Eighth Brigade of the Portuguese Army under William Carr Beresford. This was, as he happily wrote to his uncle, a "peculiarly desirable" position. The pay was nearly 24 shillings per day, 6 shillings and sixpence more than a staff surgeon in the British army. Moreover, he had been jumped two steps in rank, from a subaltern, as an assistant surgeon, to a major, as staff surgeon, "nor," he wrote, "is this matter left to doubt. . . . For every rank, there is a peculiar arrangement of the epaulets, which, by distinguishing the officer's situation, wisely prevents a thousand disagreeable consequences." Only a position in the Portuguese army conveyed such advantages, and Lesassier had finally obtained that position after three years of persistence. He thanked his uncle "for the additional obligation you have thus been pleased to confer on me" in getting him the position, but he well knew James Hamilton had had nothing to do with it. It was the chain of contacts he had made starting with Bolton in 1806 and extending through Halliday, Fergusson, Tegart, and McGrigor. It was also his early, if unmilitary, recognition that hospital duty, not regimental service, was the key to eventual promotion.

# CHAPTER 8

# Arrived at Wealth and Dignity

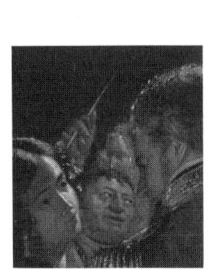he allied army was successful in its drive to the northwest. The French force holding Salamanca had to retreat on 24 May 1813, falling back with the main army to Burgos; Burgos in turn had to be abandoned on 13 June for the city of Vitoria; the allied victory at the Battle of Vitoria on 21 June turned the French retreat into a rout and left the allied army in control of Spain. The extended blockade of Pamplona in the first two weeks of July was, Lesassier wrote, "of infinite service to me; for it had afforded me time to become acquainted with the duties of my new situation & to arrange in some measure my scattered ideas." Lesassier was now staff surgeon of the Eighth Portuguese Brigade, in 1813–1814 deployed in the Third Division and commanded by General Manley Power. The brigade consisted of the 9th and 21st regiments of infantry and the 11th Caçadores, light, or skirmishing, troops. Neither the 9th or 21st had been very strong in 1811, but they had fought well at Bussaco and subsequent battles. Power's brigade was one of two singled out for special commendation by Marshal Beresford's general orders after Vitoria, and "it was extraordinary to observe," Wellington noted by the summer of 1813, the conduct of the Portuguese troops: "nothing could be like their forwardness now, and willing, ready, tempers." It was, then, an active and successful brigade on an active and successful campaign that Lesassier joined as *cirurgião mór da brigada* on 5 July 1813.

The topic of Lesassier's first recorded comments on his new position was, characteristically, his own comfort, for as the Eighth Brigade moved from village to village on the borders of France, he discovered the "real luxury of a staff situation." "Now was the time to envy the comforts of the staff," wrote Captain John Blakiston when encamped with his Portuguese regiment, "who are seldom or never doomed to sleep in a bivouac. Though they may have a little hard riding during the day, they are pretty sure to have a good dinner, and tolerable quarters for the night. They get the first and best of everything: in short, they enjoy the sweets (if such there be) of the campaign." As staff surgeon to the brigade, Lesassier was usually billeted at headquarters, where he "wanted none of the necessaries of life." He could arrive late in the evening without worrying that the best quarters would be all taken, because his quarter was reserved for him. "What a vast change this was! It is probable that there is not an instance of any other appointment bringing with it advantages so comparatively great as this one it has been my peculiarly good fortune to obtain." For the first time, he had a salary sufficient for his needs and desires, and he was even able to buy the "superb English horse . . . I had long wished to have; & now I had the pleasure of being better mounted than even many Generals in the country." Horses formed an important topic for conversation and status among the officers: "nothing," Lesassier was sure, "gives an appearance of so much meanness as a person who enjoys a lucrative situation going about mounted on a miserable horse."

And now that the army had finally bestowed upon him his long-anticipated promotion, he was prepared to reward it by his own good behavior. As he wrote to James McGrigor, offering his "sincerest thanks" for McGrigor's "condescending kindness" in appointing him staff surgeon, "it shall be the object of my unwearied attention, by diligence & unremitting zeal, at once to prove my gratitude, & merit a continuance of your good opinion." In McGrigor's vision, staff surgeons attached to brigades or divisions were middle managers whose chief responsibility was the allocation of medical staff and supplies, and the processing of the weekly and monthly returns. Though they supervised the medical care of soldiers, they were not primarily practicing surgeons: the only class of patients they were expected to treat directly were senior officers. They thus had a distinct set of adminstrative duties which "fully occupy their time . . . in the same manner as the Assistant Adjutant General, the Assistant Quarter Master General & the Assistant Commissary General." It was for that reason that Lesassier's billets had improved so much, for he had to "constantly be at . . . headquarters" in order to be apprised of brigade movements, so as to properly supervise the formation and breakup of hospitals. The regimental medical staff followed his orders in carrying out the actual medical work and Lesassier detested remaining behind with the hospitals while the brigade moved forward: "The anticipation of another banishment to the rear—far from society—from forage—from every comfort made me tremble." To prevent this, Lesassier appointed a staff officer of his own, José Joaquin de Souza, assistant surgeon to the Ninth Portuguese Infantry, "an active, meritorious officer," to act as his assistant in carrying out his official duties and supervise the hospitals in his absence.

Now Lesassier, too, was admitted into the councils of the Great Men, for the commanding officer of the brigade, General Power, received him always "with his accustomed politeness," and "wished me to come to his house & repeated this very often afterwards however I did not but dined every day with him." He did not always enjoy the dinners, but that was not the point: as he well knew, dining with the general was a perquisite of his new rank. Power also rewarded his professional competence by consulting him on the disposition of the sick, saying "I place the utmost confidence in you; & shall, on no account, interfere with your arrangements." And Lesassier, in turn, privately rewarded Power for treating him as well as he felt he deserved: in contrast to his former epithets against Blantyre and Stirling, General Power was always "my General" in his journals.

But all these advantages of Lesassier's new rank had their cost, and as we imagine him riding off on his "superb" new English charger we should remember that *soberbo* is the Portuguese word for pride. The high pay and double rank was necessary to attract

British officers to the Portuguese army, for at the beginning of the war the army was "without discipline and without subordination. The soldiers were lacking in confidence in their officers who were negligent in their duties." The Portuguese government had not provided enough funds for the army, despite British subsidies; the result was frequent desertions of men and officers. It had taken Marshall William Carr Beresford most of 1810 to accustom soldiers and officers to British standards of discipline, and the British officers appointed to maintain those standards were often resented by their Portuguese equals as well as their subordinates. Few of the British learned to speak Portuguese and Andrew Halliday's comment on the Portuguese peasantry can be as easily ascribed to his own countrymen: "Devoted to the spot which gave them birth, they cannot be brought to believe that any country in the world is superior or even equal to their own." The British officers in the Portuguese army often formed an insular little band, or, as Captain Blakiston put it, "a little mess among ourselves; for the habits of the Portuguese are so very different from ours, that there is no associating with them, more particularly at meals." By 1813 the Portuguese brigades had proved themselves in battle many times, but personnel problems remained one of the major administrative difficulties for officers in the Portuguese service.

They were especially marked in the medical service. Each regiment of fourteen hundred men was supposed to have one surgeon, the *cirurgião mór,* and four assistant surgeons, the *ajutants de cirurgião.* At the start of the war the regimental surgeon ranked as the most junior of the officers and his assistants as noncommissioned officers, similar to the British medical service of twenty years previously. In 1810, when William Fergusson had been appointed to reorganize the medical department on British lines, his first step was to increase the rank and pay of the regimental medical staff so that it was equal to that in the British army, with the cirurgião mór holding rank of a captain and his ajutants ranking with ensigns. He also required any man appointed to a medical position to pass an examination administered by a medical board. The salary of surgeons and assistants was increased to equal that of British regimental medical officers. Regimental surgeons were responsible for the same set of returns of the sick and wounded, the same tickets and case books, as in the British service. In all other medical matters, too, regimental medical officers were to follow British practice by placing themselves under the authority of the staff surgeons at brigade, with whose directives, Lesassier wrote in his first set of departmental orders, they "were to observe the utmost exactness in complying."

From the first, the British medical staff were at loggerheads with the Portuguese and with each other. Like Lesassier and the former medical cadet David MacLagan, they were ambitious assistant surgeons looking for a shortcut to higher pay and promotion rather than seasoned administrators: though McGrigor recommended that they take time "to learn the language & become acquainted with usages of . . . the Portuguese service & the manners of the people who become their patients," few followed this mild advice. Andrew Halliday took advantage of the British interest in the Portuguese army after the battle of Bussaco to publish his *Observations on the Present State of the*

*Portuguese Army*. Though probably written with the intent of praising Fergusson's reforms, it also publicly derided the Portuguese medical service as incompetent and ineffective. The reviewer in the London-based Portuguese newspaper *O Investigador* refuted his assertions concerning medical care point by point, calling them either "false, or greatly exaggerated," while Halliday's attribution of the sorry state of affairs to the corrupting influence of the Catholic Church on Portuguese character, the reviewer said, was "truly infamous." Halliday's fellow staff surgeons were also angry, branding him "a Judas among the doctors attached to the Portuguese army"; Halliday responded with equally "vindictive but childless slander," and the matter was referred to Wellington himself, who effectively quashed the "idle, foolish, and mischievous" name-calling by desiring that the medical gentlemen "reconcile their differences, and carry on the service together as men ought who make the good of the service their object." He might have taken no further steps, but Halliday had also ascribed defects in the Portuguese character to "the tyranny of a faithless government," and "Though as far as I can learn," McGrigor noted, "Dr Halliday has been an industrious officer & been actuated by zeal His Excellency the Commander of the Forces, will not consent to any officer remaining in the country who has rendered himself so obnoxious to its government." Halliday was placed on half-pay, and though he soon returned to active service as staff surgeon, it was not in the Portuguese army.

Lesassier was unusual in his ability to speak Portuguese; he was always ready to converse with civilians of the "better sort"; and his comments on countryside and antiquities reveal a romantic, but intelligent and sympathetic interest. Though not immune from the anti-Catholic bias of his countrymen he at least did not share surgeon Charles Boutflower's opinion that no one professing the Catholic faith "appeared to be touched with a coal from the Holy Altar of God." He happily scrambled over the ruined castle at Ourem with a priest as guide, and though "the Inquisition with all its horrors presented itself to my imagination" when he descended into a cistern—"Now thought I shuddering what is there to prevent him from casting me headlong . . . into the abyss of water below us"—his own haphazard religious instruction led him to regard religion in a picturesque, not moral, light, and his shudders were clearly for literary effect.

We might have expected, then, that he would be an intelligent and sympathetic staff officer on a difficult service, and it is possible that he was appointed for just that reason. But he had first heard of the Portuguese service from Halliday, who no doubt conveyed his opinions, as well as the facts. He was also the last man we could expect to be immune from the pervasive British attitude that they had saved the Portuguese from their own medical service, as well as the last to use any tact in conveying that attitude. Certainly he showed no tact in making his first official communication to General Power a report of the "gross negligence & professional incapacity of cirurgião mór Mathias Garcias, 21st Regiment. His conspicuous ignorance, together with his obstinate perseverance in a marked system of the most shameful carelessness—have led me to represent the utter impossibility of the 21st Regiment having their sick properly attended to, as long as Señor Mathias Garcias is their surgeon." This was a harsh judgment to make of an experienced medical officer after only one week as brigade surgeon. The specific evidence Lesassier gave of Garcias's carelessness was his having "left his medicine chest, instrument case & hospital bedding in Vitoria," and as Lesassier may soon have found, Garcias could have had a good reason for doing so. At the time of his complaint to Power, only two of the medical officers for the three regiments in the Eighth Brigade were presently with him. Power's brigade had fought gallantly at Vitoria, leading "the march with satisfaction and gallantry never surpassed on any occasion," according to Wellington, but the cost had been high. Between the Ninth and 21st regiments, 104 officers and men had been killed, and 289 were wounded. The number of wounded was comparable to that of the 42nd at the siege of Burgos, and at least one of the assistant surgeons of the Ninth Regiment was in Vitoria; the assistant surgeons of the 21st may have been there as well, in which case Garcias would have left the regimental medical supplies, not out of carelessness, but for the use of his regiment. As Lesassier knew, Garcias should have brought the supplies with him, leaving the sick and wounded of the regiment to be treated with the supplies furnished for the general hospital. But there were a great many sick and wounded in the allied armies during the summer of 1813, and the Spanish authorities were reluctant to provide accommodation and supplies for them. Medical officers in the British army had to use portable field hospitals to supplement the general hospitals, and regimental surgeons may also have had to dip into their regimental medical supplies.

Moreover, the British reorganization of the Portuguese medical service, whatever its merits, had also introduced the same divided allegiances that beset the British service: Garcias had served as surgeon to the 21st since at least the beginning of the war, and may have felt his duty to his own wounded outranked his duty to the medical service, at least until he had to face an angry staff surgeon at brigade. But Lesassier had his own set of allegiances. One of the most important of the British reforms had been to ensure that each regiment was allotted medical supplies comparable to those of British regiments. The expense had been considerable, for the Portuguese regiments had almost nothing to begin with, and regimental surgeons were held responsible for the value of any lost articles. McGrigor had placed high on his list of responsibilities for staff surgeons to ensure "that each medical officer in charge of a corps is at all times complete in medicines & materials," and Lesassier himself would have risked a reprimand had the 21st Regiment suffered from shortages. He had still been too quick to condemn Garcias, but perhaps we can excuse such overzealous behavior from a newly appointed staff surgeon anxious to distinguish himself for attention to duty.

If only the rest of his command had not been marked by such intemperance! Nearly all Lesassier's new staff were, like de Souza, active, meritorious officers, though he never admitted it, preferring to take all the credit for the Eighth Brigade's medical successes. The Portuguese medical staff were perhaps not as well educated as the British, and the low rank and pay prior to 1810 had not attracted the best men to the service: the assistant surgeon of the royal police guard who, together with two privates, faced a court-martial for robbery was not an ornament to his profession. But he was not typical, and his case was balanced by the assistant surgeon of the 14th Portuguese Infantry, whose "zeal and activity" while engaged on that detestable duty, escorting sick cars, "prevented 54 of the wounded from falling into the hands of the enemy." Few of the Portuguese medical staff had had any difficulty passing the British medical examinations instituted by Fergusson, and they were much less likely to receive reprimands than the junior officers of comparable rank in the Portuguese service. The most common reprimand they did receive reflected the peculiar administrative structure in which they worked: it was "neglect of . . . duties . . . and lack of subordination to the Staff Surgeon at Brigade."

The most frequent source of conflict had to do with hospital administration, for it was here that the regimental surgeons came most directly under the supervisory authority of the staff surgeon. Prior to British reforms, Portuguese military hospitals had been notoriously bad. Portuguese soldiers preferred remaining on duty than reporting themselves sick, and even one of the Portuguese military physicians admitted that it was "almost impossible for a soldier who enters the hospital to escape death." Under Fergusson, hospitals were completely reorganized. From the vantage of the twentieth century there was little to choose between the actual medical treatment prescribed by the British or the Portuguese. But British medical supplies certainly would have had an effect, and so would vaccination for smallpox, instituted by Fergusson. So too would attention to hygiene, enforced everywhere under McGrigor's command and the professional specialty of staff surgeon Lesassier of the Eighth Portuguese Brigade, "for nothing," he wrote in his first set of departmental orders, "more decidedly contributes to the health of the sick-soldier than personal cleanliness." He therefore insisted on standards of cleanliness equal to those he had administered in the British service. "On the admission of a patient," his orders state "his whole body must be washed; his hands & face every morning . . . ; & his legs & feet twice a week." Actual washing of the patients was the duty of the hospital orderly, not the medical staff, but it was the regimental surgeon's job to make sure that it was carried out properly.

By August, Lesassier observed "with sufficient disgust" that there were irregularities in his regimental hospitals. Regimental surgeons, here as elsewhere, delegated the most unpleasant tasks to the assistant surgeons, who in turn left them to the orderlies whenever they could get away with it. Lesassier himself had done the same on his way home from Gibraltar but he had no intention of letting it happen under his command. He therefore ordered all medical officers to visit twice per day, at 7 A.M. and 5 P.M.; they were also ordered to be in the hospitals at 10 A.M. to supervise the cleaning of the patients. They were to cease prescribing extras for their patients contrary to orders, and they were to make up medicines themselves, and not entrust the task to an orderly. In case of further irregularities, the cirurgião mór da brigada would castigate the medical officer involved, not the orderly. In order to more closely supervise the staff, Lesassier decided to establish hospitals at the brigade, rather than the regimental level. It was a sensible decision, in keeping with practices in the British service, for McGrigor was convinced that "frequent and minute inspection" of military hospitals at all levels was essential to prevent abuses, and brigade hospitals both facilitated that inspection and the allocation of medical work during an actual engagement.

Yet while the brigade hospitals constituted one administrative success, they set the stage for Lesassier's biggest administrative failing, his talent for acquiring—creating, we might say—enemies who stood in his path. It was the brigade hospitals that provided the occasion for the first of Lesassier's long-running quarrels with Lieutenant Colonel Charles Sutton, who commanded the Ninth Portuguese Infantry Regiment. Colonel Sutton had been with the Ninth Regiment since 1809; Power had a high regard for him, and Wellington had cited him in his dispatches. Sutton was also, according to Lesassier, "a man well known for his peculiarly strong prejudices & singularly obstinate opposition to the opinions of others." He was not a man to take lightly a perceived affront, and he perceived one in a series of letters Lesassier wrote to General Power on 24 August on the subject of hospital orderlies from the Ninth Regiment. Lesassier had asked for two orderlies, but, he wrote to General Power, "after a delay of eighteen hours, the commanding officer of that corps has sent an answer that he will allow no such servants without orders from you." Sutton had, in fact, sent some already, but these were "a sergeant & assistant, a cook, who is barely capable of doing his duty from wanting the use of one of his hands; and two orderlies; one of whom being epileptic, was unfit for the situation; & the other was sent to his duty—Thus, between 20 & 30 patients have been left unattended to."

Lesassier had to apply to Sutton for soldiers to act as bearers for carrying the wounded and hospital orderlies for "attending the sick, administering the medicines and comforts, and keeping the wards clean," because medical staff had no subordinate staff of their own: all authority over soldiers rested with their commanding officer. Since any soldier thus sent was in turn unavailable for fighting, commanding officers required convalescents to act as orderlies, or sent the least able of their soldiers. Corporal Costello attributed his recovery from fever to his good constitution, not "the brute of an orderly, who, during the delirium of the fever, beat me once most furiously with a broom stick." In sending only those soldiers he did not really want himself, Sutton was thus following a common practice among commanding officers, one that was a frequent cause of friction between general and medical officers. Lesassier's letter would have done enough to exacerbate that friction if he had stopped with a complaint about orderlies, but he did not; instead, he "solicited permission to submit for your consideration, that if commanding officers of regiments—thus oppose obstacles to the execution of my duty, notwithstanding my unwearied exertions for the good of the brigade, the consequences must, eventually, be highly injurious to the service." He followed this up with two further letters to Power, one complaining that the sick of the Ninth Regiment had been without orderlies for "forty hours," and the other stating that "the sick of the 9th Regiment are without orderlies—having now been in that unprecedented situation between sixty & seventy hours."

There was nothing wrong in Lesassier wanting to ensure that the sick of the Ninth

Regiment had competent orderlies; indeed, it might be considered highly laudable for him, a junior major of barely two months' standing, to take on the senior lieutenant colonel in his brigade. Even if, as is likely, he had rather less beneficent motives—a desire for retribution at Sutton's neglect of his request, say, or the wish to protect the prerogatives of the medical department from what he termed "the insidious encroachments of military tyranny"—the sick of the Ninth Regiment stood to benefit from his provision of better orderlies. But he was clearly going about the matter in the wrong way, for medical men could do nothing without the good will of general officers. Again, the medical service was formally a civilian department within the army, and medical officers could formally command neither soldiers nor necessary supplies like transportation and food. Even James McGrigor received a sharp reprimand for forgetting that medical officers had no authority to act independently: "Who is to command the army? I or you?" exclaimed Wellington when he found McGrigor had made arrangements to feed, shelter, and treat wounded men beyond the army's supply lines. "As long as you live, sir, never do so again; never do anything without my orders." It was for that reason imperative for his proper functioning as staff surgeon that Lesassier stay on good terms with the general officers in his brigade, just as it was imperative for the good of the medical service in the Peninsula that McGrigor stay on good terms with Wellington.

Lesassier's complaint to Power regarding Sutton, therefore, was as tactless as his letter regarding Garcias, and as he soon found, much more dangerous. Colonel Sutton was furious, and Lesassier found that "amidst the peaceful pleasures & refined luxuries" of his "new situation," he was "nearer irretrievable ruin than ever I was before. A very hairbreadth saved me from being tried by a court-martial. I shudder at the bare mention of the word. . . . In an affair purely connected with duty in which I repeatedly reported to the Brigadier the gross negligence of a favorite commanding officer, & in which everything, on my part, had been conducted with the refinements of official correctness, except one single incautious expression, the exasperated Colonel instantly seized hold of my words, & insisted on a court-martial for me to prove them." Sutton particularly objected to the last of Lesassier's letters, which stated that his sick had been without orderlies "for between 60 & 70 hours—all this I could have proved with ease," Lesassier went on, though strictly speaking the sick had not been left without orderlies, but merely without orderlies who were, in Lesassier's view, competent to carry out the tasks, a much trickier point "but as a court-martial in my opinion must leave an indelible disgrace behind it I ended the affair by waiting on the Colonel. An explanation took place in which I used the same firm dignified language which I hope has never failed me on important occasions—The result of which was the affair being compromised—But can I forget that such has been!!!—Oh—no—till memory forsake her seat. The impression is deep—it is indelible—Not the whole ocean itself could wash it out." Indeed, on 27 August Lesassier wrote the first of many letters to his administrative superior, William Wynn, inspector of hospitals, asking to be removed from the brigade and appointed to a general hospital station. He wrote to his uncle, too, to prepare him in case he had to return to his old position as assistant surgeon, claiming, however, that this was due to a reduction in the number of surgeons on the Portuguese staff, rather than his own imprudence.

Lesassier's letter to Sutton was conciliatory, with no hint of his "rage & grief at my proud spirit being so signally lowered—leveled indeed would be a better term." He stated that "he had the honor of acknowledging the receipt of your communication . . . in which you state your having transmitted to Major General Power a letter I wrote you . . . from its being supposed to convey a complaint about the practice in my own brigade of removing the hospital orderlies." He "begged leave, however, to assure you that no other object whatever was in my contemplation in writing that letter than the general view of wishing that the circumstance should be remedied for the good of the service." The effect would seem to have been ruined by Lesassier's additional, rather confused comment that as, several days previously, General Power had issued a brigade order that all commanding officers were to provide orderlies, no complaint could possibly have been applicable. Presumably, Sutton was to read between the lines that as he had disobeyed Power's order, Lesassier was in the right all along, but Sutton let it pass, and the matter was dropped.

Lesassier's rage and grief at having his orders interfered with by his superior officers was nothing compared to his anger at disobedience from his subordinates. He had never had much experience of command outside the well-established structures of medical and regimental service. The hospital assistants who had been under his authority at hospital stations no doubt grumbled at the unequal distribution of menial tasks, but they did their duty. "On no service were there ever fewer idlers," McGrigor wrote to the Army Medical Board, and in any case Lesassier's junior medical staff would have been as anxious as he had been to demonstrate their fitness for promotion. The only soldiers he had ever commanded were those assigned to be his own servants. Again in the well-established army tradition, they without exception served him faithfully and well, taking as much care of his baggage and animals as of their own. On one occasion when Lesassier's horse ran away, a "former faithful servant" from the 42nd, recognizing the animal, tried to recover it, receiving "a kick that cut his head severely." The horse eventually returned "very peaceably" on its own while Lesassier was examining the man's wound. Lesassier himself probably recorded it as a mere backdrop to the return of his horse, but that single act of dressing the wound was imbedded in twin obligations, that of his medical rank, requiring him to look after his men, and that of his military rank, requiring him to reciprocate faithful service with patriarchal care.

Once outside the army's well defined patterns of service and reciprocity, though, Lesassier's relationships with his subordinates became more volatile, as the sequel to the episode with the horse makes clear. For he was so angry at his Portuguese servant, Manoel, for "thus leaving the horses unguarded" that his "rage . . . got the better of my judgment, & no sooner did he return than I knocked him down, & beat him unmercifully. This was highly rash & reprehensible—for the poor fellow had been employed in fetching our rations. My secret repentance formed a severe retribution." The picture becomes more unpleasant still when it is remembered that unlike Lesassier's British servants, Manoel was not protected by military law from corporal punishment without trial. Lesassier struck, then, the most vulnerable target, hardly an attractive trait in a commanding officer or a gentleman. And yet Lesassier's repentance was sincere, for he and Manoel were usually on excellent terms and remained so even after this incident. British officers' accounts of the war are full of examples of their being taken advantage of by their villainous Portuguese servants, but Manoel served Lesassier as faithfully and more resourcefully than the British soldiers. What provoked Lesassier's ungovernable rage was the suspicion of insubordination and the certainty of his own impotence in preventing it.

Once again it was the brigade hospitals which became the backdrop for a series of conflicts with his subordinates. His first official letter to the surgeon general describing them took the opportunity to criticize "the singular professional ignorance & negligence of the medical officers in my brigade" in terms as harsh as those he had used for Garcias. He or his assistant, de Souza, had to be always present to completely control the practice, "it not being in my power to have the Surgeons in charge of sick so completely under my constant inspection as their obstinate attachment to their own visionary systems would require." He complained, too, of the Portuguese soldiers under his authority, particularly the convalescents who "make their way into the surrounding field unmolested," despite his "confining them" and "changing their diet to deter them." Soldiers roaming beyond the confines of hospital and regiment were notorious for plunder and other crimes, and it was precisely this situation that led to Wellington's exasperated and often-quoted statement that his solders were "the scum of the earth." Lesassier's own solution to this problem was that the commander of the guards of the hospital should be "an active man—& empowered to inflict immediate corporal punishment—the most beneficial results might be expected from the judicious exercise of so vigorous a measure." Perhaps he felt the commander of the guards should knock down and beat unmercifully anyone who disobeyed orders. He was presumably unaware that such punishment was contrary to army regulations. In 1811 Lord Blantyre had had the commandant of a hospital station arrested for doing precisely what Lesassier suggested, ordering the flogging of a convalescent soldier of the 42nd who had sold his equipment—a crime, certainly, but one that Blantyre, not the commandant, had the authority to punish. The only authority Lesassier could exercise was to reduce the soldiers' diet to make them more amenable, an unpleasant, though not unusual use of medical treatment as social control. Perhaps even this authority was circumvented, or so we might interpret his departmental order for the regimental surgeons to "cease prescribing extras"; perhaps Lesassier was not altogether wrong in seeing his staff as engaging in a kind of medical guerrilla war to maintain control over their own patients.

Once again, however, any direct chastisement even of his own staff required him to go through official channels, and it was Lesassier's bad fortune that the one truly negligent member of his staff was the assistant surgeon of the Ninth Regiment, Luiz Bento Garcao, "the avowed protégé of Colonel Sutton" who might otherwise eventually had his attention diverted from Lesassier "to some other object." Bento joined the brigade in September, having spent, according to Lesassier, "four months in Vitoria in gambling & other like amusements," though his own explanation for his absence was probably that he was on detached duty with the many sick of the Ninth Regiment. It is likely that he preferred remaining in a general hospital station to returning to the regiment, but then so had Lesassier, and Lord Blantyre, had he known of it, might have murmured something about the pot calling the kettle black. Not that this made Lesassier, in his new position as staff surgeon, disposed to be tolerant of the practice. He may have been warned about Bento by the other regimental officers, or the previous surgeon at brigade, or even General Power, from his "longer acquaintance with the young man," for, he wrote in his official complaint, "his private character for incessant intrigue was well known to me." He also complained of Bento's "gross professional ignorance," which he had "detected in several purposely directed conversations." Indeed, if Lesassier's precise accusations are correct—and since he knew there would be an official inquiry, they probably are—Bento was inexcusably negligent. Within a month of his arrival, he had, Lesassier wrote, "been guilty of disobedience of (written) orders—& gross neglect of duty . . . viz. 1. In leaving a case of fever 24 hours without medicine although I had prescribed for him. 2. In leaving an important case of erythema a whole day without the application ordered for him; & not paying the evening visit. 3. In having neglected an often repeated order that the patients' shoes should be cleaned & for telling me in a loud insolent tone of voice that it was no business of his—& if the hospital sergeant did not do his duty it was nothing to him."

Lesassier, had, in his time as assistant surgeon, disobeyed orders to suit his own comfort, and indeed he continued to do so by arranging to carry forage for his own animals on sick cars, contrary to general orders. But he had never disobeyed a direct order, and though he hated being reprimanded, he was not fool enough to respond with obvious insolence, or to refuse to modify his behavior afterwards. He was therefore furious to find Bento so disobedient and even more furious to have no recourse for punishing him, for Colonel Sutton sheltered Bento, either because Bento really was his avowed favorite or because he had developed a thorough dislike for Lesassier. The result of Bento's "public insubordination, his often repeated & contemptuous disobedience of my departmental orders, & his notoriously incendiary spirit," Lesassier complained, was that "the example has been widely extended," and the rest of the medical staff refused to follow his orders either. This latter statement was almost certainly not true, but it reflects Lesassier's own equation of power and punishment: conscious of his own impotence in chastising Bento, he was too ready to believe the rest of his staff would see it as a sign that they need not obey him. He was soothed by "receiving a highly flattering letter . . . hinting that perhaps I might succeed in obtaining an hospital station," but the months went on, and no appointment was forthcoming.

Alas for Lesassier, these letters to his superiors show no understanding of his own best interests, for a smoothly running brigade would be a better recommendation for future administrative positions than a steady stream of complaints. In fact his brigade did run smoothly, with Lesassier himself appearing every inch the exemplary medical man on active service. "Any self-respecting medical officer naturally feels he cannot refuse to go forward to the front line when the demand comes," wrote the medical historian Lieutenant General Sir Neil Cantlie of his own experience in World War I, "and would be branded as a coward if he did not comply." Lesassier made a point of riding into battle with the brigade, riding up the mountains "to *show myself*," arranging to be "amongst the foremost; resolving that the usual sarcasm of Surgeons' being always out of sight should not apply to me." Staying with the brigade in battle had clear professional advantages for setting up field hospitals as well, like the one established after the Battle of the Nivelle, "a few paces, only, from the scene of action." In Lesassier's activities on this occasion we can once again catch some glimpse of his efficient medical administration; we can also watch him putting his prior experience into practice. At 2 A.M. on 10 November the brigade marched, leaving the sick well in the rear, under the care of one of the regimental surgeons or assistant surgeons. During the battle, another of Wellington's successful thrusts deep into the French lines in the Pyrenees, Lesassier wrote that "About midday our brigade advanced up the hill & I accompanied it as far as a house which from its convenient distance I selected for the reception of the wounded. In a few minutes we took the Fort with the trifling loss of about 60 men killed & wounded, & four officers slightly wounded. . . . In about two hours, the wounded being dressed, I rode after the brigade."

"We were extremely fortunate," he wrote in an official letter a few days later, "not a single capital operation having become necessary." The next day, the brigade hospital was "established near the village of St. Pée," and Lesassier ordered all the sick and wounded to be sent there. It took several days to convey the sick to the new hospital, because "our means of transport were very limited, being confined to three cars & eight mules." By 13 November, though, "our sick and wounded were collected & comfortably accommodated in the hospital near St. Pée under the care of five assistant surgeons." He, too, was comfortably accommodated in a "farm house near the hospital," though he didn't mention that in his official report; it had been abandoned, and he had "employed twelve men" to clean it out; though the owners returned in a few days, they were "unconcerned" at Lesassier's presence. Owing to his convenient accommodation near the hospital he "had never been absent . . . except during part of the 19th; having then accompanied the brigade." He was, in fact, thoroughly bored and lonely staying near the hospital, spending "the solitary hours between business & study," though he didn't mention that in his official letter either. "It was then," he noted, "in a situation like this, where secluded from society, & surrounded by uninterrupted gloom, that without some resources within myself my existence would have dragged along with all the lethargic torpor of an animal."

Obedient to McGrigor's directives, Lesassier had not sent any men to general hospitals in the rear until the day before, and even that was because his hospital could only accommodate 150 patients, and was "almost daily receiving more wounded from the frequent skirmishes between the outposts." His hospital should have been moved to brigade headquarters, but the brigade "was so closely crammed together that it was found totally impracticable to establish an hospital there. Indeed, had there, even, been more space still the situation would have been improper, in consequence of the continued alarm in which they were kept by the Enemy. Many days passed before General Power durst venture on having his Canteen unpacked." Lesassier ensured, however, that each regiment had with it a surgeon, an assistant, and a temporary hospital. He also took the opportunity to slip in a complaint about Bento, attributing to his influence the regrettable fact that "my medical officers, on this occasion, have afforded me little or no assistance." Once again he might have left a better impression if he could have brought himself to leave Bento out of it, for there is every evidence that otherwise his medical staff worked very well with him. According to his own official letter, the hospital was under the management of five assistant surgeons; his "old assistant" de Souza accompanied him in supervising them, and transmitting the most severe cases to the rear; Matthias Garcias—the assistant surgeon of the 21st whom Lesassier had been so quick to criticize—made a "careful examination and rigorous separation of the sick from lightly sick." Neither Bento, Sutton, nor his own irascible temper, then, disrupted the smooth functioning of Lesassier's department.

Though it was not, strictly speaking, one of their official duties, staff surgeons were expected to attend the senior officers of the brigade, who naturally felt they deserved the best medical care possible. In early December, Lesassier was summoned to attend to the colonel "of our Caçadores," probably Colonel Duizbeck. This visit required Lesassier to leave his house near the hospital and proceed to brigade headquarters in Arrauntz. "Aware of the distance, & acquainted with the nature of the roads," he wrote, "it may be supposed I did not commence my journey in very high spirits. It was nearly 5 in the evening—the wind & rain beat in my face in violent gust—I could not proceed faster than merely a walk; for every now & then my large horse would plunge in the clay of this infernal road up to the knee." To make matters worse, his new English horse was "high mettled & impatient of restraint," and stopped as soon as the road entered the forest of St. Pée, refusing to move on for at least half an hour. "He at last became perfectly furious & unmanageable," Lesassier wrote, "& reared & plunged with such violence that I fancied myself becoming unsteady in my seat—The wind blew so hard— that my cloak served to impede me the more—It rained in torrents; & a solemn silence—combined with the hideous darkness of the night all served to render my situation exquisitely unpleasant." He would have been very happy to return, but prudently realized that "this step might be the future basis of incalculable inconvenience. It was requisite to show the General that I esteemed my own personal inconvenience infinitely less than the duties of my situation. I know his temper of mind to be such, that if he once had reason to suppose me of indolent habits, he would never cease tormenting me ever afterward." Attending a wounded colonel was as much a part of his position as dinners with General Power. He was lucky enough to meet up with one of the guides attached to the brigade, who had lost his way and could be persuaded to return to headquarters, and he eventually made it to the colonel's quarters, two miles further on. His patient, it turned out, "was perfectly out of danger," the house "was magnificent & the stabling excellent," and the next day he could fulfill his official duty, and highlight his devotion to duty, by "waiting on the General with a report on the Colonel's health."

By the end of December Lesassier was comfortably settled in winter quarters in "the lovely town of Hasparren" in the Pyrenees. Aside from some skirmishing, the brigade saw no action, but the winter was anything but peaceful for Lesassier, since the Bento affair finally blew up. Lesassier had received an order from the Surgeon General for Bento, together with one of the assistant surgeons of the 21st Regiment, to go on detached duty. It was, according to Lesassier, "precisely Bento's turn for detachment as all the Assistant Surgeons have now performed that duty since I joined the Brigade except himself"; moreover, Bento had been specifically named in the order. Busy in writing out the sick reports for the brigade, and wishing to give the two men as much time as possible to prepare for the trip, Lesassier said, he simply wrote out and sent the orders for the two men.

Lesassier's motives for transmitting the orders directly may not have been as benevolent as he stated—he probably liked giving orders and was pleased to be getting rid of Bento for a time—but he was acting according to the customary practice of the medical department, which operated under under the useful fiction that it had the authority to dispose of its own officers. The problem, as Lesassier was quickly reminded, was that customary practice was only a courtesy extended to the medical staff by general officers, who alone had the authority to issue orders. Bento, like Lesassier, may have wished to stay in the lovely town of Hasparren; it is clear he did not wish to go on detached duty; and it was "not within the recollection of any medical man in the brigade," that Bento "was ever permitted to go on detachment unless to suit his own individual views." Bento complained to Colonel Sutton, acting at that point as brigadier, since Power was commanding the division, and Sutton, Lesassier wrote, "attacked me in the most violent matter, asserting that I had no authority to communicate such orders without their being in the first place submitted to him so as to be published by the Brigade Major." Sutton also complained to General Power on his return to the brigade, with the result that Lesassier was "publicly reprimanded in brigade orders," a tremendous blow to him. "I have been many years in the army," he wrote to the surgeon general, "& thus far had escaped this humiliation." Lesassier attributed Power's reprimand to Sutton's "never ceasing intrigues," claiming that his orders to Bento were "no new case—no assumption of undelegated authority. . . . Every assistant surgeon in the brigade had now successfully been detached in various directions without Power's ever deigning to enquire their names—or warning me, previous intimation of such arrangements should in future be made to him."

A better explanation of the reprimand is that Power had, indeed, been pleased to let Lesassier make the arrangements for his own department as long as no difficulties arose. When they did, as happened when Sutton challenged Lesassier's authority, Power had to uphold the letter of military law. Indeed, Sutton may have been acting only out of a desire to enforce military law in his temporary command and protect his regimental officers against imposition, though it is as hard to believe that he disliked seeing Lesassier receive a reprimand as that Lesassier disliked sending Bento on detached duty. We only have Lesassier's evidence for his quarrel with Sutton, but even that evidence does not show Sutton to be as vindictive, or unprincipled, as Lesassier claimed: when "scandalous & unfounded assertions" were circulated about Lesassier in December, Sutton apparently investigated them and had them dismissed.

"How visionary the supposition," Lesassier wrote in his journal, "that there exists any situation of life free from its own peculiar portion of trouble! . . . I cursed the day I first entered the Brigade; and again I attempted, in a personal interview with the Surgeon General, to obtain a removal to a General Hospital Station." Again he was unsuccessful, and he does not seem to have been cheered up by the general order issued 28 January 1814, suspending Bento from rank and pay for six months, a result of the charges he had forwarded against him in the fall. "Arrived at wealth & dignity that rendered me an object of envy," he wrote, "still how far was I from true happiness. Yet was not all this attributable to the uneasy workings of my own restless disposition?" In part it was, in the sense that a different man would not have created the same conflicts. He had been arrogant and high-handed, resenting any opposition; more attention to what he had called the "refinements of official correctness," would have saved him both much private anxiety and a public reprimand. But his difficulties can also be attributed to the organization of the medical department: a different medical service, we might say, would not have created the same conflicts either. If Lesassier had had trained orderlies and hospital sergeants under his own command, instead of having to rely on soldiers from the regiments, the first conflict with Sutton would not have arisen. If regimental medical officers were not torn between the authority of their commanding officer and of the staff surgeon, neither would the second.

The medical department tried to assist Lesassier in his many conflicts, offering him the position of staff surgeon to the Third Portuguese Brigade, "but such a change could have been a palliative only," he wrote, "as I still looked forward to rest from the long remembered bustle of a campaign; & was resolved not to lose sight of a general hospital." He got one, but not in the way that he meant: after the Battle of Orthez on 27 February 1814 he was ordered to set up a general hospital there for the Portuguese troops. By now, Lesassier was practiced in setting up hospitals, and all the medical officers of the army were practiced in staffing them. Indeed Surgeon George James Guthrie, otherwise highly critical of the medical service, went so far as to say that as the allied army "reached the summit of the Pyrenees . . . its Medical Department approached perfection." Lesassier did not have time to write in his journal between 21 February and 14 March, but we can follow his activities through the series of orders he issued. Immediately after the battle on 27 March, the wounded were sheltered in the nearest available structures, for one of Lesassier's orders on setting up the hospital on 2 March was to send, "without delay, an Assistant Surgeon to search for wounded in the houses near the site of the late action; taking care to report in writing the exact hour of that officer's departure, arrival, & the result of his enquiries." Four buildings in the hospital were allotted for the use of the Portuguese army, each under the authority of a specified regimental medical officer, with "a sufficient number of Assistant Surgeons . . . attached to the above gentlemen; so as to afford them every facility in the execution of their official duties." Surgeons were also "ordered, in the most positive manner, to instantly collect together the sick & wounded that are, at present, dispersed through various parts of the town," and forbidden to issue rations to the sick who were not actually in a hospital. For each hospital, daily returns of the sick and wounded were to be sent to Lesassier by 7 A.M.; surgeons for each hospital were to appoint sergeants and orderlies in proportion to the number of patients; a noncommissioned officer was to be attached to each hospital to send in the usual returns, tickets, case books. Dressing of wounds was to begin at 7 A.M.; breakfast was served at 8 A.M., and dinner at 1 P.M. By 4 March there were enough convalescents to be moved to a separate hospital, under the charge of an assistant surgeon, assisted as usual by "a due proportion of noncommissioned officers and orderlies."

By 14 March Lesassier could write that "Vast & incessant efforts had, at length, given an appearance of regularity to the misshapen hideous spectre of a newly formed general hospital after a battle," and McGrigor reported "the satisfaction" he had with the hospital staff at Orthez, where "all of the officers evinced the greatest zeal for the service, and have got much credit with the army for their exertions." In Lesassier's case, his exertions were rewarded with official praise. On General Power's recommendation, Alexander Lesassier, cirurgião mór of the Eighth Brigade, was publicly commended in Marshal Beresford's general orders of 26 March 1814, "for his activity and his excellent measures for dressing the wounded." Thus he found that he had been wrong in his fulminations years earlier: victory could, indeed, crown even medical officers with praise. He was one of only two British surgeons in the Portuguese army to achieve the distinction of being cited in general orders; the other was the Edinburgh M.D., medical cadet, and staff surgeon since 1810, David MacLagan. In this instance, at least, Lesassier's proud boast in Edinburgh was proved right: he could, indeed, rank "with the highest of them."

Lesassier had been relieved at Orthez on 14 March, and returned to his brigade "accompanied by a party of between 70 & 80 of our men, a subaltern officer & two of our assistant surgeons." Power received him warmly, and "as we now approached to Toulouse," Lesassier wrote, all were "anxious . . . to visit so celebrated a town." But, Lesassier noted on 26 March, the very day of his commendation in general orders, "I would gladly have dispensed with all this military pomp; & would delightedly have returned to Orthez, there to enjoy the inestimable luxury of repose, far from the restless scenes in which I so long, had borne a part." He still hoped for a general hospital appointment, and when, after a hard-fought battle, the allied army entered Toulouse "triumphantly" on 13 April he was "seized on for a General Hospital+April 14 evening relieved April 16th seized again April 17th again relieved—a busy bustling anxious time." But his hopes for a hospital situation, which had lasted as long as the war itself, came to an end at the same time with the news of the abdication of Napoleon, signed on 6 April but not completely believed until 17 April. On 18 April 1814, Lesassier began the long march back with his brigade the way they had come, noting, characteristically, both that the towns "had been laid waste & houses almost all deserted" and "my quarter most excellent." They reached their halting point, "and here," he wrote, "ended the military movements of the wars on the Peninsula."

# CHAPTER 9

# Thrown on the Wide World

The war was now over. At 6 A.M. on 10 June 1814, "the two English brigades" of the Third Division "were formed in the great square, & the Portuguese brigade"—preparatory to beginning the long march home—"filed through them whilst the air was rent with huzzas & mingled with the mellow sounds of music and thus we parted," Lesassier wrote. "It was an affecting scene. . . . The very soldiers were in tears—Not a single division had done this except ours." Lesassier himself moved on to follow his brigade at 7 A.M. It was not a particularly difficult march for him: he still had his servants, his horses, and his mules, and the few petty difficulties involved in caring for the sick and extracting proper respect from the nonmedical officers were no more than he was used to. In his journal, however, the trip through the pretty scenery of southern France, over the mountains and down the coast became a long march toward an uncertain and perilous future, which "presented itself in the tenfold obscurity of anticipated horror & again & again I would brood over the probability of my too soon wandering on the wide world a forsaken outcast." What was he to do now that the war was ended? He had hoped he might be kept on in the Portuguese service on full pay, but the British establishment in Portugal was greatly reduced at the end of the war, and Lesassier, like most other British officers, was told he could "return to England when it suited me." But "What should I do in England?" he wrote, "For it was too true that thenceforward I should have no earthly means of increasing . . . my half-pay, except by attempting to establish myself in practice, and . . . it was clear nothing could now be more difficult than for a man of my profession to settle in Britain." Each mile closer to Portugal was a mile closer to "the frightful fate that seemed to await me." And when his dog, Capitano, died en route, it seemed "a melancholy coincidence. . . . During eight years of toil he had been my constant companion, and now, that all was over, he was taken suddenly ill, & died amidst cruel sufferings. . . . I buried him with my own hands; and I felt—ah! how acute a pang! It seemed as if I were now more forlorn, more destitute than ever. As long as I had been . . . in the enjoyment of affluence, we had never parted, but now I was thrown on the wide world he likewise was taken from me."

After some initial uncertainty, Lesassier was confirmed in his rank as full surgeon, entitled to half-pay for life of £120 per year, an income that would have seemed beyond his wildest dreams ten years earlier. Now, however, he knew better: while he "most devoutly" returned "thanks to The Almighty" that he was better off than many, he regarded his half-pay as no more than a "miserable and uncertain pittance" compared to what he needed to live on. It was in this mood of doubt that Lesassier made his first attempt at private practice since his ill-fated Rochdale venture. The home base of his brigade was the "beautiful little town" of Viana, Portugal, and there he decided to establish himself, rather than returning to Britain, where he "was as complete a stranger as if I were to drop from the Moon." In Viana, in contrast, "I undeniably possessed a high public rank from the elevated military situation I filled in the very brigade belonging to that town. I was, consequently, not merely known, but at the same time, looked up to as occupying the very first place in my profession." In Britain, his meager salary would confine him to "the isolated situation of a petty village . . . or the thinly scattered population of a rude barbarous unpracticable country" in Wales or the Highlands or western Ireland, whereas in Viana, he could mingle with "the first family in the province . . . keep a first rate house & garden, a cook & a groom, and a superb English charger on my half-pay." In other words, he hoped that settling in Viana would enable him to keep up the lifestyle he enjoyed in the army: supporting "a peculiarly genteel appearance absolutely independent of private practice."

Alas for Lesassier, his judgment in these matters was no better than it had been in Rochdale. All his life he looked for patronage from patients rather than professional contacts to increase his practice, and all his life he was disappointed. Professional success, he wrote in an echo of his comments in Rochdale, was impossible to predict, "much depending on public caprice, much on accident." His entry to the "illustrious family" of the region had been achieved through "an accident, & that too of the simplest kind." That accident, whatever it was—for he never described it—had earned him "a reputation for talents probably I was not possessed of—It was a natural conclusion, then, that what casualty had once brought to pass, might again take place by the same means." As Lesassier found over the next few months, however, such accidents were not replicable. As at Rochdale, the genteel families of the province were happy to see him socially, but made no efforts to consult him professionally. His "elevated military rank" was not a help but rather a positive hindrance, as he might have realized if he had more talent for considering matters from other people's point of view: the first families of Viana might have had doubts about consulting an army surgeon for their family practice, and the lower orders would have found a British practitioner much too expensive. Besides, the war was over; "the public opinion . . . was so very very much against the English"; the medical profession, in particular, would have no reason to encourage an interloper, and in Lesassier's three months in Viana he never mentioned, much less consulted, another medical man. The result was a repeat of Rochdale: he never "procured one single patient." Moreover, he found, "my half-pay would not keep up my present style of living," and by December, "The weather . . . set in with all the gloomy inclemency peculiar to the northern climate of Portugal. . . . I used to pass the dismal rainy days, by walking to & fro in my huge uncomfortable house, wrapped up in my boat-cloak." He had had enough, and "now abhorred Viana—I refused mixing any more with the brilliant society there, and every day I was compelled to pass in the place seemed, of more than twenty times its natural length." He sighed for England; rather opportunistically considering his Portuguese favorites, he sighed for Ella. And in early December, when he unexpectedly was offered a place on a ship, he packed up his things and was on board in a matter of hours, saying a last farewell to Manoel. "I made him a present. Alas! far too little for his service & with tears in his eyes, the faithful creature bade me farewell forever!"

Five days later, Lesassier was back in England. It was the wealth of consumer goods that struck him first, or, as he put it, "the comforts & embellishments of social life! The paper of the apartment in which I sat at breakfast; its stuccoed ceiling; its carpet; the beautiful tables, & chairs; the fire-grate; the windows, & curtains; all successively filled me with astonishment & delight." The beautiful women, too, "& the symmetrical neatness of their dress, charmed me; & again I felt amazed how I could have ever admired the women of other countries." It was an unexpectedly welcoming homecoming. He called at his tailor's in London, and was "as usual, fitted out, at a very short notice with clothes of the most fashionable description." He heard from Ella, "and, with a generosity found only in the female heart; she insisted on my sharing all she had. Poor, & friendless, & abandoned as she thought me by all the world; I was dearer far to her than ever. Already, she said, she had devised a mode by which were I even thrown aside without half-pay, we could live together comfortably on her own little pittance." "Ah!" he exclaimed at this new proof of her willingness to serve him, "clasping my hands together in the fervor of enthusiastic gratitude, "then I have still one friend left!"

Ella's offer paled, though, beside the much more advantageous one he received from his uncle. James Hamilton wrote an "exceedingly friendly" letter inviting him, once again, to Edinburgh to continue his studies. He had even sent along a letter for the medical board asking for permission, not realizing that Lesassier had been discharged from the service. It was a liberal offer, and Lesassier's "joy & gratitude were strongly excited" by it. They were the more excited as Lesassier realized that he had behaved with "want of foresight & calculation"—we might add, with want of affection or respect as well—with regard to his uncle. In 1812, he had been furious at what he regarded the callousness of his uncle, "who with the undoubted power of procuring my promotion, should allow me to languish for so long in an obscure situation." In a kind of retaliation, Lesassier had borrowed money from Hamilton, promising to repay with interest, but had never done so, and had probably never intended to do so. It had been, he now realized, a foolish way to treat a prospective patron, for no doubt Hamilton would have "concluded me as unprincipled & as thoughtless as the most improvident of his own relations." His return to England had made it his "imperious interest to attempt reconciling my uncle," and for that reason he decided to repay "both the capital and interest." He had actually sent the money before receiving his uncle's letter, and congratulated himself that things had worked out so well: he could gain all the credit for remitting the money on his own initiative, while Hamilton "himself will not be ill pleased, at having done so generous an action without the possible imputation of interest." The result, he hoped, would be to "make him more my friend than he had ever been before."

Unfortunately the friendship was not to be. Lesassier's good intentions of keeping on good terms with his uncle for his own interest's sake could not long survive his arrival in Edinburgh. He hurried there, spending only a few days with Ella, so as to take advantage of the rest of the winter session. Disillusion set in almost at once. Lesassier, like many a soldier returning from many a war, had expected a hero's welcome, but there were no ticker-tape parades for the Peninsular Army. "Were you at Waterloo?" Private Gunn of the 42nd was asked by a French sergeant, long after the war. "Yes," Gunn replied. "What did you get for it?" the sergeant wanted to know. "A medal and two years added onto our services and pension too." "Bah," was the rejoinder, "look here, I have a franc a day for wearing the beautiful ornament, the Cross of the Legion of Honor." In Britain, in contrast, officers and men found themselves thrown upon a civilian population that had apparently done perfectly well without them. This was particularly marked for returning medical officers, for they were regarded as inter-lopers by civilian practitioners, who were happy to support the prevailing prejudice that army surgeons were ill-educated and too quick with saw and lancet. "Few honours came the way of the Medical Department," its historian, Cantlie, has noted of the Peninsular War; its members were eligible for half-pay, but rarely for medals and clasps; and they soon found their military rank carried no weight at all in peacetime practice. Among his Edinburgh relations, if anywhere, Lesassier expected to be treated as a prodigal son, but instead he found himself relegated to the status of a mere nephew, offered only meals in his uncle's house while he paid for lodging and classes himself. "The professor's early breakfast" interfered with his first class; tea and supper interfered with his studying. "Thus, my dinner came at last to be the only meal I ate in their house. At first, a gentle remonstrance was made;—but so gentle—it was just worse than saying nothing at all. By this *inimitable* method, I was living as expensively, with far less comfort to myself, than if I had . . . actually, never gone near the man!"

Thus began a tug-of-war in which Lesassier pulled the hardest, only to find that all the weight was on his uncle's side. James Hamilton's intentions seem clear enough, even when viewed through the increasingly acrimonious pages of Lesassier's journal. Hamil-ton had every reason to be pleased with his nephew, who had made good in the army, certainly much better than he would ever have done in Rochdale. He had every reason, too, to feel he deserved some credit for his nephew's success. He had also been success-ful during the intervening eight years; his practice had expanded to include the highest families in Scotland, many of whom wintered in Edinburgh, and both his lectures and Lying-In Hospital, a private charity for delivering poor women, had grown as well. He was, if anything, too successful: births could not be scheduled outside of lecture hours, the administration of the Lying-In Hospital took up much of his time, and so, too, did the management of his property. An assistant would be very welcome, and what better assistant, he may have thought, than his own nephew, a man who owed his current professional success to his, Hamilton's, efforts? He had earlier proposed that Lesassier change his name to Hamilton, which would have promoted the scheme. It was a proposal both benevolent and shrewd, in keeping with the rest of his relations with his nephew; if it succeeded, it would be of benefit to both parties, while if it failed, it would have cost him nothing.

Hamilton discussed the matter with Lesassier one evening after dinner, saying "that if I could submit to the fatigues of an *accoucheur,* he could get me into practice in Edinburgh; but that there was no haste; he did not wish me to do any thing in a hurry; & so on." Lesassier should have been grateful; prudence, if nothing else, dictated that he be amenable; instead his proud spirit and his temper flared up at the implication that he should be Hamilton's assistant. He had wanted more, much more, from this, his ideal and his only patron. He had expected Hamilton to take him into his home, to make him his junior partner, to introduce him to practice, to save him, in other words, from having "to toil the remainder of my life away amongst the filth, impertinence, & ingratitude, of the mob. Alas! What an example my poor father was of this." It was all too much for him: his uncle's prosperity, his influence, his professional practice amongst the highest classes of Edinburgh society, contrasted to his own "contemptible character of an humble, needy, relation.—Heavens!" He made the firm "resolution . . . to be established with all the respectability attached to my family connections, & high official rank," by extorting from James Hamilton, if it was not given willingly, every drop of patronage he felt was his due.

His first step was to graduate at Edinburgh. This was a reasonable ambition, and Hamilton, once he had had time to consider the matter, was inclined to support it. But Lesassier wanted more than Hamilton's moral support: he intended that his uncle should pay the expense of additional education. He borrowed forty guineas from Hamilton the first year, and an additional fifty guineas the next; he ended up owing £640 to his uncle over the course of the next six years, with no sign that he ever intended to repay it. Within three months of Lesassier's arrival, Hamilton was obviously regretting his decision to invite Lesassier to Edinburgh. In March 1815, as Napoleon approached Waterloo, Hamilton suggested "that if a proposal were sent me to reenter the full-pay-list, he recommended me to accept of the offer"; for he did not believe that Lesassier was up to "the immense exertions required in his most arduous department of the profession!"

Lesassier was furious. "I protested, unequivocally, against so absurd a step, as a measure, at least, of my own choice; assured him I could reckon on my own strength to encounter any fatigue I might meet with; & added, that I should never have dreamed of settling myself in practice unless I had been certain of *his* assistance & protection; but, that I was most ready to embrace any other plan he might point out." Hamilton "replied to all this, that my settling here, was an object of my own consideration; but that, his assistance I should, of course, have." Hoping to receive an invitation to move in with Hamilton, Lesassier "here rejoined that it was now become highly important to decide on my future views; as I had, he well knew, nothing but my half-pay to commence my future professional career with." But Hamilton "coldly answered that . . . my half-pay would keep my pocket & put clothes on my back"—"Had I consulted the impetuous passions, that almost threatened to suffocate me," Lesassier continued, "I should have told him I despised him, as a scoundrel; & I would instantly leave him."

This was idle rhetoric, for where was he to go if he left Edinburgh? Britain "was ere this choked up by myriads of half-pay medical men from every branch of the Service," many of whom flocked to Edinburgh. David MacLagan returned to become a fellow of the Royal College of Surgeons; John Erly, deciding his St. Andrews degree was not prestigious enough for civilian life, attended classes to obtain his degree from Edinburgh. The "laid-up fleets and armies" from the late war, according to one civilian writer who had spent much of the war setting up his own practice, had "diffused over society" so many medical men that there "scarcely seems any vent for the overstock." Many flocked to medical schools like Edinburgh to refurbish their medical qualifications and, they hoped, to gain an entry into civilian practice.

The transition proved a difficult one for many. "Medical gentlemen who had been in the army," James Hamilton told Lesassier, "were totally uncalculated for private practice. Their manners he always thought far too unaccommodating & unpracticable for such a *difficult task*." They were too used to drawing a salary whether they saw patients or not, to pulling rank to enforce their treatment, to long periods of professional inactivity when not on campaign. Lesassier himself had written something along the same lines on the march back to Viana: "it was a sorry fate to be forced to groveling by suiting oneself to every one's caprice, in order to earn a petty livelihood, after the affluence ease & splendor of my present situation. . . . How far more enviable my situation would have been, had my father made me an apothecary's servant; or had confined me within the modest boundary of any other honest trade—for, it was not merely my present ease, or total annihilation of the best portion of my life, but what was still worse, habits of luxury & indolence had unhinged me for the humble efforts of future industrious poverty."

It is a measure of the success of Edinburgh as an academic institution that it had an effect even on these unpromising students. Returning military men flocked to Edinburgh, they said, because of its academic reputation, and to some extent that was true. But they also flocked there because they could build on their former studies: Edinburgh required three years of study in order to graduate, but the years did not have to be consecutive. Former students, like Lesassier, who had first matriculated many years earlier could count those years toward graduation. In fact, since students only had to take each course once, they could count any courses they had formerly attended, as long as they thought they could pass the examinations for graduation. They could, in other words, pick up their studies wherever they had left them, a much more economical way of working toward a degree than beginning again somewhere else. Along the way, they might also pick up the long-neglected habits of industry and application common to Edinburgh students. In Lesassier's case, the steady routine of classes, study, and long walks reasserted its hold, as the imperious staff surgeon recovered the schedule of the young student Alexander. "Nothing more effectually promotes happiness, than occupation," he wrote,

About 6 o'clock in the morning, my daily task began; & I seldom retired before ½ past 11 at night. During the whole of this time, every hour was passed strictly according to an exact distribution of the day, previously noted on a Card. Of these 18 hours, 4½ were dedicated to the Classics—; the remainder was spent between the four Lectures I attended, & my reading . . . my Notes, alone, amounted 1249 close written large octavo pages. Thus busied, it must be avowed, that the time never seemed half so short before; & the future prospect of establishing myself slowly . . . by the gradual efforts of my own industry, insensibly assumed a more pleasing appearance. I become somewhat reconciled to my situation; & looked around me with a more unprejudiced eye.

Yet even Edinburgh could not work miracles. The university might make him a student, but it could not make him a scholar. He studied hard for graduation—"As a proof of the efforts my memory made—I repeated the Nosology of Cullen"—a standard classification of diseases and their symptoms—"about 100 times by rote before I was summoned"—and passed without difficulty, graduating in August 1816. Yet his thesis makes clear how little he had internalized the values traditionally associated with academic study—truth, accuracy, scholarship—let alone those coming to be associated with medicine—scientific research or clinical observation. Ostensibly a clinical description of the fever that afflicted the troops during his detached duty at the hospital in Elvas in 1809, it is chiefly interesting for its literary style, for it prefigures some of his later case histories with its highly colored description of the patient. "For several days," Lesassier wrote, "the person who is attacked with this complaint feels merely an unusual languor, and incapability of applying himself to his common occupation. At length, toward night, he complains of a peculiar heaviness and anxious lassitude, stiffness of the joints, pain in the loins, transient rigors, frequent yawning and stretching, slight flushing of the face, trifling giddiness, uneasiness in moving the eyes with an irritating susceptibility to light and noise." Other symptoms present: "A depraved smell, unusual taste, thirst, and want of appetite. . . . The tongue is moist and lightly streaked with bands of white fur. The skin is dry; the heat increased; and the pulse full, soft, and frequent. There is constipation; and the urine is of a deep red color." After three to five days, the tongue becomes hot, the pulse more frequent, "and hurried respiration; with frequent sighing and anxiety, succeed." The tongue becomes dry, there is nausea and vomiting, and the patient "starts with terror" from sleep. In following days, he "gradually is roused with more difficulty; his impatient, hurried, incoherent answers evincing a marked confusion of thought." After nine to ten days,

the nausea and vomiting increase. Shiverings, tremors, anxiety, deafness, vertigo, stupor and coma come on. The features begin to collapse and the eyes to look dull and watery and the countenance is strongly marked with dejection. The prostration of strength is excessive. The thirst and heat disappear; and the pulse is frequent, quick, and irregular, and weak. A clammy sweat oozes out on the forehead and neck; and the skin feels loose, cold and moist. His voice is changed in tone, is rapid and tremulous. Constant dozing, hurried, difficult respiration, and oppression at the epigastrium, intermixed with low, muttering delirium, picking at the bed-clothes; and catching at hairs, supervene; followed by singultus, diarrhea, and a discharge of serous blood from the nose. . . . A peculiar oppressive smell proceeds from the patient's breath, skin, urine, and stools. He lies on his back, and slides to the bottom of the bed. His face, nose, and ears shrink; his temples become hollow; his eyes fixed and glassy; his nails livid; and his extremities cold.

These symptoms, together with increasingly difficult breathing, "usher in the closing scene."

As a piece of medical literature, this makes compelling reading, with its rapid alternation between formal medical discourse and the dying patient. As clinical description, however, it has little value. Lesassier may or may not have ever seen the fever he described, but we cannot tell, since he gives no information about it that he could not have picked up through reading. Nor can we tell what the disease is, even in nineteenth-century terms, for the thesis lumps together all symptoms ever seen in any fever, and even their limited precision is impaired when he adds, "These symptoms, however, vary according to the climate, time of the year, nature of the season, source of the disease, and age, idiosyncracy, and constitution of the patient. In some cases there is cough, hemoptysis, yellowness of the skin, incessant vomiting, abscesses, gangrenous spots from pressure, &c. In others we find little diarrhea; the fur on the tongue neither dark nor considerable . . . a recovery from the coma &c takes place; yet nevertheless, the patient dies." Nor is there any section on differential diagnosis, distinguishing this disease from others with similar symptoms, integral to clinical descriptions in his period and in ours.

But then Lesassier was not really writing for the medical professors, but rather for two ideal types of potential patrons. The first type was his intended genteel patient. Bloodletting, particularly the kind of severe bloodletting used by army surgeons, was out of fashion in the period just after the war, and Lesassier took pains to distance himself from the practice. It "prevailed on the Peninsula to an extent, that would scarcely be credited now," he wrote. "As an indiscriminate practice, it must have been bad. . . . How, in fact, should it have been otherwise than pernicious." The second was James McGrigor, now Sir James and director general of the Army Medical Department. Among other reforms, McGrigor recommended that military surgeons use hospital cases for clinical trials. Lesassier obviously had this in mind when he described an experiment proving the pernicious effects of bloodletting, in which "Mr. Anderson, the intelligent and amiable Surgeon of the 61st Regiment, myself"—"the amiable & intelligent Assistant Surgeon" of the 42nd—"and another, who supported the ordinary practice"—that is, bloodletting—"treated 366 cases of this diseases, with a view of comparing the result. It had been so arranged, that this number was admitted, alternately, in such a manner that each of us had one third of the whole. The sick were indiscriminately received, and were attended as nearly as possible with the same care and accommodated with the same comforts. One third of the whole were soldiers of the 61st Regiment, the remainder of my own. Neither Mr. Anderson nor I ever once employed the lancet. He lost two, I four cases; whilst out of the other third [treated by bloodletting] thirty-five patients died."

There is no evidence of such a clinical trial, or antipathy to bloodletting, in Lesassier's journals from the war. The account is an evident fabrication, made up for the purpose of obtaining a degree and impressing his readers. That he did obtain the degree may help to explain Edinburgh's declining reputation for academic rigor in the early nineteenth century, for it is kinder to assume the medical faculty passed the thesis without reading it than to infer that they believed the trials had actually been carried out. Nor was it Lesassier's thesis alone that was passed despite obvious flaws. John Erly's thesis on respiration, too, was apparently written only to satisfy requirements, and quite possibly was never read by the medical faculty; it lacked the usual convention of footnotes but boasted a long dedication to Sir James McGrigor. Even David MacLagan, once back in Edinburgh, was not immune from the general instrumentalist, not to say opportunistic, approach to requirements. His M.D. thesis of 1805 had been a perfectly solid discussion of the traditional subject of preserving health, but his essay on tetanus for admission to the Royal College of Surgeons of Edinburgh, written in 1816, is noteworthy primarily for its prominent mention of Sir James McGrigor and Professor John Thomson, the latter a medical hero after his assistance at Waterloo, and much caressed by the Whig ministry.

However flawed by our standards, an Edinburgh degree was still a medical degree, "the highest academical dignity" Lesassier had ever hoped to attain. Prudently, he dedicated his thesis to his uncle, and presented James Hamilton with "a magnificently bound quarto copy" of it. Hamilton was used to receiving such gifts from students but this one, he may have felt, had cost him too dear: he never congratulated Lesassier on either his graduation or his thesis and "at an after period he one day muttered something between his teeth about 'the pity of going to such expense in the binding.'"

The tug-of-war was far from over. Having obtained his degree, Lesassier wanted to be introduced to practice. He had had ample opportunities in Rochdale and Viana of finding out what it was like to sit at home and wait for patients to call, and he had no intention of repeating the experience in Edinburgh. If he could not get his uncle to make him his partner, he would compel Hamilton to introduce him to practice by "goading my uncle into a consent that I should become one of his annual pupils in order that I might obtain a practical knowledge of my new profession and at the same time become known to & respected & esteemed by the people." Once again, Lesassier was looking to his uncle's patronage as a magical formula that would lift him above other medical men. "The very labor," he wrote, "to which I must necessarily be exposed, would soon make me known to a very large portion of the lower classes. By them alone must a medical man, destitute of interest, hope to ultimately obtain more reputable practice."

Indeed, Hamilton did more than merely make Lesassier his annual pupil: he also made him assistant director of his own Lying-In Hospital. Like many similar private charities, it served its director well by providing clinical material for his students, and also by bringing Hamilton into contact with the Edinburgh gentry who served on the board of directors. Appointing Lesassier as his assistant obviously assisted Hamilton, for the director's duties required him to visit the hospital at least once a week— Lesassier went punctually every Monday—to keep the books, and to be on call for difficult deliveries, tasks Hamilton was happy to delegate. It was also an excellent opportunity for a young practitioner, one that many others might have envied. It was as assistant director that Lesassier laid the basis of his eventual professional reputation as a kind of a consulting accoucheur, to be called in difficult cases. He enjoyed, too, the contact with directors, reporting that he was "very much charmed with my general reception" after one dinner with them at his uncle's house.

Nor was that all Hamilton did. The arrangement he finally offered Lesassier was to be his assistant in his private practice, paying periodic visits to his patients, and receiving half the fee for any case at which he was actually present at the delivery. It was, again, an arrangement that was of benefit to both parties: it relieved Hamilton of the need to constantly be on call, an impossible task for him in any case during the academic session, while providing Lesassier with at least a quarter of his eventual professional income, and all of his professional contacts among the gentry and nobility. He greedily noted the latter down in his journal: dinner with Lord and Lady Elibank, tedious as it was; his "supreme pleasure of being sent for to the lovely & fashionable Mrs. Hastings Anderson"; his "superb patient—Mrs. Dunlop, George Street—It is the first family I have got in town, who keep a man servant." All of these were owing to his association with his uncle, an association strengthened when Lesassier changed his name officially to Alexander Hamilton in 1817.

But his position at the Lying-In Hospital was not salaried, and the patients there were poor. James Hamilton steadfastly refused to pay Lesassier (as I will continue to call him) a salary for his assistance, rather than payment by delivery; he neither made him joint professor nor junior partner but continued to recommend him, as merely one of several other practitioners "as he would a tooth-drawer or an apothecary." Lesassier never forgave what seemed to him incredible meanness: "the Doctor," as his family referred to him, was one of the most prominent medical men in Edinburgh, while his nephew was expected to be grateful for such medical crumbs as fell his way. "I had, to be sure," he wrote, "made some few acquaintances amongst the dregs of the mob, by dint of unwearied assiduity & the most abject attention to them. What had this, however, to do with my permanent success amongst those who would be able to remunerate me for my services!" Moreover, once Lesaassier finished his classes, Hamilton took steps to remove him permanently from his dinner-table. He was having his house painted, he told his nephew, and the entire household would have to go to lodgings, "& really he did not know how they were to live, they would be in such confinement." "I understood the hint," Lesassier wrote, "& remarked merely that I should accordingly live at home." Yet how was he to live on his half-pay! he wrote furiously. Had he not possessed "a kind, disinterested landlady . . . it would have been folly to venture on anything so hazardous as endeavoring to live like a gentleman in a capital—on seven shillings a day." He would be revenged, he decided: he would show Hamilton neither gratitude nor affection, and he would bide his time. "For I might reasonably look forward to the day when by the death of this man, I should at last obtain much higher practice, if I exerted myself, in the mean time, to deserve it." "What is the world"—or my uncle—"to me," he might have agreed with William Melmoth, the ungrammatical villain in the novel *Death's a Friend*, "I do not stand indebted for one single benefit. I am a being wholly abstracted from the rest of mankind, and was I to forego one advantage, which either fraud, or force could bring me the enjoyment, I should be an enemy to myself."

It was dangerous to make an enemy of James Hamilton, a man known for his many and pugnacious attacks on colleagues; it is a wonder, indeed, that Hamilton put up with his difficult nephew for so long. Perhaps he did it out of family affection, or, more likely, the fear of a family scandal: "preposterous," "absurd," "how would it appear?" he exclaimed when Lesassier offered—threatened, really—to no longer dine in Hamilton's house. Edinburgh was a small and gossipy world, and the quarrel between Hamilton and Lesassier soon became well known. It was a quarrel in which, as everyone but Lesassier himself could see, he would inevitably be the loser, and his friends did their best to dissuade them from continuing it. His aunt Isabella, now Mrs. Hodgeson and living with her husband and family near London, pointed out that "if a certain person patronize you—your fortune, is made," and his half-cousin Archy Campbell acted as peacemaker on more than one occasion when Lesassier's temper had gotten the better of him. Even Lesassier later admitted he had behaved with "gross want of policy, toward my uncle. . . . In fact, a little self-control, & a little common sense in my intercourse with that envious & petty-spirited man"—we may see some projection in this description—"would have placed me this moment as high in practice as my heart could desire."

But self-control and indeed common sense were just what were lacking on his return to Edinburgh. He had been in the army too long, where he could punish his enemies by currying favor with his superiors; it exasperated him beyond measure that in civilian life there was no superior officer to protect him from the "cabal" ranged against him. Chief among these he counted his grandmother and her three daughters, who, he felt "had taken advantage of every petty incident"—his sitting down, for instance, while his uncle remained standing—"to represent me in the worst possible colors." Families are delicate webs of interaction. His Hamilton relatives had welcomed him home to Edinburgh, but for continued intercourse they expected deference and respect; doubtless a few presents would not have come amiss. Yet Lesassier gave them nothing, while demanding everything the Hamilton family had worked for in return. "Be sure you keep on good terms with *all the family*," Isabella counseled him. "This, is of the utmost consequence to your future welfare—a little civility, & attention, on your part will secure, their good will, towards you." But this Lesassier refused to do. Now twenty-eight, he was no longer as malleable as he had been, and the army had reinforced the most imperious of his character traits: the agreeable, if self-centered youth had become instead an unyielding gentleman, convinced it would be a breach of honor to put up with anything other than the respect owing to his rank and dignity.

Lesassier preferred to devote himself to his great-aunt Campbell, the only one of his relations to give him the uncritical love he felt he deserved. Even Isabella, attached as she continued to be to Lesassier—"no one" she wrote, "is half so deeply interested about you as myself—ask your own heart, can they have the same affection, or love, that I have? purely disinterested"—was miffed at hearing that he had had a miniature made for his aunt Campbell while neglecting her own request for one, and his grandmother Hamilton was even less inclined to condone a slight. "One of the principle sources of vexation with them," Lesassier wrote, "was my so seldom visiting them, while they knew how very frequently I was at my dear aunt's—The storm that had been long collecting at length burst on me." One night when the family were all visiting James Hamilton, Lesassier went home, "instead of waiting, & escorting them, in the wind & rain, about a mile, to their house. Nothing more than this was wanting" to estrange him from the Hamilton family.

The circle of friends and relations surrounding his great-aunt Campbell and her daughter Mary, who lived with her, therefore provided much of Lesassier's social life during his first few years in Edinburgh. It was perhaps through them that he met Catherine Jane Crokatt. She was the daughter of Captain Crokatt of the East India Company, and she had £2,000 held in trust that gave her an income from dividends of about £90 per year. She was probably between seventeen and twenty when they met. Her father was dead, and her mother had remarried and had a son. In a parallel with Lesassier's own mother, Catherine may have been looking for a way to leave home. She may have fallen in love with the handsome young physician, for Lesassier never had any difficulty in attracting women. He may have fallen in love with her as well: "*Dearest Catherine*," he wrote to her in a letter two years after their marriage, "I long to press you to my breast for I love you, since we parted, a thousand times more than ever," and we have no more reason to suspect irony in his than in Alicia Irwin's letter. Yet affection and interest always went hand in hand for Lesassier. He was desperately seeking some way of supplementing his half-pay, and an addition of £90 per year could hardly fail to attract him. "Never sacrifice your future happiness to the shrine of avarice," he had written as a boy, but this noble sentiment had long since changed. "As I could not consult my taste & feelings," he wrote soon after returning to Edinburgh, "I would consider my interest alone; and, as necessity compelled that Deity, not only the statue, but the pedestal also should be gold!" Ninety pounds per annum was hardly gold, but Catherine had, in the phrase of a later novelist, great expectations. She was "heiress to an ample fortune at her Mother's death," at which time she would receive the principal of her trust fund as well as other moneys, "worth," Lesassier wrote, "fully £700 a year!!!" They were married on 9 April 1817.

The marriage was only intermittently happy. It may have started off well, for the gap in the journals in the early years of their marriage suggests that Catherine had supplanted Lesassier's notebooks as his confidant. Kate, Kitty, Kitten, he called her, nicknames suggesting affection; he acknowledged that she could be "quite unremitting in her attentions & kindness to me"; they took long walks together every day and sang together in the evening, Lesassier "teasing his poor Kate Dawdlums . . . who like a true Kitten, ventures occasionally to return a pat, or even a gentle *scratch*, as a practical proof of her gratitude." But he had wanted a "young lady . . . with a large fortune" to show off as an acquisition, not an India Company official's daughter with £90 per year, whose mother showed no sign of dying and leaving her daughter money. He regarded Catherine as lower in station than he, and Isabella tried to console him for what he called "the indelible blot of my disproportionate marriage," by assuring him that "under the guidance of such a husband—she will ultimately become all you can wish her, to be." But Catherine remained Catherine, young but not beautiful—as can be inferred from the absence of physical description in Lesassier's comments—devoted but not deferential, emotional but not romantic, and irretrievably middle class.

Their quarrels were fierce and frequent. He was no more tolerant of insubordination in a wife than in his Portuguese medical staff, and he was quick to hand out a "well-merited scolding," "kept up till she begs for quarter," for each offense: when she "walked out alone" despite his positive orders against it, when she visited her mother even though he forbade it, when, worst of all, he caught her "boasting of her influence over me." He was easily enraged by her "arrogant boldness and assurance," independent action in matters ranging from inviting friends to dinner to adding her own consent to his decisions regarding her trust fund. It was, indeed, her trust fund that was at the heart of the matter, for though she never questioned Lesassier's management of her dividends, paid directly to him, not her, they both were aware that the fortune was hers, not his. He could reduce Catherine to tears, but not to absolute dependence, and as in Portugal the realization of his own impotence drove him wild over apparent trifles. The Hamiltons apparently never heard of separate spheres of influence for men and women: though for the most part Catherine managed the household independently, Lesassier always abrogated final authority to himself. On one occasion when Catherine tried to countermand his decision to allow one of the maids to go out for the evening—saying, "*she* would let her know who her mistress was"—"Of course all the man & husband were roused within me," Lesassier wrote, "& I gave Catherine a tremendous reprimand." Catherine's own response to the quarrels were "hysterical paroxysms," according to Lesassier, increasingly emotional scenes which had the effect, whether intentional or not, of putting an end to the scolding. During one quarrel, Catherine "attacked me in such a way that I retort, & at last, she attempts suicide by cutting her finger, & seems to be bordering on madness. With much soothing, I get her to bed, & asleep." And during another, in which Catherine, "called me a *wretch*," because Lesassier would not allow her to go out with a friend, "I was forced to threaten her with a strait-jacket!!" Yet after each outburst, the two made up: "We are friends again" was Lesassier's usual comment within a day of the precipitating offense.

Lesassier had never regarded constancy as a goal, and meeting Catherine did not change his mind. As the historian Anthony Fletcher has noted, beneath the facade of sophistication of Georgian society "was a deeply selfish set of sexual mores and an unabashed male hedonism." In Armagh, Lesassier had combined courtship of Alicia Irwin with a sexual liaison with the servant Betty, and in Edinburgh, while courting Miss Crokatt, undoubtedly taking her on long walks through Edinburgh, he got Isabella Allan, the daughter of his "kind, disinterested landlady," pregnant. His child was born in 1817 and can be presumed to be a boy from later comments about his apprenticeship. Lesassier himself refers to the child as "it" and mentions him only to complain about Mrs. Allan's importuning him for money for the boy's upkeep: "Such, alas! is the retributive chastisement of vice; & I bow beneath the scourge I have so amply merited." He had a second child by one of his servants, Catherine Monroe, also known as Kitty. He arranged for her to deliver the baby in the Lying-In Hospital—an almost incredible act of imprudence, but there would be others—and paid for her nurse. Kitty and her baby remained in the Hamilton household for several years.

Lesassier's sexual relations with his servants quickly became something out of a bedroom farce. During his affair with Kitty Monroe, he also carried on a regularly scheduled liaison with his other maidservant, Christian McKenzie, every Sunday morning while his wife went to church. Indeed, he may have have slept with them at the same time, in the same bed, for the two servants shared a bed "in a little room off the kitchen," and when McKenzie was later formally interrogated whether on any occasion her employer came into the bed while both girls were in it, she "depones affirmative. Depones that this occurred frequently." On one occasion while Kitty was away having her baby, McKenzie shared the bed with a less accommodating servant, who was awakened one night on hearing "a third person in the bed—That on her awaking this person got up and flew out of the room; and that she had occasion to know it was a man, because he was taking improper liberties with McKenzie." Monroe and McKenzie eventually left the Hamiltons' service, to be replaced by Helen More and Anne Smith, with whom Lesassier once again had "improper connections."

Catherine may not have known of Lesassier's affairs with his servants. But she was certainly aware of, and resented, his interest in other women. Lesassier cultivated both pretty married ladies within his social circle and their equally pretty unmarried sisters. Ostensibly he did this because the ladies "may be of use to me perhaps at some future day," by either becoming or recommending patients. The real reason, though, was that Lesassier's marriage did not keep him from enjoying the "unaffected vivacity of a cheerfully social party" dominated by lovely young women. Indeed, the respectable role of married man and physician may well have encouraged the intimacy, romantic and at times explicitly erotic, that Lesassier viewed as essential in a female friendship: "How delightful," he might have said with Rosamond Lydgate in *Middlemarch* "to make captives from the throne of marriage." He acquired "favorites" among his young lady friends, with whom he carried on dangerously affectionate conversations in person or by letter: we can tell when a young lady reached this stage when Lesassier recorded his comments about her in his journals in rudimentary Portuguese or slightly more fluent French, often with Greek transliteration. His affection required devotion in return and any perceived slight led to quarrels and reprimands. He at first would "not be reconciled" to a young lady who had shown herself insufficiently appreciative of his friendship, and he called on her "to lecture her for her behavior the other evening &c." The lecture was successful: "The high spirited, haughty girl, at last yielded, & promised to be every thing I could wish." He saved another of his favorites from an imprudent promise of marriage, and he had "the delicious feeling of being looked up to as the savior of the unhappy girl." But he quarreled with her, too—"a ingrata!"—when she slighted him by taking someone else's arm after a dinner party, an episode reminiscent of his quarrel with Joseph Jordan years earlier. Lesassier did not sleep with his young unmarried lady friends, or any woman whose resulting pregnancy would be his ruin, but his courtships were as intense as he dared make them, replete with kisses and caresses.

Catherine often became jealous, and for good reason. Propriety required that the Hamilton couple had to jointly befriend their young ladies: unless on a professional visit, Lesassier could not see them alone, a circumstance that indeed added a certain piquant intimacy to his house calls. Catherine, in other words, had to participate in Lesassier's acquisition of favorites. In general she was happy to do so, for she, too, enjoyed the cheerful social parties at dinner, supper, or tea, at the theater or races, in town or in the country. But the "fancy," not unfounded, that one of their young friends "is fond of me, leads to a tremendous quarrel between me & Catherine, which went so far that, I gave her money & she gave up my keys, & went to the door to leave me. A reconciliation, however, again follow & again another quarrel before we retire to bed." Each new friendship with a new set of young ladies, brought on "an altercation about the old subject," Lesassier wrote, "of my not caring so much for Catherine as others &c &c, but, she comes round again almost immediately; although a full hour elapses, before I myself am appeased." Nor was Catherine the only one to feel slighted as Lesassier became enamored of one young lady after another. His cousin Mary Campbell was "enviously jealous" of his patient and favorite Anne Walker, and another patient—and favorite—Fanny Maitland was jealous of his attentions to her sisters Catherine and Anne.

So much sexual activity, as we may term it whether or not actual intercourse took place, calls for some explanation beyond hedonism, and an obvious one is that Lesassier did not sleep with his wife very often. He had decided from the first not to have children. He was not fond of them, an odd trait in an accoucheur who was also expected to treat diseases of young children: babies were "squalling urchins," older children were "noisy & unmannerly" or "ill-bred cubs." His affections always followed the gradients of social status, and he and Catherine disapproved of his friend John Maitland's "dandling & nursing" his newborn child—whom Lesassier had recently delivered—"like one of the lower orders." Indeed he delivered a "torrent of argumentative invective" directed against both John and Fanny Maitland to prove that "a feeling of yearning & intense love for early infancy, is the peculiar, & wisely ordained, attribute of woman, & not of man," and it was only to attract a new patient that he caressed her ten-month-old son. Besides, he was essentially selfish. His aunt Isabella was willing, she wrote, to "deprive myself of many comforts—for the sake of educating my children," but Lesassier was no more inclined to such sacrifice than his own father had been. He became terribly worried when Catherine's period was delayed, and was wild with delight when she "was seized with what *she* imagined to be miscarriage, but, which I have no doubt is her menses returned!!! My joy at this unlooked-for good fortune, was greater, more rapturous, by far, than if I had gained a prize of 500 guineas in the Lottery. At once, I am my own master again & free as air, can move unshackled whithersoever my fate may lead me!!!"

He had additional motivation. He had every reason to know that childbirth could be dangerous: if Catherine died before her mother, he would lose her £90 per annum, money that had rapidly become essential to his income. He would lose any chance of inheriting the rest of her fortune, too, for that would remain with her mother. He would also lose the chance if she lived and bore children, for her trust then devolved upon their living offspring. Only if they had no children would the money be Catherine's to dispose of as she wished, and Lesassier was sure she would give it to him. He was also sure she would leave it to him in her will, and the prospect of Catherine, first becoming an heiress, then conveniently dying while he was still young and vigorous, was a pleasing fancy, for it would at once elevate him to the status of a young gentleman of independent fortune. In the meantime his "unsettled state" made it desirable for him to avoid children if he could, he told Isabella, who concurred, "thankful" as she was in her own case "to say—number *four*, is not likely *to be increased.*" "You manage *those things* better than any one I know," she wrote, "do you really adhere, to your *resolution*? and without *murmurings*, on *her side*? I do think you are the most *extraordinary* creature, in *some respects.*"

Catherine did murmur, in fact, and loudly. It is possible that she bore Lesassier one child who died in infancy, for Lesassier kept a bill from a carpenter for "A full mounted child's coffin . . . Burying ground expenses . . . Two coaches" from March 1819. Her desire for a child was a frequent cause of their quarrels, especially as she grew older, "For, this darling wish, Catherine seems resolved never to abandon, until, some day or other, it leads to a final separation." Whenever "the fatal subject of ladies having children, was introduced . . . all further harmony was at an end." Catherine gave way "to a fit of weeping . . . from her incessant desire to have a family," and she was "exasperatingly sullen & captious." Finally she told him she would leave him unless she had a child. "Unfeeling & selfish wretch!" he wrote, and "dared her to do so." But Catherine learned over the years that if she could withstand her husband's fierce reprimands, she could wear him down; a separation, moreover, would be at least as disastrous for him as for her. "At last," therefore, Lesassier agreed to compromise, "and I promised her a child if we continue in Edinburgh under favorable circumstances."

# EDWARD NEVILLE;

OR,

## THE MEMOIRS

OF

# AN ORPHAN.

---

*IN FOUR VOLUMES.*

## VOL. I.

---

## LONDON:

PRINTED FOR

LONGMAN, HURST, REES, ORME, AND BROWN,

PATERNOSTER-ROW.

### 1823.

The title page of Alexander Lesassier's novel, published anonymously.

Left: Alexander Hamilton, professor of midwifery at Edinburgh University and grandfather of Alexander Lesassier. It is tempting to speculate that the two ladies are his wife and eldest daughter, Christina, but in fact the artist was merely providing a discreet allusion to Hamilton's profession. American Philosophical Society. Right: James Hamilton, professor of midwifery at Edinburgh University and uncle of Alexander Lesassier. Silhouette by A. Edouart. National Gallery of Scotland.

The cluster of buildings on the left comprised Edinburgh medical school in 1815. Reproduced with the permission of Edinburgh University Library (B.B.3.24).

Male physicians often competed with female midwives for obstetrical practice, claiming their education and technical expertise with instruments gave them professional superiority. But men who intruded on the female world of childbirth could be accused of "crudity & indecency," as this print shows. Isaac Cruikshank, *A Man Mid-wife*, 1793. Yale University, Harvey Cushing/John Hay Whitney Medical Library, Clements C. Fry Print Collection.

This engraving was done twenty years after Lesassier's apprenticeship in Manchester, but the apprentice looks as busy with inconsequential tasks as young Alexander, and just as bored. Henry Heath, *Physic*, 1825. Philadelphia Museum of Art: The William H. Helfand Collection.

During Lesassier's attempt at practice in Rochdale, his bout with the "blue devils" (a contemporary expression for depression) led him to contemplate suicide. George Cruikshank, *The Blue Devils*, 1823. Philadelphia Museum of Art: The William H. Helfand Collection.

"Since here we are met
And a Jolly set
A fig for sack & sherry
Once came we'll clink
Over liquor well drunk
And will be wonderous merry"

Lesassier bitterly complained at the prospect of practicing in a little village, his social life restricted to visits to the local tavern, "forming a smoky trio with the curate and the exciseman." This engraving plays on a similar image of the village doctor, while suggesting that his "friends" also included Death and the Devil.

This caricature suggests that the pompous examiners seated behind the table are hardly more qualified than the young surgeon standing before them. Though Lesassier was examined individually—and more professionally—before joining the army, he surely shared the anxiety of the visibly quaking candidate in this engraving. George Cruikshank, *The Examination of a Young Surgeon*. Photograph courtesy of the National Library of Medicine, Bethesda.

Dress uniform of an officer in Lesassier's regiment, the 42nd Foot (the Black Watch). Lesassier did not spend his years on the Iberian Peninsula in a kilt; this uniform would have been for formal occasions only. American Philosophical Society.

View of the Serra d'Estrella mountain range in Portugal, where Lesassier's regiment was quartered during the war.

Depiction of the Battle of Salamanca, which conveys the sense of theater described in Lesassier's journal: "a brilliant overwhelming sublime spectacle."

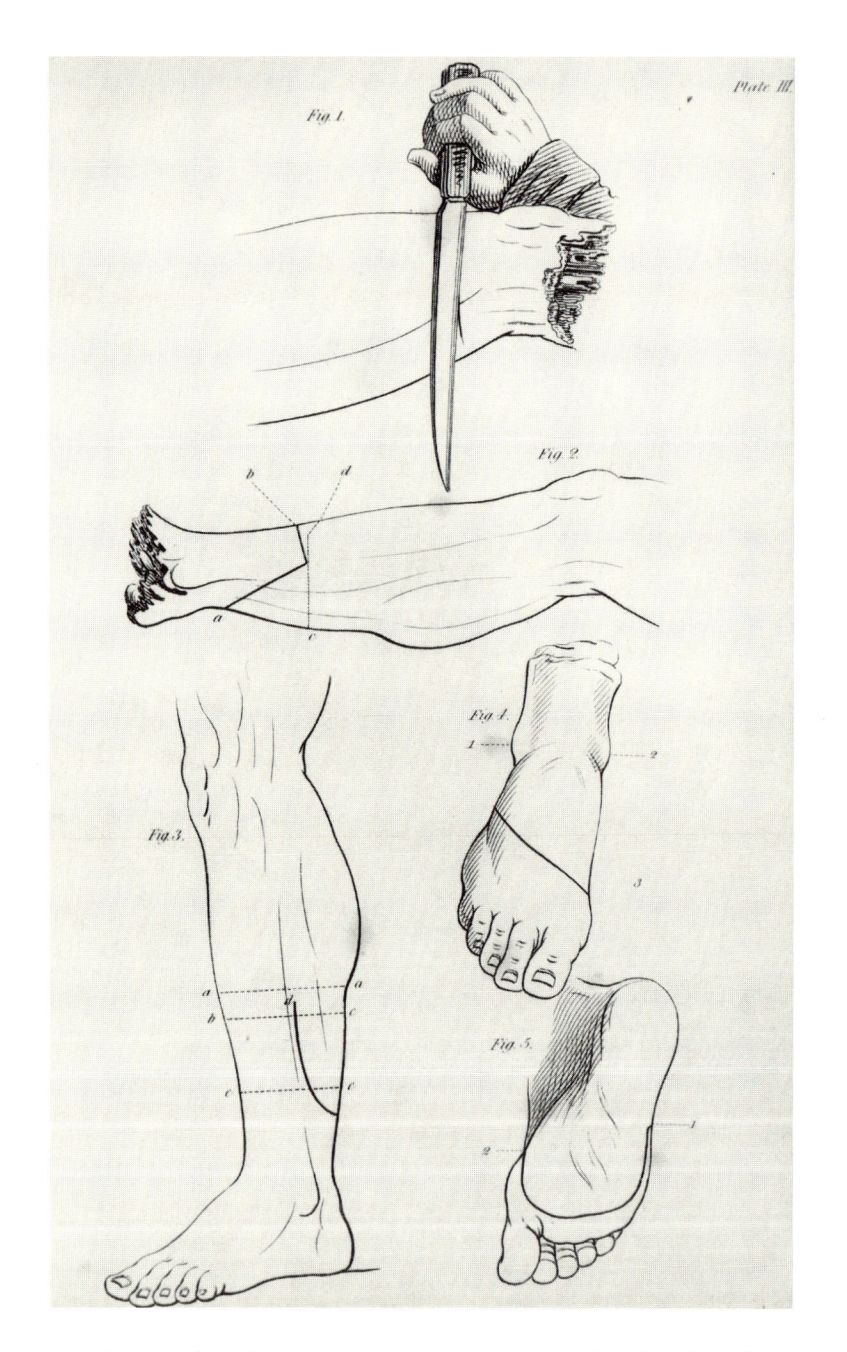

George James Guthrie's book on gunshot wounds was largely based on the author's experience of surgery during the Peninsular War. These illustrations convey one of the most important medical lessons to come out of the war, that prompt amputation was often the only way to save lives. Library of the College of Physicians of Philadelphia.

**MEDICAL DISPATCH** OR

**DOCTOR DOUBLEDOSE KILLING TWO BIRDS WITH ONE STONE.**

A doctor's house calls. Lesassier's behavior brought him a particular notoriety, but this caricature reveals a more general distrust of the uses to which a physician might put a patient examination. Thomas Rowlandson, *Medical Dispatch, or Doctor Doubledose Killing Two Birds with One Stone*. Photograph courtesy of the National Library of Medicine, Bethesda.

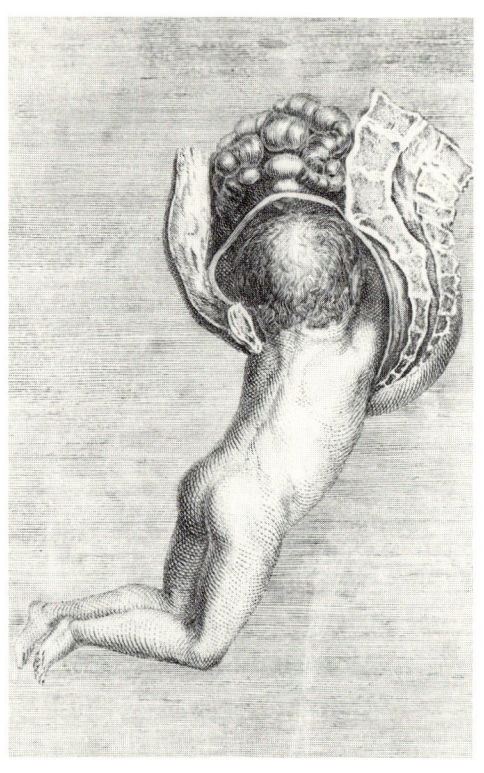

James Hamilton published his *Collection of Engravings, Designed to Facilitate the Study of Midwifery* in 1798. These engravings of a footling breech birth (above) and a posterior breech (right) depict two conditions for which a male physician like Lesassier or Hamilton himself might have been called. Though Lesassier often reviled his uncle, he faithfully followed Hamilton's midwifery teaching. Library of the College of Physicians of Philadelphia.

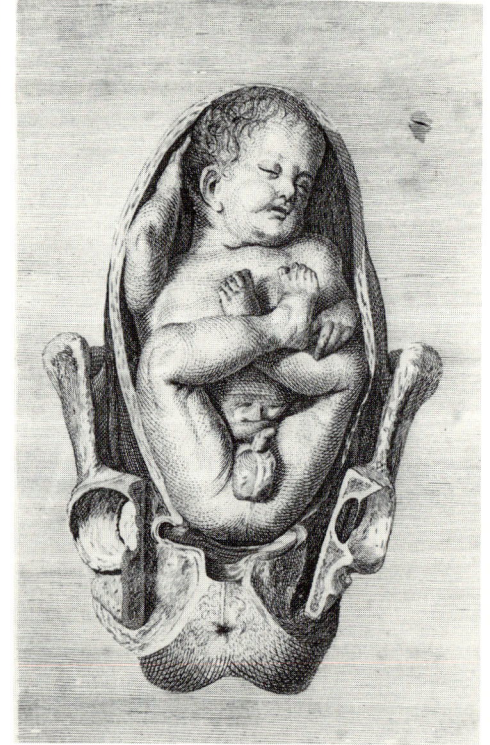

MODERN NURSING 342

Fashionable new mothers in Edinburgh, ca. 1796. Though accoucheurs like Lesassier were sometimes asked to recommend wet nurses, many genteel young ladies chose to nurse their own babies, and did so in style. American Philosophical Society.

Ladies and gentlemen of style promenading in Edinburgh, with the less fashionable Old Town in the distance.

Lesassier's "castle of a house" at 57 Northumberland Street, still an elegant address.

Lady Louisa Kintore. When her husband, the seventh Earl of Kintore, intercepted a letter to her from Lesassier, the ensuing scandal was the talk of Edinburgh. Painting by B. R. Faulkner. Photograph courtesy of the Scottish National Portrait Gallery.

CHAPTER 10

# Appearances Are of Essential Consequence

Lesassier commenced practice on his own shortly after his marriage in 1817. Through the Lying-In Hospital, he had made contacts among the poor, and it was through them, as he had thought, that he was able to ultimately obtain more reputable practice. He had delivered the wife of a poor cobbler without charge, through whom he met a young gentlewoman, Mrs. Veitch, who "had been accidentally affording charitable assistance" to her. Mrs. Veitch, in turn, recommended him to his first paying patient, Mrs. Cleland, the wife of "an obscure house-painter"; more important to Lesassier, she also recommended him to her sisters-in-law, his first patients of the better sort. His next patients consisted of his own tradesmen—Mrs. Tait, wife of the baker, and Mrs. Adams, a dressmaker whose husband was an ironmonger. Eventually it consisted of about seventy families, most of whom Lesassier described as "the lower or inferior orders of the middle classes," "shopkeepers, petty clerks, etc." Their occupations mark urban Britain's changing social structure, for among them we can find both the lower reaches of the traditional educated class—solicitor, law agent, accountant, government clerk—and the upper ranks of tradesmen—grocer, flour dealer, coachmaker. Newly able to pay for the consumables, including medical attendance, that had once been limited to the gentry, they were still ready to accord the traditional respect to a properly graduated physician. Yet "How different is this circle . . . from the one, to which I had once a right to look!" he lamented after a party given by one of his patients, a "cheerful, kind-hearted, blundering Irish girl . . . young and lovely"; how different was his bourgeois practice from his uncle's patronage by those of rank and fortune. Lesassier blamed his uncle for his own failure to establish a prestigious practice, but alas, as Jane Austen wrote, "there certainly are not so many men of large fortune in the world, as there are pretty women to deserve them," and there were not so many duke's wives having babies in Edinburgh as there were accoucheurs who wished to deliver them.

Was Lesassier a good doctor? the inquiring reader wants to know. Not as good as his uncle, is the obvious reply; not as good as the other medical professors, or the Edinburgh graduates who had not fabricated their theses. But a more useful answer is that he was good at some things. In the army, he had become a competent hospital administrator, rather than either a good clinician or a skillful surgeon. In civilian life, he was a good consulting obstetrician, competent in natural births, resourceful and just a little bit callous in difficult cases requiring active and painful intervention. Like all obstetricians, he preferred the "nine hundred and twenty" out of "a thousand labors" which were "accounted natural," that is, in which the head presented down and facing front: "Thank God! the baby was coming right," he wrote after one examination of his patient Anne Walker. But he was proud of his ability when more active measures were called for, and at one point considered establishing a lying-in hospital for difficult and dangerous cases only. "I was called at 6 A.M. to a poor woman at Stockbridge, whom I successfully delivered with the forceps. More such cases," he wrote, "might be of service to me." The Lying-In Hospital provided an outlet for his talents, where he applied the forceps "with great facility, & extracted the head in the course of a few efforts. The infant was alive; & the mother had a rapid recovery." He was adept, too, "in cases where the head presents, and for several hours we expect the child will be delivered in the natural way; but . . . the woman has not strength enough to force down the child's head into the pelvis." The procedure in such a case was to give the mother a large dose of opium to stop the contractions, then push back the head while bringing down the feet. Extracting the baby might require some force; moreover the child might be stillborn. Animation, in the form of "breathing . . . & an occasional feeble cry" might still be restored, "by artificially inflating lungs for upward of half an hour . . . and by friction with ardent spirits, the application of hot flannel," continuing for another hour. In the worst cases, the child could neither be delivered naturally nor turned. "Considering that I had no choice left me," Lesassier wrote on one such occasion, he "resolved to open the infant's head," that is, break open the skull to extract the fetus. As in amputation, he had to get the patient's consent, even though she was a charity patient at the Lying-In Hospital. She eventually gave it "most reluctantly," and she, at least, "had a rapid recovery." He detested such cases, like the "horrible operation at the Hospital" which prevented him from attending church one Sunday. On another occasion "At 20 minutes to 6," he wrote, "I am called to a patient of the Doctor's"—that is, James Hamilton's—"& am not at liberty till ¼ past 3 P.M. never having tasted any food, & having to perform a hateful operation on a lovely girl." But in these cases standard medical opinion was that "instead of destroying, you are really saving a life; for, if the operation be delayed, both mother and child are lost." As these cases make clear, it was the mother who was the patient in midwifery cases, not the child: "Doubtless it is our duty to save both mother and child," noted one medical writer, "but, if that is impracticable, to pay our chief regard to the parent"—a dictum reinforced in one of Lesassier's cases by the patient's husband, who vented "the most brutal threats against us in the next room if we did any thing to hurt his wife."

Lesassier's care of the mother began well before delivery. His routine care included frequent visits: "How getting on in your pregnancy?" he asked. "How's your general health?" He also visited twice per day for about three weeks after delivery: "Does the nurse please? Is infant thriving?" He made additional visits, if called, for any problems. He distinguished between the social backgrounds of his patients in his journal—"I am called to a woman forenoon, & to a lady in the afternoon," runs a typical entry—and there is no doubt that he was less pleased with his "low patients" than his ladies. He did not, however, distinguish between them in his professional care. Though he was generally called to poor patients only when they were in labor and therefore did not make his usual prenatal calls, he never refused to attend even those he was sure would not pay him, and he visited them after delivery twice daily for the regular time. Though he was much more sensitive to the feelings of his well-born patients, his deference to their social position may even have made him less effective in difficult cases. As he noted, "To be told by a beautiful woman & an excellent patient, that one is hurting her, & that, one must surely be forgetting oneself, every time one attempts to discover the actual position of the infant's head, actually makes one timid, & afraid of doing one's duty."

Once the infant was born, he or she did become a patient. Lesassier's first medical treatment was to vaccinate for smallpox, carried out within the first few months of life. The precise time depended on Lesassier's practice, for he tried to use the postules from one recently vaccinated baby he had delivered to vaccinate the others. The operation was not without its dangers. One infant was "attacked with such frightful inflamation of its arm . . . that I still dread lest it should not struggle through. Should it die, the event will make a great noise, & will injure me excessively." He was "exceedingly anxious" respecting his "little patient" and visited her every day. Within a week she was better, but, he wrote, she "will still require a good deal of farther attendance, &, what is still worse, its illness arising from vaccination, I cannot receive a shilling for my trouble!" Lesassier also visited patients for problems that arose during weaning, for many of his patients nursed their own children, and he cut babies' gums when they were teething.

Maintaining his practice involved some paperwork. He made lists of when he expected his patients to be delivered and tried to insure that he would be in town for the delivery. If some other medical man was present he would have to share the fee, and he might even lose the patient if she decided she preferred the other attendant for her subsequent pregnancies. He also drew up occasional lists of when infants were to be vaccinated, perhaps for the same reason. He was often consulted for wet nurses, some of whom he obtained from among the patients at the Lying-In Hospital: "I shall . . . be much obliged to you, if you will procure me a good mouth nurse, whom you can depend upon," one of his patients wrote, "& engage her for me . . . as *wherever* I am, I am determined to have an Edinburgh nurse." Even between his patients' pregnancies, Lesassier would make the occasional "gratuitous" visit, pretending that he was merely paying a call, but really to remind his patients of his existence.

In his obstetrical practice, Lesassier was perfectly professional: in reading his case histories, we feel that we are in the presence of a capable, if self-centered, physician. His heroic efforts were often successful in saving mother and infant, and his analysis of more complicated cases is in the cold, but precise language of anatomy and physiology, in terms of "toughness of the *os uteri*; rigidity of the membranes; want of sufficient uterine action; an unfavorable presentation of the head; & a lateral, instead of a general, contraction of the uterus." In turning to his general medical practice, however, we are on less sure ground. By modern standards the medical treatment of the early nineteenth century could not be very effective, since there was neither knowledge of the germ theory nor any effective antibiotics. A patient's only recourse, we would say, was his or her own constitution, and many remedies of the period—bloodletting, purging, and the like—in our view, would have weakened, rather than strengthened, the ability of the patient to recover from the disease. Still, there were excellent clinicians in the early nineteenth century; there were practicing physicians who were also excellent anatomists, particularly in obstetrics; there were practitioners who took every opportunity to attend hospitals and keep up with the medical literature. Any of these, we have to admit, would have had greater knowledge of medicine than Lesassier.

One way to measure professionalization is the extent to which the knowledge of a professional differs from that of a layman. There will always be some overlap: modern physicians share with the general educated public a knowledge of bacteria and viruses. We expect physicians, however, to have much more detailed knowledge of the impact bacteria and viruses can have on the human frame; we also expect their diagnosis of one or the other class of microorganisms to affect treatment. A comparable example from Lesassier's period has to do with knowledge of what were called nervous diseases. Physicians shared with the general educated public the knowledge that weakness of the nerves could make one more susceptible to illness, and that sudden shocks could kill an already weakened patient. This idea, the physiological basis for the cult of sensibility, was common to both medical and literary works from William Cullen to Mary Wollstonecraft. What distinguished the understanding of the physician—what was, indeed, the core of his claim to professional expertise—was detailed knowledge of the anatomy and physiology of the nervous system and the ability to apply that knowledge in the diagnosis of nervous diseases.

We can examine this distinction between the lay and professional knowledge of the period by constructing a case history based on the death of the Matilda, the heroine of the Marquess of Normanby's novel *Matilda; A Tale of the Day*, published in 1825. Matilda falls in love with a young man but through the usual contrivance of novels is prevented from marrying him. Instead, she marries a man she could not love. Encountering her true love again, she runs off to Italy with him. He has to return to England to take care of his affairs, and leaves her pregnant with his child, but during his trip finds that her husband has been persuaded to grant her a divorce and they are finally free to marry. The story might have had a happy ending, but Matilda, watching for the ship carrying her beloved back to her, sees it dashed to pieces before her eyes. She first falls unconscious, then goes into premature labor, giving birth without awakening. Not even the realization that her lover survived the wreck could restore her "weakened frame" when she did regain consciousness. A contemporary lay reading of the novel would have been that, in fact, the "renewed energies" she felt on seeing him still alive, prompted by "the strongest of human passions," would only have served to use up the vital force she needed to recover: "she was now," her author tells us, "utterly exhausted," and soon died.

A contemporary medical reading of Matilda's case would not have been incompatible with her author's, but it would have been more detailed. A physician called to Matilda's sickbed would have diagnosed her disease as an apoplexy, "a sudden abolition of all the senses, external and internal, and of all voluntary motion, commonly attended with a strong pulse, laborious breathing, a deep sleep, and snorting." Alert to the need for differential diagnosis, the physician would note that the main distinction between "a person asleep and in an apoplexy" is "that the one can be awaked, and the other cannot"; this distinction would have supported his initial diagnosis, for the unhappy Matilda could not be "awaked" even when in labor. So, too, would her state of mind and nerves, for apoplexy could be brought on by "violent passions of the mind." The physician could have gone on to trace the action of the passions in causing the blood to rush to the brain, "which by its pressure hurts the origin of the nerves," ten pairs of which were located in the brain. There were three degrees of apoplexy, and a sympathetic physician might have hoped that Matilda would fall victim to the first, which "may be cured by timely bleeding," or the second, which "generally rendered the patient infirm." Alas, her author felt a tragic ending would better uphold the moral responsibility of the novel, and afflicted her with an apoplexy of the third degree, "which was almost always mortal."

It may seem incongruous to apply a medical diagnosis to a death in a sentimental novel: it appears a violation of decorum, an unwarranted cross-over of genres, a misapplication of clinical expertise to write a case history for a scene that was never intended to support such weighty language. It is with the same sense of incongruity that we turn to Lesassier's description of the deaths from disease that occurred in his practice, for where we expect the clinician's gaze we find instead a novelist's sensibility. When Mrs. Banner became ill with a persistent diarrhea after Lesassier "delivered her . . . at seven months of a male infant, who died," he became "uneasy" and left "the most pointed injunctions" for her to be sure to take her medicine. "I am excessively apprehensive they will call in some other medical man," he wrote, and he was "driven half frantic with my patient's perverseness; for, through neglect of my directions, the complaint still continues unsubdued." After a few days, Mrs. Banner became better, and Lesassier was much relieved, but apparent recovery was not unusual in the last stages of fever following childbirth, and his patient died eleven days after her infant. "This was the first patient in private practice I had ever lost," Lesassier noted; "the shock was considerable," and he was immediately worried about his reputation. However, "the extreme imbecility displayed by the parties concerned, shifted the odium, as much as, under such circumstances, it could possibly be, to them instead of me." He had left positive orders that Mrs. Banner's mother should not be admitted to her while she was in such a weakened state, and it was to that cause that he attributed her death. "The mother had been again admitted to her, between 12 & 1, & never left her, till the excessive emotion produced by her presence, her passionate embraces, & her repeated & heartrending farewells, actually overwhelmed the wretched victim's delicately balanced nervous system, &, by a species of moral assassination, put an end to the miserable sufferer's existence!!"

In the overwhelming of the "wretched victim's delicately balanced nervous system" we can hear the echo of Matilda's death, as well as the deaths of countless novel heroines from Lesassier's day to our own who expire from unnamed diseases with no clear etiology or pathology. It may take some effort to remember that Mrs. Banner was a real patient, not a fictional character, and that Lesassier has here neglected the first duty of the physician to name the disease by pronouncing a diagnosis, with its attendant discussion of history, treatment, and prognosis. He has neglected, in other words, to transform his individual patient into a case history, literally embodying the progress of her disease rather than merely her own experience of illness.

In this, as in other things, Lesassier chose to go against the current of medical professionalization, and we can tell that this was a deliberate choice by turning once again to his novel *Edward Neville*, in which first the hero's father, then his mother, succumb to fatal illnesses. Major Neville was attacked by something like Matilda's apoplexy—ranking with fatal but noncontagious fever as the most versatile of all fictional illnesses—on hearing that he had lost his entire fortune of £6,000. A doctor was called, and the ensuing scene becomes a pointed attack on the medical man as unsympathetic, insensible expert. "After minutely enquiring into the Major's lamented attack and present condition, the Doctor"—perhaps modeled on James Hamilton— "insisted upon giving Mrs. Neville what he was pleased to term a summary sketch of the history, nature, causes, and cure of his patient's disease, in which he persevered with unwearied volubility, notwithstanding her marked impatience, and repeated interruptions. At last, however, having completed what he had to say, he wound up his learned discourse—rendered utterly unintelligible by technical phraseology, and interminable episodes,—with the direct conclusion, that his patient would be quite himself again the following morning." But the doctor was quite wrong, and the major soon died. The physician had paid too much attention to the disease, Lesassier implied, and not enough to the patient.

Mrs. Neville's physician did not make the same mistake. Her disease ran true to its genre in having no clear etiology or pathology that would allow a diagnosis, and indeed her own physician "hesitated in assigning a name to a disease, which, he said, had all the air of being a complicated affection, arising from causes not less of a moral, than of a physical nature." He prescribed only "light nourishment, and absolute tranquility," while sparing "neither time nor exertion in his professional services," whatever they may have been. Mrs. Neville, too, died of her unnamed disease, but this time no blame was attached to her "humane and enlightened physician": he had displayed the requisite sympathy for the patient.

Critics of aspects of modern medicine have come to regret the dominance of technical phraseology in clinical encounters and would like to see more sympathy for the patient's point of view as well as "causes not less of a moral, than of a physical nature." But even the fiercest critics would hesitate before consulting a medical practitioner who traded technique completely for sympathy, and there is evidence that Lesassier's own patients hesitated as well. He never built up a general practice outside of midwifery, and even families who regularly employed him in deliveries did not call him in their other illnesses. He was in any case difficult to deal with. Mrs. Banner's mother could hardly have been happy to find herself accused of a species of moral assassination. The young mother who watched her child die as she tried to feed her, and who exclaimed "in an agony of grief . . . Oh! my child is suffocated—& with my own hand," would not have been pleased to be told it was "chastisement . . . for her double-faced perfidy & ingratitude" in following the advice of another medical man instead of Lesassier. "I tremble" for my fee, he wrote in the latter instance; he eventually was paid, but he was never called to that family again. More professional detachment would have been in his own interest, but Lesassier had never been able to cultivate the easy, obliging, and attentive manner recommended for physicians and could not begin now.

Lesassier's other professional blunders are legion. He persisted in regarding his "real" life as his leisure for study or pleasure: every time he had to deliver a patient, he complained that it "broke in on his time": "I went a long round of calls today—visits which I had deferred so long that I forced myself to go—though the consequence was, that I lost my whole day." He took his wife along when he went to visit his patients, and though she seldom came in unless she knew the patient socially, it was still an unwarranted mixing of the private and domestic with the public and professional. There was no harm in merging personal and professional life: many a doctor's practice arose out of his family and social connections, and the ideal doctor was also a friend of the family. David MacLagan, whose practice flourished thanks to his assiduous cultivation of his professional contacts, including his father-in-law, was on excellent terms with his patient Susan Ferrier, and the charm of her conversation "invariably led him to spend three-quarters of an hour on his visits to her instead of the conventional quarter of an hour." But MacLagan never confused his professional calls with social calls, and Lesassier, too, knew perfectly well that professional visits were to be paid by himself, alone, in the morning or early afternoon, with social calls left for the late afternoon or evening. "Catherine accompanied me to Mrs. Cairns, a patient," Lesassier wrote. "It was provokingly too early, however, to be walking with her. We met Cousin Mary, too, which was a pity, as she would think it so unprofessional."

Lesassier made other professional mistakes. Anxious to be popular, he displayed "want of tact, of common sense," by conversing too freely with patients when he should have "paid shorter visits, & behaved with more dignified reserve." He violated— "incurable imbecility"—the confidentiality of the consultation by discussing his patient's ailments with their friends. He became too involved in his patients' affairs. He agreed to act as a mediator between Mr. Banner and his wife's mother, who "vows . . . never to forgive him." Banner later "imposed upon me the detestable, laborious, & responsible task of writing to . . . the clergyman, such an explanatory letter respecting his wife's illness & death, her mother's behavior, & his conduct & his origin & family, & the share I myself bore in the whole affair, as might assist as a counterpose to his mother-in-law's scandalous allegations." Still later he asked for Lesassier's assistance in persuading another young lady of fortune to marry him. Lesassier should never have gotten so involved in the matter; having done so, however, he should not have asked

Banner "to buy me an Oriental pearl for a breast-pin—hoping he will take the hint, &, for the trouble I have taken in his private affairs, make me a present of it!" The end result might be called a fitting chastisement for Lesassier's unprofessional greed, for Banner, instead of making him a present of it, "brought me a pearl, to be sure, but a most diminutive one it is, & he has made me pay the enormous sum of £3 18s. for it."

These were not just ethical lapses but an entire misdirection of Lesassier's professional efforts, for he cultivated his patients because he believed that it was through them that he would expand his practice. His assumption that the more his patients liked him personally, the more they would refer him to others appears almost a caricature of modern scholarship on the importance of patients as patrons. A few referrals did come from patients, but never to the extent he expected. Though he was "roused . . . from my despondency" when one of his prized patients bowed to him, "by the conviction which it gives me, that, if *he*"—his uncle—"were dead, I should, through her . . . powerful influence . . . unquestionably get into the higher ranks," neither she nor his other ladies were able or willing to use their influence in his behalf. This conviction that referrals would come through his patients persisted despite his own experience to the contrary. "For instance," one friend "recommended a lady to employ me," he wrote, but she chose "the rascal," his uncle, instead. Even more mortifying, his own neighbors across the street chose "to employ the rascal for their newly married daughter!" instead of him. The fact that his own uncle was regarded in Edinburgh as the "chief of his department" was an obstacle to patient patronage. But even more was Lesassier's public reputation—which he cultivated himself—of being a fine gentleman, "proud and inaccessible . . . a man of fortune . . . and consequently careless about any increase of business."

Most of his own cases were in fact acquired through his medical connections, primarily that "rascal," "wretch," "scoundrel" his uncle, his only "professional patron." His other medical associates had little business to spare. The most active professionally, the best tempered, and the most helpful of his contacts was Edward Milligan, who had received his M.D. from Edinburgh in 1815. His efforts to succeed by professional endeavors form a striking contrast to Lesassier. A one-man competitor for the university professors, he gave extramural lectures on physiology, proposed a "Lady's Charity for delivering poor women at their own houses," with Lesassier to be senior physician, and founded a medical review. The Lady's Charity failed because Lesassier and Milligan could not find any ladies willing to serve as directresses, a prerequisite to the success of any charitable enterprise in Edinburgh; so, too, did the review, unable to compete with other medical publications. But despite these failures, Milligan continued his professional efforts, and he encouraged Lesassier whenever his professional affairs took a turn for the worse. Milligan is the only one of Lesassier's medical associates whom he referred to as "my old friend," and the only one whose good fortune he did not begrudge: when Milligan moved to a new house, Lesassier "was surprised & gratified to find him removed from the small flat he occupied so long . . . & . . . at the elegance, as well as the substantial nature, of his furniture."

Among other Edinburgh medical men, Lesassier had allies, but no real friends. John Mackintosh was, like Lesassier, a returning army officer who received his medical degree from Marischal College, Aberdeen, in 1820. His own professional quarrels with his colleagues began in his probationary essay on midwifery for entrance to the Royal College of Surgeons of Edinburgh, where he was asked to remove offensive paragraphs. His quarrels continued throughout his practice, and he acquired the reputation of "one of the wildest men in Edinburgh." Lesassier was also briefly associated with Robert Knox, an Edinburgh graduate and fellow of the Royal College of Surgeons, who gave extra-academical lectures in anatomy, notorious for both their popularity and their attacks on other Edinburgh anatomists. Though not marginal in the sense of being unlicensed or illegal practitioners, all three were, like Lesassier himself, lean and hungry physicians prowling on the margins of medical life, enviously contrasting their own "want of respectability" with the apparently gilded "eminence" of the university professors.

Lesassier's own life-style was far from gilded, though he worked hard to make it appear so. His half-pay amounted to £120 per year, and Catherine's dividend brought his income up to £210. Many practitioners would have envied so substantial a financial cushion, and in reflective moments, he knew he ought to be grateful "to the Almighty— of whose divine & unspeakable mercies, I am so utterly undeserving"—for his "independence." But the truth was that his income was never enough, not even when augmented with practice. He earned perhaps £100 in 1817, the year he began seeing patients on his own, and his practice increased to £262 by 1821; his income, therefore, amounted to over £300 even in his worst years, and nearly £500 in his best. If only he could have lived on that! But Edinburgh was expensive; more to the point, Lesassier was fiscally irresponsible, imagining from the first that his uncle must die in a year or two, when, he assumed, his money worries would be over.

The marriage that had added £90 per year to his income had also added to his expenses. In 1817, Lesassier moved from lodgings to a small house in St. James Square, hiring a manservant, a maid for Catherine, and a cook. In 1819 his father came to live with him, for Pierre's own practice in Manchester had nearly disappeared, either through scandal or lack of attention. "I am very much astonished, at hearing, that your Father's means are so limited," Isabella wrote from Chatham, "when I had always, conceived them to be most flourishing. Your intention of affording him, the comforts of life, in his old age, are highly commendable & do credit to your kind heart." Pierre, in himself, would not have added much to Lesassier's expenses, but his arrival prompted Lesassier to do what he had long wished to, move to a larger, more fashionable house on Picardy Place. Isabella may have had some influence in this decision "as I consider your present house," she wrote, "very unfit—for the practice you now have, *appearances*, are of essential consequence to you, & never can be more so, than at this period. All your *wellwishers* rejoice, that you are going to quit your present one . . . for one more worthy of you. Depend upon its being an unspeakable advantage to you, the change of situation." But appearances were expensive. The new Hamilton household had two maidservants and a footman, an establishment which, if we use Jane Austen's novels as a guide, required a clear £500 per year. Lesassier also purchased a carriage and expensive furnishings. Catherine's family may have provided some of the money to defray the "numerous expenses which attend furnishing a house." But most of them—upholstery, carpentry, and the like—were simply purchased on credit, Lesassier assuming that the appearance of the new address would be so useful in attracting practice that he would soon be able to purchase all he wanted.

His practice did increase, but not enough to cover his expenses. "Alas! how much evil is my unhappy portion, & how little good!" he wrote much later. "That day was an unlucky one, in which I left the humble obscurity [of his previous lodging] & took a mania for so much finery—I have never prospered since, nor, apparently, ever will again in this world! To it, I must, in fact, attribute all my sufferings." He bemoaned, too, that he had not persisted in the habits of prudent economy that would have enabled him to pay off his debts. Only after some years did he attempt to calculate, let alone reduce, his living expenses, and then he found that, at frugal best, he needed over £400 to maintain his household. His real expenses were probably £50 to £75 higher, because he always neglected to figure in household repairs, new clothing, and his own enormous love for shopping. It was so tempting to spend money! His practice required him to be out in all weathers, and he therefore needed "a great-coat, although God knows how I am to pay for it." He and Catherine saunter out "looking for a Shawl for Catherine, as she has had her present one three years. We meet with an *India* one at 6 guineas (credit till December) which is such an amazing bargain, that I cannot resist buying it, for *she* must be well dressed," any more than he could resist the Dutch paintings, "three good things for a mere song (55 shillings)." Then there were theater tickets, and the races, and suppers with friends, all those trappings of a genteel lifestyle that he could neither forego nor afford.

In order to pay his bills, Lesassier began to devise expedients. He could balance some of his tradesmen's bills against his own, for example his baker's, who was willing to barter free bread for free medical care as long as the two roughly evened out. His friend Maitland, a solicitor's clerk, gave him free legal advice in exchange for medical care for his family. But the majority of his creditors wanted money, and though debts could be postponed for an astonishingly long time—up to ten years, in some cases—they had to be paid eventually. Lesassier granted bills—that is, wrote post-dated checks—for payment of his debts, but if he did not have the money to "take them up," that is, no money to pay the check, he had to negotiate a new set of bills to extend the debt for a further period. His old friend Richard Jenoway, who moved to Edinburgh with his family in 1822, suggested another method of paying the most pressing of his bills. In an early nineteenth century version of debt consolidation, Lesassier could borrow money in £400 or £500 increments to pay off his tradesmen's debts. Many of these loans were from private parties, contracted through his man of business, Thomas Syme, and granting them seems to have been a reasonable, if risky, way of investing disposable capital. Since Lesassier never had the money to pay off the loans, he was compelled to pay the interest, usually 5 percent per year. A £500 loan, therefore, deducted £25 from his income. Since his expenses always outran his income, he found himself compelled to pile loan on loan, the interest from which, he bemoaned, "is a severe tax upon me."

Much of this was simple financial irresponsibility. He was living well beyond his income, hoping for a death, either his uncle's or Catherine's mother's, to save him from the continual threat of bankruptcy, of having to sell all he had at public auction and to leave Edinburgh in disgrace. Syme, "soft & heavy" as Lesassier considered him, lent him considerable sums and did his best to save his client from his own imprudence, only once tendering the exasperated "advice that I should retire to a cottage in England, after selling everything, & live in future on my half-pay!!" But not all of Lesassier's financial straits were his own fault. Perhaps half his patients did not pay their bills, and most paid only after several months, while his expenses, of course, accrued daily. Medical etiquette frowned upon his actually presenting a bill, and his usual practice was simply to keep calling until the patient offered to pay him: "pay my last visit to Mrs. McPherson, Leith," he wrote on one occasion, "I was in hopes she would pay me, but she did not which disappointed me, for, I am almost penniless." If pressed, he could take a patient to court who did not pay, but the trouble and expense made it hardly worthwhile, for he could not recover the legal costs associated with the suit. Nor could he charge patients interest or a late fee for late payment of bills, though he had to pay interest on loans contracted to repay his own creditors. The loans of the day did not include principle and interest in the repayment schedule, so he could not look forward to working them off over time. "Nothing short of a miracle," it seemed to him, could extricate him from his financial embarrassments.

The miracle could not come from increased practice. The seventy families that constituted his practice by 1821 meant that he delivered one or two children every few weeks. His average fee was four guineas for attendance leading up to an actual delivery, but he followed standard medical practice in charging more or less if he thought his patient's circumstances warranted it. Mr. McKenzie paid £2 for his wife's delivery, while Lord Elibank paid £21; Mr. Banner paid £30, and Mrs. Siddons paid £50. When one patient "had the assurance" to send merely £2 for her fee, he "wrote to her . . . affecting to suppose it a mistake, as I never accepted less than £5 or 5 guineas from a lady; & she immediately sent me £3." In some cases he even had to accept payment in kind, like the "two cheap pictures" he received from "Mrs. Kay or rather Mrs. Alexander mistress to Kay landscape painter." For Lesassier to have supported his establishment while paying off his debts he would have had to earn at least £500 per year, nearly double the £282 he made in 1821. That meant either delivering at least one patient every two or three days, a quite incredible increase in practice, or exchanging all his four-guinea for fifty-guinea patients, a calculation which gives some perspective to his rapture over his patients' footmen. Indeed, his patients' financial status directly affected his own, for the "lower ranks of the middle classes" were as liable as he to be rich in consumer goods but cash-poor and unable to pay their bills. They were liable, too, to consider a physician a luxury item when times grew hard, and though they might call Lesassier in emergencies and in the first anxious pregnancy, they were apt to choose the less expensive midwife in subsequent normal pregnancies. "Mean, deceitful wretch," Lesassier wrote in fury at one such recently delivered patient. "It was only on Monday last I called upon her. She made me believe, she was only six months pregnant. What consummate duplicity . . . what a loss to me, who, at present, am so miserably poor, besides the injurious report, that she employed Dr. Alexander Hamilton once, but, in her next confinement, she called in a woman!" He had no alternative financial resources: the furnishings, plate, and paintings so essential to appearances had little resale value, and the persistence of his debts made it impossible even for him to follow Syme's advice and leave Edinburgh. Small wonder that he hoped so fervently for one of the two deaths that would end his financial anxieties once and for all; small wonder that it was impossible for him to forego the transitory pleasure of a hundred and one trivial purchases, for what was an additional £2 or £5 or £10 to his ever-increasing financial burden. He tried to acquire another £100 per annum by asking Catherine's mother for the money, offering to maintain her son in exchange; he also tried asking his uncle for first £100, then £60, as a salary, instead of his payment of half fees. In both attempts he was unsuccessful, and the concerned reader can only note that such an increase would have made little difference: he would have required at least £135 per annum to maintain his existing expenses, including interest on loans, let alone pay any of his loans off. Each quarter he went to the bank to draw his half-pay and Catherine's dividend, "all of which instantly alas! melts away amidst my countless debts like snow before the fire."

With so little hope of increasing his income from practice, Lesassier tried other expedients. He bought Catherine a piano, and she briefly tried to give piano lessons, the only respectable way a physician's wife could earn money. Jenoway, whose finances were as "horribly embarrassed poor fellow" as his friend's, proposed several unlikely schemes for restoring their finances: investing in a technique for calico-printing, though Lesassier "doubted any such discovery," lending his name "to a book proposed to be published by the claimant for the Crawford peerage," or, if all else failed, "retiring to pass our lives in Jersey."

Prudently, Lesassier rejected all of these for a more successful expedient of his own, applying for a disability pension from the War Office. According to his application for a pension, "While accompanying the magistrates of the village who were endeavoring to secure carts for my sick, resistance was opposed to their authority, & I received a violent contused wound on one leg from a large angular fragment of granite, which was thrown at the escort by an enraged peasant (November 30, 1811)." This wound "produced excessive pain and almost wholly disabled me from walking." He "disregarded it so far as to proceed in the performance" of his duty, but took the opportunity of his leave to return to the care of his father, "a physician in the north of England." There, under his father's care, he slowly recovered, but returned to his regiment against his father's advice. The wound was such that only his love of duty enabled him to make it through the rest of the war, for "as might naturally be expected," he wrote, "I always suffered extensive uneasiness & pain afterwards, whenever I underwent any unusual fatigue." Of course, his arduous duties, first as acting regimental surgeon during the campaigns of 1812, and later as staff surgeon in the Portuguese army—which he took care to detail, referring to "Sir James MacGregor's personal recollections" for support—required immense exertions on his part, but "instead of taking the smallest advantage of the injury I had sustained in the performance of my duty, I never once contemplated the possibility of my ever being forced to submit my claims for a provision." It was only now, when he had acceded to his uncle's "repeated representations" and set up in practice in Edinburgh that he found himself "at once disabled from gaining a subsistence by my profession & maimed for the remainder of my life," for he could hardly walk the many miles required for visiting his patients. For that reason, he most respectfully requested a pension.

This account was, to say the least, a great embellishment of the truth. As a boy he had injured his Achilles tendon—it prevented him from learning to dance during his first stay in Edinburgh in 1805—and his journals for November 1811, though incomplete, refer to a blow to his leg, apparently caused either by a kick from a horse or by some other accident received while mounting or dismounting. But the journals also make very clear that by that time Lesassier had set his heart on a leave of absence. Certainly he did not record being hit by a rock—there is no mention of any ill treatment by Portuguese peasants at any time—and receiving a blow that at first led him to imagine "that the tibia was shattered to pieces." As for the rest of his application for a pension, it was an outright lie. In December 1811, Lesassier had set sail from Lisbon to England, and had spent the next three months with Ella in Manchester, not under his father's care. There is no sign that he was ever inconvenienced at all by the injury to his leg. To support his story, though, he enlisted Pierre's aid. He wrote a letter purported to come from Pierre, and requested that his father copy it as though he had written it on 30 March 1812. Pierre's letter gives a detailed account of Lesassier's wound, but despite showing that Lesassier had some knowledge of injuries to the bone, it is not very convincing, ending with the stilted sentence "Under these circumstances, I therefore consider his leaving me at present (March 30th) to join his regiment again on Foreign Service, as an injudicious, rash, & dangerous experiment."

Lesassier's account of his present disability was, again, completely untrue: he went for a daily walk of several miles around Edinburgh, and he had no trouble making rounds from Princes Street to the far-flung suburbs of Leith, Newhaven, and Stockbridge. He even walked to the seaside town of Portobello when necessary, a distance of at least eight miles each way. It is hard to see how anyone could have believed his story and even the medical board did not merely accept it, requiring Lesassier to go to London on two separate occasions to have his leg examined. "So much is my mind occupied with my approaching business at the Board," he wrote, "that I feel—rightly, too, as if all my future comfort & respectability, not to say even my personal safety, depend on my success! . . . & begin to tremble for the decision." Perhaps the medical board examined the original injury to the achilles tendon, or perhaps the injury in 1811 had left some visible sign. In any case he was "so supremely successful" that his pension of £70 was "granted for life, an advantage, I never even durst hope for!! . . . What a glorious piece of good fortune," and he celebrated, characteristically, by spending money: "I immediately buy Catherine some valuable presents."

"I cannot rest satisfied," Isabella wrote, "till I impart part of the pleasure I feel to you, My Dearest Alexander for the glad tidings, conveyed, in your letter of last night. . . . We are truly & sincerely happy—at your complete success . . . which was well worth the journey." The journey had been worthwhile to her for another reason: she and Lesassier had finally had an opportunity to meet again after so many years. To all appearances, it was a cheerful family party, for Lesassier got on well with Isabella's husband, Thomas Hodgeson. "I had heard so much of you," Hodgeson wrote, "I know how dear you were to Isabella, I longed to see, to regard, to esteem you—*I now do all*—I am no flatterer— Sincerity is my motto," and "it gratifies Hodgeson & me," wrote Isabella "to find our home, proved so happy a one, to you." But beneath the surface, the sexual tension must have crackled, and Lesassier and Isabella had at least one private conversation late at night after Hodgeson and the children had gone to bed. In a formal letter, written at home, Isabella merely noted that she was "gratified beyond expression that your senti- ments of affection, were in such perfect unison, with my own." Away from her family at a spa, she could be more candid. "What would I give—to have you with me, at this moment—*facing me sitting alone in my room* half undressed—& every soul in the house asleep!" she wrote. "What an opportunity—for *renewing* our vows of unalterable affec- tion. . . . I have lately dreamt often, that we were *together*, I attribute *that feeling*, to my *sleeping alone*." Their visit "was short in time, but how *truly transporting* . . . you may guess my feelings—burn this—& always write affectionately, but *with caution*, God bless you."

The addition of £70 per annum brought the Hamiltons' yearly income up to £280, independent of practice, but it was still not nearly enough, and it was as much from desperation as inclination that in 1821 Lesassier turned to writing *Edward Neville; or, The Memoirs of an Orphan*. The hero had several changes of name. His first name went from Henry to Edward, and his surname from Derwent to Neville. The former is the more important, since it is clear that a major requirement of the young hero's name is that it might have, like Alexander himself, a nickname rather different from the formal name: instead of Sandy for Alexander, the hero was called either Harry for Henry or Ned for Edward. Young Edward is orphaned at an early age, and his mother dies without revealing the name of her wealthy family. He is raised by a Mr. Melburne, a character who begins the novel as a wealthy gentleman, but soon comes to resemble Pierre Lesassier both in improvidence and financial misfortune. In the novel, Mr. Melburne is fooled into marrying Dorothy, his foolish, vulgar housekeeper, who speaks in an outlandish idiom and schemes to alienate her husband's affection from his charge. The marriage alienates Mr. Melburne himself from the affections of his lifelong friend, Sir Charles Grosvenor, who has a haughty wife and a lovely daughter, Sophie. As his fortunes decline, Melburne is forced to leave his home and go to Paris with Doro- thy, young Edward, and their servant, Timothy. On the way, Mr. Melburne is impressed as a common sailor, Dorothy abducted and taken to a brothel, and Edward dumped out onto the road. Edward obtains help to rescue his guardian and rejoin Dorothy, who—in an episode sure to gladden the heart of any modern reader of *Clarissa*—gave her would-be rapist and his accomplice "a spice of her mind; and, when she had said all she had to say, she took the poker out of the fire, red hot . . . and so, flourishing it about their ears, she frightened them in such a way that they durst not follow her, and she got safe into the street." The quartet continue to France, where they meet the Marchioness de Montsalve, her lovely daughter Emily, and her Scottish nurse, Mrs. Henderson. Their coach is attacked by robbers, which Mr. Melburne and Edward fend off. In the manuscript, Edward rescues the fair Emily from rape, but after successive rewrites this was softened to a mere rescue from being bruised by her would-be abductor; she is also allowed to demonstrate her exquisite sensibility by the length of time it takes for her to recover from the overwhelming fright of being attacked. There is less action in the second volume. Emily and Edward fall in love, assisted by Mrs. Henderson, but are separated by Emily's mother, who disapproves of the match. Edward is bereft, but continues to seek his fortune. He saves the life of a wealthy Scottish gentleman residing in Paris, Dr. Macintosh, is befriended by him, and finally acquires some education. Mr. Melburne, finding his fortunes worsened, rather than improved, by their stay in Paris, decides to return to his own small estate.

In the third volume Edward, still searching for some means of earning his living, decides to volunteer for a regiment bound for the Peninsula, hoping for the opportunity to display some obvious bravery that will procure him a commission. Poverty forces him, accompanied by the faithful though extremely stupid Timothy, to walk to London. On the way he rescues a lady in a carriage with runaway horses. He is successful in his plans to volunteer for the regiment, and leaves for the Peninsula to serve in an unnamed regiment, clearly based on the 42nd, which in 1812 did include at least one volunteer, John Lane. Edward quickly demonstrates conspicuous bravery and is commended for it to the colonel of the regiment, who turns out to be none other than Sir Charles Grosvenor. It is at this point, too, that he learns that the lady he rescued on the way to London was Lady Grosvenor. He is given a commission and gallantly charges up the ladder during the fateful siege of Burgos, but he is treacherously attacked from behind by one of the soldiers in his regiment, an officer he had quarreled with on the way out to Portugal who had subsequently lost his commission and been forced to enlist as a private. The quarrel, we may note in passing, is based on the one concerning Mrs. Geddes's dog, while the demoted officer is based on Ryan, a hospital mate who did lose his commission. The wounded Edward is cared for by "the amiable & intelligent Assistant Surgeon" of the regiment, just as was the real John Lane, also wounded at Burgos. Edward is soon invalided back to England. Thus ends the third volume, and Edward's wartime experience, which is a pity, for as the *Monthly Review* observed, the "history of the hero's campaigns in the Peninsula" is "the best portion of the whole"; indeed, it went so far as to suggest that they "may perhaps be read with interest."

The final volume sees the hero back in England and brings the novel to its denouement. Edward finds his beloved Emily is betrothed to another, and after an awkward confrontation, in which Edward again saves her life, learns that she has agreed to this only because her mother had assured her that Edward had married another lady and had taken the trouble to have the deception published in the newspapers. Edward also finally learns of his mother's family by being befriended by an elderly Scotswoman who notices a peculiar birthmark on his arm. The Scotswoman turns out to be the dowager Countess of Harlington and his own grandmother, while the birthmark turns out to be the family motto, "Revirescam" (Let me be young again). If it seems improbable that so distinctive a birthmark would have remained so long unnoticed it is no more than the reader has come to expect. Edward is welcomed to her family as "Edward Desmond, Earl of Harlington"; Emily's haughty mother gives her consent to their marriage; and even Sophie Grosvenor, Lord Grosvenor's beautiful daughter, is rewarded by her author with a growing affection for one of Edward's faithful friend Stewart.

"We apprehend this book was written by a very young author," the *Monthly Review* noted; the reviewer was wrong in fact—Lesassier was thirty-four—but right in principle, for the author of the book obviously saw himself in his hero, and young Edward does not display a single adult characteristic. His education, a major theme of the first two volumes, appears never to have been completed, but instead remains in a state of suspension from around his seventeenth year. He displays no commitment to his regiment, which he makes no efforts to return to after being informed of his noble birth, and certainly no constancy to his beloved: once he believes she does not love him any longer, he happily pursues young Portuguese ladies. Despite the trend for bathos in contemporary novels, there is no sorrow that touches him or the reader, no tenderness toward any character, no responsibility toward any higher principle. It is as though Lesassier, in recasting his own youth and wartime adventures into the hero's, has rethought himself back to age twenty, and then brought himself no further. The result is that though the book is filled with incident, plot contrivances, and contemporary novelistic clichés—how often in novels of the period was the course of true love put asunder by false information presented to the hero or heroine!—it is exceedingly monotonous, "a long and dull tale," as the *Monthly Review* states, "about a number of vulgar and foolish people."

Yet however limited in literary quality, *Edward Neville* is a marvelous vehicle for showing the contradictions and ambiguities in Lesassier's world. He wrote it very quickly, writing as many as ten pages a day, and completed the whole in eleven months. In writing he fulfilled the advice given by a modern romance writer, Phyllis Whitney, that the "first necessary ingredient" of writing romantic novels is to love reading them. "While I am in the process of writing, I am submerged in my heroine and her problems—and having a wonderful time. Me and all those dark-browed heroes!" Lesassier, too, became submerged in his hero, his problems, and—in his case—fair-haired heroines. Though *Edward Neville* is not a true story, it is passionately, intensely based on the author's own life and "innermost practical feelings," as novels were expected to be. Sometimes this commitment to Lesassier's own experience is tedious, as when he gives vent to his boyhood resentment of Ann Collins or his boyhood "exasperation" at his father's "good natured weakness," "rustic air and old fashioned clothes." Sometimes it is pedestrian, as when the young hero takes time out from brilliant heroism to transport sick soldiers, as the young assistant surgeon Lesassier had done. But often it is revealing: in the description of the many ways in which a gentleman of independent fortune could be driven to penury, or in the narrator's anxiety about his own social status, made explicit in the fear of being insulted and imposed upon by both ends of the social spectrum, "stared, and pointed, and grinned at," by the lower orders, and passed over by the great, whose servants are instructed to "fairly shut the door" in the hero's face. Lesassier's passion for clothes and admiration for his own appearance is here, in the description of young Neville's dress for the dinner party at which, unexpectedly, his true identity will be revealed: "the gorgeous new jacket, and scarlet waistcoat, richly embroidered with gold . . . the profusion of lace that covered his uniform, the two massive gold epaulets . . . which gave him so dazzling an appearance, that he could not help smiling when he looked at himself in the mirror," just as the reader cannot help smiling at the disclaimer that it was for good manners, "and not for the sake of displaying the exquisite symmetry of his leg, that he put on silk stockings and shoes."

Lesassier's passion for consumer goods is also here, as well as his conviction of their value as a medium of exchange in relationships. Edward gives Mrs. Henderson, as reward for her many faithful efforts, "a superb folio-copy of the Bible, and a pair of richly mounted spectacles, which the worthy and venerable gentlewoman received from him with tears in her eyes." Emily gives Edward, as a sure sign of her love, "a little green velvet case, containing a diamond brooch . . . which enclosed a beautifully braided lock of hair, and with the little magic word *Emily* engraved on the back of this valuable ornament." At their clandestine parting in Paris, she even offers him money "in a hesitating and embarrassed tone of voice." "Angelic girl!—adorable Emily!" he responded, "while he clasped her in his arms, and gently impressed a kiss of pure and spotless innocence upon her timid cheek. 'A thousand and a thousand thanks for this additional proof of your affection.'" Yet though he would not accept such a "practical mark of her attachment . . . until no resource remain"—"Had you offered me your miniature, I should have prized it above everything I have in the world; but money— no, no, Emily, that I could never bring myself to receive"—young Edward, like his author, had no qualms about accepting the usual financial rewards for true love. "Deign only at some future day," he told his beloved, "to give me a claim to share what Heaven has blessed you with, and then, I shall be reconciled to what, till then, I should hate myself if I could be capable of."

The hero's final apotheosis to the aristocracy is paved with possessions. It is deliberately presented as a journey, as Edward, his patron Dr. Macintosh and friend Stewart wind their way toward the Harlington castle, where they have been invited, as they think, for a dinner party. "In proportion as they drew nearer, the prospect became more and more interesting," and Edward "repeatedly declared that, even in Portugal itself, he had never seen any thing more beautifully picturesque." The situation of the castle certainly owed more to the author's experiences in the Iberian peninsula than the Highlands: in the foreground, "a green meadow, studded with . . . wild flowers," and sloping "down before them to the rocky brink of a shallow mountain-stream," while in the middle distance, "crowning a loftier and more rugged height, . . . the castellated mansion, which they were about to visit." On driving up they were met by a servant dressed with a magnificence that, to the irreverent reader, appears to rival Edward's, "of white, faced with scarlet, and richly trimmed with broad gold lace." They "ascended a noble staircase, and were shown into a sumptuous drawing room." The dining room was huge, and decorated by "real Gobelin tapestry," as Edward could see "by the artificial light that was profusely shed on every side—from a superb diamond-cut lustre, with frosted Argand lamps, which hung from the centre of the room, besides four large silver candelabras on the table." The dinner plates "were beautiful specimens of painting and gilding, on the most costly china; but the tureens, dishes, wine-coolers, and every thing else, were composed of massive chased silver." During dinner, which "comprised every thing that was either rare or delicious," the guests were attended by no less than five servants and a butler. Surrounded by such profusion, it is no wonder that Edward was so "intently admiring the exquisite landscape that was painted on his dessert-plate" that he almost missed the entrance of his grandmama. Rising with the others, he was struck with surprise when she "pressed him in an anguish of tenderness to her bosom," informed the company of his true identity, and called upon them to join with her "in a bumper,—to the YOUNG EARL." "Edward," she summoned him, "take your proper place at the foot of your own table," thereby celebrating his elevation from the devoted admirer to the rightful owner of the luxury goods so lovingly depicted.

The novel also reveals Lesassier's attitudes toward his own actions, for it shows that he knew perfectly well when he had himself violated the conventions of good behavior for a novel hero. The novel includes many incidents based on these violations, transmuted to cleanse them of any equivocal character. In real life, for example, he had shown no interest in constancy to his beloved Ella, certainly not in the Peninsula, where he had pursued any available woman. He wanted to include some of these incidents, and so had his hero pursue two young Portuguese ladies on his arrival in Lisbon. Yet this posed a problem: how was this flagrant infidelity to be explained? Tom Jones had been similarly unfaithful to Sophia, but novel heroes had grown more refined over the years, and Reginald Dalton, on his knees before his heroine in a novel published the same year as *Edward Neville*, swore "I ask for nothing, Miss Hesketh, I hope for nothing, I expect nothing. . . . But since I do kneel, I will not rise till I have said it—I love you, Ellen—I have loved you long—I have loved you from the first hour I saw you. I never loved before, and I shall never love another." Certainly Lesassier felt that his hero's conduct required some explanation, and so he made Edward the recipient of a letter, ostensibly from Emily but really forged by her mother, in which she informed him she was married. This perfectly justified Edward's seeking "some other and more deserving of her sex. Emily had certainly, thought he, merited a still harsher return, for so much inconstancy and caprice; and, at all events, he was henceforwards at liberty to act in that respect as he himself thought proper." In the novel, too, Edward beat his faithful and devoted servant Timothy out of mere bad temper, directing "his blows with such velocity and effect, that Timothy's eyes were speedily closed up, and he began to bellow out with pain and terror," just as Lesassier had sometimes beat Manoel in Portugal. Unkindness to servants had respectable literary precedents—Roderick Random had often been thoroughly unpleasant to the faithful Sprat—but by the 1800s ingratitude was no mere foible but a real sin, hard to countenance in a hero. So was aggression without a substantive cause: the hero of Richard Cumberland's novel *Henry* beat up the local bully only after much provocation, then quickly demonstrated his noble character by saving his antagonist's life. Lesassier's justification of his hero shows his own uneasiness with his past behavior: whereas the real-life Manoel was almost certainly smaller than his real-life attacker, the fictional Timothy is deliberately made "older and stronger" than young Neville.

Lesassier had great hopes for his novel as a solution to his financial problems: "All my comfort depends on my book selling well." He hoped to get £300 for it, but worked his expectations down to £200, or even £100: "even that sum will delight me; & I then may think of attempting another which I trust in God will finally extricate me from all my painful embarrassments." But the Edinburgh bookseller to whom he sent the first version of the manuscript sent it back "with an impertinent note, rejecting it & almost telling me to burn it!! as it would merely add to the number of books, without '*any redeeming qualities*' & would neither do them 'service' nor me 'credit'?!!!" This was a blow with which any prospective author may sympathize. "I may safely say that I never was so shocked in my life," Lesassier wrote, "& really, don't well know how I got through the evening. Still, however, I do not despair of getting £100 for it in London, if they won't buy it here. I know what to expunge, & it will be strange, indeed, if I cannot make it a good book. But I must say that it has depressed me excessively; so much, indeed, that I can scarcely undertake the alteration of the book at all." He rallied his spirits, sent it to London, and received "my ill starred book again from Longman and Orme with rather a gratifying criticism, holding out the probability of its being published at last!!" Alas, it was never the financial success he had hoped, though he tried to help sales by inquiring "for my book at the Circulating Libraries, so as to make them buy it." He read sections of it aloud to his friends in the evening "to their infinite delight. Alas! if the public had only been of the same opinion"; but it was of no use in helping him clear his debts. It had been published "on the plan of sharing the profit & loss," but Longman and Company, who published many forgettable novels in the 1820s, did not intend to lose either their money or their space. Three hundred of the five hundred copies printed sold in 1823 at the price of 18 shillings 4 pence, enough to recoup the expenses of printing and advertising. In 1824, therefore, the book was discounted to three shillings in order to sell off most of the remaining copies quickly. There was no call for a new printing, and in 1825 Longman and Company sent Lesassier word that his share amounted to £15, 11 shillings, and 4 pence, half the total profit of £31/2/8. This "profit" actually came in the form of a new bill, for Lesassier had ordered fifty copies of the book at a cost of £51/1/0, and his publishers called on him to pay the £35/9/8 remaining. They agreed to cancel the debt in return for the thirty-five copies of *Edward Neville* that Lesassier still had, much to his relief: "It would be hard, indeed, first to have all the trouble of writing the book, &, then, lose money by it!" Immediately after finishing *Edward Neville*, he had "begun another novel. . . . It amuses me & distracts my attention from thinking of my debts; & after all, there is no harm done; for, God knows I have time enough on my hands." But the failure of the first to remunerate him dissuaded him from going beyond the preliminary plans for a second. It remained a wistful dream: "Ah!" he wrote on reading *Chelsea Pensioners*, like his, a novel with a military hero, "if I could have written such a book!"

Oliver Goldsmith noted in one of his reviews that the novel at hand "concludes, as they all do: 'Thus, before I was thirty years of age, I saw myself completely happy, beloved by my family, and more especially so by a wife whose lover I am as well as husband. From that happy moment no misfortunes have intervened to intercept our tranquility. Our family has received the additional increase of several children, and I have now six alive, all well provided for and thriving in the world.'" But "Reader," Goldsmith apostrophized, "if thou hast ever known such perfect happiness as these romance-writers can so liberally dispense, thou hast enjoyed greater pleasure than has ever fallen to our lot. How deceitful are these imaginary pictures of felicity! and, we may add, how mischievous too! The young and the ignorant lose their taste of present enjoyment by opposing to it those delusive daubings of consummate bliss they meet with in novels; and, expecting more happiness than life can give, feel but the more poignancy in all its disappointments." In his own romance, Lesassier had indeed liberally dispensed perfect happiness. It remained to be seen whether he could ever arrange for real life to live up to it.

# CHAPTER 11

# Consecutive Chain of Corroborative Evidence

By 1822, Lesassier realized that his establishment on Picardy Place was too expensive, and he made the decision to move to a cheaper one in the Old Town, in Argyll Square. It was a prudent decision, for he reviewed his "affairs; & I find to my infinite satisfaction, that they promise to be completely redeemed by our change of residence." If he could also have brought himself to reduce his establishment to two female servants, while cultivating the middle classes rather more assiduously, he might eventually have freed himself from all financial embarrassments. If he had, in other words, been able to give up the appearance of a gentleman, he might have been able to achieve that handsome independence that he had earlier considered the essential feature of one. But where his perceived rank was at stake, Lesassier found it hard to be prudent, and he was "wretchedly low at the thought of leaving this beautiful house," especially after having put so much money into it. The Old Town had become déclassé, and in moving there he had to rely on his manservant and carriage to "enable us to hold up our head." The move made him unhappy for another reason as well: his cousin Mary Campbell received an anonymous letter accusing Lesassier "of going to Argyll Square, merely to be nearer Anne." Anne Walker—Mrs. Colonel Walker—was one of his "favorites," and rumors had already been circulating about his "improper intimacy" with her. Though he dined often with her and her husband, he could "not walk home with her," after paying a professional visit to her younger sister, "lest it should seem as if I had met her purposely."

Lesassier's intimacy with Anne as well as other patients was indeed improper and unprofessional, and it gives some point to the continued prejudice against male midwives. He enjoyed having his beautiful young lady patients look up to him as a physician and as a man; he became their confidant in their most intimate concerns; and he encouraged their falling in love with him, both for the gratification it gave him and from the conviction it would lead to renewed visits and referrals. It is not clear how often Lesassier actually had sexual intercourse with patients, though since a pregnant woman could not become pregnant by him, one of the main checks on his pursuit was removed. It is clear, however, that his relationships with his long-term patients went through the same cycle of intense involvement, Portuguese comments with Greek transliteration, and often bitter quarrels as those with his young lady friends. The repeated intimacy, emotional as well as physical, conspired to drive him to that extreme of passion that, in his view, absolved him of all responsibility. It also robbed him of all prudence, and, except for using Portuguese to mask his remarks, he made little attempt to hide his attraction. Scandal, to borrow his earlier phrase, was poised to attack him openmouthed, and in the fall of 1822 he set a consecutive chain of events in motion that linked his name with scandal for years to come.

The trouble began just after Lesassier moved to Argyll Square, when James Hamilton became so ill with "a severe cough which has required various violent remedies," that he could not see his patients for nearly three weeks. He called on Lesassier to assist him, and though Lesassier fulminated at the timing ("The Doctor is confined to the house. But, except two patients, I get nobody to visit for him, & I have no deliveries!!! He might almost have purposely made choice of this particular time for laying himself up, so little is there to do for him in that department") he did end up delivering several high-paying patients, so that he got "several large fees, than which, at present, nothing could be more acceptable. In fact, this month, I make £48.16!!" Hamilton recovered from his illness enough to resume his responsibilities, but his cough continued, especially at night, and for the first time he had to miss several of the lectures for his spring course on midwifery. It continued through the summer, and he decided to take his first vacation from practice by spending the month of September in his country house. He left his patients in the care of Lesassier, "my nephew," he wrote to Mr. Hastings Anderson, whose wife was due in September, "who has for several years been my assistant, and I can truly say that unless I could place every reliance on his skill and attention I should never devolve such an important task on him." A flattering recommendation, but Hamilton was no fool: he was not about to give up his practice to his nephew and was careful to refer to Lesassier as "my substitute." Moreover, he added in a paragraph that could serve as a model of shrewd patient management, since "Mrs. Anderson ought on every account to be indulged in her wishes on such an occasion," he would "not take offense if Lesassier be not employed," and recommended two other "respectable gentlemen in the same line . . . Dr. Beilby and Dr. Minto," concluding that "the interest I take in Mrs. Anderson's welfare leads me to hope that her choice may fall on one of the three." Lesassier's own methods of dealing with patients would have benefited from more attention to his uncle's, but that did not keep him from being enraged by this letter: instead of "specifically recommending, and personally introducing, me to them," Lesassier later complained, his uncle had "mixed up my name with that of other medical practitioners, whom they had never before even heard speak of." As always, a perceived affront absolved him, he felt, of any responsibility toward the perpetrator. In this case, his resentment toward his uncle led him to the greatest of his professional blunders, attempting to steal his patients.

Lesassier had been anxiously watching the progress of James Hamilton's illness since April, when he and Catherine had amused themselves one beautiful moonlight night, "by anticipating the consequences of the Doctor's death." Each new intelligence regarding Hamilton's illness brought them hope that "His day . . . will come," while each sign of recuperation led to the "fear . . . that all will be in vain, & that, as usual, he will soon recover." At the end of August, his uncle out of town, Lesassier lost no time in ingratiating himself with Hamilton's patients. "I have the gratification of again being engaged to attend that capricious woman Lady Elibank," he wrote the day after James Hamilton left, "which I never looked for, & am again in such favor that I am unfortunately asked to dine with her & Lord E. at the Royal Hotel on Friday!" He was also "engaged to attend Mrs. Anderson"—the recipient of Hamilton's letter—"(one of the first Ladies here, though poor at present) who is so exasperated with the Doctor, that she declares she will always employ me in future!!" In all, seven of his uncle's patients called upon him during the month, and three asked him to continue his attendance even after James Hamilton's return on 25 September. In fact, he noted with complacency on 26 September, "my Uncle returned yesterday evening (in better health than ever!!). I fancy he will not be much gratified with my getting so many of his patients. . . . Such is the punishment due to cold-hearted grasping!"

James Hamilton was not in the least gratified, and he made that point at once during a consultation for a dangerously ill patient, Mrs. Cockburn. Though Lesassier was called first, "After a day of toil, & her getting better, I have to undergo the mortification of having my uncle sent for. We have high words about my getting his patients." They had high words, too, about Mrs. Cockburn's treatment. Lesassier claimed to be "triumphant; for, she actually is better in the morning," but his "uncle's exasperated feelings & opposition" continued, and he succeeded "by dint of pushing & independence, . . . to exclude me almost from attending." Mrs. Cockburn recovered; "He will gain little by it I hope," Lesassier wrote, sure, now, that his fortunes were on the rise independently of his uncle. Even though "The Doctor's spite manifests itself more than ever," he was unconcerned, "I despise it, & him too."

There is no sign that he was aware he was playing with fire. James Hamilton had forgiven much, but he was not about to forgive this: perhaps he even welcomed the opportunity for a final break. Hamilton "had not been forty-eight hours in Town," he told Lesassier, "before several of the chief medical men here"—perhaps including Drs. Beilby and Minto—"had called on him to express their detestaton of Lesassier's conduct, and to say that they could no longer consider" Lesassier as his nephew. "From the old rascal," Lesassier wrote, "it is quite evident that I have nothing more to expect in this world," and it became even more evident a few days later, for Hamilton acted swiftly and efficiently to sever relations with his errant nephew. On 30 October he sent Lesassier his share of the payment for his patients, amounting to nearly £200. As a result, Lesassier earned nearly £500 during the year, the largest income he ever had. On the same day, however, Hamilton sent Lesassier "a Promissary Note, at one day's date, for the money which he had lent me at different times." In an excess of naiveté, Lesassier assumed that the promissary note was merely to replace his former notes, that is, a mere bookkeeping matter, and signed it. "What, however, was my astonishment, terror, and indignation," he wrote, "on receiving, in three days afterward . . . a most violent and abusive letter . . . in which he withdrew all connection with me, and expected, *an immediate settlement of the debt* I owed him." The debt amounted to £624, and as Hamilton well knew, Lesassier had no money to pay it. As Hamilton may also have known or guessed, Lesassier never had any intention of repaying it, since he considered Hamilton's many loans as no more than his due: part of his "astonishment, terror, and indignation" must have come from the realization that he had been completely outmaneuvered in their private tug-of-war. His man of business, Syme, was able to raise a £900 loan for him at the usual 5 percent interest—he had been trying to raise a loan in any case, to help pay off his other debts—and with that he repaid his uncle. He tried, after much hesitation, to come to a reconciliation, "in order to get as much practice from him as I can," but though Hamilton consented to a meeting, Lesassier refused to admit he had ever been in the wrong. Though they parted "to *appearance* friends," the "little wretch" answered a later letter "by saying that he will not employ me for some time to come. Or, in other words, not at all!"

James Hamilton took advantage of further imprudence on Lesassier's part to remove him from the Lying-In Hospital as well. Lesassier's associate, John Mackintosh, had become embroiled in a fierce quarrel with several Edinburgh physicians, including James Hamilton, and wrote a series of pamphlets attacking Hamilton's obstetrical teachings and the management of the Lying-In Hospital. Hamilton "endeavored," he wrote to Lesassier, "to bring under your review, the extraordinary fact of your being the *intimate* friend of a person who had *falsely* & *wantonly* attacked your uncle. In saying this I have no occasion to express what I feel—I leave you at liberty to choose your own friends and ever am, my dear nephew, yours affectionately, James Hamilton Junior." But Hamilton made it clear that in choosing Mackintosh, Lesassier had chosen against his uncle, and he did not shield him when one of Mackintosh's charges descended on his head. Mackintosh had alleged, among other criticisms of the Lying-In Hospital, that no patient records were kept, probably on information from Lesassier himself. Hamilton claimed that the records had been kept as long as the hospital had been under his sole direction, and blamed Lesassier for their current neglect: "I fairly own," he wrote to Lesassier, "that I never was more surprised and shocked at any want than when I found that no proper account of the cases of any of the patients had been kept." With the excuse that Lesassier's residence "is so far removed," Hamilton dismissed him from the Lying-In Hospital, writing, "there has been . . . *no public* nor *extraordinary* measure of *severity* in finding that it is easier for myself and probably better for the Institution that *I* should take the sole charge of the Hospital." "In short," Lesassier wrote, "he genteelly gets rid of me. Well, I am well rid of a very troublesome & responsible office." Perhaps. But he had lost the only professional patron he had in Edinburgh, and no other physician of comparable influence would consult with him.

Lesassier could afford to flout his uncle, he was sure, because of the relationships he had formed with two of his uncle's patients, Lady Mary Ann Portsmouth and Lady Louisa Kintore, who, like many of the aristocracy, preferred to deliver their babies in town rather than in the country. Once again he was looking to patient, rather than professional patronage. More dangerously, he was relying on his personal influence rather than his professional skill, for the ladies were young and beautiful, and he was sure he could make conquests of them both. Lady Portsmouth was his first: "I have gained such amazing ascendancy over her," he wrote, "that she has actually engaged me to attend her in London if ever she be again in the family way!!! What a stroke this would be! What a noise it would make here. Why it would put an immense sum in my pocket, perhaps £200 or £300." He made every effort to increase his influence over her. He accompanied her on the first stage of her journey home, even though it meant leaving his other patients; and after taking "an affecting leave of her," he continued to correspond with his "sweet Lady Portsmouth; so that I hope she may not forget me." This was far from disinterested affection. He wanted her to employ him in her subsequent deliveries; even more, he wanted to become her personal physician, so that she would grant him an allowance of, he hoped, as much as £100 per year. By ingratiating himself with her, by being attentive, by—though he never quite says this—having her fall in love with him, he was sure that she, like his faithful Ella, would be happy to make him the master of both her heart and her possessions.

It was a flagrant breach of professional relations to try to take such advantage of a patient, and we could hardly fail to censure Lesassier were it not that in clear-headed pursuit of self-interest he was clearly outmatched. Lady Portsmouth came from the class that had literally written the book on it, Lord Chesterfield's *Letters*, widely regarded as advising readers to put their own advantage above conventional morality and "betray . . . a friend," as one parody put it, "If you find, to your int'rest, 'twill visibly tend." Lady Portsmouth was pleased to have Lesassier as a suitor, for she could use ever-attentive friends. Like the Marchioness de Montsalve who initially made use of Edward Neville and his guardian on their travels to Paris, Lady Portsmouth "had discovered the extreme inconvenience to which females are subject . . . without the countenance, protection, & assistance of the other sex." She was temporarily bereft of such countenance, protection, and assistance from her own family: her own husband had been confined for insanity, and his brother had brought suit to annul the marriage, in which case the title would pass to him, rather than Lady Portsmouth's child. Lady Portsmouth and her family contested the suit, and the case was brought before the House of Lords. She lost the case, and the marriage was annulled shortly after her daughter's birth. Though she was given an allowance that would have seemed princely to Lesassier— £1,200 per year and £500 for expenses—it was much less than she was used to. Her consequence, and her reputation, suffered badly as well, aided by her own imprudent behavior, and the former Lady Portsmouth became the mere Miss Hanson with a newborn baby. A well-spoken physician to dance attendance was very welcome.

Lesassier found it was no easy matter being a courtier. It was as if a character from *Edward Neville*, with its careful delineation of how £300 per year could decline to £150 per year, had been thrust into the world of Susan Ferrier's aristocratic characters, where the £700 per annum that Lesassier considered an ample fortune was not even enough for the "cottages, curricles, and good family dinners" despised by a London grande dame. The young Lesassier had referred slightingly to shopkeeper's daughters as "seulement des Bourgeoise," and bemoaned his own middle-class practice, but for Lady Portsmouth, one suspects, he himself was merely a "bourgeois that nobody knows." "Mild, timid, gentle, dignified, & kind," she nonetheless kept Lesassier dangling for the next two years without giving him anything more than was absolutely necessary to retain his services. A grande dame herself, Lady Portsmouth demanded unlimited devotion. Lesassier had to visit her when she called, or risk a total break, and during the visits "every moment was devoted to my noble & generous hostess, as well from courtesy, as sound policy." Whenever he saw her—or when he, in turn, threatened to "have done with her for ever"—she would promise him an annuity of £100, or even £200 per year; but whenever he tried to obtain the money, he wrote, "I could never bring her to the wished-for point."

But Lady Portsmouth was not his only equivocal conquest, for after she left town that fateful September, he increasingly devoted his attentions to the beautiful Lady Kintore. It was inevitable that he fall in love with her. She was lovely and responsive and had been unhappily married for about a year. Just before her confinement, she had quarreled with her husband, while the "whim for a separation was in his head, only that he might enjoy more hunting," a whim to which Louisa had "joyfully acceded," according to her sister Emmeline Hawkins. From the first, Lesassier was attracted to Louisa, and his attraction was increased by the manner of her delivery, for the need for active intervention had transformed him from substitute physician to savior. "I am hurried & fatigued to day beyond all conception," he wrote, "I am called to the Countess Kintore, sit with her seven hours, &, after all, am forced to apply the forceps!!! Thank God as yet, every thing is safe. Never did I feel so much exhilirated in my whole life at such success! If things only continue to do equally well, what a glorious business it will be." He paid his usual two visits per day, but before long his second visit extended all evening, and he began to chaff if any other company was there, even her sisters Emmeline and Isabella. By 10 October, two weeks after her delivery, he was hopelessly in love with Louisa, and writing in Portuguese, "O Deo! que divina prazer" (What divine pleasure), with a large star in the margins. The next day he wrote "a secundo vez" (a second time), with another star, and the stars recurred as his intimacy with Louisa grew.

What did the stars signify? Though intercourse seems improbable so soon after delivery, we cannot rule it out, for Lesassier was sexually aroused by the sight of naked women no matter what their stage of pregnancy. "What an exquisite beauty! What iridescent symmetry!" he wrote of a patient he had delivered the day before; "Oh! what a matchless leg" he wrote of another who became his lover when six months pregnant, "then, too, what rapturous pleasure, actually kept up for ¾ hour." When aroused by a pretty girl Lesassier longed to place his hand, he wrote in Portuguese with Greek letters, in her beautiful and chaste vagina. He rhapsodized over one patient's "swelling, beautifully-turned throat, & bosom, & waist, & haunches, & feet . . . her matchless & blushing timidity." And how he could see, he wrote of another, without trembling with emotion, open to his view, her beautiful legs, her thighs, firm and palpitating, white and polished like ivory. Perhaps Louisa Kintore responded like that patient, her beautiful eyes, full of tears of love and tenderness, a small smile playing on her mouth, and all illuminated by a vivid, yet modest, blush; perhaps she pressed his hand to her heart and her lips, clasped him to her breast and passionately kissed him. Certainly there is every reason to believe their relations were passionate and sexual, even if they did not proceed to the "ultimate favors." And when Lady Kintore finally left town, "Oh what exquisitely poignant feelings were mine," Lesassier wrote, in a farewell reminiscent of his parting from his aunt Isabella years earlier. "I call on Louisa from 11½ till 12.10; & bid her farewell. I am almost shaking with grief, & hardly knowing what I do. I return home! Alas! poor Louisa!!!"

There is no reason to wonder at his passion. Louisa was precisely the young lady he had been longing for all these years, precisely the noble heroine to validate his sense of himself as a hero. Their affair was the fantasy of his novel come to life, lacking only the revelation of his own noble birth. As for Louisa, he was the dear, trusted friend, "my beloved Daddy," as she and her two sisters referred to him, but a daddy whose passionate attentions formed a marked contrast to her own husband's apparent neglect, for Lord Kintore was not even in Edinburgh when his child was born. It is clear enough what Louisa and Lesassier wanted, and what they discussed, at such great length each evening alone together. Louisa would get a separation from Lord Kintore and come to live in Edinburgh; Lesassier would be her personal physician, on whom she would settle £100 per year. His love for her, however passionate, was no more disinterested than his affection for Lady Portsmouth: Louisa, now, was to be the young lady he literally dreamed of, whose overwhelming love "relieves me from difficulties." As with Ella and his fictional Emily de Montsalve, his proof of her devotion was her willingness to serve him financially. She offered to sell her pearls for him during his final quarrel with his uncle, and, as with Ella, his affection led him to financial metaphors: "divine, matchless girl," he wrote, "what homage, what affection do I not owe thee. The services of a long life would not be more than a poor return for such goodness." He would not accept such a sacrifice, and for perhaps the first time, even registered scruples about accepting the £50—"What noble & disinterested generosity!"—she later sent him, refusing, like Edward Neville, to "take advantage of such devoted liberality until I have no other resource left." Indeed, the correspondences between his novel dialogue and journal entries are not accidental, for Lesassier was in the process of revising *Edward Neville* for Longman and Orme during the fall of 1822, precisely at the period of his affair with Lady Kintore. Life, it may have seemed to him, was imitating art in a most satisfactory manner.

His passion for Louisa was no better guarantee of his constancy than his marriage to Catherine. As always, he preferred young ladies in groups, playfully assuming the "character of *Turk*" and supposing the Hawkins sisters "the fair ones in an imaginary harem." His attentions to Emmeline Hawkins were marked and reciprocated. She had little "genius for *matrimony*," she told him, for "I grow horribly qualmish at the idea of being chained for life to one tiresome animal, who I know would never do half as much for *my* amusement, as I should for *his*." But Lesassier, safely married and delightfully and improperly affectionate, was another matter: though with "the generality of men, I find it quite impossible to relish their society, or care for them in return," she told him, she loved to dwell on "the delightful *thrill* of a kiss from lips I love"—his lips—even when "he to whom those lips belong is far away." When Lesassier extended his kisses to her sister Isabella, though, it made all three sisters acutely jealous of one another, destroying, Emmeline complained—though for her sisters, not Lesassier—"in some degree the harmony of our happy trio." As usual, Catherine was pressed into service as chaperone when the sisters came to call or went on drives, and as usual she, too, grew jealous of his new favorites. And throughout this period Lesassier continued his regular Sunday liaison with his maid Christian McKenzie.

Whether Louisa's and Lesassier's scheme could ever have succeeded is not certain; what was certain, to everyone but themselves, was that the whole affair was horribly imprudent, particularly as it continued in their correspondence, with Louisa pledging "eternal constancy." When part of that correspondence fell "into Catherine's hands," Lesassier complained, "she had taken up the thing in its most distorted form, & a violent rupture was the consequence. . . . I was almost distracted at such perfidy, ignorance, & folly. However, by that very evening's post, I brought Catherine to a proper view of the matter." The "proper view" must have been that he was no more than Lady Kintore's physician, and that she would relieve them from their financial embarassments, for when he discussed with Catherine a later letter from Louisa, again offering him £100 per year if she lived in Edinburgh, "Catherine is infinitely delighted at my good fortune!"

Catherine turned out to be the least of their worries. Emmeline sent an early warning of looming disaster. Rumors of Louisa's attachment for Lesassier had spread to their relatives, and "I told you," she wrote, "*that I had been quite thunder-struck at some remarks, made by my Aunt & Isabella, about poor Louisa's conduct; her alienated affections from Lord Kintore, her wish for a separate establishment, to enjoy more liberty & show, and her chief attraction to Edinburgh your increasing attentions.*" Had "Louisa carried the matter through, I believe more odium would have attached to me, than herself even . . . because at first—looking on the thing as unavoidable, and during Lord K's absence feeling highly indignant against him, *in consequence of Louisa's representations*—I defended her conduct, & did what I could to prove, that a separation could conduce to her happiness, and not be a discreditable thing if amicably arranged." Now back home, she was made aware by her family of the danger of their private fantasy, and began to draw back. In truth, she wrote Lesassier, she had been against the matter from the start, and had privately tried to use all her influence to persuade Louisa that "Lord Kintore . . . behaving so very affectionately to Louisa, & his baby *even she herself was obliged to own, it would really be sinful to forsake* so generous, and really kind hearted a man." Rather contradictorily, she added that Louisa "has dear girl been often greatly tried." Still, she insisted, "*had she not known you*, she would never have allowed herself to be so very indignant, *nor have thought of a separation*, but as a wretched, a humbling thing, and an expedient to which nothing but absolute necessity should drive her."

Lesassier was excessively enraged against Emmeline for this letter, "for, she again insinuates that Louisa's separation is all owing to me." He was even more upset after another letter, written in October 1823, in which Emmeline mentioned that Louisa again "is in the family way, & is not to be confined here in Edinburgh!" This was a severe blow to him, either from jealousy—for Lady Kintore had obviously resumed sexual relations with her husband and a separation was therefore unlikely—or from financial hardship, for if she were not confined in Edinburgh he would not get the fee for delivering her. "Thus, are instantly dissipated all my dreams in that quarter for ever. But, after all, it was only a dream, a short & feverish dream." In retaliation he turned back to Lady Portsmouth, as Edward Neville had turned to his Portuguese conquests to punish Emily: "Let me then forget what is past," he wrote, "in the consolation of what I possess in Mary Ann's practical affection," the latter a phrase with its own echoes from *Edward Neville*. Lesassier retaliated further by sending an angry letter to Louisa, and another to Emmeline. The latter elicited an explanation from Emmeline that Louisa would probably be confined in Edinburgh after all and protestations of affection from Louisa that "all is so far well, at least, that *she* is unchanged. I write to her, divine & thrice incomparable girl. . . . What a load off my spirits." He had received a promising letter from Lady Portsmouth the same day, filled with assurances of her "practical affection" though as usual vague about the terms in which it was to be paid. "Que singular fortuna, de ser tas tem amante amada de *duas* Condessas a mesma vez, e a minha idade!!" he wrote, What singular good fortune, to be the beloved lover of *two* Countesses at the same time, and at my age!!

This was hubris that the gods were quick to punish. Lesassier's letter addressed to Louisa Kintore, beginning "Is it possible Louisa you are again in the family way?" and written with a "bitter mixture of rage, & contempt," was intercepted by Lord Kintore. It was unsigned and written with feigned handwriting, but Lord Kintore had no difficulty deducing who it came from. He claimed it as proof that Louisa and Lesassier were conducting an illicit affair, and used that circumstance as the reason for demanding a separation from his wife, declaring that "to preserve his own honor and dignity" "he cannot receive back Louisa." He was, he said, "quite willing to settle an aliment on her, but that that must be arranged by the private arbitration of mutual friends, not according to his rank, and fortune, but after a due investigation of all the facts, and circumstances leading to the separation." Louisa's brother, James Hawkins, took on the task of defending her, and refused to go along with private arbitration: what was necessary to clear Louisa's reputation was "formal recantation," which, alas for Louisa, "Lord Kintore refuses to give." To compel him to do so, James Hawkins brought an action against Lord Kintore. The ensuing scandal dominated Edinburgh society for the next six months.

James Hawkins was placed in the difficult situation of having to defend Louisa and Lesassier against their own imprudence, for though they never admitted their illicit passion, they had been obviously guilty of, at best, the most flagrant impropriety. Lesassier had addressed all the sisters, both in person and in correspondence, by their first names. His doing so with Louisa had been made abundantly clear by the "unhappy concluding sentence," of the intercepted letter: it was one part of the "consecutive chain of corroborative evidence," that, Lord Kintore claimed, proved his case against his wife. James Hawkins never knew that Lesassier had called Emmeline by her first name as well. "For my part," she wrote to Lesassier, desperate to exculpate herself after the scandal broke, "I used to tell you, and I still feel the same, my brother would never forgive my having wished to be called Emmeline by any man," but of course she had never told Lesassier any such thing, delighting instead in their intimacy. "Need I say who I shall think of during those hours, which have often stolen away so quickly and so deliciously in Louisa's room?" she had written to him in Edinburgh when he could not pay his usual evening visit. "No my own dear Daddy you know enough of my feelings towards you, to be certain of occupying a large portion of my thoughts in whatever place or company I may be. . . . I would not for any thing in the world give up that very retentive memory, or strong imagination which I possess: the one faithful to its trust brings up past scenes in all their glowing colors before me—makes me catch every look, hear every word, and feel every touch, which ever gave a zest to hours spent with those I love."

Emmeline, as she had feared, found herself in an especially awkward position. She was "her sister's only companion," for much of the time they were in Edinburgh, expected to help look after her during pregnancy and delivery; but convention required that she, as an unmarried woman, appear completely innocent of any knowledge of reproduction. Lesassier, in his own exculpatory efforts, wrote to James Hawkins that he had always stood at the folding doors between Louisa's bedroom and the next room when the servants brought tea. "James colored up," when he read this, Emmeline wrote, "and he said to me, with some sharpness, 'Honi soit qui mal y pense,' but I wonder Emmeline, what the world will say to a young unmarried woman understanding appearances so well, and being so very cautious as to what servants may think of a gentleman taking tea with you." Of course, Lesassier should not have been taking tea alone with Louisa at all, and Emmeline urged Lesassier to state "that you always had a third person in Lady Kintore's room at tea, or went into the next room, where the other ladies were, & this was almost invariably the case, as I used to bring you in a cup myself, along with my own into Louisa's room, that the party might not be broken, during the few evenings that you spent alone with us two." Emmeline also was at some pains to try to explain away her letter telling Lesassier that Louisa was again pregnant, since her brother had "expressed himself uneasy, as to the opinion which would be formed of a young lady writing on such subjects to a physician." What would he have thought if he had seen her earlier letter, in which she described Louisa's discomfort, "and" she went on, "don't be shocked at my *writing* a word, we have so often used in *conversation*—. . . you said it must be attributed to a bearing down of the womb."

The conventions may strike us as absurd and contradictory, for how was Emmeline to avoid impropriety if she was not supposed to understand appearances? Why wasn't she allowed to mention pregnancy when writing to a male midwife? What could be the harm in using first names? Certainly Lesassier insisted all along that he was blameless.

But of course he was not blameless, and though the specific rumors that were spread about him were untrue—"that Lord Kintore had secured a *number* of your letters written in the most abusive strain of Lord Kintore, and of distracted tenderness towards Louisa—that you had spent a fortnight with Lady Kintore in St. Andrews, and as the crowning piece of villainy, that Lord Kintore declares, he has never inhabited the same apartment with his wife, since her confinement, and will consequently disown her next infant"—Lesassier could not deny the basic fact, that the case between Lord Kintore and his wife was "occasioned by a love intrigue, & letters intercepted between her & Dr. Alexander Hamilton!!!"

Lesassier did not stand up well to the pressure of the unfolding events. Emmeline's letters drove him wild, for she hoped for a vindication from an open, public trial: "our character will be cleared at once as well as Louisa's," she wrote to Lesassier, "from the private slanders, I have no doubt, that he has circulated of both; & we often amuse ourselves with arranging the praises & esteem of you, which we four ladies shall certainly bestow on your whole conduct in court—when you are set up as a bright example of all a man can be, the skillful, humane physician, the prudent adviser, the kind the modest friend, why should you dream of leaving a town where I think every lady ought to worship you?" But an open trial would ruin him; as it was, he was told, "nothing else is talked of in Edinburgh!!!" "The story of Lady K. is very amusing," wrote the Marchioness of Stafford to the Edinburgh antiquarian and gossip Charles Kirkpatrick Sharpe, "I remember a succession of mad Lord K.'s, and conclude this to be quite equal to his predecessors." Lesassier was ashamed to appear in public, and it required a great act of courage for him to visit his patients and go to church, where he would see his uncle and his other Hamilton relations. "Never Oh! never," he wrote, "did I suffer such mental torture" and "my heart quite sinks within me, when I reflect what a public object of suspicion, odium, & derision I am become."

As the interests of the trio began to diverge, their conspiratorial trust unraveled. Lesassier tried to shift the blame: "I begin an exculpatory letter to Emmeline, to prove that if I was familiar with them, they were the same with me," and "Woe be to them" if he were called as a witness in the Kintore suit, "for, I must contradict much of what they the sisters have sworn to, which, assuredly, will ruin them here." We may condemn Lesassier for such self-interested and unchivalric behavior—his contemporaries did—but we are better placed than they to recognize how overwhelming were the forces working against him. Lady Kintore may genuinely have loved Lesassier, but she, like Lady Portsmouth, belonged to a class that had had generations of experience of protecting themselves from the consequences of their own actions. Her own interest required that she deny all guilt, and treat Lesassier "with indignation for writing the letter": the "skillful, humane physician" had become a presumptuous servant. Social distinctions had meant little when "the girls," Louisa, Emmeline, and Isabella, came to call on the Hamiltons during their happy days in Edinburgh, and Lady Kintore continued to express concern for "dear Mrs. Hamilton." But as the scandal deepened and spread the Hawkins family closed rank to protect themselves, leaving Lesassier outside their circle to fend for himself and his own household. After some consultation with her brother, Louisa finally wrote Lesassier two very formal letters concerning her expected confinement, though she forgot herself once and had to write "Dr. H" over some more affectionate appellation. She could not be confined in Edinburgh after all, she wrote, as "It would be highly indelicate, & improper." But Lesassier was in despair in reading this, for in his view his defense of his own character depended on Lady Kintore's continued patronage, to show that all was open and above board: "such selfish time servingly base ingratitude were destruction to *me*."

Lesassier had other reasons to despair, for the scandal destroyed forever his dreams of Louisa's "annual allowance," an allowance that had become essential to his financial calculations. In January 1823, in anticipation of the patronage of his "duas condessas," Lesassier had moved to a magnificent and very expensive house at 57 Northumberland Street, in the most fashionable part of the New Town. He was delighted to have left Argyll Street: "I again & again admire the magnificence of the rooms, & walk through them, in solitary musing. . . . Oh! how my heart expands, as it were, with pleasure, at the idea of once again becoming respectable in the eyes of the public, instead of being exiled to the Old Town, as I feared I should be for many years." But the house was much too expensive for him, especially since the owner decided to sell it after a few months. In an excess of financial imprudence, Lesassier decided to buy it at a cost of £2,000. Even Jenoway, who usually supported all his plans, "dissuades me from buying the house; as I have not the money; but, he is wrong. It never would do for me to move again—although it is so very hazardous to purchase when one has no funds." He was able to do so with the help of another loan obtained from Syme, this one from Syme's own family. Mortgages in Lesassier's day were not calculated so that principal was repaid with interest; instead, Lesassier simply paid the interest to retain the house. It was a magnificent residence—"a castle of a house," his cousin Mary Campbell called it. But without his hoped-for money from Louisa and Lady Portsmouth, an increase of professional income, or—faint hope—Catherine's mother's death, he could not possibly pay the expenses. He had to depend on a windfall, and where that windfall was to come from was anybody's guess.

It would not come from Louisa. Only Lesassier could have continued to believe that she would give him money after the scandal broke, and when none was forthcoming he was "irritated & low spirited, at such apparent selfishness. . . . I suspect the firmness of her sentiments, & must, in future, leave *her* out of all my future calculations. She will be perfidious & changeable indeed, if I do not, at all events, get one year's payment from her of £100; & with that, I shall content myself." But Louisa was in no position to send him money, even if she had wanted to. Instead, he received an additional blow: Louisa was after all to be confined in the nearby suburb of Portobello "& . . . my great rival Beilby is absolutely engaged to attend her in her confinement! Such monstrous folly & want of heart quite unhinged me all day." He wrote to her, through Emmeline, insisting "that she dismiss Beilby, & employ a midwife, or I have done with her for ever. Yet, I daresay she feels so anxious to retrieve herself with the public, that she will treat my proposal with ineffable contempt." The reader exasperated with such selfishness in the matter of his former beloved's health and safety may be as disappointed as Lesassier was delighted to hear that Louisa did "as I requested, by dismissing Beilby, & empowering me to send her a midwife. This is as it should be, & is an immense relief to my mind." Louisa later "incautiously tells me, she *repents* not having taken Beilby!" Lesassier, still hoping for "future remuneration from her," sent a mild reply; but he could "no longer brook" the "canting tone" of her letters, "& at once break off with her forever." Not quite forever: he met Louisa by accident one more time, and though he later rubbed out most of the Portuguese words "*Bellissima e Divina Creature*" (most beautiful and divine creature) can still be read.

But the beautiful and divine creature could no longer be the one whose overwhelming love relieved his financial difficulties, difficulties that only increased as the scandal grew. Lesassier's great aunt Campbell and his cousin Mary continued to support him in this crisis, but they were alone among his relations. James Hamilton expressed "the deepest affliction at my *horrible* conduct & laments that anyone should so much disgrace his name." "Scoundrel!" Lesassier cried and wrote demanding an explanation for this statement, as well as for "the revival of reports respecting any former alleged misconduct." "My dear nephew," James Hamilton responded, both were "the necessary consequence of the prevalent rumors in regard to a certain unsigned letter." He himself "must feel the most poignant distress at having been the innocent cause of introducing you to that Lady, who now suffers, from a letter which probably she would have rejected with indignation, had it reached her. It would indeed relieve my mind from a load of distress, if you could prove that the letter in question was not written by you; and in the hope of this I remain, Yours affectionately, James Hamilton Junior." This answer, and his uncle's refusal to accept any further letters from him, led to another of Lesassier's acts of folly: publishing what was intended as an exculpatory pamphlet explaining the circumstances of the quarrel between himself and his uncle. It described those circumstances in every detail, and reproduced all the letters he had received from his uncle or his uncle's patients. Lesassier printed and distributed a thousand copies, with a special seal for those intended for the nobility. The public reaction was not what he expected. His patient Anne Walker "hurts & irritates me, by saying that, perhaps, people may wonder why I trouble them with my quarrels with my uncle," and Lesassier found that his uncle's "loan of £624"—mentioned in the pamphlet—"is looked upon as a strong proof of his former kindness to me." He realized, much later, how foolish he had been to publicly attack James Hamilton: it was like a son defying his father in public, "For, a child, in respect of a parent, can scarcely be considered in the right, when an appeal is made to the tribunal of public opinion." Indeed, the main result of his vindication was that anyone who might have been unaware of the scandal could now read about it in exhaustive detail. "All future respectability of character, is gone for ever," he wrote, "& with it, are dissipated all those gay dreams of happiness, which have buoyed me up through so many calamitous circumstances. . . . I do not complain, however; because, in fact, my fate has been the effect of causes over which, generally speaking, I have had perfect control. It would be a needless loss of time to review the errors of the past. They have been the errors of a fervent imagination & impetuous feelings, that have obained an ascendancy over my judgment." It made matters worse that these were "very nearly precisely the same errors, to which my poor old father owes *his* ruin also."

Fortunately for Lesassier, the Kintore scandal blew over: in December 1824, his man of business, Syme, "arrived to transport & transfix me with the intelligence, that Lord & Lady Kintore are again living together in perfect harmony!! I need scarcely remark that few events of my life ever occasioned me such a burst of pleasure, as this most unlooked-for change." Yet between the notoriety of the Kintore scandal and his very public quarrel with his uncle, his professional character was largely ruined. His practice went from seventy families to only twenty, and over time the "principal part" of those "almost entirely ceased bearing children—while, on the other hand, their family having most of them passed the period of infantile diseases, & their mothers having acquired experience in the treatment of their complaints," seldom called him in. He could acquire only a handful of new patients, and without his uncle's half-fees, his income from practice sank to only about £100 per year.

His medical associates were of limited assistance in this crisis. Robert Knox, as intent on rank as Lesassier, proclaimed him to be "the most talented physician here & a perfect gentleman," but Knox was soon involved in his own scandal, created by his purchase of bodies for dissection from the murderers Burke and Hare and burned in effigy. John Mackintosh "told me of so many scandalous stories to my disadvantage, & said so much about that infamous rascal my uncle, that I feel plunged in despair." It was left to Edward Milligan to encourage Lesassier in his one sensible method of raising money, taking a medical student to live with him as a private pupil. His first was Henry Ludlow, whose father was willing to pay Lesassier £100 per year for two years while his son was studying medicine at Edinburgh. Lesassier bitterly resented the necessity—"Ah! If poverty did not force me—I would spurn, with indignation, the thought of my house being thus converted into lodgings"—but Ludlow turned out to be, on the whole, an unobtrusive addition to their household. One can only wonder if he, or his father, felt their money was well spent, for £100 per year was very expensive to pay for mere lodgings. Lesassier was supposed to act as a kind of tutor as well as to show Ludlow his practice, and on Ludlow's arrival he made out a schedule for study that would have taxed the most industrious pupil. But he had little taste for tutoring and his practice was much diminished, though Ludlow did accompany him on occasion.

His second pupil turned out to be more troublesome. As his affection for Louisa waned, Lesassier began to devote himself more and more to Lady Portsmouth, whom he visited twice at her country home during the winter and spring of 1824, each time leaving his patients but acquiring a fee of £50. In the second of these visits, he wrote, "her brother," Newton Hanson, "is persuaded to come & study under me. My feelings at so astonishing a change!!" Lesassier's feelings were at first of delight!! here he had his second pupil, a true young gentleman, adding more than £100 per year to his income.

His delight should have been tempered with caution, for Lady Portsmouth's patronage was variable and Hanson was not an obviously promising pupil. He had been studying law, and though his father felt "flattered and obliged by the proposition you have made to take him under your guidance and protection in the new career," he could not "conceal . . . deep regret that after so great a loss of time and waste of expence he should at so late a day withdraw himself from the profession he had embarked in and fly to another in my opinion equally, if not more abstruse and laborious." Newton himself was "full of fears & alarms," he wrote Lesassier prior to his arrival. "I am coming to Edinburgh a town of all towns I have every reason to dislike. I am going to commence a course of study which will expose to your view, what a consummate ignorant fellow I am. I am going to put myself under discipline which I have not been subjected to for eight years past."

We may wonder, then, why young Hanson chose to come to Edinburgh, but his letters furnish some clues: devoted to his sister, perhaps too much so, he had no great ambition to work, and may have intended to study medicine in order to serve as her personal physician. In some respects, Lesassier and young Hanson were perfect foils: both anxious to show good fellowship at the expense of unbending rectitude, both actively vying to engage Lady Portsmouth's affection and interest. Certainly they did each other no good. Lesassier was supposed to be Hanson's patron and mentor, for which privilege Hanson's father was willing to pay £140 per year. He even began examining Hanson: "I hope soon to get into the proper mode of teaching," he wrote, "& if he himself relish the thing, I shall do." But he also confided his financial embarrassments to Hanson, who, in a gesture of Georgian male bonding reminiscent of Lord Berridale's loan of a horse years earlier, suggested that Lesassier contract a two-year loan with his own moneylender in London. From the start there were peculiarities involved in the transaction that should have made both parties wary. Hanson took care of all the correspondence, telling Lesassier that his "money-lender will not advance any money except to him," and raising the suspicion in our minds, though not Lesassier's, that he had some undisclosed stake in the matter. The rate was high, and the interest had to be paid in advance, so that the actual amount Lesassier could receive was only £424. Even worse, this loan had a fixed term, unlike Lesassier's previous ones, which could be floated indefinitely as long as the interest was paid. But Lesassier was in desperate financial straits, desperate enough to agree to the terms, even though "the great question is, how shall I be able to pay £500 in two years." Hanson obtained the money on 29 May 1824, and turned it over to Lesassier in return for a promissary note dated May 1826. Lesassier was exceedingly obliged for this favor, and made it a point to do one in return: he wrote to James McGrigor, director of the Army Medical Department, pretending great knowledge of Hanson's professional abilities in order to recommend him.

Once again, Lesassier was out of his league, for what had a struggling Edinburgh physician, with a declining practice and no family backing, to do with dissolute young gentlemen and London moneylenders? The only resource he had left for repaying the moneylender, as well as his other creditors, was Lady Portsmouth. She had already given him around £100 and had promised him more, but this was not enough to pay his bills, even with the fees from his two pupils. He made further efforts to extract money from her, efforts that might almost be called heroic if they were not so unprincipled. His first scheme involved Lady Portsmouth coming to live with him incognita. This would have been disastrous, if detected, for Lady Portsmouth's reputation was in shreds. Moreover, it involved innumerable arrangements: expensive remodeling of the house to impress his noble guest, hiring an additional servant "so that there are now ten persons in my family." It also involved much negotiating, for Lesassier would not allow Lady Portsmouth to bring her baby daughter to his house, and had to arrange with Fanny Maitland to take "the little mysterious girl"—not even his friends could be told of Lady Portsmouth's identity—when she was to come later in the year. But the potential rewards were great:

> Mary Ann actually gave me £600 for the first half year's board, & promises to give me her whole £1,200 per annum out of which I have merely to pay Fanny £100 a year for Mary Ann's child, £60 to Newton, & her own pocket money & clothes. In short, I shall be in the clear receipt of nearly £1,000 a year!!! In addition to all this, she gave me £500 of her own to place in the bank, in my own name. . . . So that I have now the glorious reflection that I can, at any moment, pay off all my tradesmen's debts, & shall very soon relieve my £900 loan also, & diminish the mortgage on my house—while, in the meantime, I can never more be annoyed for money, as I have it, in future, in my power to merely send a check on my account for the amount of any claim that may be made upon me. As may readily be imagined, I can think of nothing, & talk of nothing to Catherine, but my astonishing good fortune; & indeed, we both of us sometimes think it a dream.

So indeed it proved. It was not easy sharing his house with Lady Portsmouth, from "her love of deference, & magnificence, & slavish attention": they quarreled over her daughter, over her servants, over her desire to speak privately to Newton Hanson in his room, a propensity sure to lead to discovery of her identity. John Hanson heard she was in Edinburgh, and wrote to Newton "expressing such amazement . . . & evincing so exasperated a feeling," that Lesassier "became excessively alarmed lest he should actually write to my uncle, & produce an explosion." Catherine resented having an imperious stranger in the house, and had a "violent quarrel" with Lesassier "about the manner in which she disposes of Mary Ann's maid's time." Indeed, from Catherine's point of view, it was like having one of Lesassier's favorites in permanent residence, and "jealous of Lady Portsmouth's rank," as Lesassier put it, "envious, & suspicious of my attentions to her, & detesting her for being superior to herself in manners, as well as situation & fortune, she is perpetually boiling up, and taking fire." The Hamiltons had to hold onto Lady Portsmouth for at least six months in order to keep the £600, but

Lesassier had come to believe this was unlikely even before his quarrel with Catherine: "How this rash experiment will terminate, it is difficult to know."

Concerned that Lady Portsmouth would take offense and leave, Lesassier decided on a further intrigue, convincing her to make an "irrevocable will" in his favor, leaving him £10,000 out of the £20,000 she was to inherit when the Earl of Portsmouth died if her own child did not survive. In this way he would have obtained his windfall, for "when should *I* gain £10,000 by my practice here, even if I were to practice for ever!" Lady Portsmouth, in fact, promised to leave him everything she had, but by now, Lesassier's daydreams had clearly run away with his common sense, for he founded quite incredible hopes on the success of his schemes. "In the singular friendship of Lady Portsmouth," he wrote in the beginning of July 1824, "I have met with the only means of restoring me to liberty, for, with *her* income at my disposal, nothing now remains but to pay off every thing." When she finally agreed to make a will in his favor, he added, "I may simply remark that she has done all that any woman can do for me, & more than ten thousand would have done." Once again, only Lesassier could have believed she would really do it: to the reader of his journals it seems clear that Lady Portsmouth was ready to promise anything that Lesassier wished, but that she had no intention of compromising her own financial security by following through. Even Lesassier had his doubts, writing that the purpose of the will was merely to "tie her down to live with us" until he established a practice and paid his debts. Lady Portsmouth's own agenda became clear in the course of the summer, when she persuaded Lesassier, his father, and Catherine to set up a household for her in Paris. At the end of July they moved to France.

For the first time in his life, Lesassier had plenty of money to spend as he liked, but there were costs: "What a life this is," he wrote. "Alas! . . . to be dependent on so capricious, & so useless a woman." Living with "that ill-fated Lady" was excessively tedious: "Rising late;—breakfasting between 9 & 10—sauntering out, without any definite purpose, at 11 or 12 in a scorching sun, that aggravated our mutual irritability & ill will;—lounging along the Boulevards, & gazing once more at the china ornaments, upholstery, & prints, which we had already become familiar with." They were, in fact, living the nobly idle life of gentlefolk he had always aspired to, and within a month he found he could not stand it: "It is really little else than a tiresome repetition always to enumerate the dissensions & quarrels which seem alone to distinguish the days of this extraordinary visit one from the other. . . . Never in my life did I find myself so often opposed & thwarted, or so often & so thoroughly miserable." By the end of September he and Catherine returned to Edinburgh, leaving Pierre with Lady Portsmouth until November.

The quarrel with Lady Portsmouth proved to be irreconcilable and had important financial ramifications. Lesassier had been living largely at her expense; in addition, he retained a large portion of the money—perhaps the entire £1,200—which she had given him to deposit under his name. Lady Portsmouth demanded her money back, and Lesassier retaliated by sending in his account to her for medical attendance, amounting to £53 more than that sum. He tried to get her to sign a release, but to no avail, and he remained haunted by the fear that she, or her former husband's trustees, would try to take him to court. Nor was that the only result. After Lesassier's quarrel with his sister, Newton Hanson left Lesassier's house as well, "telling the Doctor plainly he must now support the strongest party." In May 1825, he called upon Lesassier, becoming "importunate to get back the money"—that is, the £434—"adding, very ingenuously, that, as there seemed to be so many claims between his sister & the Doctor, he had better be paid now lest there should be nothing afterward to pay him with." But Lesassier had no money to repay the loan, and Hanson, in a burst of folly of his own, forged Lesassier's signature to the promissary note, and altered the date from May 1826 to May 1825. He was able to cash the note at the Kinnears' bank in Edinburgh, and thus obtained £434; the Kinnears then called on Lesassier to pay the money. Lesassier insisted that his signature on the note was a forgery, and wrote a series of discreditable letters to John Hanson—many of which were never sent—to disown his own part in the transaction. Once again Lesassier found himself involved in scandal; "again & again" Jenoway urged him "to fly instantly into concealment"; and it took Syme's best efforts to keep Lesassier from doing "harm, instead of good," by appearing in court himself. The case came to court in June 1825, and "This was a day of tumultuous & conflicting emotions—of anger, disappointment, terror, & unutterable joy," Lesassier wrote, for the signature on the note was declared a forgery, which meant that he had no legal obligation to pay it at all.

Lesassier had been saved from his own fiscal irresponsibility—for he had, after all, received the money from Newton Hanson, and he never paid it back—by the equal irresponsibility of Hanson. The amount of money he had acquired through his schemes was considerable: at least £70 from John Hanson, £100 from Lady Kintore, over £1,200 from Lady Portsmouth, as well as a diamond pin that Lesassier claimed as a present but Lady Portsmouth insisted was a loan. Lady Portsmouth had also paid around £500 for the Hamiltons' expenses while they lived with her in Paris. To this we can add £434 from the Kinnears, eventually paid by John Hanson to save Newton from prosecution, or by Newton himself out of his allowance or inheritance. Lesassier had thus acquired an enormous sum by his adventuring, far more than he could have made in practice in the three years, but we can calculate the cost, too: loss of professional reputation, loss of his uncle's patronage, cut off from the majority of respectable medical practitioners who might have patronized him. Even Lesassier may have eventually acknowledged that much of this money was obtained by very dubious means. He never forgave Anne Walker for making "scurrilous"—but true—"remarks about my connection with Lady Portsmouth, proceeding even the length of telling me I had received *supplies* from her," and though he was legally clear of the Kinnears' debt it remained an uneasy moral obligation. "Oh! Hamilton is this the way you repay him who has assisted you," Newton Hanson wrote, "well will this apply, 'He who is ungrateful has no fault but one all other faults are virtues in him.'" And we can look to John Hanson for the clearest statement of Lesassier's professional lapse: while deploring his son's behavior, he wrote, "It does appear to me to be extraordinary, that you, Sir, should have been an instrument in the transaction, placed as he was as your pupil, inmate, and under your protection and guidance."

There were other costs. Newton Hanson made a point of complaining to James McGrigor concerning Lesassier, and Lesassier was on tenterhooks as to whether Mc-Grigor would investigate further. Hanson spoke to Catherine's mother, too, and told her "a plaintive story of the whole affair from the very commencement—Lady Portsmouth being here—the money & diamond, journey to Paris . . . in which I am made as black as soot. Armed with this tale, she has made it her business—the infernal hag—to spread the story far & wide," so that his reputation suffered another assault. He had become so notorious that several of his former young lady friends would not call on him; his early patrons, like Mrs. Joanna Home, née Stirling, would no longer acknowledge him on the street; and he never again was employed by the higher ranks as a physician. It is true, he wrote, "I owe somewhat less than I did three years ago, still, deprived of practice, & society, what comfort remains! Large & elegantly furnished as this house is, who sees it? No one!" His debts still amounted to fully £1,200, not including his mortgage of £2,000, and he could not even hope for the salvation of his uncle's death with the same confidence, for "it strikes me," he wrote, "when I see myself treated with such contemptuous indifference by the people of this town, that I *could not* succeed, even although the fiend did die. Oh! God what a mortal stab these two last years have inflicted on my future peace of mind!"

# CHAPTER 12

# Compare What I *Might* Have Been
# with What I *Am*

Lf Lesassier were a novel's villain, he would have died here, as a just reward for his ill behavior; if he were its hero, his uncle and Catherine's mother, repenting on their deathbeds, would have left him a fortune. He himself looked for a speedy change: either he would sell everything and leave Edinburgh, or Catherine would inherit her mother's money—by now increased to £1,000 per year by her grandmother's death—or he his uncle's practice. It was inconceivable that things could go on as they were. "One thing is quite clear," he wrote, "my affairs have obtained their ultimate climax, & ruin, or a favorable change, must now speedily take place." In medical language, it was as though he had reached a crisis in an acute illness, which would soon resolve itself in a cure or in death. In his own preferred language of the theater, "The closing scene of the last act in this eventful drama is fast approaching; & much may hereafter be hoped from the hand of time." But Lesassier's life and his difficulties were more like a chronic complaint, never fatal but never cured, more like a serialized novel than a drama that respected the unities. He always wrote as though he could not bear to continue, but continue he did, year after year, pacing "in silent neglect up one street, & down another for an hour—unheeding & unheeded. Oh! What a fate for so proud a spirit as mine! Good God did I ever think I could have endured existence in any part of the world under such circumstances!"

These were years marked with financial crises. He was never again close to paying off his major loans, and without his uncle's assistance he was hard-pressed to pay for his ordinary living expenses. He had to put off his tradesmen and negotiate with them to take up his bills until he could afford to pay them; the negotiations take on their own drama. His upholsterer refused to take up his bill for £50. "Shocked at so unlooked for a blow," he wrote, "I leave Catherine . . . plunged in despair—for, she insisted on knowing the cause of my distress—& proceed to that worthy man's myself. After my very short, but, powerful statement, the kindhearted creature agreed to accept of £10 & my promissary note for the remainder. . . . Being left alone in his ware-room—as he had accompanied some customers to another room—I could not refrain from shedding tears at the mournful state of ruin, exposure, & desolation to which I am reduced!!"

But tradesmen had their own debts to pay. "Sir, it is with extreme reluctance that I send this to you," wrote one of Lesassier's many creditors, "but really necessity compels me to state that I have been much disappointed by your not paying the money you promised at the end of last month. The truth is that I have a bill to pay on Monday fortnight, and I shall take the liberty of calling on you on that morning when if you cannot give the full sum you expected you must at all events give me a part of it in the interim. You must not really take this amiss—for what can I do?" Negotiations could become more heated, especially after Lesassier kept putting off payment time and time again. One of his debts had been carried on so long that the creditor, Aitchisson, had died, and the account was now due to his estate. Aitchisson had also consulted Lesassier for venereal disease, and Lesassier had the disreputable and unprofessional idea of calling that fact to the attention of his son, with the implied threat that he might make it public, in order to assist his negotiations over his bill. As usual in Lesassier's life, the crime of unprofessional behavior was promptly punished, for young Aitchisson consulted with his solicitor and responded that "he felt but slender inclination to enter into any transaction with *me* . . . & that he was amazed at my want of delicacy, in disclosing to him the nature of his father's complaint; but, in fact, he was incredulous respecting my claims, for any such thing!" As always, realization of his own impotence to command drove him to fury: "Anger, humiliation, & despair took possession of my mind by turns upon finding my self treated with scurrilous contempt by a petty clerk, a boy, the very son of one of my tradesmen."

Here was he, a physician and a gentleman, forced by poverty to put up with insubordination not only from young Aitchisson but from others as well "for, of course, in him I too plainly hear the opinion of a great body of the people of Edinburgh." Each month, each week, brought its crises: "I am . . . annoyed at want of money. I have only 5 shillings;—owe Catherine, for the house expenses, at least 10 shillings—& have nothing to give her for the market tomorrow, although Saturday! Who could endure such pinching poverty as this!" Even picturesque walks around Edinburgh, formerly one of his favorite pastimes, could not console him: on walking up the hill with his father from Stockbridge to the New Town, with the Old Town and Castle before them, he wrote, "My father is charmed with the distant prospect . . . while I, on the contrary, cannot raise my eyes to it without a mingled emotion of execration, rage, & despair: And how is it possible to be otherwise, when I cannot fail of conjuring up to my too faithful memory all the scenes in which I have been so luckless an actor. What, in fact, must be my feelings, when I reflect that, here am I, strolling idly along the byroads & lanes, of a town; where my successful rivals are rolling in their carriages from patient to patient—& making rapid fortunes."

There were other sorrows. His aunt Isabella Hodgeson had died in November 1823; much embroiled with his "duas Condessas," he had recorded the fact in his journal in capitals, but otherwise made no comment. His beloved great-aunt Campbell died in 1826: "Poor old lady! With her has departed the only friend I had in her accursed family," except her daughter Mary. To add to his distress, he was not invited to the funeral. The death of his hated grandmother the following year also ended by adding to his distress, for his father was invited to the funeral, but he was not. Of course, since there is no sign he had made any effort to mask his feelings toward her—"How shall I express the delightful emotions of triumph which I experienced at learning that the old wretch the rascal's mother, died yesterday!!! It would be very difficult to convey an adequate idea of the immense exultation I experienced at the event"—it is hard to see why he should have been.

He thought of going on active service at full pay, and rapidly built all his hopes upon the plan. The sound of the regimental band of the gallant 42nd, playing in Edinburgh Castle one evening, brought no memories of his former execrations against his regiment but only the hope of escape from his present miseries. "Nothing could be finer than the gray twilight faintly lighted by the new moon," he wrote, "& while the soul-stirring notes swelled on the breeze, I could not help exclaiming to Catherine that I would rather be again upon full-pay . . . than enjoy the best practice Edinburgh can bestow!" He wrote to Sir James McGrigor, confidently expecting a favorable reply; but Sir James wrote and "abruptly told me that, referring to my two examinations for my wounded leg he could not think himself authorized to submit my name again for employment! Thus, then, in a breath, all my air-built castles sink into eternal annihilation." The letter was clear enough: Lesassier had received a pension because his wounded leg made him unfit for future service. That meant, to Sir James, that he was unfit for future service. If, however, his leg was well enough for him to think of applying, his pension would be forfeited since the conditions under which it was awarded—extreme disability preventing medical practice—obviously no longer existed. In James McGrigor's response we can hear the approach of a new age, Victorian moral rectitude coming to supersede easygoing Georgian interest. Perhaps alone among Lesassier's acquaintances, McGrigor put duty to his office before the desire to oblige particular individuals, believing that regulations were to be upheld, not set aside when it suited the convenience of a petitioner. Lesassier's own response to McGrigor's letter indicates how little he understood such a view, for he instantly tried "to examine Sir James' reasons for acting so extraordinary a part" as to insist he give up a disability pension before going on active service. "The fact is, he could appoint me, if he chose, & has nothing to do with my pension, which is a concern entirely of the Secretary at Wars." That Sir James felt a responsibility to the War Office, rather than merely regarding it as a source of additional income for former army officers, was obviously a foreign concept to Lesassier, who felt no such responsibility. He concluded that McGrigor's decision was based on his own self-interest: "Most likely he actually recommended me, & was reprimanded for endeavoring to bring forward a person who had been pronounced quite unfit for service, in consequence of disease." Or perhaps Newton Hanson's complaints had succeeded in ill-disposing McGrigor to him, and had thus deprived him of his former patron.

On hearing that Sir James was to be in Edinburgh, then, Lesassier took care to call on him, "still fearing I might hereafter accuse myself of having supinely allowed Sir James McGrigor to be actually in Edinburgh without doing everything in my power to set the question for ever at rest respecting the grand point of my being replaced upon full-pay." For once, he carried off the rapprochement—as he perceived it—quite diplomatically. "I go straight to his hotel. He is out at breakfast," but the two men ran into each other in George Street. "I suspect he knew me," Lesassier wrote, "though he affected not to do. However, I stopped him, & introduced myself; upon which, he somewhat drily shook hands with me, & hoped I had been well; for his own part, he had such a headache, that he was going home to lie down." Lesassier took the point, "that I must not annoy him with my affairs," and responded mildly "that his numerous visitors I feared had increased his distressing complaint . . . &, indeed, although merely, for five minutes, to personally offer my respects to him, I had quite dreaded to intrude." McGrigor, "Perceiving how adroitly I had taken his hint, . . . now smiled, & assured me how happy he was to see all his friends." Lesassier took this as a favorable sign, "& expressing my satisfaction at seeing him look so well, I took leave, & he cordially shook me by the hand!!" And "thus," he remarked, "I am perfectly warranted in concluding that he is quite reconciled to me again . . . a most important step . . . even as a mere matter of feeling."

It had to remain a mere matter of feeling, for McGrigor remained adamant in the matter of full pay. With that option gone, Lesassier began to think of moving to another city; indeed, why should he hesitate, when he lived "under such glaring circumstances of scorn, hatred, & neglect . . . the scene of so many, many years of infatuated indiscretion—wretchedness, exposure & insignificance." Many another physician had had to leave after years of effort, foiled by the entrenched practices of Edinburgh professors and elite surgeons: William Fergusson, for example, though later physician to the king and eminent in London medical circles, could make little headway in Edinburgh. Lesassier's own plans included returning to Manchester and lecturing on midwifery, where his former friend Joseph Jordan "who is clearing £1500 a year could assist me very much." True, he had not seen Jordan for years and had hardly parted with him on the best of terms, but he gave no thought to that, preferring to dwell on his projected social and professional status. Manchester "is not a polished place; but, what of that—was I not brought up among them, & consequently, am I not prepared for all their boorish rudeness! There, a physician is a dignified personage;—here, he is a cipher. There, my expenditure will be so much reduced, that a single £100 a year from my practice—so as to make up my income to £300 a year—will maintain us in a comfortable manner: And surely, I shall be able to gain £100 a year." He might also be able to get an appointment as physician "to a factory (if a physician might accept of such a thing), which would perhaps bring me £100 a year." With this move in mind, he began working on a set of lectures on midwifery. Compiling them occupied most of his largely free time for the next few years and gave him something to work on, together with the illusion that he was furthering his professional career: "Now that I have fairly begun the task of writing by dictation," he wrote, "I have a nearer prospect, as it were, of my great undertaking—that of lecturing—being carried into complete effect. That my lectures will be incomparably superior to any thing of the kind in Britain. Yes, it will, indeed, be some compensation for all my mortifications & disasters, to know that, as far as the Manchester newspapers are circulated, I shall be looked up to as the head of my profession. Surely with such claims to public confidence & the support of a strong body of friends, I must speedily obtain practice. Then, all this misery will be forgotten." Thus he spoke in his euphoria, but in more sober moments even he had to admit that his lectures were "too palpable a plagiarism" from his uncle's lectures, and the reader cannot help feeling that he might have saved himself much trouble by merely copying them.

Lesassier also began a correspondence with his "old and tried friend Ella," now living in Manchester with her second husband. She was overjoyed to hear from him—"At last we are united—thanks to God for this—thus I am repaid for years of agony and suspense"—and in raptures that he might be coming to live in the same town. He and his family could, she suggested, lodge with them. "We have a very handsome bed room and sitting room for *you*—and if I can serve you on my *knees* command Ella . . . don't pretend to others you are my friend for although we are in a respectable line of business you must not in your rank *say* you have *friends* in *business*." "And I am confident," Lesassier mused, "poor thing, that she would study my interest, comfort, & happiness, to the utmost. At the same time, she would serve both as an example & check to Catherine, & thus render me more independent of her. . . How wonderful if we were to live together in Manchester again after a lapse of nearly twenty years."

Yet he didn't want to go to Manchester, "an odious climate, & a most vile illiberal place." He hated the thought that he "must begin the world again in lodgings!" And he hated still more the thought of ending up like his father, sinking back down to "the circle to which my father's old housekeeper, & all that slanderous set belong: For, it is their tongues I should most dread." His father raised his fears concerning Manchester "in consequence of its vicinity to Edinburgh facilitating the communication of scandal about poor me—in addition to the revival of old stories concerning my father in the place." Indeed, his father posed a problem for moving to Manchester, for Pierre might "again degenerate into habits of intoxication." They had "high words" on the subject one morning at breakfast: "In short," Lesassier wrote, "I find it utterly vain to think of going there; as nothing could prevent him from practicing—drinking would follow—& then a quarrel & a public exposure by his leaving my house." Indeed, he continued, "as the old gentleman is confident of his being employed in Manchester, & is so thankless for all that has been done to make him happy & respectable, I shall," perhaps remembering his father's words to him so many years earlier, "supply him with a little money, & leave him to make his way thither again." Jenoway, that faithful and injudicious echo, concurred "that if I went to Manchester, my father's conduct would disgrace me, & prevent my success." For that reason, Lesassier wrote, "I am fully determined to give up all thoughts of Manchester," and he left Ella's increasingly frantic letters unanswered.

If he did not settle in Manchester, perhaps he should try Liverpool, where he had "the moral certainty, that I should fall into practice" almost immediately: "For, I would be bound to say, that, in less than six months, my name would be known far & near . . . by . . . establishing a course of lectures, a Lying-in Institution, & a Dispensary, for the

Diseases of Women & Children—With such powerful instruments as these in my hands—in a place so populous & liberal & wealthy, & enlightened as Liverpool—my rapid success among the lower orders, at least, must depend entirely on my own assiduity & popular manners—in other words, upon my positive determination, as my father says, to close my eyes, tête basse head lowered, & to succeed in spite of all opposition." He must have known that positing such a burst of professional energies at this stage in his career was as much a dream as gaining fame by his lectures; in any case he decided against Liverpool because "it wears a beggarly, degraded, air to leave such a celebrated metropolis as Edinburgh, & sneak away to Liverpool." Nor did he want to go to Paris, or Boulogne, despite the almost daily conversations he had with his father. Catherine grew very tired of the subject and refused to join in, "professing a firm belief that we shall never leave Edinburgh." Indeed, she tried to convince Lesassier, if not to stop speaking of it, at least to stop worrying so much over which was the right path to follow: "Force nothing, says she. Don't continue brooding over your situation perpetually, & thus making yourself ill. If we *be* to go, no exertion on our part will prevent us. Therefore, try to bend your thoughts to something pleasant, as I always endeavor to do; & just let things take their chance." This was, "certainly, good, sound, common sense," he had to admit, "& is worthy of a more judicious head," by which he meant the advisor, though we might think his remark more applicable to the advisee.

Lesassier approved any advice, "grasped any floating straw," that suggested he was right in staying in Edinburgh. He began to look to superstition—"poor credulous fool" as he called himself—for signs that his harsh fate would be ameliorated. He took to writing down the psalms at chapel each week to use them to predict his future, his hopes for which centered around the death of his uncle or his mother-in-law. "From all this," he wrote after perusing one set of psalms, "I should feel inclined to suppose that the Arch Scoundrel is either to die in October, or not at all while I am in Edinburgh. Indeed, I should almost be disposed to conclude that I am fated to leave this town next spring." He kept track of his dreams, too, certain they helped him predict the future, particularly when they reflected his own hopes. Dreams of his hanging meant his own elevation, he was certain; dreams of a funeral meant his uncle's death, and he became so convinced "that the little Doctor is going to die, that I feel astonished & disappointed whenever I now see his vehicle in the street." This conviction prevented him from making up his mind to move away: if his uncle were to live, moving to another town was his only sensible option, but if his uncle were to die, moving would rob him of the chance of a lifetime to take over his uncle's practice. He found it impossible to get anything done; "The fact is, that my mind fluctuates so incessantly between going away from this, & remaining; between fully expecting his death, & altogether despairing of it." Months went by in this uncertain state: "As to the never failing topic of the rascal's death, I cannot look for any thing else than continual, & irritating, hope, until a few weeks more have elapsed without any confirmation of my dreams, & then I shall no longer trust in them, but treat them with the contempt they deserve."

The hope inspired by his dreams prevented him from making up his mind to leave, and, we may say, perhaps that was their psychological purpose, for he didn't really want to go. "Quand tu ne sais si l'action que tu medites est bonne, ou mauvaise, abstiens-toi," he wrote on the inside cover of his journal: if you don't know whether the action you meditate is good or bad, abstain. His later journals are full of thanksgiving for divine providence, but it is divine providence of an especially self-centered sort, for he took the fact that he had weathered so much, and was the beneficiary of so much good fortune, as a sign that he could expect still more, in the form either of his uncle's or his mother-in-law's death. One evening after dinner, his father mentioned that "Catherine's mother is just recovering from a severe illness which had confined her some weeks to bed. Of course, much less than this was quite sufficient to set us to work in disposing of the increase of fortune. . . . However, upon sending to inquire, all our dreams of prosperity were instantly dissipated by learning—she was perfectly recovered! The good which I expect, seems to mock me. Yet, how merciful—oh! how merciful Divine Providence has been to poor me!!" Surely it was not too much to hope that Divine Mercy would be shown him yet again, in the form of one of the longed-for deaths, "& surely, in another year, or two, with such a constitution as they both of them have, they cannot long hold out."

The financial exigencies of remaining in Edinburgh drove Lesassier, finally, to reduce his expenditures. He sold his carriage for £65, and he gave up his manservant, "for alas! what have *I* to do with a footman, to open the door, when no person knocks at it, but some importunate creditor!!" He rented his carriage house and stable. He managed to have the trustees of Catherine's money changed from his uncle and two legal advisers from her family, to his friends Jenoway, Syme, and Maitland. The new trustees agreed to remove the money from the funds and lend it, with the interest to go toward paying the interest on Lesassier's mortgage bond. He made use of the genteel alternative to common pawnshops, depositing his jewels as security at the Equitable Loan Company, to pay unexpected bills, and developed the habit of redeeming them whenever he had spare cash, "to prevent me from spending the money, as I might do, if it were lying beside me." He deposited his plate and silver there, too, though this created difficulties in keeping up appearances before servants and acquaintances. One evening "Having engaged my good friends . . . to tea & a small supper," he wrote, "I thought it most politic to relieve the silver, so as to raise our diminished consequence a little. It was a troublesome affair. At 10 and ¼, my father & I taking a porter with us . . . relieved the tea-set, for £13/8/4, &, making such a parcel of it as could not be recognized, my father carried it to a neighboring stair." In the meantime, Lesassier himself "went for the porter, who was waiting in the street, & brought him to my father; so that he [the porter] could have no suspicion of what I had been doing." The porter took the parcel and "preceded us home & I took the parcel myself from him at the door, having admitted myself privately with my pass-key. Thus, no one is aware . . . that I have been driven to this disgraceful extremity." These financial makeshifts were by no means uncommon even for the most genteel of households: as the clerk at the Equitable Loan Company told him, they were common among "many families of consequence here."

Lesassier also tried playing the lottery, but found that his shares "were all blanks!" and he concluded, prudently, that "No, no, the experience of years, proves, that it is not by such means as this, that we are to get money!"

It was, finally, his cousin Mary Campbell who came to his aid. Hearing his plans to leave Edinburgh in the fall of 1826, she offered him a loan of £100 per year for the next three years. Though her mother's death made it impossible for her to continue this loan beyond the first year, she did provide considerable financial support for the next few years, "one of the most unexpected pieces of good fortune," Lesassier marveled, "that can be imagined—especially from such a quarter." He never asked himself her motives, assuming it must come from the pure, disinterested affection that would lead any woman to come to his aid, but we can consider them more closely. Her brother warned her that Lesassier "had a design on her purse," and certainly Lesassier's own increasing demands—including a £700 loan on her house and a £400 loan raised on a £700 life-insurance policy taken out for that purpose—provide evidence for this. He also tried to persuade her to make her will in his favor, and her financial status soon figured prominently in his schemes: "Besides plate, linen, furniture, & a handsome house, she will have fully £6000 to bequeath! . . . and I am quite certain if she once made her will in my favor, she would never alter it—But, she is so stern, & impractica-ble, and self-willed, that I do not believe she will ever do so, unless she be again taken ill." He suggested that she move in with them to "secure to him the bulk of her fortune," and he was fearful of losing his influence over her when she spent the winter with her sister, who felt, like the rest of the family, "that Mary was ruining her character by her connection with me!"

Mary may not have cared what her family thought, for Lesassier was not the only one of her relatives to put his own interest before hers. She, like other unmarried women, had been left by her siblings to look after her mother alone for many years, and she was already involved in a lawsuit with one brother concerning her inheritance. Moreover, she was genuinely fond of Lesassier, assuring him often that "no attempt should ever succeed in weaning her affection" from him. Like her mother, she deplored the way he had been treated by the rest of the family: when the legacy of £50 left him by her mother was overturned through her brother's action, Mary paid it herself, believing it to be her mother's wish. In addition she may, like Lady Portsmouth, have been happy to have a kind, devoted friend to dance attendance on her, for Lesassier realized that he risked offending her "by apparent neglect" and "every motive—of policy, not less than grati-tude combines to make me exert my utmost to please her." Mary may also have reflected on the fact that James Hamilton was getting older, and had never shown himself very generous to the female members of the family; Catherine's mother was also growing older, and Catherine's chances of inheriting a fortune and thus becoming a connection to be prized were therefore rather better. Catherine herself was getting older, and it was more and more likely that she would die childless, leaving her money to her husband. Whatever her motives, though, Mary, again like Lady Portsmouth, made no positive commitment to giving Lesassier whatever he asked for, promising only "whatever she should be able to spare," and having to be coaxed into each loan or gift. He deplored what he called "her natural pusillanimity"—"When I . . . reflect upon Mary's abominable conduct, how can I fail to be low spirited—for, had she behaved towards me as any other woman would have done, I should, long ere this, have been relieved from all further anxiety respecting the future"—but what we would call the determination of an affectionate, fair-minded, but stern and self-willed woman to keep tight control both over her own money and her cousin. Lesassier's lack of power over her frustrated him beyond measure, as any form of independence among those he considered his subordinates always had: it was one thing to rely on the sacrifice of a devoted young lady but "what could be more revolting than for *me*, to live upon the eleemosynary assistance of an old maid!" Mary eventually decided to leave him £1,000 in her will, and she agreed to word the bequest so that he would not be required to repay to her estate the £1,100 she had lent him. Lesassier was grateful and did his best not to hope for her death. "Yet," he could not help noting, "it would be the making of me."

However revolting to his feelings, it was with Mary's assistance together with his own economizing that he made it through another year, and then another, and then another, so that he had, "once more, extending before me, the cheering prospect of a much tranquillity for a couple of years to come, as I have any right to expect in this transitory life." By 1827 his acquaintances began bowing to him again "after . . . years of cold neglect." He attracted a number of new patients, and he began to hope that he might, "within the space of four or five years, by dint of incessant toil, & good fortune, at length make my guinea a day—that is to say, between £300 and £400 a year." But his feelings were still easily hurt. New acquaintances, he found, were likely to have heard his story from their other Edinburgh connections, and even old friends might make remarks that cut him to the quick. One of his friends "absurdly & thoughtlessly" told him "how she had been defending me . . . against the charges respecting taking the scoundrel's practice, & Lady Kintore," charges he would much rather have forgotten ever existed. "A physician might succeed in London, although he failed here," said another, "granting he only possessed a good address & *character*," that character that Lesassier had so thoroughly lost. Any trifle could make him low spirited. "After all," he wrote, "surely, I have still abundant reason to be so, when I look around me, & reflecting on the past, compare my present situation with what it might have been— contrast my neglected & forlorn condition with the arrogant prosperity of those professional opponents, who were once so far behind me on the great road to eminence."

We can trace, in these years, a series of what can be called emotional makeshifts to maintain Lesassier's shattered self-esteem, running parallel to his financial makeshifts for paying his bills. It would have been prudent to sell or let his house and move to a smaller one, but just as in his army service, fine lodgings with many comforts became his compensation for his low professional rank, and he, Catherine, and Pierre all agreed that "it would sink us to the dust were we to remain in Edinburgh after parting with this house." He continually looked for ways to make his "splendid mansion" more elegant. He bought six vases for evergreens; called the smith "to metamorphose the shabby grate for the card-room into a brass-grate"; had the French chairs painted imitation oak and gilded. He learned to play chess and became passionately concerned both with winning and with possessing the finest accoutrements: "a superb set of indian chess, for four guineas, well worth twenty guineas," "perhaps 25 shillings—for a rosewood box to contain them & a gilded board to play upon," "a beautiful large set of bone chessmen at 24 shillings to save my . . . ivory ones." "I doubt," he wrote, "if any thing more elegant, appropriate, or superb, should be met with." He took care that he and Catherine were better dressed than ever before. He bought Catherine "a new silk cloak, lined with brown squirrel," though hard-pressed to know how he would pay for it; as for his own clothes, he had "never before, since I was married, dressed fashionably till now." The two of them were "so superbly dressed, that we are the objects of general notice," and their walks through town took on a new point, "to shew the execrable wretches, that I am still here; & that we are better dressed than nineteen out of twenty of the beggarly pack amongst whom, we are carelessly & contemptuously moving."

In 1827, Pierre revealed to his son that he, Pierre, was the illegitimate son of the Count de Rochepaliere; since the count had had no legitimate children, the title, Pierre claimed, thus devolved upon Pierre and his issue. Lesassier was only too happy to believe this extremely unlikely tale—for it is thoroughly doubtful that Pierre was the count's son, that the title would descend through an illegitimate line, or even that Monsieur de Rochepaliere was actually a count—which so strongly reinforced his most dearly held daydream. Certainly there was no external evidence for it and even he doubted "exceedingly . . . that I shall ever be able to make good our claims to the actual title." He tried to look up the count in the *Almanach de Gotha* and entered into a correspondance with the Marquis de Lafayette on the subject, a correspondence cut short by the events leading up to the revolution in France in July 1830. Lesassier took to wearing "the full arms & supporters" of the putative Count de Rochepaliere and had them engraved on the brass door plate at his house, writing that "notwithstanding my abject poverty, & forlorn uncertainty of my future prospects—I now feel a certain pleasing elevation of secret feeling, when I muse upon the lofty personage from whom I am descended." He tried, too, to get the French Cross of the Legion of Honor, as well as an English knighthood, for if he received either, he wrote, "I should certainly set instantly about dispatching to the different newspapers a paragraph, announcing to the news-loving people of Scotland the rankling & astounding intelligence of my being exalted for ever above their heads." Those attempts failing, he at least hoped to "satisfy my little circle of friends here," as to the justness of the claims and had the Coronet engraved on his tea-knives "to remind our guests of my title." But, he lamented, "it has produced no improvement" in the behavior of either Catherine or his friends, who still refused to treat him with appropriate "deference & respect."

His relationship to Catherine had in fact worsened under the strain of the many affronts to his self-esteem. For the most part they lived together amicably, for "peace at home," wrote Lesassier, "is the first blessing in the married state" and he was always "dejected . . . during my quarrels with Catherine." They still spent part of every day taking their "usual stroll," "idle, but laughing & enjoying our remarks"; they spent happy evenings "reading and conversing," occasionally taking "some hot negus together"; and they frequently went out for tarts and cookies at Ridpath's and lunch at Littlejohn's. But Lesassier's increasing irritability meant that their quarrels, when they came, were increasingly violent. Once, during the worst period of the Lady Kintore scandal, he had actually struck Catherine: "Aggravated by her shaking her clenched fist in my face, I knocked her down!!" But he was immediately sorry. "Never, since we married, had I been so cruel to her, & accordingly, I instantly perceiving my fault, expiated it on my knees to her. Poor thing, with her characteristic affection, she immediately forgave me. But, I never can forgive myself." Both were shocked at this episode, and there was no repetition, but they became increasingly less able to bear each other. "Oh! what man, in his senses, would be married, if he did but know the wretchedness to which, in nineteen cases out of twenty, he subjects himself for the remainder of his existence!" Lesassier wrote after one quarrel, and Catherine might have had similar sentiments after a violent scene occasioned merely by her wanting to read in bed. Lesassier tried to control his temper, or else, he wrote, "I do not know what rashness I might not be driven to commit" during his quarrels with Catherine. "I must just . . . avoid throwing myself into those paroxysms of rage . . .—lest they should end in either apoplexy, or paralysis; or what would be far worse lest, in a moment of frenzied passion, I should maim, or even kill her. Answering her deliberately, & in a gentle tone of voice—& walking out of the house, or taking up an amusing book till the emotion has subsided—is indeed, precisely, what I ought to do." He succeeded to some extent in cultivating this emotional detachment, and though their quarrels continued—"this low, vulgar, unmannerly, & foul-mouthed living-disgrace of mine," he called her in one of the worst of their altercations—so did their reconciliations.

In the meantime, though, Lesassier's attentions to other women became more insistent. He had learned his lesson "as to ever writing to any lady again!!" but he had not learned to be more continent, and he began to form sexual liaisons with most of his patients as well as any other woman who showed any interest. One of his patients, Mrs. Ramsay, was in delicate health, and he worked out a contract with her husband whereby he was paid five shillings per week to attend her whenever she might need it. His relations with her became a long-standing sexual liaison—her part, we may say, of his contract. He had another long-term liaison with another old patient, Mrs. Scott, and more intense, short-lived love affairs with nearly all the new ones he acquired: Catherine Hill, Euphemia Maugham, Margaret Wallace, Catherine Johnson, and Isabella Ross. The speed at which he was able, in many cases, to progress from attendance to examination "with the hand" to intercourse—leading, in the case of Euphemia Maugham, to her bearing his child (ugly, but with my eyes, he noted in Portuguese)—suggests that his disreputable reputation may have been one reason why he was called. He continued regular liaisons with his new servants May and Mary as well as a former servant Margaret, the latter leading to the fear of gonorrhea for the first time in fifteen years. The profusion is bewildering—it even included Catherine—for Lesassier consoled himself with rebuttal or failure with one woman by turning to another. To have so many liaisons was, once again, courting disaster through another scandal: "Self-reproach for my reckless folly—to give it no other name," he wrote on returning from a visit to Mrs. Scott, "rendered my walk home a very disagreeable one." Moreover, his sexual activity made no professional sense. Perhaps he assumed that love for him would attach his patients to him and make them, like Ella, more ready to serve him. But the course of true love for Lesassier never did run smooth: his patient-lovers grew tired of him, or they quarreled over his fee, or they grew jealous of his attentions to other young ladies in their circle, for Lesassier was always restlessly on the lookout for new conquests.

Acquiring women had become, like acquiring possessions, an outward sign of Lesassier's heroic aspirations. This was particularly marked as he began to show signs of age. "This is my birth-day," he wrote on 12 September 1827, "& I am shocked to say I am forty!! . . . I blush to think how very old I am, & how little good I have done either for others or myself." What vexed him "incomparably more than any thing," was finding he was "growing bald!! I who justly boasted of my strong, thick hair"; Edward Neville's family motto, "Let me be young again," had become his own. It reassured him to attribute Catherine Hill's love for him to "a triumph of manners and address over age," for she was only twenty-two, and he at that point, forty-one. He considered an equal triumph his affair with a poor, but genteel young lady companion of Euphemia Maugham's, Alicia Williamson. It was unusual for Lesassier to sleep with an unmarried lady, but he believed her unable to have children and was unable to resist her "shrinking trembling, blushing modesty . . . her artless fondness, . . . innocent and fascinating caresses!" Their liaison disturbed his conscience. "Oh! what must that monster deserve, who could abuse such unsuspecting affection," he wrote at the beginning of their affair, and repeatedly reproached himself throughout: "libidinous, gray-haired, old, goat." But he could not stop himself: is it astonishing, he wrote in French, that at my age—at forty-two—I am vain of being the object of the most tender love of such a beautiful and amiable child?

Such emotional investments in his love affairs brought with them concomitant loss of self-esteem when they went wrong. He was "excessively depressed" when Catherine Hill refused him the ultimate favor. He was able to "embrace" Margaret Wallace in secret, under pretext of an examination, but when he tried to have intercourse he failed to have an erection three times in succession. And she a mere coachmaker's wife! "At times, the recollection of what has occurred, makes me almost stamp with rage at such a failure. It will haunt me during the remainder of my life," he wrote. Who could imagine, he went on in Portuguese, that I, of all men, I so powerful in love, so magnificently formed, would suffer . . . the indignity of not being able to satisfy the most beautiful girl in the world. It was foolish, he continued in French as his Portuguese vocabulary failed him, to hope that a beautiful, and young, and voluptuous girl like her would come to love a man of my age, who had the misfortune—Ah! I blush from shame—to appear impotent! The emotional ups and downs of these affairs took him out of himself and gave him something to live for, for the rest of his life held no appeal for him, "so languid, heartless, & spiritless do I find myself, that I am unhinged & unfitted for every thing—even for light reading. At times, I almost tremble for myself; for, I shrink alike from a retrospect of the past, & an anticipation of the future; the one presenting to my view an appalling prospect of poverty, embarrassment, & final ruin; the other, a long & sickening train of improvidence, folly, & error!" Previously he had at least been able to hope for his final apotheosis, if not, like Edward Neville, into the aristocracy, at least into the forefront of his profession, but now he saw "the very individuals"—like that "ignorant upstart . . . Dr. Beilby"—"who had not even dreamed of practice long after *I* had commenced . . . riding through the Town while *I* am still walking in the rain & mud! But, I deserve it all ! Yet, I often wonder that my courage does not completely sink within me, when I compare what I *might* have been, with what I *am*."

And yet it was in this period, when his professional reputation was largely in shreds and his persona as a romantic hero had faded, that he gathered together the writings that best speak to the emerging image of the physician as romantic hero: his midwifery case histories. Case histories as a genre have existed since Hippocrates. By the eighteenth century they were enshrined in academic medicine as a test of diagnostic skill. In Lesassier's day, they mirrored the gradual transformation in medicine from a focus on the history of the sufferings of an individual patient, to the history of the disease as an entity in its own right, with the patient merely one example of the progress of that disease. Yet as the individuality of the patient retreated from the case history, the individuality of the physician describing the case advanced. In what we may call the romantic case histories of nineteenth-century medical and popular literature, the physician appears as hero, the disease or condition as his adversary, and the patient's body as their battleground. Instead of beginning, as earlier case histories did, with a description of the patient—"man, stout, plethoric, with ruddy complexion, aetas 40," they begin at the moment the doctor is sent for, as though the patient had no real history up to that point, or as if that history required the doctor to interpret it. They take the patient through the course of the doctor's treatment, and end, generally, with the end of the doctor's involvement with the case, sometimes but not always coterminous with the end of the condition for which he was called. It is, again, the physician who is the hero of the story; the history chronicles his activities; and it is those activities that bring the story to its climax and successful denouement. The most famous example of this genre is the history of the Elephant Man, told by Frederick Treves, so dramatic a case that it has been presented in film and stage a number of times. But similar examples can be found in the writings of the nineteenth-century American neurologist and author Silas Weir Mitchell as well as in the recent books of physician Oliver Sacks.

In its presentation of the physician as hero, the romantic case history was part of the process of collective self-fashioning that we call professionalization. The process as a whole was largely carried out by increased educational standards, creation of medical journals, and state licensing requirements, but the case history as exemplary act of the well-educated physician also had a part to play. It is the case history, rather than the novel, that first represented physicians as heroes. Traditional heroes of novels were gentlemen who led nobly idle lives when they were not being beloved by heroines; doctors were often rather disreputable figures of fun, like Susan Ferrier's Dr. Redgill. In this, as in so much else, Lesassier reflected his time. His own hero, Edward Neville, had been a sometime soldier and gentleman, not a physician; in the novel, we are still a long way from George Eliot's Tertius Lydgate or any of the dedicated young doctors of twentieth-century fiction. To find the shorter path to the physician as hero, we must turn to case histories.

Lesassier's case histories often have a dramatic power absent from his novel. They show his medical competence to best advantage, since they document successful cases of active intervention in delivery. In each case history, the protagonist is Lesassier himself, as the young physician called to the bedside; each case has its own woman—more or less beautiful—in more or less distress. He only wrote about cases where active intervention was necessary: this is of course part of the tradition of case histories, but it also means that Lesassier—the physician—is always presented as coming to the rescue. Like most of his writings, they began as rough notes, which he later expanded into a continuous narrative, complete with running headings. "Unusual adhesion of the placenta . . . but eventually I extract the whole," or "After great difficulty, I succeed in turning, but the infant is still born." Being sent for under those circumstances was certainly consistent with his practice as consulting physician, but so was being sent for too early and having to wait "without stirring, except once to swallow some slight refreshment," an event mentioned only once in the histories.

The persona of the physician in Lesassier's histories is much more attractive than in his journals: he is competent, careful, a little too quick to believe that a case is an easy one but equally quick to admit his mistake and determine the appropriate solution. Typically he came as a savior, bringing clarity and vision where there had been only distress and confusion. Like any hero, he had obstacles to surmount. The patient and her attendants could give him no useful information: he "could learn no distinct previous medical history of the patient," or received only "a vague account . . . of the previous duration of labor." Other practitioners had already tried to deliver the child and failed. Even the patient was an uncertain ally, for her pain and sensibility could get in the way of his efforts. In some cases initial difficulties even made Lesassier lose heart for a moment, so that he was "near abandoning" one case before rallying and bringing it to a successful conclusion. Faced with these obstacles, the physician was on his own, forced to rely on his own "energy and resources" as surely as a man contending with the elements, adrift at sea or alone in the wilderness.

Each of the case histories can be read as following the structure of a novel, with Man against Nature in the form of an obdurately adhering placenta or a too-narrow cervix constricted around an infant's neck. Unlike many of the episodes in Lesassier's novel, the case histories hold the attention of the reader, who wants to know how they will turn out. "On Friday the 20th of August," for example, Lesassier was sent for by a surgeon for help in removing the placenta after an otherwise successful delivery. The surgeon had been called in by the midwife who was attending the case, but "had been completely foiled in his endeavors to bring it away." "On introducing my hand into the vagina," Lesassier wrote, he found that "the placenta was partially separated . . . but the adhering portion seemed so intimately united to the uterus as to form part of that viscus. Every attempt I made to detach the adhering portion was completely fruitless. . . . I then resolved . . . to bring away as much of the placenta as I could, & leave the rest to be thrown off afterward. Yet, when I attempted to press away all that hung loose, it proved too firm for me to make any impression on it." In fact, it seemed to him that he had only two choices: "I must either leave the placenta absolutely in status quo to be extracted by some more fortunate operator, or do my best to pass up my long . . . scissors & cut off the detached piece."

What will Lesassier do, the reader wonders. Will he succeed in removing the placenta? And will the patient, "who had all along been very restless," survive the process? In fact he did succeed, by first removing the partially separated section by cutting, or rather, by "gnawing it through, fiber by fiber, with the nails, such as they were, of my thumb & forefinger." And he was subsequently able to remove even the adhering portion, as, "with the risk before my eyes of pushing my fingers through the sides of the uterus, I proceeded carefully & slowly to destroy the uniting medium which joined the adhering fragment to the uterus." In this case, the patient herself has almost vanished, and it takes effort to recall that the placenta is actually merely a body part inside a woman: it seems to have expanded to fill a universe of its own. Only at the end, the conflict resolved, does the patient herself partially reappear. A good deal of bleeding followed the operation, Lesassier tells us, but "At last the hemorrhage became diminished, a glass of spirits was exhibited to the patient . . . and I left her," he concluded, "doing well."

The "case of turning attended with great difficulty" had its own drama. Once again, Lesassier was called in at the request of a less experienced operator; once again, he could learn nothing material from the patient or her attendants. In this case, Lesassier appears as smug as Major Neville's physician in his novel as he advised the younger man "to turn; as I looked upon this to be a very favorable case for a beginner." He smiled, too, at the "imaginary difficulty" when the practitioner "after many fruitless attempts . . . was compelled to desist, as the feet, he said, always slipped out of his fingers." Taking over himself—and we can fill in the indulgent "Here, I'll show you how"—he found that "the uterus, especially the cervix, was very strongly contracted," even though the patient had been given a substantial dose of opium to stop the contraction. "I could not secure more than a single foot," he wrote, "and even that I could not, with all my force, bring down lower than the brim of the pelvis." As in the early case, all seemed lost, but again he found a way out: "I endeavored to slide a ligature over the foot that I had hold of." By this time it seemed clear that the infant was dead, and "by pulling steadily at the ligature . . . &, at the same time, pushing the head back with two fingers of the right hand," he succeeded in extracting it. The delivery accomplished, the patient again reemerged, "timid & uncommonly irritable & impatient," but recovering well from her experience.

Lesassier's life is full of might-have-beens, and nowhere are they so tantalizing as in these case histories. We must be honest: these cases do not indicate hidden brilliance in either literature or medicine. Lesassier was not a great writer, nor a great anatomist, nor a great clinician. He was merely a competent obstetrician whose interest in medicine formed a conjunction with his vision of himself as hero of his own life story, as when he was "sent for to a poor woman" whom he "happily snatched from inevitable death with her infant." "What a triumphant proof of my professional superiority," he wrote; he would get no fee from it, but the "feeling, however, is no mean reward for my trouble." And we may imagine this feeling multiplied throughout his generation of physicians. Men like Lesassier formed the backdrop to the educational and professional reformers of the mid-nineteenth century, who promoted the values of hard work, long years of study, public service, and absolute moral rectitude. What is tantalizing about Lesassier's cases is that they show him looking forward to those reforms as much as his historically absurd belief in his noble birth looked to the past. Could he not have rid himself of the latter, and concentrated solely on the former? the reader cannot help asking, thereby committing an historical absurdity of his or her own. Could he not have cut himself loose from any historical or emotional baggage that encumbered him, and dedicated himself solely to his profession?

Perhaps Lesassier's last chance to free himself from the past came on 24 January, 1829, when his father died. Pierre's presence in the household had not been an unmixed blessing. He made wrong diagnoses, appeared on public streets while tipsy, and stole books from Lesassier and Catherine to sell for drink. But he was still courteous and charming. He had helped support his son's spirits in the worst of his "pecuniary embarrassments . . . and domestic wretchedness," and Lesassier felt the loss keenly. "How could I have felt otherwise towards an only parent, who was so kind, so conciliating, & gently inoffensive, & well bred, & cheerful, as my father!" whose only fault was that, "with the characteristic improvidence of his countrymen," he had left "nothing whatever of the smallest value . . . and not even a single sixpence in money." By that time Lesassier's economizing and Mary's loans had reduced his debt, and the Kintore scandal had died down. The former ill feeling against him among many medical men, he was told, had been removed by his "correct & consistent conduct." His bad fortune seemed to be in remission. His financial agent actually went bankrupt while holding Catherine's entire trust fund of £2,000, threatening the Hamiltons with total ruin, but they were able to recoup nearly all the money. "Never did I hear of any one so fortunate as you," Catherine exclaimed to him. "You may do anything you choose now: I declare you are a second Faustus, for, you must have dealings with the evil one." With his father dead, Lesassier seriously considered moving to less expensive lodgings, and had he been able to bring himself to sell his "darling house," and keep from first courting and then alienating his patients, he might have had one last chance for professional success in civilian life.

But he could do neither, and the result was that his debts mounted again while his patients, old and new, drifted away. Mrs. Ramsay died: "Thus I lose an old & affectionate patient, & £12 a year!" Mrs. Rennie, whose child had died under his care, found another physician; Mrs. Hill and Mrs. Maugham grew tired of paying for his attendance when accompanied by protestations of love punctuated by quarrels; Mrs. Wallace left Edinburgh. In all his troubles, Lesassier's journal remained the perfect confidant he had proclaimed it as a boy, and his increasingly detailed daily entries catch the many small ways in which the eighteenth-century world that shaped his own perceptions was "gliding away," as he wrote of his own life, "like sand through the silent hourglass!" while a new society grew up around him. His patients, wives of petty clerks and shopkeepers, began to summer in the newly built suburbs south of the city, and his own housemaid had the "provoking assurance" to ask him to visit her married sister's infant. Gas lighting became available, and Lesassier had it installed in the kitchen, lobby, and bedrooms with elegant "large, frosted, vase-shaped glass-globes." The London mail cab began regular service to Edinburgh, delivering the London newspapers within "41–3/4 hours" of their issue; among other news they brought word of the Revolution of 1830 in France and of King Louis Philippe receiving "at his dinner-table, his new subjects in plain frock coats." And on 26 June 1830 Georgian Britain came to an end with the death of George IV; a few days later Lesassier and Catherine "stroll to High Street . . . expecting William IV."

By 1830 Lesassier was simply failing, for his fees from patients amounted to barely £70 per year: "What a professional finale!" He had to pile an additional loan, based on a life insurance policy taken out on the ever helpful Jenoway, on top of Mary Campbell's £1,100, and he was no longer paying many of his tradesmen's accounts. It was at this point that Fortune supervened, this time in the form of a letter from Sir James McGrigor. The War Office had grown tired of providing half-pay to surgeons whom it had not employed for fifteen years, and Lesassier, like all the others, was given a choice: go into active service, or have his half-pay replaced with a lump sum of £500. "Insane proposal!" he wrote, for that amount would not begin to pay his debts, and his life in Edinburgh could not possibly support a loss of £120 per annum. Despite his earlier response from McGrigor he had never given up hope of a return to the army as his "safest & most honorable asylum"—the military rank was the only one, he wrote on dining at Edinburgh Castle with his old colleague Swinton McLeod, "for which, I have any true respect"—and so he applied for active service. "Oh! that I may be called on full pay," was his frequent comment during the long, anxious wait which ensued. Though Jenoway gave him good advice for once—"Thinks I still shall be called upon full pay in my proper turn"—Lesassier could not keep from writing letter after letter urging all the officials whose names he knew to use their interest in his behalf. He recorded his dreams, too, with even more than usual assiduity. "I am standing, with nervous agitation, on a perilous height at the brink," he recorded on 2 September 1830, "& above, a large & very deep reservoir, which, however, is now dry; & the bottom is grown over with grass. Seeing a smooth, sloping foot-path, descending from where I stood, I leave my dangerous position, & walk down this road." Two days later his anxious wait was over, as he noted, "This dream verified by the Medical Board again placing me among the candidates for full pay, after so long refusing to do so, & by my escaping the peril of the £500 commutation."

On 12 April 1831 Lesassier was appointed surgeon with the 41st Regiment, at that point stationed in the pretty town of Moulmein, in Madras, where Catherine and Lesassier joined them. Most of their household effects may have been disposed of by auction to pay their debts and provide a cushion for their arrival in India. The castle of a house at 57 Northumberland Street was probably rented with Syme as agent, for it had several occupants in the next few years, including Lesassier's hated rival Dr. Beilby. Here we must leave a firsthand account, for Lesassier's journals after 1830 have not survived, so that we do not know how the long-projected removal from Edinburgh was accomplished. Our last word in Lesassier's own hand is a brief note dated 24 March 1831. "All the books to go with me," it reads, listing a few still to be picked up at the bookseller's. And it includes a few allusive fragments concerning the disposal of the journals, letters, receipts, and manuscripts that chronicled his life story: "Letters & Papers" gathered together, "Red Tape" for sealing them, and "Oak graining on trunk-cover" for packing them away.

# One Series of Hardships and Privations

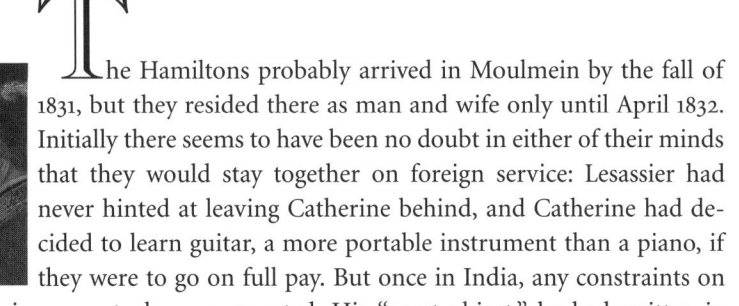

The Hamiltons probably arrived in Moulmein by the fall of 1831, but they resided there as man and wife only until April 1832. Initially there seems to have been no doubt in either of their minds that they would stay together on foreign service: Lesassier had never hinted at leaving Catherine behind, and Catherine had decided to learn guitar, a more portable instrument than a piano, if they were to go on full pay. But once in India, any constraints on Lesassier's behavior seem to have evaporated. His "great object," he had written in Edinburgh during one of their bad quarrels, was to become financially independent of her trust fund, "so as to put her away at the first opportunity;" "patience, patience, till I am fairly clear of this country, &, then, let her beware!" Now, on full pay, he may have made good his threats to make her miserable. He "gave himself up to adulterous practices and carnal dealings with other women," she charged, "and in particular . . . he so gave himself up to adulterous practices and carnal dealings with a native female"— probably his servant the "faithful Christian girl Ignatia," whom he kept as a mistress at Moulmein all winter and early spring. Catherine might have had some intimations of his earlier affairs, but this "criminal intimacy and adulterous intercourse" was "carried on so openly and avowedly," that she soon had full details. By April she had had enough, and she returned to her mother's house in Edinburgh. Perhaps at her mother's urging, and certainly with her encouragement, Catherine began the long, slow process of obtaining a divorce in June 1834.

Her decision to sue for divorce was a shock to Lesassier: Jenoway, acting as his agent, claimed he had "understood that a proceeding of a different kind was in contemplation against him," perhaps legal action to get him to send the money he had "solemnly pledged" to pay her when she left. Her choice of attorney may have shocked him as well, for it was James Ivory, husband of one of Lesassier's long-term patients. Catherine's solicitor, John Gibson, acted as her agent in obtaining incontrovertible proof of adultery, and she gave him Lesassier's personal papers, together with any information she had about his extramarital affairs. Gibson spoke to Isabella Allan, on the point of taking a position as servant in a household leaving for the West Indies, and he tracked Christian McKenzie, now married to a weaver, Allan, through the mill towns in Fife. He also spent "upward of 12 hours" at a time "perusing Autobiographical sketches by Dr. Hamilton in which he detailed all the incidents of his own life," translating "the Greek into the English characters," and employing a Portuguese translator for help where necessary. He had copies made of Isabella Hodgeson's letters "to lay before counsel"; and he spoke about the journal references to Isabella Ross who "peremptorily denied all that was there stated concerning her." Ross was the only unmarried mother among Lesassier's liaisons, which may explain Gibson's choice of her: perhaps he had no wish to provoke another divorce while trying to obtain this one. In the end Gibson was able to get enough testimony from the servants to prove Lesassier guilty of adultery without disturbing any of his more genteel mistresses, and Catherine filed her summons for divorce in 7 November 1834. The suit was not contested, and her divorce was granted in 25 May 1836, with Lesassier ordered to pay the expenses amounting to £230, 30 shillings, and 3 pence. Catherine brought one more suit against Lesassier for aliment from the time she left him until the divorce was final; this suit, too, was successful, and she was awarded a sum of £600, as well as an additional £13 for expenses.

With the divorce, and the loss of Catherine's money—for she would have been entitled to her trust fund, though it is not clear how this was effected—Lesassier had lost all chance of resettling in Edinburgh. Perhaps he found some happiness with his Christian servant, whom he called Anna Maria Ignatia Hamilton after his divorce, probably as a form of retribution against Catherine. He may have aspired to the love of young ladies, but had always been most at his ease with his servant-mistresses from Ann Dean onwards. It is likely, though, that his restless disposition came into play once again, for on 23 December 1836 he transferred to the surgeoncy of the 17th Regiment, based in Poona. He transferred once again, this time to the 57th Regiment, as of 1 March 1839. The 57th was stationed in Madras; perhaps Lesassier had decided he preferred it to Bombay, for Madras was generally considered the more desirable location.

Lesassier never returned to Madras. The 17th spent much of the early years of Victoria's reign peacefully garrisoned in one or another imperial outpost, but in 1839 it was one of the Queen's regiments to join forces with the East India Company's men in what became known as the First Afghan War. It was an inglorious war, fought to support the unpopular Shah Sujah on the throne, a move carried out despite the claimant's own desire to live in luxurious exile. Conceived with the idea of registering a strong British presence in Afghanistan, the war chiefly succeeded in arousing the warring factions to unite against the British troops, ending in the virtual destruction of the entire army of the Indus by December 1841.

No historian has cared to provide the same loving chronicle of the First Afghan War—"the Road to British Disaster," as one historian called it—as Charles Oman did for the Peninsular War, but we can still trace Lesassier's movements, for the long march across Afghanistan that marked the opening phases of the war acquired its own notoriety. Surgeons traveled in some luxury, and the account of Richard Kennedy, chief of medical staff of the Bombay division of the army, is as jaunty as some of Lesassier's Portuguese journals, pausing to describe their "rest in a noble orchard" while their "tents arrived and were pitching," where the trees were "surmounted and overhung with gigantic vines, which wreathing round the trunks, and extending to the remotest branches, festooned from tree to tree in a wild luxuriance of growth such as I had never dreamt of seeing in fruit-trees and the vine: it was the first month in spring, and they were covered with blossoms which perfumed the air, and presented a picture of horticultural beauty surpassing description." For most commentators, however, the march was long, hot, and exhausting, marked by dissension among the leaders and forebodings for the future: "Instead of the fancied party of pleasure," one officer wrote, "it has been one series of hardships and privations." The trip over the Bolan Pass in March 1839 was a nightmare. "Our cattle destroyed, the men worn out with fatigue, and want of proper food and rest. One of our marches, from the ignorance of the guide, perhaps, was in length forty miles nearly; seventeen, twenty, twenty-two miles, were distances which were perfectly common to us, and these in a country now become hotter even than India, and without *any halt*, and the soldiers on half rations, and those of the worst description. Every soul, soldier, officer, and servant had dysentery." Perhaps Lesassier had seen a gazette, and perhaps he was aware that he was now officially attached to the 57th. As in Portugal, though, he could not join his own regiment until his replacement arrived, but no replacement was available in the midst of the Bolan pass, "seven days' march, among mountains whose sides are nearly perpendicular in many places, without a vestige of herbage for the cattle to feed on."

Lesassier had been guilty, in his life, of many professional sins of omission and commission; his present situation was in large part "the effect of causes over which, generally speaking," as he had written earlier, "I have had perfect control." But it was still a hard fate for a man of fifty-one to have to toil on "again day after day, over a wretched road covered with loose flint stones," closer to genuine starvation than ever he had been on the Peninsula, "as men looked at the shrunk frames and sunken cheeks of each other, and in their own feebleness and exhaustion felt what wrecks they had become." He, like the rest of the army, must have been "heartily sick of this expedition"; no doubt he cursed his bad fortune; and it is possible that even the relief of his journal writing was denied him, for as the camels died or were carried off by marauders all excess weight had to be left behind: "the way was strewn with baggage—with abandoned tents, and stores; and luxuries which, a few weeks afterwards, would have fetched their weight twice counted in rupees, were left to be trampled down by the cattle in the rear, or carried off by the plunderers around them." The main body of the army arrived in the town of Kandahar on 4 May 1839, and a triumphant display of support for Shah Sujah was stage-managed by the British. We cannot say if Lesassier saw it, for he may already have been ill, and he died in Kandahar on 21 June 1839. In doing so he just missed the one military triumph of the war, the capture of Ghazni, the main fortress guarding the capital of Kabul, on 22 July 1839. It was therefore his successor, surgeon Smith of the 17th, who was publically crowned with laurels in surgeon Kennedy's published account of the battle, an unintentionally fitting conclusion to Lesassier's military career.

In Edinburgh, Lesassier's death made few ripples. Years earlier, trying to secure a legacy from Mary Campbell as well as release from paying back her loans, he had agreed to make Mary his own chief beneficiary after Catherine. "Oh! that it were in my power to do by her as she has done by me!" he had apostrophized after one of her loans, counting, in fact, on her dying first, for the £1,000 she had left him would have rescued him from all his financial embarassments. But it was Mary Campbell who survived him and thus became the executrix of his will and his chief beneficiary. His estate, after a legacy to his servant Ignatia, amounted to £700, so Mary was finally repaid at least part of the money she had lent him. We do not know what became of Catherine—there is certainly no mention of her in his will—nor whether to attribute the sale of the magnificent house at 57 Northumberland Street in 1867 to her mother's death or to her own. Emmeline Hawkins was married in 1830. In March 1840, Lady Kintore divorced her husband for adultery. She married again one month later, and died in 1841.

Among Lesassier's medical connections, the most eminent, Joseph Jordan, practiced with great success in Manchester until his death in 1873. Joseph Brown practiced in Sunderland until his death in 1868, late in life writing religious works in which no trace can be found of the apprentice who kept fireworks in his master's house so many years earlier. Lesassier's Edinburgh associates were less fortunate. Robert Knox's reputation never recovered from the Burke and Hare scandal, and he left Edinburgh in 1842. John Mackintosh was involved in scandal similar to Lesassier's: it was "alleged of him, that, in two instances, he has been detected in an attempt to enter his patients' houses, during night by the window!—that he made an open assignation with another married patient at a hotel, & actually took her to a bed room." He nonetheless remained in Edinburgh, operating a small medical school in Argyll Square, and died in 1837. Edward Milligan did not live to enjoy his fine house for too long. He was already going blind when Lesassier visited him in 1829, and he died in 1833.

James Hamilton died in 1839, just a few months after his nephew. His successor in the chair of midwifery was not the successful extra-academical lecturer John Thatcher, as Lesassier had thought, or anyone of his generation, but instead James Young Simpson, a baker's son, the last and most talented of the protégés of that same Professor John Thomson, whose recommendation the young Lesassier had been so anxious to get in 1806. Simpson, like Lesassier, read novels, and like Lesassier he was appointed by James Hamilton as assistant director of the Edinburgh Lying-In Hospital after receiving his M.D. in 1832. But there the similarity ends. Supported by a loving family, and embued with all the love of his profession Lesassier lacked, Simpson was appointed professor of midwifery in 1839, at age twenty-eight, and he, with his colleagues James Syme and Joseph Lister, did much to restore the Edinburgh Medical School to its former eminence. After Hamilton's death, his family sold the Lying-In Hospital, but Simpson bought it back for his midwifery classes, not without some private grumbling at their meanness—"Dr. Hamilton would blush to see what his family have done"—at his being thus obliged to buy back even the furnishings he himself had purchased for it. He renamed it the Royal Maternity Hospital, and one of his earliest uses of chloroform in childbirth was on a patient there. It is still possible to find the entry in the hospital case book, for Simpson, unlike Lesassier, kept very good records.

The records of Lesassier's own life are kept in the library of the Royal College of Physicians of Edinburgh, whose unsurpassed collection of Edinburgh medical manuscripts includes materials from his famous contemporaries, including James Hamilton and James Young Simpson. In his archive, if not in life, Lesassier finally ranks with the leading lights of his profession, sharing accommodations in an elegant neoclassical building in Edinburgh's New Town. Interested readers can examine professors' lecture notes and class lists, official correspondence, and case histories; or they can place all these polite and respectable sources to one side, and travel on the back roads of history with Alexander Lesassier's "most trusted friend," the journals of his life. He imparted every thought to them, confided every misfortune, sought consolation, commanded their secrecy. Whether in the end they served faithfully, or betrayed him, I leave to you, Dear Reader, to decide.

This book is largely based on the manuscript writings in the Alexander Lesassier Hamilton Collection of the Royal College of Physicians of Edinburgh. The collection as a whole consists of twenty-five archive boxes holding thousands of pages of correspondence, journals, and drafts of books. In 1987 it was liberated from the trunk in which Lesassier had placed it and put in order by Joy Pitman, then archivist at the Royal College. Lesassier's daily journals from 1803 to 1830 fill seventy-eight notebooks. Thirty-one small notebooks, with separate books for official letters and orders, cover the period of the Peninsular War, 1809–1814. Eighteen larger memoranda journals, with often lengthy daily entries, detail Lesassier's Edinburgh practice from 1821–1830. In addition to the daily journals, there are separate medical ledgers and cash books as well as ten "Somnia" notebooks describing Lesassier's dreams from 1825 to 1830. The manuscript of *Edward Neville* comprises approximately two thousand pages, and the manuscript of Lesassier's lecture on midwifery, nearly four thousand. Most of the material is not paginated, though Lesassier was usually consistent in dating his daily journals. I have tried to provide the most precise references possible, but in some cases interested readers will simply have to pick up a particular notebook and start reading. I promise they will not be bored.

Lesassier was a fluent and vivid writer, and I have not had to do much work to make his own words accessible to the modern reader. I have expanded all abbreviations, for example substituting "would" for "wd," "Edinburgh" for "Edinh." I have also modernized and Americanized the spellings: "the" for "ye," "labor" for "labour." I have generally kept his own words in quotation marks to indicate that they are his perceptions, not mine, but in cases where he appeared to be merely reporting, not interpreting, I have removed the quotation marks but included a citation to his journals.

The following examples indicate the changes I made to the manuscript. The first is from the "General Outline" for the manuscript of *Edward Neville*, Box 7, Folder 50: it is the description of Edward Neville I drew on for the portrait of Lesassier in Chapter 1. In this section, the character called Mr. Melburne in the final version is referred to as "the Doctor," and Dorothy of the final version is referred to as Susan. There are small inserts in this section, which I have transcribed within brackets.

> Am left unprovided for; but taken home by the Doctor, who, agreeably with my mother's last wish, resolves to adopt me. His family establishment described; with a sketch of his own life. Susan undertakes to teach me to read, whh I am

utterly ignorant of. Susan's history, Sam. He amuses me (ª) by, & gives me an early love for old chivalrous, & romantic ballads [while I steal beer of him]. I resolve on being a coachman; as being, I conceive, the grandest profession. My disposition exemplified by threatening to turn Susan out of doors, [& for what]—persuading a young woman, (a patient) to let me get on her back, while I pilfer sugar;—& an old man to go with me to the pantry, ~~while~~ & reach me down an apple-pye, whʰ I am found eating, with his old wig on; by helping a tall girl & some romping boys, children of a neighbour, an Attorney, in soaking up [every day yᵉ] gravy of [our] roasting meat.—Am treated with great harshness, instead of the contrʸ; hence, I become sullen, capricious, obstinate, [indolent] & liable to gusts of passion. Conseqˢ of my being always in the kitchen such as hearing my ~~father~~ Uncle & the most respect[able] persons & things ridiculed.

The second example illustrates Lesassier's use of Greek transliteration of Portuguese and French, in this case in his notes on his liaison with Margaret Wallace, discussed in Chapter 12. A section from the journal entry on 16 October 1828 looks like this:

Transliterated into uncorrected French, this reads:

"Ha! ma pauvre Margaritte, j'ai te dis adieu, et, peut etre, pour jamais! Mais, apres tout, c'est etre bien sot de vouloir q'une belle, et jeune, et voluptueuse fille, comme elle, voulait parvenir a aimer un homme de mon age, qui a le malheur—ah! que je rougis de honte—de lui paraitre impotent!"

# NOTES

The following abbreviations are used in the notes:
*EN*     [Hamilton], *Edward Neville*
"EN"    Mss. of "Edward Neville"
Frequently cited names of people in exchanges of correspondence are abbreviated as follows:
AH      Alexander Hamilton
AL      Alexander Lesassier
ALH     Alexander Lesassier Hamilton
CH      Catherine Hamilton
IH      Isabella Hodgeson
JH      James Hamilton
JM      James McGrigor
PL      Pierre Lesassier
All box and folder numbers in the notes refer to the Alexander [Lesassier] Hamilton Collection unless otherwise specified.

### Preface. A Journal of Life

ix    *self-construction* Seavey, pp. 1–9; Barker-Benfield, pp. 37–103.
      "*It is a work . . . reflections*" Boswell, "On Diaries," p. 259.
x     *modern British identity* See Colley.
      *professionalization . . .* There is a large literature on the professionalization of medicine, but useful starting places are P. Starr; and Friedson. For the eighteenth century, see Pelling, pp. 90–128; G. Holmes; and Lindemann, pp. 176–191.
      "*desirous . . . medicine*" Lawrence, " 'Desirous of Improvements in Medicine,' " pp. 171–192.
xi    *were aimed at women* As Mitterauer and Sieder described gender and middle-class culture, men are responsible for production, and women, for reproduction and consumption. This point is implied, less starkly, in Davidoff and Hall.
xii   "*let me have . . . hearts*" Sarah Fielding, *The Governess, or, Little Female Academy*, ed. Mary Cadogan (London: Pandora, 1987), p. 174, cited in A. Richardson, p. 136.
      *Benjamin Franklin* Seavey, p. 44.
      "*wholly virtuous . . . heroes*" O'Brian, p. 8.

### Chapter 1. Interest or Love

1     "*Nelly . . . outstretched in death*" "EN," Box 8, Folder 55.
      *novels like* Tom Jones There is an extensive literature on eighteenth-century novels. See Tompkins, *Popular Novel in England*, pp. 1–33; Tompkins, *Polite Marriage*; Mayo, pp. 273–358; Kenner, p. 65. Readership is discussed in Altick; McKeon.
2     "*September 12 1787 . . . & 20 days*" The note is slightly inaccurate: it records her age at death as 19, not 20. According to a note, "Mrs. LeSassier wrote this at this date viz 1789." Leaf from family Bible, Box 6, Folder 44.
      "*toiling . . . without receiving any thing*" Journal 1814–1816, pp. 55–57, Box 13, Folder 81.
      *father of ten children* One had died in infancy. Leaf from family Bible, Box 6, Folder 44.
      "*My father's inexplicable mystery . . . conclusion*" 30 June 1827, Box 14, Folder 85.
3     *excellent preliminary education* PL to AL, copy of letter dated 1 Jan. 1812, Box 2, Folder 12.

*"was perfectly disgusted"* PL to AL, Manchester, 1 Jan. 1812, Box 2, Folder 12.

*His travels* PL to AL, copy of letter dated 1 Jan. 1812, Box 2, Folder 12.

*From 1780 to 1782 . . . Edinburgh.* Pierre LeSassier, Class Tickets, Box 6, Folder 45.

*"by all means to marry . . . connections"* 15 July 1805, Box 11, Folder 72; on marriage as an economic strategy, see Davidoff and Hall; MacFarlane.

*"by which he had frequent opportunities . . . success"* Alexander Hamilton, midwifery class certificate for Pierre Lesassier, 12 July 1784, Box 6, Folder 45.

4 *"Every thing . . . amiable"* General Outline, "EN," Box 7, Folder 50.

*professors' unmarried daughters* For example, Professor Andrew Duncan's three unmarried daughters were buried with him in the churchyard in Buccleuch Place, and Professor Adam Ferguson's three daughters were likewise unmarried. Ferguson, 1:100.

*the beauty of the family* 11 Nov. 1805, Box 11, Folder 73.

*"eldest daughter . . . with [his] father"* Table drawn up by Lesassier of characters in his novel, "EN," Box 7, Folder 50.

*they were married* Marriage certificate between Peter Le Sassier and C. Hamilton, Musselburgh, 1 Sept. 1786, Box 6, Folder 44.

*"I . . . Gretna Green"* Austen, *Pride and Prejudice,* p. 257; Pool, pp. 183–184.

*"is never forgiven . . . her family"* Table drawn up by Lesassier of characters in his novel, "EN," Box 7, Folder 50.

*more respectable ceremony* Marriage certificate, 11 Oct. 1786, Box 6, Folder 44.

5 *"natural and acquired abilities . . . unparalleled"* 10 Nov. 1805, Box 11, Folder 73.

*"had for sometime before . . . recovered his health"* Letter from JH and AH to Rev. Dr. Ashton of Middleton, Edinburgh, 7 May 1788, Box 6, Folder 45.

*"the word Accoucheur"* PL to ALH, Manchester, 25 Sept. 1818, Box 2, Folder 12.

*taught women midwifery* PL to ALH, Manchester 16 Sept. 1818, Box 2, Folder 12.

*"Their view was selfish . . . connections"* PL to ALH, Manchester, 25 Sept. 1818, Box 2, Folder 12.

*"it was objected . . . trials"* 24 May 1787, minutes 1771–1793, pp. 310–311, Royal College of Surgeons of Edinburgh, Surgeons Hall, Edinburgh.

*"A sacrifice . . . whole family"* PL to ALH, Manchester, 25 Sept. 1818, Box 2, Folder 12.

6 *"If I had married . . . York"* PL to ALH, Manchester, 26 Sept. 1818, Box 2, Folder 12.

*Edward Neville's father. . . family* "EN," Box 8, Folder 55.

*sufficient courses to apply for graduation* Edinburgh University Library ticket, 12 July 1784, Box 6, Folder 45.

*Alexander Hamilton provided one* Letter from JH and AH to the Rev. Dr. Ashton of Middleton, 7 May 1788; diploma from St. Andrews University, December 1787. Box 6, Folder 45.

*"the still contracted . . . entitled him to it"* Letter from JH and AH to Rev. Dr. Ashton of Middleton, 7 May 1788, Box 6, Folder 45.

*"seized with consumption"* PL to AL, copy of letter dated 1 Jan. 1812, Box 2, Folder 12.

7 *"who behaved . . . tenderness"* 10 Nov. 1805, Box 11, Folder 73.

*"sweet boy . . . reluctantly"* JH to PL, Edinburgh, 2 Oct. 1792, Box 2, Folder 12.

*"crying on the attic stairs"* Austen, *Mansfield Park,* p. 15.

*"How often . . . inalienable right"* 4 July 1827, Box 14, Folder 85. For a more notorious version of a young man's belief in his noble birth, see Holmes, *Dr. Johnson,* p. 150.

8 *competing for limited resources* For an example of this kind of competition between mother and daughter, see Nancy Woodforde's diary, printed in Woodforde, pp. 37–85.

*"abilities . . . business"* Letter from JH and AH to Rev. Dr. Ashton of Middleton, 7 May 1788, Box 6, Folder 45.

*"professional zeal . . . tipsy"* General Outline, "EN," Box 7, Folder 50.

*George Eliot . . . loan* See Eliot; for other ramifications of the theme of guaranteeing a loan in eighteenth century literature, see Ziff, p. 57.

*fathers lost their fortunes* 15 March 1808, Box 11, Folder 74.

*"that uncertain, casual, precarious . . . encounter"* Hazlitt, "On the Want of Money," in *Complete Works,* 17:176.

*"I regret . . . none"* 25 Jan. 1806, Box 11, Folder 73.

*Pierre's housekeeper* Journal Jan.-March 1812, Box 13, Folder 79.

"*Suspicious to excess . . . scold*" Table drawn up by Lesassier of characters in his novel, "EN," Box 7, Folder 50.

9    *climbing on a patient's back* General Outline, "EN," Box 7, Folder 50.

*learned to read . . . application* "EN," Box 8, Folder 55.

*Manchester Free School* J. F. Smith *The Admission Register*, 2:206; Mumford, pp. 205–242; Hans, pp. 19–41.

"*what could be easier . . . reward*" "EN," Box 8, Folder 55.

"*Idleness . . . I acquire*" General Outline, "EN," Box 7, Folder 50, "pilfering" crossed out on the page, but still legible.

*Roderick Random* Roderick Random's character has been seen by commentators from the eighteenth century to the present as mirroring Smollett's own, but Smollett himself wrote "that (the account of the expedition to Carthagena excepted) the whole is not so much a representation of my life as that of many other needy Scotch surgeons whom I have known either personally or by report." Smollett, pp. 6–7; Knapp.

"*I become sullen . . . passion*" General Outline, "EN," Box 7, Folder 50.

*a host of characters* Such characters were a common feature of the novels of the period. Michael Warner has called attention to the "chorus of minor characters" who "admonish" Eliza Wharton, the heroine of Hannah Foster's *The Coquette*, "to a more republican comportment." Warner, p. 174.

"*To a father . . . Instruction*" JH to PL, Edinburgh, 2 Oct. 1792, Box 2, Folder 12.

"*he always had urgent business . . . shoes*" "EN," Box 8, Folder 55.

10    "*(absurdly) . . . persuasions*" General Outline, "EN," Box 7, Folder 50.

"*of utterly neglecting . . . tasks*" "EN," Box 8, Folder 55.

"*I'm sure my father . . . any more*" 31 Jan. 1806, Box 11, Folder 73.

"*be prevailed upon . . . advantage to him*" "EN," Box 7, Folder 53.

*She had him arrested* Notes at end of Journal, Nov. 1806-Feb. 1808, Box 11, Folder 73.

"*in his french . . . greek*" "EN," Box 7, Folder 53.

*He was taught to ride* General Outline, "EN," Box 7, Folder 50.

"*all attention . . . boxes*" EN, 1:193.

"*Lord . . . called to mind*" 17 March 1808, Box 11, Folder 74.

"*gardens . . . amusement*" 23 June 1805, Box 11, Folder 72.

"*For a long time . . . Milliners Girls &c there*" General Outline, "EN," Box 7, Folder 50.

11    *He left his grandson . . . estate* JH to PL, Edinburgh, 3 June 1802, Box 2, Folder 12.

"*In consequence . . . thoughtless disposition*" "EN," Box 7, Folder 53.

"*Dr. — . . . to a patient*" Alcock, p. 8.

"*splendid Highland uniform*" McGrigor, *Autobiography*, p. 4. See Chapters 7 and 8.

"*a love for his Profession . . . shine in it*" 17 Nov. 1804, Box 11, Folder 72.

12    *equally moody adolescent* Chatterton's biographer E. H. W. Meyerstein makes the point that it is not clear what sort of place Walpole, or other patrons, could have found for him that would have been a reasonable outlet for his talents. For studies of adolescence in early modern Europe, see Ozment; Hanawalt.

*one influential educator* See Edgeworth.

"*afterwards enable him . . . elegant manner*" "EN," Box 7, Folder 53.

"*I would gradually . . . all who knew me*" 20 Aug. 1805, Box 11, Folder 72.

"*scene . . . wreck behind*" 26 Oct. 1803, Box 11, Folder 72.


Chapter 2. Born to Misfortune

13    *distance to foreground* This phrase is taken from William Gilpin's discussions on picturesque landscape. See especially Gilpin, *Observations on the Mountains and Lakes*, pp. xxiv–xxxi. Gilpin's influence on Lesassier is discussed in Chapter 5.

"*One in whom . . . secrecy*" 10 June 1805, Box 11, Folder 72.

*And yet his journals were . . . addressed* For illuminating discussions of the relationship between writer and intended audience, see Pascal; Spacks; Raoul.

*Commentators . . . from Clara Reeve* See Reeve; Brownstein; Radway; Radford. Most recently

Richter, p. ix, has asserted, "Though some men clearly read the Gothic, its primary appeal, then as now, was to women; it was typed as 'female reading,' " but the type of evidence he cites, book reviews, diaries, and contemporary fiction (pp. 109–124), can also be marshalled to show that men were avid readers of novels.

"*I myself . . . hundreds and hundreds*" Austen, *Northanger Abbey*, p. 107. Henry Crabb Robinson certainly read novels: see *Henry Crabb Robinson on Books and Their Writers*. Young Charles Dickens also read novels and imagined himself to be his favorite characters: cited in Kelly, ed., pp. 366–367. And as Richter, p. 196, notes, "Thomas Babington Macaulay . . . used to frequent . . . the circulating library, and it is suggestive that . . . he read at least one romance closely enough to have kept a tally of how often the various characters fainted."

*Lady Emily and Mary Douglas* See Ferrier, *Marriage*, p. 314; Caracciolo.

"*not always . . . improvement*" "EN," Box 7, Folder 53. Dickens read the *Arabian Nights* as well. Kelly, p. 366.

"*fix their eyes . . . own practice*" Cited in Kelly, p. 44.

"*Where . . . Novels I suspect*" Austen, "Love and Friendship," p. 81.

"*His features . . . produced*" EN, 1:124.

14    *prize his exquisite sensibility* Like the "amiable and refined Laura" of Austen's "Love and Friendship," who had a "sensibility too tremblingly alive to every affliction of my Friends, my Acquaintance and particularly to every affliction of my own." Austen, "Love and Friendship," p. 78. There is substantial literature on the cult of sensibility. See, for example, Tompkins, *Popular Novel*, pp. 70–115; Barker-Benfield.

"*alive to impression . . . trouble to conceal*" "EN," Box 8, Folder 55.

"*Some . . . born for misfortune*" 30 Aug. 1805, Box 11, Folder 72.

"*the tricks of Fortune*" 21 Sept. 1805, Box 11, Folder 72.

"*aristocratic notions*" EN, 1:4.

"*manly figure and deportment*" EN, 1:111.

"*shed tears . . . vexation*" EN, 1:227.

"*September 12th 1803 . . . move to*" 12 Sept. 1803, Box 11, Folder 72.

"*of all pleasure . . . studying hard*" 26 Oct. 1803, Box 11, Folder 72.

"*Such expense . . . an only son*" This example is taken from a later quarrel; Lesassier never said precisely what precipitated the first entry in his diary. 10 Sept. 1805, Box 11, Folder 72.

"*a Quaker . . . respectable man*" 12 Sept. 1803, Box 11, Folder 72.

"*where every branch . . . taught*" Mary Hewson to Thomas Tickell Hewson, 9 July 1795, Hewson Papers.

"*the metropolis . . . practical medicine*" Samuel Powell Griffitts to Benjamin Rush, London, 10 Aug. 1783, Rush Mss, cited in Bell, p. 15.

15    *University of Glasgow* Rosner, pp. 11–24.

"*Now on full conviction . . . absurd*" Parkinson, pp. 37–38.

"*Apprentices . . . whole shop*" Duncan, p. 414.

"*instruct them . . . perfect way*" William Brown, p. 83.

*teaching them botany . . . bandages* This ideal picture is implied by Lucas; Chamberlaine; William Brown.

16    "*By which step . . . God only knows*" 12 Sept. 1803, Box 11, Folder 72.

"*house which was furnished . . . Gentleman*" 20 June 1805, Box 11, Folder 72.

"*a very intelligent . . . opinions*" 14 Sept. 1803, Box 11, Folder 72.

"*exquisitely formed . . . teeth*" 26 Sept. 1803, Box 11, Folder 72.

*nearly burning . . . in their room* 27 Feb. 1804, Box 11, Folder 72.

"*surrounded with practice*" 20 June 1805, Box 11, Folder 72.

"*not strict . . . extremely well*" 26 Sept. 1803, Box 11, Folder 72.

"*over some mere . . . three days ago*" 21 April 1804, Box 11, Folder 72.

"*harsh . . . dislike her*" EN, 1:252.

"*my respected Master*" 27 Feb. 1804, 11, Folder 72.

"*an infamous Rascal*" 21 April 1804, Box 11, Folder 72.

"*slavish task . . . medicines*" Dec. 1804, Box 11, Folder 72.

"*I wish he . . . insupportable*" 26 March 1804, Box 11, Folder 72.

"*I began . . . Brown had ever been*" Dec. 1804, Box 11, Folder 72.

"*a little boy . . . very comfortable*" 1 June 1804, Box 11, Folder 72.

17    "*is a curse . . . patient*" Baxandall, pp. 38–39.

"*the vocabulary . . . others*" Baxandall, p. 39.

"*business . . . in my power*" 24 April 1804, Box 11, Folder 72.

"*a fickle one . . . through life*" 23 June 1805, Box 11, Folder 72.

"*a Lieutenant's Commission . . . for life*" 20 March 1805, Box 11, Folder 72.

"*What perseverance . . . example*" 5 March 1805, Box 11, Folder 72.

"*The most perfect . . . occasions*" A. Smith, *Moral Sentiments*, p. 119.

"*natural pride . . . sentiment*" 10 June 1827, Box 14, Folder 85.

"*young nobleman . . . ever arrive at*" A. Smith, *Moral Sentiments*, p. 117.

18    "*nonchalance . . . ease*" Ferrier, *Marriage*, p. 273.

"*a scheme . . . Spain*" 1 July 1804, Box 11, Folder 72.

"*May independency . . . reward*" toast to Jenoway, 16 Sept. 1804, Box 11, Folder 72.

"*Young men . . . gallantry*" Fielding, p. 119.

"*a more corrupt work*" according to Hannah More's *Memoirs*, 1780, cited in Henderson, p. 42.

"*obliging . . . general*" Fielding, p. 119.

"*Villain, seducer . . . towards me*" 21 April 1804, Box 11, Folder 72.

"*This independent . . . benefit to me*" 1804, Yearly Retrospect, Box 11, Folder 72.

"*My spirit . . . independent*" Austen, *Northanger Abbey*, p. 147.

19    "*I send my love . . . Cunt*" Chatterton, 1:686–687.

"*To my ear . . . pride*" Meyerstein, p. 98.

"*partly . . . request*" 21 April 1804, Box 11, Folder 72.

"*my master's daughter . . . was mad*" 24 April 1804, Box 11, Folder 72.

"*filles de joie . . . hint at*" 23 June 1805, Box 11, Folder 72; Stone, pp. 318, 343–344, 353–354.

"*Good heavens . . . her*" 25 June 1805, Box 11, Folder 72.

"*be imprudent . . . apprenticeship*" 27 Feb. 1804, Box 11, Folder 72.

"*from a single heedless . . . shape*" 25 June 1805, Box 11, Folder 72.

"*perfectly happy . . . in town*" 1804 Yearly Retrospect, Box 11, Folder 72.

"*May the honest heart . . . distress*" His response to Lesassier's toast. 16 Sept. 1804, Box 11, Folder 72.

"*resorted . . . mortals*" Dec. 1804, Box 11, Folder 72.

20    "*in Mr. C's . . . dangerous*" 1 Jan. 1805, Box 11, Folder 72.

"*A complete study . . . experiment*" 20 March 1805, Box 11, Folder 72.

"*From the time . . . the garden*" 20 March 1805, Box 11, Folder 72.

*Jordan's first indenture* Jordan, p. 19.

"*took the first . . . companion*" 20 March 1805, Box 11, Folder 72.

"*defiance . . . slavery*" 2 March 1805, Box 11, Folder 72.

"*no fear . . . master*" 20 March 1805, Box 11, Folder 72.

"*frequented . . . a separation*" 20 March 1805, Box 11, Folder 72.

"*Thou'd better . . . Alexander*" 12 March 1805, Box 11, Folder 72.

"*They best . . . dare!!*" Attributed to Ossian, on cover of Journal 21 Feb-12 March 1805, Box 11, Folder 72.

"*bold decisive step*" 12 March 1805, Box 11, Folder 72.

"*laconic letter . . . So that I live*" 20 March 1805, Box 11, Folder 72.

21    "*Jordan . . . before us*" 4 April 1805, Box 11, Folder 72.

"*telling him . . . attends me*" 16 April 1805, Box 11, Folder 72.

22    *Pierre . . . refused to pay* 27 March 1805, 4 April 1805, Box 11, Folder 72.

"*behaves to me . . . accounts*" 16 April 1805, Box 11, Folder 72.

"*that absolutely . . . studying*" 30 April 1805, Box 11, Folder 72.

"*How fickle . . . young men*" 20 May 1805, Box 11, Folder 72.

"*we ended . . . serious manner*" 28 May 1805, Box 11, Folder 72.

"*We never take . . . strangers*" 20 June 1805, Box 11, Folder 72.

*weeping, sentimentality* The growing body of literature on men's studies has concentrated on the

Victorian period, but for general statements on the variety of masculinities see Sussman, p. 8; Stearns, pp. 10–11, 13–38; Watson. Sherrod discusses the modern assumptions that men's friendships are less emotional and include less physical intimacy than women's.

"*the sooner . . . the better*" 4 April 1805, Box 11, Folder 72.

*A position as apothecary . . . Saddleworth* 28 April 1805, Box 11, Folder 72.

"*a project . . . the world*" 15 July 1805, Box 11, Folder 72.

"*an old gentleman . . . assistance too*" 27 July 1805, Box 11, Folder 72.

23   "*I am . . . happy manner*" 4 June 1805, Box 11, Folder 72.

"*Last night . . . necessary*" 10 June 1805, Box 11, Folder 72.

*telling him to make up a medicine chest* 30 Aug. 1805, Box 11, Folder 72.

*offering to introduce him . . . amount* 4 Aug. 1805, Box 11, Folder 72.

"*easy obliging . . . skill*" John Bard to Samuel Bard, New York, 11 Dec. 1765, Bard papers. On the intricacies of patient management, see Porter and Porter, pp. 85–95, 139–143.

"*It was well known . . . reverse*" 6 Oct. 1805, Box 11, Folder 73.

"*The town . . . world's opinion*" 27 July 1805, Box 11, Folder 72.

"*Young medical practitioners . . . resort*" 7 Sept. 1805, Box 11, Folder 72.

*He dressed as well . . . "quality"* 4 Aug. 1805, 14 Sept. 1805, Box 11, Folder 72.

"*we find . . . must be seen*" 7 Sept. 1805, Box 11, Folder 72.

*Cinderella Complex* See Dowling; for a discussion of how women's academic success is derailed by visions of romance, see Holland and Eisenhart.

24   "*as follows . . . to bed*" 5 Oct. 1805, Box 11, Folder 73.

"*independancy . . . my living*" 14 Sept. 1805, Box 11, Folder 72.

"*I have . . . Lord!*" 2 Oct. 1805, Box 11, Folder 73.

*local gentry . . . ability* Digby, pp. 172–174.

"*that such questions . . . service to me*" 22 Sept. 1805, Box 11, Folder 72.

"*had heard . . . placid smile*" 14 Sept. 1805, Box 11, Folder 72.

*Pierre . . . "succeeded with me"* 21 Sept. 1805, Box 11, Folder 72.

*advance on the interest* 10 Sept. 1805, Box 11, Folder 72.

*James Hamilton . . . £10* 28 Sept. 1805, Box 11, Folder 72.

"*that I was . . . undertaking*" 6 Oct. 1806, Box 11, Folder 73.

"*anxiety . . . midwifery*" 6 Oct. 1806, Box 11, Folder 73; Lesassier did have some obstetric patients, though it is not clear who they are. See 25 Oct. 1805, Box 11, Folder 73.

25   "*Such a plan . . . in the world*" 6 Oct. 1806, Box 11, Folder 73.

"*Bravo! Bravissimo!*" 30 Oct. 1806, Box 11, Folder 73.

"*This piece of news . . . delightful*" 25 Oct. 1806, Box 11, Folder 73.

"*my library . . . connections with women*" 20 June 1805, Box 11, Folder 72.

"*Young men . . . destruction*" 25 June 1805, Box 11, Folder 72.


Chapter 3. Hot from Your Studies

26   "*Edinburgh . . . place*" 5 Nov. 1805, Box 11, Folder 73.

"*with a most . . . garden*" 8 Nov. 1805, Box 11, Folder 73.

"*ran forwards . . . in turns*" 5 Nov. 1805, Box 11, Folder 73.

"*the lady . . . joy*" 10 Nov. 1805, Box 11, Folder 73.

"*was so different . . . dear*" 5 Nov. 1805, Box 11, Folder 73.

"*great incentive . . . idleness*" The quote is from George Bell, in *Evidence, Oral and Documentary*, 1:448.

"*Who . . . spoken about*" 10 Nov. 1805, Box 11, Folder 73.

"*a little man . . . old*" 5 Nov. 1805, Box 11, Folder 73

27   "*one of the liveliest . . . gentleman*" 10 Nov. 1805, Box 11, Folder 73.

"*a fat plain . . . countenance*" 5 Nov. 1805, Box 11, Folder 73.

"*very agreeable . . . housewife*" 10 Nov. 1805, Box 11, Folder 73.

"*fine dashing lady . . . stone*" 5 Nov. 1805, Box 11, Folder 73.

"*a sweet retired . . . Edinburgh*" 27 April 1806, Box 11, Folder 73.

"*in his carriage . . . connections*" 5 Nov. 1805, Box 11, Folder 73.

"*the sprightly . . . gentleman*" 25 Jan. 1806, Box 11, Folder 73.

"*the merriest . . . knew*" Emmeline Hawkins to Catherine Hamilton, 7 Jan. 1823, Box 1, Folder 9.

"*advanced me . . . pleased*" 17 Nov. 1805, Box 11, Folder 73.

"*That I should . . . supper*" 5 Nov. 1805, Box 11, Folder 73.

"*I have . . . possess it*" 29 Nov. 1805, Box 11, Folder 73.

28    "*the first . . . empire*" Duncan, p. 424.

"*This week . . . manner*" 17 Nov. 1805, Box 11, Folder 73.

*Leisure for study . . . vain* See Dierks.

"*will not allow . . . studies*" 25 Jan. 1806, Box 11, Folder 73.

*lived like . . . uncle* 3 Dec. 1805, Box 11, Folder 73.

*going to church* 25 Jan. 1806, Box 11, Folder 73.

*writing his journal* 13 Dec. 1805, Box 11, Folder 73.

"*by constantly attending . . . formerly did*" 29 Nov. 1805, Box 11, Folder 73.

"*a mere dream . . . School*" 25 Dec. 1805, Box 11, Folder 73.

"*What can . . . delightful thought*" 10 Nov. 1805, Box 11, Folder 73.

29    "*forming . . . exciseman*" n.d., Journal 1814–1816, p. 98, Box 13, Folder 81.

*same income bracket* There is an extensive literature on the limits of education as a vehicle for social mobility. For this period, see A. Richardson, pp. 25–33; see also Bourdieu and Passeron; Willis; Macleod.

*Alexander Hamilton's will* JH to PL, Edinburgh, 3 June 1802, Box 2, Folder 12.

"*led a dissipated life . . . enraged*" 15 Dec. 1805, Box 11, Folder 73.

"*a sister . . . deserted me*" IH to ALH, Liverpool, 3 Jan. 1822, Box 1, Folder 10.

"*very young looking*" 5 Nov. 1805, Box 11, Folder 73.

"*as active . . . son*" 10 Nov. 1805, Box 11, Folder 73.

"*his unnatural . . . sisters*" IH to ALH, Liverpool, 3 Jan. 1822, Box 1, Folder 10.

*far from fashionable* IH to ALH, Liverpool, 16 Oct. 1822, Box 1, Folder 10.

30    "*paternal conduct . . . to me*" 27 April 1806, Box 11, Folder 73.

"*there is nothing . . . more*" 25 Jan. 1806, Box 11, Folder 73.

"*My father . . . they give*" 29 Nov. 1805, Box 11, Folder 73.

"*a Scotch Pebble . . . shillings*" 13 Dec. 1805, Box 11, Folder 73. On Scotch pebbles see Ferrier, *Marriage*, pp. 378–380.

"*present . . . guineas*" 15 Dec. 1805, Box 11, Folder 73.

"*the first present . . . hand*" 1 Jan. 1806, Box 11, Folder 73.

"*My life passes . . . on them*" 25 Jan. 1806, Box 11, Folder 73.

"*You condemn . . . emotions*" *Death's a Friend*, 1:1–2.

31    "*A fine . . . creature*" 5 Nov. 1805, Box 11, Folder 73.

"*the first . . . relations*" 13 Dec. 1805, Box 11, Folder 73.

"*Egad! . . . body or other*" 15 Dec. 1805, Box 11, Folder 73.

"*the most lovely . . . aunt*" 11 Nov. 1805, Box 11, Folder 73.

"*I never . . . sister*" 15 Dec. 1805, Box 11, Folder 73.

*Herman Melville* See Melville.

"*much resemble . . . heart*" 15 Dec. 1805, Box 11, Folder 73.

*incestuous passion . . . death* Henry Seymour in *Death's a Friend* dies in duel; a closer parallel is Hillaston in John Chater's *The History of Tom Rigby* (1773), who attempts suicide because he is haunted by the love of his sister. See Tompkins, *Popular Novel*, pp. 62–66.

"*blew his brains . . . suicide*" 7 Nov. 1810, Box 12, Folder 77.

"*but oftener . . . otherwise*" 20 April 1806, Box 11, Folder 73; see J.C. Robinson.

"*We must not . . . decrees*" IH to ALH, Chatham, 28 March 1820, Box 1, Folder 10.

"*the moon . . . affection*" 20 April 1806, Box 11, Folder 73.

32    "*ever Dear Laura*" 21 Oct. 1807, Box 11, Folder 73.

*she married* According to a newspaper clipping kept by Lesassier, they were married 7 Jan. 1807. Box 11, Folder 73.

"*that there . . . constancy*" IH to ALH, Artillery Barracks (Chatham), 4 July 1820, Box 1, Folder 10.

*"best plan . . . finish"* 31 Jan. 1806, Box 11, Folder 73.

*"requesting . . . compliment"* 4 April 1806, Box 11, Folder 73.

*"had promised . . . mateship"* 24 April 1806, Box 11, Folder 73.

*"was excessively . . . Classes"* 26 April 1806, Box 11, Folder 73.

*"great numbers . . . situations"* 20 April 1806, Box 11, Folder 73.

*"went to the door . . . away"* 26 April 1806, Box 11, Folder 73.

*"of my . . . here"* 26 April 1806, Box 11, Folder 73.

*"then thanked . . . London"* 27 April 1806, Box 11, Folder 73.

33 *"heartily tired . . . until 9"* 30 April 1806, written as Wednesday April 29, Box 11, Folder 73.

*"dread . . . place"* 26 April 1806, Box 11, Folder 73.

*"You are hot . . . trials"* 26 April 1806, Box 11, Folder 73.

*"Good God . . . despair"* 24 April 1806, Box 11, Folder 73.

*Napoleonic Wars . . . entitled to half-pay* This was part of a general rationalization of military departments under the Duke of York as commander in chief and his adjutant general, Sir Harry Calvert. Ward, pp. 18–19.

34 *"create a young man . . . West Indies"* 30 April 1806, Box 11, Folder 73.

*"if I had . . . indentures"* 1 May 1806, Box 11, Folder 73.

*"pull out . . . date"* 26 April 1806, Box 11, Folder 73.

*"How long . . . got through it"* 1 May 1806, Box 11, Folder 73.

35 *David Balfour* See Stevenson.

*"sat in the greatest anxiety . . . ordered this"* 2 May 1806, Box 11, Folder 73.

*David Dundas . . . surgeons* Cope, p. 315.

36 *"These were very unfavorable . . . studies"* 2 May 1806, Box 11, Folder 73.

37 *"has received . . . rude"* 8 May 1806, Box 11, Folder 73.

*attending lectures in London . . . "over again"* 1 May 1806, Box 11, Folder 73.

*"I am now . . . starvation"* 7 May 1806, Box 11, Folder 73.

*"that the orders" . . . only eighteen* 15 May 1806, Box 11, Folder 73.

38 *"the illiberal antipathy"* 26 April 1806, Box 11, Folder 73.

*"Wiseacres . . . title to it"* 15 May 1806, Box 11, Folder 73.

*"delighted . . . rapidly"* 12 May 1806, Fox 11, Folder 73.

*"gold pencil . . . of the kind"* 22 May 1806, Box 11, Folder 73.

*"condoling . . . found"* Evening, 12 May 1806, Box 11, Folder 73.

*"particular favor . . . excellent plan"* 2 May 1806, Box 11, Folder 73.

39 *"where there is . . . expectation"* Tatler, no. 196, 11 July 1710.

*"wished so much . . . gratitude"* 2 May 1806, Box 11, Folder 73.

*"my having taken . . . Surgeoncy"* 9 May 1806, Box 11, Folder 73.

*"Well I'll not . . . existence"* 16 May 1806, Box 11, Folder 73.

Chapter 4. This Despicable Rock

40 *"Scarlet coat . . . grand sword"* 16 May 1806, Box 11, Folder 73.

*"completely uncertain . . . in it"* 7 May 1806, Box 11, Folder 73.

*"in the most . . . practice"* 16 May 1806, Box 11, Folder 73.

*"as my pay . . . long"* 7 May 1806, Box 11, Folder 73.

*"nobly idle . . . one's time with"* 7 May 1806, Box 11, Folder 73.

*"of all the places . . . to"* 24 May 1806, Box 11, Folder 73.

*from midnight* 26 May 1806, Box 11, Folder 73.

*"a devilish . . . no fear"* 18 May 1806, Box 11, Folder 73.

*"call often and inquire"* 26 May 1806, Box 11, Folder 73.

41 *final bill* 26 May 1806, Box 11, Folder 73.

*"Live always . . . ruin"* 26 April 1806, Box 11, Folder 73.

42 *eggs, bread . . . sugar* 28 May 1806, Box 11, Folder 73.

*eating . . . utensils* 31 May 1806, Box 11, Folder 73.

*tea kettle . . . pan* 4 June 1806, Box 11, Folder 73. The dating for June is imprecise, because Lesassier
did not always record the date of events.

"*looked remarkably . . . degrading*" 4 June 1806, Box 11, Folder 73.

43    "*and our little fleet . . . sail*" 14 June 1806, Box 11, Folder 73.

"*Sea . . . hills of snow*" 18 June 1806, Box 11, Folder 73.

"*chiefly on deck . . . impossible*" 14 June 1806, Box 11, Folder 73.

"*a parrot . . . her friend*" 14 June 1806, Box 11, Folder 73.

"*But of course . . . his bed*" 10 Nov. 1806, Box 11, Folder 73.

"*In coming . . . four hundred yards*" 28 June 1806, probably corrected and amended later, Box 11,
Folder 73.

"*the situation . . . stir*" Walsh, p. 8.

44    "*this despicable rock*" cited in Woodford, pp. 43–58.

"*during the flowering . . . cooped up*" 25 Dec. 1806, Box 11, Folder 73.

"*The civilian . . . uniform*" 17 Aug. 1806, Box 11, Folder 73.

"*is a most . . . most polished language*" 28 June 1806, Box 11, Folder 73.

45    "*numerous . . . sauntering about*" 25 Dec. 1806, Box 11, Folder 73.

"*whole bands . . . inebriety*" Walsh, p. 7.

"*repose . . . bed*" 28 June 1806, Box 11, Folder 73.

"*as graciously . . . admitted*" Henry, p. 24.

*the preceding set on Gibraltar* 28 June 1806, Box 11, Folder 73.

*he tried to save them* Henry, p. 30.

"*a very sulky fellow . . . voyage*" 28 June 1806, Box 11, Folder 73.

46    "*thrown into . . . language*" Fergusson, p. 66.

*leave of absence . . . "to do anything"* 28 June 1806, Box 11, Folder 73.

"*The hospital . . . mess*" 5 Aug. 1806, Box 11, Folder 73.

"*cacophonous . . . middle ages*" Henry, p. 20.

47    "*highly mutinous . . . Articles of War*" Great Britain, *General Orders*, 29 July 1810.

"*constantly reflecting . . . detected*" 4 March 1808, 9:30 P.M., Box 11, Folder 74.

"*imposed on . . . office*" 28 Feb. 1807, Box 11, Folder 73.

"*his best . . . prudence*" 10 Nov. 1806, Box 11, Folder 73.

"*days of chivalry*" 17 Aug. 1806, Box 11, Folder 73.

"*charmingly situated . . . front*" 28 Feb. 1807, Box 11, Folder 73.

"*the eldest son . . . most nobly drunk*" 17 Aug. 1806, Box 11, Folder 73.

"*extensive & tolerably select*" 13 Oct. 1807, Box 11, Folder 73; the circulating library is described in
Walsh, p. 8.

"*immortal work . . . education*" 13 Oct. 1807, Box 11, Folder 73.

"*relations . . . own terms*" 28 Feb. 1807, Box 11, Folder 73.

"*much handsomer . . . humanity*" 12 March 1807, Box 11, Folder 73.

48    "*tedium . . . language*" 30 March 1807, Box 11, Folder 73.

"*the girl herself . . . attention*" 28 Feb. 1807, Box 11, Folder 73.

"*the medical staff . . . society*" Fergusson, p. 64.

"*Poor Maria . . . heart*" 27 April 1807, Box 11, Folder 73.

"*This regiment . . . Men*" 20 Aug. 1807, Box 11, Folder 73.

"*a young lady . . . sex*" 31 May 1807, Box 11, Folder 73.

*on walks* 31 May 1807, 4 June 1807, Box 11, Folder 73.

*going to a ball* 4 June 1807, Box 11, Folder 73.

*on picnics* 21 Aug. 1807, Box 11, Folder 73.

"*I am on . . . tea &c*" 23 June 1807, Box 11, Folder 73.

49    "*I shall never forget . . . volume*" 21 Oct. 1807, Box 11, Folder 73.

"*and unluckily . . . duty*" 28 May 1807, Box 11, Folder 73.

"*my colleague McLean*" 2 Aug. 1807, Box 11, Folder 73.

"*Until I get home . . . promotion*" 28 Oct. 1807, Box 11, Folder 73.

"*to write immediately . . . recommendation*" 30 May 1807, Box 11, Folder 73.

"*his word . . . possible*" 4 Oct. 1807, Box 11, Folder 73.

*Colonel Stirling informed . . . "both times"* 4 Oct. 1807, Box 11, Folder 73.

"*very much . . . I ever knew*" 13 Oct. 1807, Box 11, Folder 73.

50   "*has employed . . . interest*" 28 Oct. 1807, Box 11, Folder 73.

*left the officer's mess . . .* 23 June 1807, Box 11, Folder 73.

"*what young man . . . jacket*" 27 April 1807, Box 11, Folder 73.

"*to my utter . . . thither*" 29 Nov, 1807, Box 11, Folder 73.

"*because he had written . . . title*" 28 Nov. 1807, Box 11, Folder 73.

*On December 2* 16 Jan. 1808, Box 11, Folder 73.

"*a veteran . . . officer*" 29 Nov. 1807, Box 11, Folder 73.

"*agreeably surprised . . . limbs*" 16 Jan. 1808, Box 11, Folder 73.

"*suffocated . . . it gave me*" 9 April 1811, Box 12, Folder 77.

"*would be the very reverse . . . infinite delight*" 16 Jan. 1808, Box 11, Folder 73.

51   *lodging house . . . tailor* 17 Feb. 1808, Box 11, Folder 74.

"*a beautiful . . . black silk*" 19 Feb. 1808, Box 11, Folder 74.

"*really so distinguished . . . Mate*" 18 Feb. 1808, Box 11, Folder 74.

*two months' back pay* 3–4 March 1808, Box 11, Folder 74.

"*forgot . . . thank me*" 16 Jan. 1808, Box 11, Folder 73.

52   "*that my having been . . . note of it*" 19 Feb. 1808, Box 11, Folder 74.

"*if it be kept . . . precision*" 2 July 1826, Box 14, Folder 84.

"*that this time . . . forever*" 4 March 1808, 9:30 P.M., Box 11, Folder 74.

"*that it was a rare case . . . nobly*" 5 March 1808, Box 11, Folder 74.

53   "*A jacket . . . exult*" 10 March 1808, Box 11, Folder 74.

*letter from a friend* 15 March 1808, Box 11, Folder 74.

"*So at last . . . Mate*" 22 March 1808, Box 11, Folder 74.

"*extremely delighted . . . wrote*" 15 March 1808, Box 11, Folder 74.

"*My views . . . perfectly happy*" 26 March 1808, Box 11, Folder 74.


Chapter 5. The Most Beautiful Man in Existence

54   "*Fare thee well . . . city*" 23 March 1808, Box 11, Folder 74.

"*I have . . . well-informed*" 22 March 1808, Box 11, Folder 74.

"*two fathoms . . .*" *per minute* 4 April 1808, Box 11, Folder 74.

*They were rescued . . . obliged* 6 April 1808, Box 11, Folder 74.

"*the preference . . . society*" IH to ALH, Liverpool, 23 May 1822, Box 1, Folder 10.

55   *sick soldier* 6 May 1808, Box 11, Folder 74.

"*from 10 . . . vagabonds*" 28 Aug. 1808, Box 11, Folder 74.

"*a set . . . drapery*" Wollstonecraft, p. 17.

"*a species . . . world*" Ferrier, *Inheritance*, p. 245.

"*labours under one . . . passing the day*" McGrigor, *Autobiography*, pp. 194–196.

56   *attempts to avoid drinking* McGrigor, *Autobiography*, pp. 198–200.

"*My dear . . . Mr. Lesassier*" William Forbes to AL, Aberdeen, 18 April 1808, Box 1, Folder 4.

"*tainted . . . any change*" 31 July 1808, Box 11, Folder 74.

*as a young surgeon, McGrigor* McGrigor, *Autobriography*, p. 45.

*could McGrigor prevail . . . officers* McGrigor, *Autobiography*, p. 278.

"*tearing from us . . . Officers*" 1 April 1809, Box 12, Folder 77.

*He repaid Captain Davidson* 26 April 1808, Box 11, Folder 74.

*Captain Fraser* 21 Aug. 1808, Box 11, Folder 74.

*subaltern* 7 June 1808, Box 11, Folder 74.

*hazards* May 1808, 6 May 1808, Box 11, Folder 74.

"*settled profession*" 26 March 1808, 1 May 1808, Box 11, Folder 74.

57   "*a little stiff . . . from me*" 26 April 1808, Box 11, Folder 74.

*refusing to accept* 5 May 1808, Box 11. Folder 74.

*lending him a horse* 31 July 1808, Box 11, Folder 74.

"*puppyish brethren*" 6 July 1808, Box 11, Folder 74.

"*enables me . . . conversation*" 7 June 1808, Box 11, Folder 74.

"*we are . . . own opinion*" 10 June 1805, Box 11, Folder 72.

"*uniform steadiness . . . contemplation*" 31 July 1808, Box 11, Folder 74.

"*barren country . . . new works*" 26 April 1808, Box 11, Folder 74.

"*equally poor . . . excursion*" 1 May 1808, Box 11, Folder 74.

"*A picturesque landscape . . . chiaroscuro*" Barbier, p. 1. A useful selection of travel literature, though Gilpin is omitted, is found in Fussell.

58    "*beauty . . . produce*" Gilpin, *Three Essays*, p. 42. On Gilpin, see Templeman; Michasiw.

*In Gilpin's view* Barbier, p. 99.

"*as many travel . . . purposes*" Gilpin, *Three Essays*, p. 41.

"*fore-grounds . . . landscape*" Austen, *Northanger Abbey*, p. 111.

"*the pen . . . observed*" 28 Feb. 1807, Box 11, Folder 73.

*The tone of the journals* See Preston.

*He did his best to be accurate* 11 May 1808, Box 11, Folder 74.

"*famous . . . Scotland*" 5 May 1808, Box 11, Folder 74.

"*It was the merriest . . . fail me*" 6 May 1808, Box 11, Folder 74.

"*superior to such trifles*" 12 May 1808, Box 11, Folder 74.

"*became extremely . . . culture*" 10 May 1808, Box 11, Folder 74.

"*Down a deep . . . extricate ourselves*" 11 May 1808, Box 11, Folder 74.

59    "*surrounded . . . Highlands*" 13 May 1808, Box 11, Folder 74.

*brand new edition* Gilpin, *Observations on the Highlands*, p. 135. The first edition was published in 1789, the second in 1792, and the third in 1808.

"*Our present inn . . . depth*" 13 May 1808, Box 11, Folder 74. Gilpin, following Edmund Burke and others, made a distinction between picturesque and sublime views, but Lesassier is not as consistent in using the terms.

"*Indeed I was . . . stage coach*" 13 May 1808, Box 11, Folder 74.

"*more amusement . . . past*" 16 May 1808, Box 11, Folder 74.

"*In a large town . . . study*" 11 Dec. 1808, Box 12, Folder 75.

*Lord Berridale* 15 May 1808, Box 11, Folder 74.

"*a poor looking . . . 2 o'clock P.M.*" 7 June 1808, Box 11, Folder 74.

*Mrs. Major Campbell* 8 Oct. 1808, Box 11, Folder 74.

"*some very . . . society*" 12 July 1808, Box 11, Folder 74.

*Atkinson* 16 July 1808, 8 Oct. 1808, Box 11, Folder 74.

*disinterested hospitality* 18 Nov. 1808, Box 12, Folder 75.

"*Armagh . . . completely*" 12 July 1808, Box 11, Folder 74.

60    *live within his salary* 12 July 1808, Box 11, Folder 74; 26 Nov. 1808, Box 12, Folder 75.

"*alas! . . . free again*" 21 Aug. 1808, Box 11, Folder 74.

"*If I obtained . . . manner*" 2 Aug. 1807, Box 11, Folder 73.

"*the Luxury . . . Affection*" Austen, "Love and Friendship," p. 84.

*Lord Blantyre* 16 July 1808, Box 11, Folder 74.

"*seulement des Bourgeoise*" 2 Jan. 1809, Box 12, Folder 75.

"*failed in my attempts . . . love*" 3 Nov. 1808, Box 12, Folder 75.

"*Because it is taken . . . conquest*" William Hazlitt, "Why the Heroes of Romances Are Insipid," in *Complete Works* 17:246–247.

61    *a friend of* 8 Oct. 1808, Box 11, Folder 74.

"*the only young lady . . . know her*" 31 Oct. 1808, Box 12, Folder 75.

*reflect well* He had been careful to note Lord Berridale's approbation of another young lady he had briefly paid attention to in Fort George. 4 May 1808, Box 11, Folder 74.

"*handsome and accomplished . . . extremely*" 8 Oct. 1808, Box 11, Folder 74.

"*Last night . . . laid aside*" 3 Nov. 1808, Box 12, Folder 75.

"*I wish your heart . . . too little*" Austen, *Northanger Abbey*, p. 147.

"*I fear ... conceited*" 3 Nov. 1808, Box 12, Folder 75.

*restrained materialism* The importance of the manipulation of material possessions in the social world of Jane Austen's novels is emphasized in Spring.

"*I sat by her side ... thought*" 14 Oct. 1808, Box 12, Folder 75.

62    "*Never since ... error*" 14 Oct. 1808, evening, Box 12, Folder 75.

"*How could you ... sight of her*" 22 Oct. 1808, Box 12, Folder 75.

63    "*had ... been ... gallantry*" 23 Oct. 1808, Box 12, Folder 75.

"*although she knew I was ... she kept them*" 31 Oct. 1808, Box 12, Folder 75.

64    "*sweetly ... the giver*" 1 Nov. 1808, Box 12, Folder 75.

"*Scandal ... ourselves*" 31 Oct. 1808, Box 12, Folder 75.

"*Two hazel nuts ... burnt*" 1 Nov. 1808, Box 12, Folder 75.

"*I must say ... inseparable*" 31 Oct. 1808, Box 12, Folder 75.

"*a kind friend ... what to say*" 1 Nov. 1808, Box 12, Folder 75.

65    "*In a fit of rage*" 3 Nov. 1808, Box 12, Folder 75.

"*not feel any ... indifference*" 1 Nov. 1808, Box 12, Folder 75.

"*felt a most pungent ... General*" 3 Nov. 1808, Box 12, Folder 75.

"*A free ... agreement*" 5 Nov. 1808, Box 12, Folder 75.

66    "*in charge ... each other*" 11 Nov. 1808, Box 12, Folder 75.

"*against her ideas ... circumstance*" 13 Nov. 1808, Box 12, Folder 75.

"*I should think ... truly loves*" EN, 3:10.

"*If my own ... short a time*" 13 Nov. 1808, Box 12, Folder 75.

"*unless I could state ... eloquent language*" 16 Nov. 1808, Box 12, Folder 75.

67    "*took leave ... again*" 20 Nov. 1808, Box 12, Folder 75.

"*Contrary to her promise ... misfortune*" 22 Nov. 1808, Box 12, Folder 75.

"*He insists ... business*" 2 Dec. 1808, Box 12, Folder 75.

"*I was agitated ... joined in*" 22 Nov. 1808, Box 12, Folder 75.

68    "*With great trepidation ... merit*" 26 Nov. 1808, Box 12, Folder 75.

"*whichsoever way ... her regard*" 24 Nov. 1808, Box 12, Folder 75.

"*The spell ... loved Alicia*" 2 Dec. 1808, Box 12, Folder 75.

"*She lived ... left her*" 3 April 1809, Box 12, Folder 75.

"*She was young ... delusion*" n.d., Journal, 4 Feb. 1812-March 1812, Box 13, Folder 81.

"*Alexander ... watch*" Ella Anderton to ALH, Manchester, 3 June 1828, Box 1, Folder 2.

" *the* most *beautiful ... existence*" Ella Anderton to ALH, Preston, 5 July 1826, Box 1, Folder 2.

69    "*Ella wore a veil ... dear girl*" 3 April 1809, Box 12, Folder 75.

"*She bade me ... 1809!!*" 6 April 1808, Box 12, Folder 75.

"*retraced the night ... table*" Ella Anderton to ALH, Preston, 5 July 1826, Box 1, Folder 2.

"*with any circumstance ... good fortune*" 3 April 1809, Box 12, Folder 75.

"*that blessed period ... my ear*" Ella Anderton to ALH, Preston, 5 July 1826, Box 1, Folder 2.

"*still ... happy*" Ella Anderton to ALH, Preston, 10 June 1826, Box 1, Folder 2.

"*a fine moonlight ... Alexander*" Ella Anderton to ALH, Preston, 5 July 1826, Box 1, Folder 2.

"*lately discovered ... dissimulation*" 28 May 1809, Box 12, Folder 75.

"*how was it ... existence*" Ella Anderton to ALH, Preston, 5 July 1826, Box 1, Folder 2.

70    "*After confiding ... girl*" 6 April 1809, Box 12, Folder 75.

"*a present ... I am of it*" 16 April 1809, Box 12, Folder 75.

"*she ... letter*" 6 May 1809, Box 12, Folder 75.

"*Alas! ... disordered imagination*" 18 May 1809, Box 12, Folder 75.

"*continued perseverance ... conduct*" n.d., Journal, 4 Feb. 1812-March 1812, Box 13, Folder 81.

*medical lectures* 11 Dec. 1808, Box 12, Folder 75; brief extracts from the lectures of Abraham Colles, anatomy lecturer in Dublin, 1809, Box 23, Folder 132.

"*Do you mean ... doctor*" Richard Jenoway to AL, Cork, 17 Aug. 1808, Box 2, Folder 11.

"*Few things ... indigence*" 6 May 1809, Box 12, Folder 75.

71    *Lindsay* 21 May 1809, Box 12, Folder 75.

*Donald McPherson* 28 May 1809, Box 12, Folder 75.

"*a worthy ... my duty*" 28 May 1809, Box 12, Folder 75.

"*Officers are rejoining . . . God knows where*" 13 June 1809, Box 12, Folder 75. The regiments were the 6th, 20th, and 88th.

"*Portugal . . . valor*" 31 May 1809, Box 12, Folder 75.

Chapter 6. Tinsel of Military Reputation

72    "*a most pleasing . . . buildings*" 2 July 1809, Box 12, Folder 75.

"*whither this Brigade . . . dispatch*" 1 July 1809, Box 12, Folder 75.

*5,363 men* Cantlie, 1:314.

"*There are five thousand . . . medicines*" 13 Aug. 1809, Box 12, Folder 76.

*The Peninsula War began* Keegan, pp. 109–110.

73    "*The Spanish Ulcer*" Gates, p. 468.

"*Every privation . . . uncomfortable life*" 8 July 1809, Box 12, Folder 75.

"*old friend Bolton*" 21 July 1809, Box 12, Folder 75.

*good quarter* Henry, p. 24.

74    "*for the reception . . . Barracks Corps*" 21 July 1809, Box 12, Folder 75.

75    "*a most magnificent . . . marble*" 8 July 1809, Box 12, Folder 75.

"*a most lovely girl*" 21 July 1809, Box 12, Folder 75.

*flying ambulances* Cantlie, 1:330; R. G. Richardson, pp. 34–8.

"*the first and peculiar care . . . stores*" Hennen, p. 23.

*setting fractures* "Instructions to Regimental Surgeons," pp. 141–144.

*treating cuts* 4 June 1813, Box 13, Folder 80.

*prescribing emetics* Costello, p. 71.

*diagnosing measles* Gunn, p. 94.

"*apothecaries' boys . . . impunity*" Sergeant Donaldson, *The Adventurous Life of a Soldier*, p. 258, cited in Cantlie, 1:329.

76    *surgeons and their assistants* Cantlie, 1:360–361.

"*The surgeon goes round . . . visits them*" Decius, p. 369.

"*Thinks I . . . campaigning*" Henry, p. 26.

"*my present duty . . . engaged in*" 24 July 1809, Box 12, Folder 75.

"*some hundreds of sick . . . consequence*" 13 Aug. 1809, Box 12, Folder 76.

"*with horror . . . motives*" 26 July 1809, Box 12, Folder 76.

"*a small though very strong . . . portmanteaus*" 8 July 1809, Box 12, Folder 75.

*Lesassier's regiment* The 42nd was now in Lightburne's brigade.

77    "*an irregular town . . . picturesque sight*" Lesassier's depiction of this scene, like almost all those in his Portuguese journals, is still strikingly accurate today. 18–20 Aug. 1809, Box 12, Folder 76.

"*My time . . . Portuguesas*" 7 Aug. 1809, Box 12, Folder 76.

"*I myself although unwell . . . miserable place*" 13 Aug. 1809, Box 12, Folder 76.

*Medical treatment . . . reecovery* See Wellington's angry comments about the failure of regiments to send their sick and wounded to general hospitals in October 1811. Great Britain, *General Orders*, 3:204; Wellington, *Dispatches*, 8:339.

"*expending . . . powder*" R. B. Long, p. 172. Long had his own reasons for being dissatisfied with Wellington and the war.

"*proper care . . . morality*" Keegan, p. 160.

"*The eternal screeching . . . carts*" Cited in Cantlie, 1:296; Blanco, p. 114.

"*I dread a removal . . . bad weather*" Wellington, *Dispatches*, 5:230.

"*So great was the suffering . . . Lisbon*" Cited in Blanco, p. 114.

78    "*after infinite labor . . . flotilla of eight boats*" 18–20 Aug. 1809, Box 12, Folder 76.

*Lesassier waited on . . .* 23 Aug. 1809, Box 12, Folder 76.

"*esteemed . . . Portugal*" 12 Sept. 1809, Box 12, Folder 76.

"*fair friends*" 4 Sept. 1809, Box 12, Folder 76.

"*No sooner . . . infernal duty*" 24 Sept. 1809, Box 12, Folder 76.

79    "*Graces à Dieu*" 30 Sept. 1809, Box 12, Folder 76.

"*perfectly eaten up . . . books*" 8 Oct. 1809, Box 12, Folder 76.

"*seeing that . . . faring ill*" 24 Sept. 1809, Box 12, Folder 76.

"*experience . . . was very great*" Guthrie, *Treatise*, p. 258.

"*a most particular friend . . . Guthrie*" Boutflower, p. 178–9.

"*The wounded were numerous . . . suburb*" McGrigor, *Autobiography*, p. 304.

"*that active . . . fever*" Halliday, pp. 94–95; McGrigor, *Sketch*, p. 50, 60.

80  "*This day our number . . . 24 hours*" 1 Nov. 1809, Box 12, Folder 76.

Surgeon Walter Henry Henry, p. 61, cited in Cantlie, 1:346.

"*threw off . . . rough towel*" 28 May 1812, Box 13, Folder 79.

"*the manner of cure . . . me*" Costello, p. 22.

"*very much disliked . . . drugs*" Gunn, p. 94.

"*I here joined McPherson . . . our Sick*" 19 Nov. 1809, Box 12, Folder 76.

"*ill built . . . poor & wretched*" 19 Nov. 1809, Box 12, Folder 76.

"*Even this obscure village . . . duties*" 26 Nov. 1809, Box 12, Folder 76.

81  "*Intermittent Fever*" 29 Nov. 1809, Box 12, Folder 76. The 24th was brigaded with the 42nd under Major General Cameron.

"*notwithstanding . . . hurried back again*" 26 Nov. 1809, Box 12, Folder 76.

"*The officers . . . men*" 29 Nov. 1809, Box 12, Folder 76.

"*mild affable gentleman . . . diminished*" 3 Dec. 1809, Box 12, Folder 76.

"*Having plenty of leisure . . . pouring in upon us*" 12 Dec. 1809, Box 12, Folder 76.

"*nearly 5000*" 28 Dec. 1809, Box 12, Folder 76.

"*I may venture . . . wines*" 27 Dec. 1809, Box 12, Folder 76.

"*Now cease awhile . . . Christmas day*" 25 Dec. 1809, Box 12, Folder 77.

82  "*So I may . . . annoyance*" 6 Jan. 1809, Box 12, Folder 77.

The trip was marked 16 Jan. 1810, Box 12, Folder 77. For another example of a race, see 14 and 18 Aug. 1811, Box 12, Folder 78.

"*celebrated . . . gratis*" 19 Jan. 1810, Box 12, Folder 77.

"*This . . . hurrying myself*" 16 Jan. 1810, Box 12, Folder 77.

"*about 200 . . . Chateau*" 24 Jan. 1810, Box 12, Folder 77.

"*How sudden . . . Elvas*" 24 Feb, 1810, Box 12, Folder 77.

"*wild & majestic . . . conspicuous appearance*" 23 March 1810, Box 12, Folder 77.

83  "*beheld . . . verdure of spring*" 19 May 1810, Box 12, Folder 77.

"*to conceal . . . sick*" 12 Aug. 1810, Box 12, Folder 77.

"*of course highly pleased . . . medical officer*" 26 Aug. 1810, Box 12, Folder 77.

was attacked . . . "*consented to try*" 28 Aug. 1810, Box 12, Folder 77.

"*pretty town . . . must go*" 29 Aug.-1 Sept. 1810, Box 12, Folder 77.

84  "*order all your sick . . . loss of time*" Wellington, *Dispatches*, 6:449.

The British Army 21 Sept. 1810, Box 12, Folder 77; Oman, *History*, 3:411–412.

"*indeed a most masterly action*" 16 Oct. 1810, Box 12, Folder 77. The militia were commanded by Colonel Trant.

"*as every step . . . occasion*" 8 Dec. 1809, Box 12, Folder 76.

"*Everything in Lisbon . . . hospital ships*" 22 Oct. 1810, Box 12, Folder 77.

sad croaker Keegan, p. 129.

"*A certain great man . . . impregnable position*" 22 Jan. 1811, Box 12, Folder 77.

"*It is impossible . . . campaign*" Great Britain. *General Orders*, 2:131.

85  "*than that which . . . obtained*" Ward, p. 45.

"*is that the Enemy . . . disgrace*" Boutflower, pp. 112–113.

"*Ah! . . . unfortunate I am*" 10 Nov. 1810, Box 12, Folder 77.

nearly seven thousand sick Cantlie, 1:325.

"*that haughty tyrannical scoundrel*" 30 Oct. 1810, Box 12, Folder 77.

"*a most . . . friend of his*" 10 Nov. 1810, Box 12, Folder 77.

"*I have been busied . . . Captain in the regiment*" 9 Dec. 1810, Box 12, Folder 77.

86  "*marquee and tent . . . for his servant*" Long, p. 22.

"*ankle-boots . . . seasonings*" Long, p. 95.

"*cannot be deemed . . . whilst with it*" 24 Sept. 1809, Box 12, Folder 76.

"*need fear . . . return to them*" 9 Dec. 1810, Box 12, Folder 77.

"*The French were here . . . desolation*" 14 Dec. 1810, Box 12, Folder 77.

"*has been a pretty town . . . without a master*" 16 Dec. 1810, Box 12, Folder 77.

"*under arms . . . placed beside me*" 22 Dec. 1810, Box 12, Folder 77.

87 "*Belemites . . . in advance*" Blakiston, 2:150.

"*And pray where . . . period*" Costello, p. 91.

"*condoling . . . officer in our Army*" 9 Dec. 1810, Box 12, Folder 77.

"*utmost disgust & detestation*" 9 May 1810, Box 12, Folder 77.

*quarrel with Lieutenant White* 28 Feb. 1811, Box 12, Folder 77.

"*I am ignorant . . . situation*" 9 May 1810, Box 12, Folder 77.

"*neither communication . . . staff*" 10 May 1810, Box 12, Folder 77.

"*most politely . . . already appointed*" 19 May, 1810, Box 12, Folder 77.

"*its numerous churches . . . Serra d'Estrella*" 6 June 1811, Box 12, Folder 78.

88 *new friend* 17 May 1811, Box 12, Folder 77.

"*uniformly correct conduct*" 17 Feb. 1812, Box 13, Folder 81.

*Lesassier's introduction* 31 May 1812, Box 13, Folder 79.

"*very flattering . . . distinction*" 23 June 1811, Box 12, Folder 77.

"*Some men . . . aspects of my situation*" 28 Aug. 1811, Box 12, Folder 78.

"*best thanks. . . .this hospital*" 23 June 1811, Box 12, Folder 77.

*Blantyre himself Royal Military Calendar*, 3:415–416.

89 "*as there is no disposable . . . Hospital Mates*" 23 June 1811, Box 12, Folder 77.

*Perston, like Lesassier* Great Britain, *General Orders*, 2:187.

"*frightful appearance . . . dreadful*" William Grattan, *Adventures of the Connaught Rangers from 1808 to 1814*, 1:104–5, cited in Blanco, p. 116.

"*highly enraged*" 31 May 1811, Box 12, Folder 77.

*always sensitive to criticism* Wellington, *Dispatches*, 5:590; Cantlie, 1:332.

"*much is to be conceded . . . specific hours*" Hennen, p. 63.

"*that he had several times . . . leaving my regiment*" 31 May 1811, Box 12, Folder 77.

"*The skulking rascal . . . that period*" 6 Aug. 1811, Box 12, Folder 78.

"*pleased to warmly express . . . doctor does*" 31 May 1811, Box 12, Folder 77.

90 "*after a long . . . galling*" 23 June 1811, Box 12, Folder 77.

"*most unpleasant . . . duties*" 2 Aug. 1811, Box 12, Folder 78.

"*the dullest . . . pine away in*" 13 Aug. 1811, Ephemeris June July Aug. 1811, Box 12, Folder 78.

"*to prevent liquor . . . excepted*" "Instructions to Regimental Surgeons," p. 145.

*nine pence per day* "Instructions to Regimental Surgeons," p. 149.

*tickets, in triplicate* Great Britain, *General Orders*, 1:249, 5:183.

*The necessaries themselves* "Instructions to Regimental Surgeons," p. 147.

*soldier would have to present* See, for example, Great Britain, *General Orders*, 2:110–111, 4:86–87.

*preliminary medical records* "Instructions to Regimental Surgeons," p. 148.

"*approbation of the Commanding Officer*" "Instructions to Regimental Surgeons," p. 144.

"*An incomplete adventure . . . English boy*" 20 Aug. 1811, Box 12, Folder 78.

91 *In ballads* An excellent discussion is in Dugaw.

*Lesassier's motive* Dugaw, pp. 121–122, discusses the view of A. L. Lloyd, *Folk Song in England* (New York: International, 1967), p. 225, that the female warrior ballads should be considered a male fantasy.

"*she was to act . . . discovery of her sex*" 12 Sept. 1811, Box 12, Folder 78.

"*in washing . . . drives me to madness*" 15 Sept. 1811, Box 12, Folder 78.

92 "*Thus Alas . . . resource*" 6 Aug. 1811, Box 12, Folder 78.

*391 men* Oman, *History*, 3: 391.

"the formidable force *of 250 bayonets*" 31 May 1811, Box 12, Folder 77.

"*interested himself . . . whole affair himself*" 23 Nov. 1811, Box 12, Folder 78.

"*Assistant Surgeon Lesassier . . . Battalion*" Great Britain, *General Orders*, 3:256.

"*burst of rapture . . . fortune*" 23 Nov. 1811, Box 12, Folder 78.

"*What have I . . . praise?*" 31 May 1811, Box 12, Folder 77.

Chapter 7. Soothing Hope of Speedy Promotion

93   *back cover of one of the journals . . .* n.d., cover of untitled rough notes, May-Sept. 1812, Box 12, Folder 78.

"*a gay—giddy . . . than before*" n.d., Journal, 4 Feb. 1812-March 1812, Box 13, Folder 81.

"*mutually lost . . . had ever met with*" n.d., notes from March 1812, Box 13, Folder 79.

"*This is affection . . . heart*" 17 June 1811, Box 12, Folder 77.

"*bewitching delicacy . . . hordes of wealth*" n.d., Journal 4 Feb. 1812-March 1812, Box 13, Folder 81.

94   "*when cockle-shells . . . bells*" Bronson, 4:424–436.

*ballad tradition* See "Hide Horn," for example, or, for a role-reversed version, "The Bailiff's Daughter of Islington." Bronson, 1: 254–264, 2:515–529.

"*one single pleasing sensation . . . lodged*" 24 Feb. 1812, Box 13, Folder 81.

"*was a grand sight . . . baggage beast*" n.d., rough notes, 30 March-30? April 1812, Box 13, Folder 79.

*One of his friends . . .* 31 May 1812, Box 13, Folder 79.

"*was amply prepared . . . brother officers*" 7 May 1812, Box 13, Folder 79.

*retrieve his horse* 28 May 1812, Box 13, Folder 79.

95   "*pitched in a few minutes . . . night*" 4 June 1812, Box 13, Folder 79.

"*This retired spot . . . in vain*" 1–2 July 1812, Box 13, Folder 79.

"*the slightest exertion . . . in the Army*" 24 Feb. 1812, Box 13, Folder 81.

"*if I were . . . right*" 24 Feb. 1812, Box 13, Folder 81.

96   "*many scenes*" IH to ALH, Chatham, 16 Nov. 1818, Box 1, Folder 10.

"*shallow pretext . . . welfare*" 24 Feb. 1812, Box 13, Folder 81.

*filling vacancies with newcomers* Cantlie, 1:358.

"*It would be . . . duty*" Wellington, *Selections*, p. 627.

"*supreme mortification*" 10–11 June 1812, Box 13, Folder 79.

*He had kept in contact* 7 May and 21 May 1812, Box 13, Folder 79.

"*most anxious . . . that I wanted*" 31 May 1812, Box 13, Folder 79.

*saving Wellington . . . a division* Cantlie, 1:357.

97   *reported directly* Ward, pp. 32–33.

*mobile medical units* Cantlie, 1:357. Blanco, pp. 134–135, cites McGrigor on division hospitals, but brigade hospitals are also mentioned by Lesassier for the first time this winter.

"*all Medical Officers . . . England*" JM to W. Hogg, 28 Feb. 1812, Mss 2166, Letter Book, 30 Nov. 1811–31 March 1812, Sir James McGrigor Manuscripts.

"*found . . . groundless*" JM to J. Weir, 26 Nov. 1812, Mss 2165, Letter Book, 26 April 1812–25 April 1813, Sir James McGrigor Manuscripts.

*instruct their subordinates* JM to J. Weir, 26 Nov. 1812, 6 March 1813, Mss 2165, Letter Book, 26 April 1812–25 April 1813, Sir James McGrigor Manuscripts.

"*has hardly done . . . country*" JM to J Weir, 4 Oct. 1812, Mss 2165, Letter Book, 26 April 1812–25 April 1813, Sir James McGrigor Manuscripts.

*painstaking notes* JM, Mss 2156, Prevailing Diseases which occured amongst the British Troops in the Peninsular, Abstract of sick in general and regimental hospitals, 21 Dec. 1811–20 June 1814, Sir James McGrigor Manuscripts; McGrigor, *Sketch*.

*John Erly* Johnston, 1:110.

"*in the most . . . serving me*" 9 June 1812, Box 13, Folder 79.

98   "*claim for promotion . . . service*" JM to A. S. McEnally, 28th Regt., 17 March 1812, Mss 2166, Letter Book, 30 Nov. 1811–31 March 1812, Sir James McGrigor Manuscripts.

"*material points . . . education*" JM to A. S. Baxter, 48th Regt., 27 Feb. 1812, Mss 2166, Letter Book, 30 Nov. 1811–31 March 1812, Sir James McGrigor Manuscripts.

*writing to Deputy Inspector Tegart* 25 June 1812, Box 13, Folder 79.

*high in McGrigor's favor* JM to S Reed, 12 May 1812, Mss 2165, Letter Book, 26 April 1812–25 April 1813, Sir James McGrigor Manuscripts.

"*To a person . . . inconsiderate folly*" 14–20 May 1812, Box 13, Folder 79.

"*old friend*" 7 Jan. 1811, Box 12, Folder 77.

"*be treated like a gentleman . . . sighed*" 2 Nov. 1811, Box 12, Folder 78.

"*Daddy" Stirling* Gunn, p. 94.

"*severely scolded*" 10–11 June 1812, Box 13, Folder 79.

"*renowned fortress . . . destroyed*" 12–13 June 1812, Box 13, Folder 79.

*taking mess with the quartermaster* 30 June 1812, Box 13, Folder 79.

99   "*the old brute*" 5th Aug. 1812, 29 Aug. 1812, Box 13, Folder 79.

*medal and two clasps Royal Military Calendar*, 3:345–348.

"*Dinner ready . . . Dined however*" 24 June 1812, Box 13, Folder 79.

*routinely ignored* 2 July 1812, Box 13, Folder 79.

"*determined to steal away . . . seen by him*" 29 July 1812, Box 13, Folder 79.

*Marmont ordered* Oman, *History*, 5:361.

"*an occasional firing . . . musketry*" 17 June 1812, Box 13, Folder 79.

*Wellington entered* Oman, *History*, 5:562.

"*narrow+houses antique . . . cathedral*" 17–19 June 1812, Box 13, Folder 79.

"*crowded with Officers . . . streets*" "EN," Box 8, Folder 55.

100   "*Much exposed . . . luxury*" 17–19 June 1812, Box 13, Folder 79.

"*afforded him . . . shop windows*" "EN," Box 8, Folder 55.

"*The rear . . . I escaped*" 20 June 1812, Box 13, Folder 79.

"*I went . . . I ran*" 26 June 1812, Box 13, Folder 79.

*Lesassier's activities* 17 July and 19 July 1812, Box 12, Folder 78.

"*a truly awful night*" [21 July 1812? "20th" written], untitled rough notes, May-Sept. 1812, Box 12, Folder 78; Oman, *History*, 5:417.

"*where we remained . . . splendid & decisive*" 22 July 1812, Box 12, Folder 78.

"*regarded . . . as his 'masterpiece'*" Keegan, p. 92.

101   "*That same evening . . . Redoubt*" 19–30 Sept. 1812, Box 13, Folder 79. Oman, *History*, 6:26, described the main assault force as Pack's brigade, assisted by the 42nd and the rest of Stirling's brigade, but Lesassier can be forgiven his emphasis on his own regiment.

"*The storm succeeded . . . suffering terribly*" Oman, *History*, 6:27–28.

"*For, you may believe . . . there*" Gunn, p. 100.

"*Having lost . . . suffering heavily*" Oman, *History*, 6:27–28.

"*The Redoubt stormed . . . very hour*" 19–30 Sept. 1812, Box 13, Folder 79.

"*and most of these men . . . memory*" Guthrie, *Treatise*, p. 4.

"*splinters of bone . . . tow or rags*" Hennen, p. 47.

102   "*rare in the Peninsula . . . mischief*" Guthrie, *Commentaries*, p. 37.

"*every man . . . several others*" Cannon, p. 128.

"*after cleaning away . . . close stitches*" Hennen, p. 48.

"*Military surgeons . . . injury*" Guthrie, *Treatise*, p. 221.

"*collecting . . . spring wagons*" Henry, pp. 155–156, cited in Cantlie, 1:361.

"*It is a very prevalent . . . trouble*" Hennen, pp. 46–47.

"*stripped to their shirts . . . blood*" Grattan, *Adventures in the Connaught Rangers*, p. 143, cited in Cantlie, 1:328–329.

"*with as little delay as possible*" Hennen, p. 45.

"*no hope . . . carried on*" Hennen, p. 41. See Guthrie, *Treatise*, pp. 468–469; Cantlie, 1:344–345, discusses this point.

"*I had officers . . . some hours*" Guthrie, *Treatise*, pp. 223–224.

103   "*If the ball . . . we possibly can*" Hennen, p. 34.

"*It was five minutes . . . hold of the ball*" Cited in Kempthorne, "Wellington's Army," p. 71; see also Guthrie, *Treatise*, pp. 94–95.

"*a certain extraction . . . circumstances*" Hennen, pp. 90–91.

"*felt at the distance . . . imagined*" Guthrie, *Treatise*, p. 94.

"*from a neglect . . . lost*" Hennen, p. 49.

"*which . . . obnoxious to injury*" Guthrie, *Treatise*, pp. 306–307.

"*anxiety at insinuations . . . him*" 19–30 Sept. 1812, Box 13, Folder 79.

104   *He went to visit Burgos* 19–30 Sept. 1812, Box 13, Folder 79.

"*became so nervous . . . operation*" Henry, pp. 152–153, cited in Cantlie, 1:360.

*Guthrie was accused* Cantlie, 1:331.

"*from that period . . . connected with it*" 18–19 Sept. 1812, Box 13, Folder 79.

*fourteen in the next Bulletins of the Campaign 1812*, pp. 503–506. These are the wounded of the 42nd only, but it is likely that Lesassier would have treated the wounded in the rest of the brigade as well.

"*and if it was not a retreat . . . call it*" Gunn, p. 100.

*Under James McGrigor's* Cantlie, 1:350.

"*A thousand perplexing difficulties . . . sick*" 19 Oct. 1812, Box 13, Folder 79.

*dreadful retreat* Oman, *History*, 6:143–161.

"*had been employed . . . several days together*" McGrigor, *Sketch*, p. 46.

"*the removal of the wounded . . . amputation*" Guthrie, *Treatise*, p. 223.

*Lesassier was detached* 13–15 May 1813, Box 13, Folder 80.

105 "*asked for the doctor . . . send for us*" Gunn, p. 101.

*medical-board regulations* Cantlie, 1:326. See the case described by Guthrie, *Treatise*, p. 96, of a soldier who "died early in the morning, having complained a good deal in the night, but not sufficiently to induce the orderlies to call [the surgeon], until symptoms of approaching death alarmed them." There is no sign from Guthrie that the surgeon was at all to blame in not attending the hospital during the night.

"*the Officers of the Medical department . . . hospitals*" Great Britain, *General Orders* 2:191.

"*Oh . . . next campaign*" Gunn, p. 107.

"*the trouble . . . get better*" Pakenham, p. 197.

"*obstinately persisting . . . interfered with*" 14 May 1813, Box 13, Folder 80.

*The long period of rest* The exception was Howard's brigade of guards in the 1st Division. Oman, *History*, 6:322.

"*My people . . . out of them*" Pakenham, p. 198.

"*our next operation . . . weaker*" Wellington, *Dispatches*, 10:372, cited in Oman, *History*, 6:304.

106 *According to Oman* Oman, *History*, 6:300–305.

*Lesassier wrote* Letters to and from J. Cole, 14? May 1813, Box 13, Folder 80.

*Regimental hospitals* Cantlie 1:355.

"*The men . . . preserved*" 16 May 1813, Box 13, Folder 80.

"*second day's march . . . ourselves*" Gunn, p. 107.

"*an excellent stock . . . whole*" 16 May 1813, Box 13, Folder 80.

"*as there was . . . Fahrenheit*" 18 May 1813, Box 13, Folder 80.

"*many advantages . . . so many years*" 14? May 1813, Box 13, Folder 80.

107 "*new & a degrading duty . . . brigade*" 21 May 1813, Box 13, Folder 80.

*cart for transporting the slightly ill . . . army* Cantlie, 1:341.

"*our great man . . . hint at it*" 3 June 1813, Box 13, Folder 80.

"*peculiarly desirable . . . confer on me*" AL to JH, Valley of the Mosta, 25 Aug. 1813, Letterbook, Service, Box 2, Folder 19.

## Chapter 8. Arrived at Wealth and Dignity

108 "*of infinite service . . . scattered ideas*" 18–19 July 1813, Box 13, Folder 80.

*Neither the 9th nor 21st* Wellington, *Dispatches*, 7:341, 419, 437; Halliday, p. 23,31.

*Power's brigade* Compilação das ordens do dia, 1 July 1813, 4:61.

"*it was extraordinary . . . tempers*" Larpent, 2:3.

*Lesassier joined* AL to JM, 6 July 1813, Letterbook, Service, Box 2, Folder 19.

"*real luxury of a staff situation*" 29 July 1813, Box 13, Folder 80.

"*Now was the time . . . campaign*" Blakiston, 2:315–316.

"*wanted none . . . life*" 13 Nov. 1813, Box 13, Folder 80.

"*What a vast change . . . obtain*" 19 July 1813, Box 13, Folder 80.

109 "*a superb English horse . . . miserable horse*" 9 Oct. 1813, Box 13, Folder 80; Blakiston, 2:268.

"*sincerest thanks . . . good opinion*" AL to JM, 6 July 1813, Letterbook, Service, Box 2, Folder 19.

"*fully occupy their time . . . headquarters*" JM to the Army Medical Board, 8 Nov. 1812, Mss 2165, Letter Book, 26 April 1812–25 April 1813, Sir James McGrigor Manuscripts.

"*the anticipation . . . tremble*" 4 Jan. 1813, Box 13, Folder 80.

"*an active, meritorious officer*" AL to Francis Burroughs, 12 Jan. 1814, Letterbook, Service, Box 2, Folder 19.

*act as his assistant* Brigade orders, Erazu, 29 Sept. 1813, Orders, Departmental, Box 2, Folder 19.

"*with his accustomed politeness*" 18 Dec. 1813, Box 13, Folder 80.

"*wished me . . . day with him*" 8 Dec. 1813, Box 13, Folder 80.

*consulting him* See 4 Jan. 1814, Box 13, Folder 80.

"*I place . . . arrangements*" AL to Francis Burroughs, 29 Jan. 1814, Letterbook, Service, Box 2, Folder 19.

110   "*without discipline . . . duties*" Marshall Beresford to Portuguese Minister of War Forjaz, cited in Vichness, p. 261.

*Portuguese government* Vichness, pp. 296–332; Wellington, *Dispatches*, 7:341, 419, 437.

*British officers* Vichness, pp. 264–283; see Bunbury, 1:69–72.

*Few of the British* Vichness, p. 273.

"*devoted to the spot . . . their own*" Halliday, p. 87.

"*a little mess . . . meals*" Blakiston, 2:286.

*William Fergusson* Vichness, p. 323.

*pass an examination* Vichness, p. 283.

*same set of returns Compilação das ordens do dia*, 10 June 1812, 3:98–39. All the British forms were translated into Portuguese.

"*were . . . exactness in complying*" Orders, Departmental, 8 July 1813, Box 2, Folder 19.

"*to learn the language . . . patients*" JM to J. Weir, 29 April 1812, Mss 2165, Letter Book, 26 April 1812–25 April 1813, Sir James McGrigor Manuscripts.

111   "*false, or greatly exaggerated*" *O Investigator*, 2:204.

"*truly infamous*" *O Investigator*, 2:208; see Halliday, p. 86.

"*a Judas . . . object*" Wellington, *Dispatches*, 7:174.

"*the tyranny of a faithless government*" Halliday, p. 86.

"*Though as far . . . government*" JM to S. Reed, 29 April 1812, Mss 2165, Letter Book, 26 April 1812–25 April 1813, Sir James McGrigor Manuscripts.

*Halliday was placed* Johnston, 1:184.

*comments on countryside* 30 Aug. 1810, Box 12, Folder 77.

"*appeared to be touched . . . God*" Boutflower, pp. 38–39.

"*the Inquisition . . . water below us*" 10 Jan. 1810, Box 12, Folder 77.

"*gross negligence . . . Vitoria*" AL to Major General Power, 12 July 1813, Letterbook, Service, Box 2, Folder 19.

112   *only two* AL to William Wynn, 11 July 1813, Letterbook, Service, Box 2, Folder 19.

"*the march . . . occasion*" Wellington, *Dispatches*, 10:450–451; *Compilação das ordens do dia*, 1 July 1813, 4:59.

*Between the Ninth* Oman, *History*, 6:760.

*at least one of the assistant surgeons* AL to Francis Burroughs, 28 Oct. 1812, Letterbook, Service, Box 2, Folder 19.

*portable field hospitals* Wellington, *Dispatches*, 11:447.

*the expense had been considerable* Vichness, p. 322.

*regimental surgeons were held responsible Compilação das ordens do dia*, 27 Nov. 1810, 1:216.

"*that each medical officer . . . materials*" JM to Staff Surgeons of Divisions, 6 March 1812, Mss 2166, Letter Book, 30 Nov. 1811–31 March 1812, Sir James McGrigor Manuscripts.

113   *court-martial for robbery Compilação das ordens do dia*, 11 Sept. 1811, 2:196.

"*zeal and activity . . . enemy*" *Collecção das ordens do dia*, 21 Jan. 1813. He was promoted to *cirurgião mór* of the 2nd Caçadores for this, one of the few examples during the war of a medical officer promoted for bravery in facing the French.

"*neglect of . . . duties . . . Brigade*" *Collecção das ordens do dia*, 25 Jan. 1811.

"*almost impossible . . . escape death*" Antonio Peisoto d'Almeida to General Miranda, Tomar, 4 Jan. 1810, cited in Vichness, p. 321.

*vaccination for smallpox* Vichness, p. 324.

"*for nothing . . . twice a week*" 8 July 1813, Orders, Departmental, Box 2, Folder 19.

*"with sufficient disgust" . . . orderly.* 14 Aug. 1813, Orders, Departmental, Box 2, Folder 19.

*Lesassier decided* AL to Francis Burroughs, n.d. but probably October 1813, Letterbook, Service, Box 2, Folder 19.

114  *"frequent and minute inspection"* JM to the Army Medical Board, 31 Jan. 1813, Mss 2165, Letter Book, 26 April 1812–25 April 1813, Sir James McGrigor Manuscripts.

*Colonel Sutton* Wellington, *Dispatches,* 6:473.

*"a man well known . . . others"* AL to Francis Burroughs, 25 Jan. 1814, Letterbook, Service, Box 2, Folder 19.

*"after a delay . . . unattended to"* AL to Major General Power, 24 Aug. 1813, Letterbook, Service, Box 2, Folder, 19.

*"attending the sick . . . clean"* "Instructions to Regimental Surgeons," p. 145.

*"the brute . . . broom stick"* Costello, p. 22.

*frequent cause of friction* Wellington, *Dispatches,* 6:531, 9:622.

*"solicited permission . . . service"* AL to Major General Power, 24 Aug. 1813, Letterbook, Service, Box 2, Folder 19.

*"forty hours"* AL to Major General Power, 25 Aug. 1813, Letterbook, Service, Box 2, Folder 19.

*"the sick . . . hours"* AL to Major General Power, 26 Aug. 1813, Letterbook, Service, Box 2, Folder 19.

115  *senior lieutenant colonel* Sutton commanded the brigade while Power commanded the 3rd Division in Picton's absence.

*"the insidious . . . tyranny"* AL to William Wynn, 24 Aug. 1813, Letterbook, Service, Box 2, Folder 19.

*"Who is to command . . . orders"* McGrigor, *Autobiography,* p. 302; cited in Cantlie, 1:348.

*"amidst the peaceful pleasures . . . wash it out"* n.d., Ephemeris Aug. and Nov. 1813, Box 13, Folder 80.

*first of many letters* AL to William Wynn, 27 Aug. 1813, 9 Sept. 1813, Letterbook, Service, Box 2, Folder 19.

*He wrote to his uncle* AL to JH, 28 Aug. 1813, Letterbook, Service, Box 2, Folder 19.

116  *"rage & grief . . . term"* 8 Sept. 1813, Ephemeris Aug. and Nov. 1813, Box 13, Folder 80.

*"he had the honor . . . service"* AL to Charles Sutton, 1 Sept. 1813, Letterbook, Service, Box 2, Folder 19.

*"On no service . . . idlers"* JM to the Army Medical Board, 8 Nov. 1812, Mss 2165, Letter Book, 26 April 1812–25 April 1813, Sir James McGrigor Manuscripts.

*taking as much care* See, for example, 26 July 1809, 3 Dec. 1809, Box 12, Folder 76. Servants had greatest discretionary power when temporarily away from Lesassier, and invariably used it to look after his interests: 24 Aug. 1810, 28 Aug. 1810, 30 Aug. 1810, 10 Sept. 1810, Box 12, Folder 77.

*"former faithful servant . . . retribution"* 4 June 1813, Box 13, Folder 80.

117  *British officers' accounts* Blakiston, 2:150–51, 286–87; Fergusson, p. 66, extrapolated on by Cantlie, 1:326.

*Manoel served Lesassier* His resourcefulness in Lesassier's interest was shown most clearly in his independent activity while in transit: 22 Sept. 1811, Box 12, Folder 78; 28 May 1812, Box 13, Folder 79; 2–3 June 1813, Box 13, Folder 80.

*"the singular professional ignorance . . . require"* AL to Francis Burroughs, n.d. but probably October 1813, Letterbook, Service, Box 2, Folder 19.

*"make their way . . . deter them"* AL to General Power, 25 Nov. 1813, Letterbook, Service, Box 2, Folder 19.

*"scum of the earth"* Wellington, *Dispatches,* 10:496.

*"active man . . . vigorous a measure"* AL to General Power, 25 Nov. 1813, Letterbook, Service, Box 2, Folder 19.

*Lord Blantyre* Wellington, *Dispatches,* 10:38.

*"cease prescribing extras"* 14 Aug. 1813, Orders, Departmental, Box 2, Folder 19.

*"the avowed protégé . . . object"* AL to Francis Burroughs, 25 Jan. 1814, Letterbook, Service, Box 2, Folder 19.

118  *"four months . . . amusements"* AL to Francis Burroughs, 28 Oct. 1812, Letterbook, Service, Box 2, Folder 19.

"*longer acquaintance . . . man*" AL to Francis Burroughs, 9 Nov. 1813, Letterbook, Service, Box 2, Folder 19.

"*his private character . . . nothing to him*" AL to Francis Burroughs, 28 Oct. 1812, Letterbook, Service, Box 2, Folder 19.

*carry forage for his own animals* 18 Dec. 1813, Box 13, Folder 80.

"*public insubordination . . . extended*" AL to Francis Burroughs, 9 Nov. 1813, Letterbook, Service, Box 2, Folder 19.

"*receiving . . . hospital station*" 8 Sept. 1813, Box 13, Folder 80.

119   "*Any self-respecting . . . comply*" Cantlie, note 13, 1:393–94. Cantlie, however, felt this was a military prejudice with bad medical consequences, for unless medical officers remained with the field hospital in the rear of the action, wounded soldiers would not know where to find them.

"*to* show myself" 18 Aug. 1813, Box 13, Folder 80.

"*amongst the foremost . . . me*" 7? Oct. 1813, Box 13, Folder 80.

"*a few paces . . . action*" AL to JM, 25 Nov. 1813, Letterbook, Service, Box 2, Folder 19.

"*About midday . . . after the brigade*" 10 Nov. 1813, Box 13, Folder 80. The fort was probably the Louis XIV redoubt, one of two redoubts defending the Bridge of Amotz. Oman, 7:189.

"*We were extremely fortunate . . . assistant surgeons*" AL to the surgeon general [probably Francis Burroughs], 25 Nov. 1813, Letterbook, Service, Box 2, Folder 19.

"*farm house . . . unconcerned*" 13 Nov. 1813, Box 13, Folder 80.

"*had never been absent . . . brigade*" AL to the surgeon general [probably Francis Burroughs], 25 Nov. 1813, Letterbook, Service, Box 2, Folder 19.

"*the solitary hours . . . animal*" Nov. 1813, Box 13, Folder 80.

*Lesassier had not sent* AL to the Surgeon General [probably Francis Burroughs], 25 Nov. 1813, Letterbook, Service, Box 2, Folder 19.

"*almost daily . . . unpacked*" 13 Nov. 1813, Box 13, Folder 80.

120   "*my medical officers . . . assistance*" AL to the surgeon general [probably Francis Burroughs], 25 Nov. 1813, Letterbook, Service, Box 2, Folder 19.

"*old assistant*" 13 Nov. 1813, Box 13, Folder 80; brigade order, 25 Nov. 1813, Orders, Departmental, Box 2, Folder 19.

"*careful examination . . . lightly sick*" Brigade order, 25 Nov. 1813, Orders, Departmental, Box 2, Folder 19.

"*of our Caçadores*" Lesassier does not give his name, but Duizbeck appears to have been commanding the eleven caçadors at this point.

"*Aware of the distance . . . health*" 13 Nov. 1813, Box 13, Folder 80.

121   "*the lovely town of Hasparren*" 29 Dec. 1813, Box 13, Folder 80.

"*precisely Bento's turn . . . himself*" AL to Francis Burroughs, 29 Jan. 1814, Letterbook, Service, Box 2, Folder 19.

"*not within the recollection . . . humiliation*" AL to Francis Burroughs, 29 Jan. 1814, Letterbook, Service, Box 2, Folder 19.

"*never ceasing intrigues*" 13 Jan. 1814, Box 13, Folder 80.

"*no new case . . . made to him*" AL to Francis Burroughs, 29 Jan. 1814, Letterbook, Service, Box 2, Folder 19.

122   "*scandalous & unfounded assertions*" AL to Colonel Sutton, 30 Dec. 1813, Letterbook, Service, Box 2, Folder 19.

"*How visionary . . . station*" 4 Jan. 1813, Box 13, Folder 80.

*suspending Bento from rank and pay Collecção das ordens do dia*, 28 Jan. 1814.

"*Arrived at wealth . . . disposition?*" 8 Sept. 1813, Box 13, Folder 80.

"*but such a change . . . general hospital*" 13 Jan. 1814, Box 13, Folder 80.

"*reached the summit . . . perfection*" Cited in Cantlie, 1:378.

"*without delay . . . orderlies*" Extracts from departmental orders, general hospital, Ortes, 2, 4, 5 March 1814, Orders, Departmental, Box 2, Folder 19.

"*Vast & incessant . . . after a battle*" 14 March 1814, Box 13, Folder 80.

123   "*the satisfaction . . . exertions*" JM to the Army Medical Board, 12 March 1814, Mss. 2157, Letter Book 25 April 1813–3 June 1815, Sir James McGrigor Manuscripts.

*"for his activity . . . wounded"* *Compilação das ordens do dia*, 26 March 1814, 5:23–24. The translation is from Giao, p. 302.

*crown even medical officers* 31 May 1811, Box 12, Folder 77.

*David MacLagan* Giao, p. 302. He was cited after the Battle of the Nivelle.

*"accompanied . . . our assistant surgeons"* 16 March 1814, Box 13, Folder 80.

*"as we now approached to Toulouse . . . part"* 26 March 1814, Box 13, Folder 80.

*"triumphantly . . . anxious time"* April 1814, Box 13, Folder 81.

124   *"had been laid waste . . . Peninsula"* April 1814, Box 13, Folder 81.

## Chapter 9. Thrown on the Wide World

125   *"the two English brigades . . . except ours"* 10 June 1814, Box 13, Folder 81.

*"presented itself . . . outcast"* May 1814, Journal marked "J," Box 13, Folder 81.

*"return . . . suited me"* 26 Sept. 1814, Box 13, Folder 81.

*"What should I do . . . taken from me"* May 1814, Box 13, Folder 81.

126   *"most devoutly . . . private practice"* 1814, Journal marked "J," Box 13, Folder 81.

*"much depending . . . farewell forever!"* 1814, Journal marked "J," Box 13, Folder 81.

127   *"the comforts & embellishments . . . one friend left!"* 1814, Journal marked "J," Box 37, Folder 81.

*"exceedingly friendly . . . strongly excited"* Journal 1814–1816, Box 13, Folder 81.

*"want of foresight & calculation"* 1814, Journal marked "J," Box 13, Folder 81.

*"who . . . obscure situation"* 24 Feb. 1812, Box 13, Folder 81.

*"concluded me . . . capital and interest"* 1814, Journal marked "J," Box 13, Folder 81.

*"himself . . . imputation of interest"* Journal 1814–1816, Box 13, Folder 81.

*"make him . . . been before"* 1814, Journal marked "J," Box 13, Folder 81.

128   *"Were you at Waterloo"* Gunn, p. 119.

*"Few honours . . . Medical Department"* Cantlie, 1:378.

*"The professor's early breakfast . . . man!"* Journal 1814–1816, Box 13, Folder 81.

129   *"that if I could submit . . . high official rank"* Journal 1814–1816, Box 13, Folder 81.

*reasonable ambition* Journal 1814–1816, Box 13, Folder 81.

*owing £640* Alexander Hamilton, "Vindicating Address to the Public," Box 25, Folder 143.

*"that if a proposal . . . profession!"* Journal 1814–1816, Box 13, Folder 81.

*"I protested . . . leave him"* Journal 1814–1816, Box 13, Folder 81.

130   *"was ere this . . . service"* 1814, Journal marked "J," Box 13, Folder 81.

*"laid-up fleets . . . overstock"* Speer, p. 40.

*"Medical gentlemen . . . difficult task"* Journal 1814–1816, Box 13, Folder 81.

*"it was a sorry fate . . . industrious poverty"* May 1814, Journal marked "J," Box 13, Folder 81.

*"Nothing more effectually . . . unprejudiced eye"* Journal 1814–1816, Box 13, Folder 81.

131   *"As a proof . . . summoned"* Journal 1814–1816, Box 13, Folder 81.

*"For several days . . . myself"* Translation of Lesassier's inaugural dissertation, "De Synoch Castrensi," Box 11, Folder 70.

132   *"the amiable . . . Surgeon"* As Lesassier described the assistant surgeon of the 42nd at Burgos in *Edward Neville*. "EN," Box 8, Folder 55.

*"and another . . . patients died"* Translation of Lesassier's Inaugural Dissertation, "De Synoch Castrensi," Box 11, Folder 70.

133   *Edinburgh's declining reputation* Rosner, pp. 175–194.

*essay on tetanus* MacLagan, *Probationary Surgical Essay*; Jacyna, pp. 105–112.

*"the highest academical dignity"* Journal 1814–1816, Box 13, Folder 81.

*"a magnificently bound . . . binding"* Journal 1814–1816, Box 13, Folder 81.

*"goading my uncle . . . reputable practice"* Journal 1814–1816, Box 13, Folder 81. Lesassier had originally written "esteemed of the lower classes," but then replaced the last three words with "the people."

134   *consulting accoucheur* 14 July 1822, Box 13, Folder 82.

*"very much charmed . . . reception"* 22 Feb. 1821, Box 13, Folder 82.

*dinner with Lord and Lady Elibank* 28 Aug. 1822, Box 13, Folder 82.

"*supreme pleasure . . . Mrs. Hastings Anderson*" 10 Sept. 1822, Box 13, Folder 82.

"*superb patient . . . man servant*" 10 May 1821, Box 13, Folder 82.

"*as he would . . . apothecary*" Journal 1814–1816, Box 13, Folder 81.

"*I had . . . services!*" Journal 1814–1816, Box 13, Folder 81.

"*& really he did not know . . . deserve it*" Journal 1814–1816, Box 13, Folder 81.

135    "*What is the world . . . myself*" *Death's a Friend*, 2:3.

"*preposterous . . . appear?*" Journal 1814–1816, Box 13, Folder 81.

"*if a certain person . . . made*" IH to AH, Chatham, 16 Nov. 1818, Box 1, Folder 10.

*Archy Campbell* 26 Oct. 1821, Box 13, Folder 82.

"*gross want of policy . . . desire*" 23 Sept. 1826, Box 14, Folder 84.

"*had taken advantage . . . colors*" Journal 1814–1816, Box 13, Folder 81.

*his sitting down* 11 Feb. 1830, Box 15, Folder 88.

"*Be sure . . . purely disinterested*" IH to AH, Chatham, 16 Nov. 1818, Box 1, Folder 10.

136    *had a miniature made* IH to AH, Barracks [Chatham], 23 April 1821, Box 1, Folder 10.

"*One of the principle . . . wanting*" Journal 1814–1816, Box 13, Folder 81.

*between seventeen and twenty* She was still thinking of having a child in 1829. 11 April 1829, Box 14, Folder 86.

"*Dearest Catherine . . . ever*" AH to Catherine Hamilton, London, 8 May 1819, Box 1, Folder 7.

"*Never sacrifice . . . avarice*" 23 June 1805, Box 11, Folder 72.

"*As I could not . . . gold!*" Journal 1814–1816, Box 13, Folder 81.

"*heiress . . . death*" Copy of letter from AH to S. Reed, Secretary to the Army Medical Department, Edinburgh, 29 March 1819, Box 1, Folder 15.

"*worth . . . year!!!*" 5 May 1821, Box 13, Folder 82; see Staves.

137    "*quite unremitting . . . to me*" 8 Feb. 1829, Box 14, Folder 86; 10 June 1827, Box 14, Folder 85.

"*teasing . . . gratitude*" Emmeline Hawkins to Catherine Hamilton, 7 Jan. 1823, Box 1, Folder 9.

"*young lady . . . with a large fortune*" 10 Sept. 1805, Box 11, Folder 72.

"*the indelible blot . . . marriage*" 6 July 1824, Box 13, Folder 83.

"*under the guidance . . . to be*" IH to AH, Staffordshire, 6 Sept. 1819, Box 1, Folder 10.

"*well-merited scolding*" 26 June 1826, Box 14, Folder 24.

"*kept up . . . quarter*" 30 June 1830, Box 15, Folder 88.

"*walked out alone*" 1 March, 13–19 March, 12 June 1826, Box 14, Folder 84.

*visited her mother*  27 May 1829, Box 14, Folder 86.

"*boasting . . . over me*" 18 June 1824, Box 13, Folder 83.

"*arrogant boldness and assurance*" Week of 9 Jan. 1826, Box 14, Folder 84; 8 March 1827, Box 14, Folder 85.

"*she would let her . . . reprimand*" 30 Aug. 1826; 22 Sept. 1826, Box 14, Folder 84.

"*hysterical paroxisms . . . asleep*" 1 Aug. 1822, Box 13, Folder 82.

"*called me a* wretch . . . *strait-jacket!!*" 16 Aug. 1822, Box 13, Folder 82.

"*we are friends again*" for one of many examples, 21 July 1822, Box 13, Folder 82.

138    "*was a deeply selfish . . . hedonism*" Fletcher, p. 345.

*Isabella Allan*  Jean Allan to AH, 11 Oct. 1830, Box 5, Folder 36.

*presumed to be a boy* 25 May 1829, Box 14, Folder 86.

"*Such . . . amply merited*" 29 Oct. 1827, Box 14, Folder 85; Jean Allan to AH, 15 April 1830, 11 Oct. 1830, 7 Jan. 1831, Invoices and receipts, Box 5, Folder 36.

*deliver the baby*  Divorce proceedings between Catherine Jane Crokatt and Alexander Hamilton, Scottish Record Office CS46/76/1836.

*paid for her nurse* July 1820-Feb. 1821, Bills from "Kitty's Nurse," Margaret McIntosh, Box 3, Folders 26 and 27.

*Kitty and her baby* 6 Sept. 1824, Box 13, Folder 83.

"*in a little room . . . improper connections*" Divorce proceedings between Catherine Jane Crokatt and Alexander Hamilton, Scottish Record Office CS46/76/1836.

"*may be . . . day*" 1 April 1823, Box 13, Folder 83.

"*unaffected vivacity . . . party*" 26 April 1823, Box 13, Folder 83.

"*How delightful . . . marriage*" Eliot, p. 475.

139 "*not be reconciled*" 27 May 1822, Box 13, Folder 82.

"*to lecture her . . . wish*" 28 May 1822, Box 13, Folder 82.

"*the delicious feeling . . . girl*" 4 June 1823, Box 13, Folder 83.

"*a ingrata!*" (the ingrate!) 14 June, 23 Aug., 6 Sept. 1823, Box 13, Folder 83.

"*fancy . . . retire to bed*" 25 June 1821, Box 13, Folder 82.

"*an altercation . . . appeased*" 8 June 1823, Box 13, Folder 83; 16 March 1825, Box 14, Folder 84.

"*enviously jealous*" 1 Sept. 1821, Box 13, Folder 82.

*Fanny Maitland* 28 March 1825, Box 14, Folder 84.

"*squalling urchins*" 8 Jan. 1828, Box 14, Folder 85.

"*noisy & unmannerly*" 9 April 1823, Box 13, Folder 83; 1 Jan. 1826, Box 14, Folder 84.

"*ill-bred cubs*" 31 Dec. 1827, Box 14, Folder 85.

"*dandling & nursing . . . not of man*" 16 Jan. 1828, Box 14, Folder 85. Thomas Carlyle also felt that paternal affection for infants was distasteful and lower-class. See Carlyle, 3:195.

140 *attract a new patient* 11 Sept. 1828, Box 14, Folder 85.

"*deprive myself . . . children*" IH to AH, Artillery Barracks [Chatham], 15 Oct. 1820, Box 1, Folder 10.

"*was seized . . . lead me!!!*" 5–11 June 1826, Box 14, Folder 84.

*Only if they had no children* 15 Sept. 1826, 14, Folder 84.

"*unsettled, state*" IH to AH, Liverpool, 3 Jan. 1822, Box 1, Folder 10.

"*thankful . . . to be increased*" IH to AH, Artillery Barracks [Chatham], 15 Oct. 1820, Box 1, Folder 10.

"*You manage . . . know*" IH to AH, Artillery Barracks [Chatham], 23 April 1821, Box 1, Folder 10.

"*do you really adhere . . . respects*" IH to ALH, Artillery Barracks [Chatham], 4 July 1820, Box 1, Folder 10.

"*A full mounted . . . coaches*" Andrew Ker's account, 30 March 1819, Invoices and Receipts, Box 3, Folder 25. The receipts suggests a funeral procession, which Lesassier would only have paid for a member of his own family. He does not mention the death of this child anywhere in his journals.

*as she grew older* 8 Nov. 1829, Box 15, Folder 87.

"*For . . . at an end*" 12 Sept. 1826, Box 14, Folder 84.

"*to a fit . . . family*" 6 Oct. 1826, Box 14, Folder 84.

"*exasperatingly sullen & captious*" 7 Oct. 1826, Box 14, Folder 84.

"*Unfeeling . . . favorable circumstances*" 14 June 1826, Box 14, Folder 84.

Chapter 10. Appearances Are of Essential Consequence

141 *he had delivered . . . families* Medical Ledger 1818–1831, note on inside cover, Box 5, Folder 39.

"*the lower . . . classes*" 29 Jan. 1829, Box 14, Folder 86.

"*shopkeepers . . . etc.*" 16 April 30, Box 15, Folder 88.

"*How different . . . look!*" 6 Mar 1829, Box 14, Folder 86.

"*cheerful . . . lovely*" 8 Jan. 1829, Box 14, Folder 86.

"*there certainly . . . deserve them*" Austen, *Mansfield Park*, p. 3; an excellent analysis of the difficulties and expedients in establishing a medical practice is in Digby.

142 "*nine hundred . . . natural*" *Encyclopedia Britannica*, s.v. "Midwifery."

"*Thank God! . . . right*" 11 Jan. 1821, Box 13, Folder 82.

*Lying-In Hospital* 19 Dec. 1829, Box 15, Folder 87.

"*I was called . . . service to me*" 26 March 1825, Box 14, Folder 84.

"*with great facility . . . recovery*" Sept. 1819, Select Cases in Midwifery from my own practice, 1819–1825, Box 23, Folder 131.

"*in cases . . . pelvis*" *Encyclopedia Britannica*, s.v. "Midwifery."

"*breathing . . . hot flannel*" 11 Feb. 1820, see also Oct. 1819, Select Cases in Midwifery from my own practice, 1819–1825, Box 23, Folder 131.

"*Considering . . . rapid recovery*" 10 Nov. 1820, Select Cases in Midwifery from my own practice, 1819–1825, Box 23, Folder 131.

"*horrible operation at the Hospital*" 14 July 1822, Box 13, Folder 82.

"*At 20 minutes to 6 . . . lovely girl*" 14 Feb. 1821, Box 13, Folder 82.

"*instead of destroying . . . parent*" Encyclopedia Britannica, s.v. "Midwifery."

"*the most brutal threats . . . wife*" 20 Aug. 1819, Select Cases in Midwifery from my own practice, 1819–1825, Box 23, Folder 131.

"*How getting on . . . thriving?*" Medical Ledger 1818–1831, Box 5, Folder 39.

"*I am called . . . afternoon*" 13 Jan. 1822, Box 13, Folder 82.

143    "*low patients*" 15 Nov. 1821, Box 13, Folder 82.

*never refused* 1 Jan. 1827, Box 14, Folder 85.

*visited them . . . twice daily* 13, 14, 17 March, 1821, Box 13, Folder 82.

"*To be told . . . one's duty*" 13 July, Select Cases in Midwifery from my own practice, 1819–1825, Box 23, Folder 131.

"*attacked . . . excessively*" 2 May 1827, Box 14, Folder 85.

"*exceedingly anxious*" 3 May 1827, Box 14, Folder 85.

"*little patient*" 4 May 1827, Box 14, Folder 85.

"*will still require . . . trouble!*" 7 May 1827, Box 14, Folder 85.

*weaning* In this case, the child was weaned at about seven months. 9 July 1821, Box 13, Folder 82.

*baby's gums* 18 Jan. 1822, Box 13, Folder 82.

*wet nurses* 26 Dec. 1827, Box 14, Folder 85; 24 April 1828, Box 14, Folder 85. In rare cases wet nurses came to him seeking employment: 20 Dec. 1830, Box 16, Folder 90. James Young Simpson also kept track of wet nurses: List of Wet-Nurses, Edinburgh, c. 1840/50?, James Young Simpson Papers, Royal College of Physicians.

"*I shall . . . Edinburgh nurse*" Louisa Kintore to Alexander Hamilton, 9 Feb. 1824, Box 2, Folder 11.

"*gratuitous*" 4 March 1828, Box 14, Folder 85; 23 Dec. 1830, Box 16, Folder 90.

"*toughness . . . uterus*" 13 July, Select Cases in Midwifery from my own practice, Box 23, Folder 131.

144    *physiological basis* See Barker-Benfield.

*Matilda falls in love* Review of *Matilda*, p. 443.

145    "*a sudden abolition . . . nerves*" Encyclopaedia Britannica, s.v. "Medicine."

*ten pairs . . .* Encyclopaedia Britannica, s.v. "Anatomy."

"*may be cured . . . mortal*" Encycopedia Britannica, s.v. "Medicine."

*clinician's gaze* See Foucault.

"*delivered her . . . died*" Medical Ledger 1818–1831, Box 5, Folder 39.

"*uneasy . . . man*" 21 June 1827, Box 14, Folder 85.

"*driven half frantic . . . unsubdued*" 25 June 1827, Box 14, Folder 85.

"*This was the first . . . existence!!*" 29 June 1827, Box 14, Folder 85.

146    "*After minutely enquiring . . . morning*" EN, 1:20.

"*hesitated . . . enlightened physician*" EN, 1:47.

*Critics of aspects of modern medicine* Two accessible examples are Arthur Kleinman and Oliver Sacks.

*families . . . did not call him* 1 Oct. 27, Box 14, Folder 85.

147    "*in an agony . . . tremble*" 18 May 1829, Box 14, Folder 86.

*never called* 29 Nov. 1830, Box 16, Folder 90.

"*broke in . . . whole day*" 10 Jan. 1821, Box 13, Folder 82.

"*invariably . . . hour*" Ferrier, Memoir, p. 15.

"*Catherine . . . unprofessional*" 15 Feb. 1826, Box 14, Folder 84.

"*want of tact . . . reserve*" 21 Jan. 1820, Box 15, Folder 88.

"*incurable imbecility*" 24 Nov. 1829, Box 15, Folder 87.

"*vows . . . forgive him*" 22 June 1827, Box 14, Folder 85.

"*imposed upon me . . . allegations*" 5 July 1827, Box 14, Folder 85.

*young lady of fortune* 11 Dec. 1827, Box 14, Folder 85.

148    "*to buy me . . . present of it!*" 16 Dec. 1827, Box 14, Folder 85.

"*brought me . . . for it*" 1 Feb. 1828, Box 14, Folder 85.

*modern scholarship* For example, Jewson; Porter, "The Patient's View".

"*roused . . . higher ranks again*" 13–19 March 1826, Box 14, Folder 84.

"*For instance . . . rascal*" 2 May 1825, Box 14, Folder 84.

"*to employ . . . daughter!*" 17 April 1827, Box 14, Folder 85.

"*chief . . . business*" 26 Sept. 27, Box 14, Folder 85.

"*professional patron*" 26 Sept. 1826, Box 14, Folder 84.

"*Lady's Charity . . . houses*" 14 Feb. 1823, Box 13, Folder 83.

*medical review* 24 Oct. 1826, Box 14, Folder 84.

"*my old friend*" 2 May 1823, Box 13, Folder 83.

"*was surprised . . . furniture*" 14 Oct. 1829, Box 15, Folder 87.

149 *probationary essay on midwifery* Rosner, pp. 101–102.

"*one . . . Edinburgh*" 12 Aug. 1829, Box 15, Folder 87.

*Robert Knox* Knox and his medical and urban milieu are vividly described in Edwards.

*unlicensed or illegal practitioners* Porter, *Health for Sale*; Ramsay.

"*want of respectability . . . eminence*" 6 July 1824, Box 13, Folder 83.

"*to the Almighty . . . independence*" 12 Sept. 1826, Box 14, Folder 84.

*£100 in 1817* Note on inside cover, Medical Ledger 1818–1831, Box 5, Folder 39.

"*I . . . kind heart*" IH to AH, Chatham, 15 July 1819, Box 1, Folder 10.

"*as I consider . . . period*" IH to AH, Chatham, 24 Feb. 1820, Box 1, Folder 10.

"*All your wellwishers . . . one*" IH to AH, Chatham, 27 April 1820, Box 1, Folder 10.

"*for one . . . situation*" IH to AH, Chatham, 2 June 1820, Box 1, Folder 10.

150 *Jane Austen's novels* MacDonagh, p. 58.

*Catherine's family . . . "house"* IH to AH, Artillery Barracks [Chatham], 4 July 1820, Box 1, Folder 10.

"*Alas! . . . sufferings*" 5 July 1822, Box 13, Folder 82.

"*a great-coat . . . it*" 19 Oct. 1825, Box 14, Folder 84.

"*looking . . . dressed*" 20 July 1826, Box 14, Folder 84.

"*three . . . song (55 shillings)*" 22 March 1826, Box 14, Folder 84.

*tradesmen's bills* 27 April 25, Box 14, Folder 84.

*Richard Jenoway* 7 July 1822, Box 13, Folder 82.

151 "*is a severe tax upon me*" 4 Oct. 1827, Box 14, Folder 85.

"*soft & heavy*" 18 May 1825, Box 14, Folder 84.

"*advice . . . half-pay!!*" 7 July 1826, Box 14, Folder 84.

*pay their bills* Medical Ledger, 1818–1831, Box 5, Folder 39. On the difficulties of collecting fees, see Digby, pp. 155–158, 193–196.

"*pay . . . penniless*" 2 July 1827, Box 14, Folder 85.

*he could not recover* 8 Sept. 1826, Box 14, Folder 84.

"*Nothing short of a miracle*" 6 June 1828, Box 14, Folder 85.

*Mr. McKenzie . . . £30* 26 Oct. 1827, Box 14, Folder 85; Medical Ledger, 1818–1831, Box 5, Folder 39.

*Mrs. Siddons* 6 June 1822, Box 13, Folder 82.

"*had the assurance . . . £3*" 10 March 1828, Box 14, Folder 85.

"*two cheap pictures . . . painter*" Medical Ledger, 1818–1831, Box 5, Folder 39.

*rich in consumer goods* 16 June 1829, Box 14, Folder 86.

152 "*Mean, deceitful wretch . . . woman!*" 25–7 April, Box 14, Folder 86.

*asking Catherine's mother* 22 Feb. 1825, Box 14, Folder 84.

*asking his uncle* 14 Feb., 25 Feb. 1822, Box 13, Folder 82.

*£135 per annum* 25 July 1827, Box 14, Folder 85.

"*all of which . . . fire*" 21 Nov. 1823, Box 13, Folder 83.

*He bought Catherine a piano* Receipt for advertising instruction on the piano, 9 Nov. 1819, Invoices and Receipts, Box 3, Folder 25.

"*horribly embarrassed poor fellow*" 18 Nov. 1824, Box 13, Folder 83.

*investing in a technique* 1 Feb. 1825, Box 14, Folder 84.

"*to a book . . . peerage*" 25 Aug. 1826, Box 14, Folder 84.

"*retiring . . . Jersey*" 4 Nov. 1824, Box 13, Folder 83.

"*While accompanying . . . my life*" Copy of letter from AH to S. Reed, Secretary to the Army Medical Department, Edinburgh, 29 March 1819, Box 2, Folder 15.

153  *prevented him from learning to dance* 3 Dec. 1805, Box 11, Folder 73.
   *"that the tibia . . . experiment"* Copy of letter from AH to S. Reed, Secretary to the Army Medical Department, Edinburgh, 29 March 1819, Box 2, Folder 15.
   *"So much . . . decision"* 24 June 1822, Box 13, Folder 82. Lesassier's first examination before the medical board was in 1819, and his second in 1822.
   *"so supremely successful . . . presents"* 25 June 1822, Box 14, Folder 84.
154  *"I cannot rest . . . journey"* IH to AH, Brompton, 13 May 1819, Box 1, Folder 10.
   *"I had heard . . . motto"* Thomas Hodgeson to AH, Chatham, 29 Dec. 1818. Box 1, Folder 10.
   *"it gratifies . . . my own"* IH to AH, Brompton, 13 May 1819, Box 1, Folder 10.
   *"What would I give . . . bless you"* IH to AH, Staffordshire, 22 Sept. 1819, Box 1, Folder 10.
155  *"a spice . . . street"* EN, 1:401.
   *"the amiable . . . Surgeon"* "EN," Box 8, Folder 55.
   *John Lane Bulletins of the Campaign* (1812): 459. John Lane was commissioned as ensign on 13 Oct. 1812. McMicking, p. 46.
   *"history . . . read with interest"* Review of *EN*, p. 106.
156  *"Revirescam"* EN, 4:385.
   *"Edward Desmond, Earl of Harlington"* EN, 4:381.
   *"We apprehend . . . foolish people"* Review of *EN*, p. 106.
   *"first necessary ingredient . . . heroes!"* Cited in Radway, pp. 68–69.
   *"innermost practical feelings"* H. C. Robinson, *Henry Crabb Robinson*, 2:787.
157  *"exasperation . . . weakness"* EN, 1:188.
   *"rustic air and old fashioned clothes"* EN, 1:212–213.
   *"stared, and pointed, and grinned at"* EN, 1:179.
   *"fairly shut the door"* EN, 1:216–217.
   *"the gorgeous new jacket . . . shoes"* EN, 4:252.
   *"a superb . . . eyes"* EN, 4:367.
   *"a little green . . . ornament"* EN, 2:406.
   *"in a hesitating . . . capable of"* EN, 3:21–20.
   *"In proportion . . . own table"* EN, 4:371–379.
158  *"I ask . . . love another"* Review of *Reginald Dalton*, p. 206.
   *he made Edward the recipient EN*, 3:326–327.
   *"some other . . . proper"* EN, 3:331.
159  *"his blows . . . terror"* EN, 1:324.
   *The hero of* Henry *Henry*, 1:57.
   *"older and stronger"* EN, 1:327.
   *"All my comfort . . . well"* 15 Dec. 1821, Box 13, Folder 82.
   *"even that sum . . . embarrassments"* 4 Jan. 1822, Box 13, Folder 82.
   *"with an impertinent note . . . at all"* 20 Nov. 1821, Box 13, Folder 82.
   *"my ill starred . . . last!!"* 12 July 1822, Box 13, Folder 82.
   *"for my book . . . buy it"* 24 July 1823, Box 13, Folder 83.
   *"to their infinite delight . . . opinion"* 20 July 1823, Box 13, Folder 83.
   *"on the plan . . . loss"* C. Orme to AH, London, 9 July 1822, Longman Papers, Longman I, 101, no. 305.
   *Three hundred* Longman, Rees, Orme, Brown & Green to Alexander Hamilton, 4 Sept. 1828, Box 5, Folder 34; Longman Papers, Divide Ledger 1813–1866.
160  *"It would be hard . . . by it!"* 4 Sept. 1828, Box 14, Folder 85.
   *"begun another novel . . . hands"* 8 Jan. 1822, Box 13, Folder 82.
   *"Ah! . . . such a book!"* 13 July 1829, Box 14, Folder 86; Gleig.
   *"concludes . . . disappointments"* Goldsmith, p. 63.

Chapter 11. Consecutive Chain of Corroborative Evidence

161  *"affairs . . . residence"* 17 March 1822, Box 13, Folder 82.
   *reduce his establishment* 6 June 1828, Box 14, Folder 85; 11 June 1829, Box 14, Folder 86.

"*wretchedly low . . . house*" 7 March 1822, Box 13, Folder 82.

"*enable us . . . head*" 13 March 1822, Box 13, Folder 82.

"*of going . . . Anne*" 1 April 1822, Box 13, Folder 82.

"*improper intimacy*" Lady Louisa Kintore to AH, Dunnichen, 3 Feb. 1824, Box 2, Folder 11.

"*not walk home . . . purposely*" 2 March 1821, Box 13, Folder 82.

*continued prejudice* See Roy Porter, "A Touch of Danger."

162   "*a severe cough . . . remedies*" Copy of letter sent from James Hamilton to William Hastings Anderson, Edinburgh, 25 Aug. 1822, Box 1, Folder 7.

"*The Doctor . . . department*" 9 April 1822, Box 13, Folder 82.

"*several large fees . . . £48.16!!*" 27 April 1822, Box 13, Folder 82.

*he had to miss . . . lectures* Copy of letter sent from JH to the Lord Provost of Edinburgh, Edinburgh, 27 May 1822, Box 1, Folder 7.

"*my nephew . . . three*" Copy of letter sent from JH to William Hastings Anderson, Edinburgh, 25 Aug. 1822, Box 1, Folder 7.

"*specifically recommending . . . speak of*" Alexander Hamilton, "Vindicating Address to the Public," Box 25, Folder 143.

"*by anticipating . . . death*" 5 April 1822, Box 13, Folder 82.

"*His day . . . recover*" 7 April 1822, Box 13, Folder 82.

163   "*I have . . . future!!*" 28 Aug. 1822, Box 13, Folder 82.

"*my Uncle . . . grasping!*" 26 Sept. 1822, Box 13, Folder 82.

*dangerously ill . . . "better in the morning"* 27 Sept. 1822, Box 13, Folder 82.

"*uncle's exasperated . . . opposition*" 28 Sept. 1822, Box 13, Folder 82.

"*by dint . . . I hope*" 2–5 Oct. 1822, Box 13, Folder 82.

"*The Doctor's spite . . . him too*" 30 Sept. 1822, Box 13, Folder 82.

"*had not been . . . consider*" Alexander Hamilton, "Vindicating Address to the Public," Box 25, Folder 143.

"*From the old rascal . . . world*" 31 Oct. 1822, Box 13, Folder 82.

*£500 during the year* 31 Oct. 1822, Box 13, Folder 82.

"*a Promissary Note . . . times*" Alexander Hamilton, "Vindicating Address to the Public," Box 25, Folder 143.

*mere bookkeeping matter* There is no mention of any suspicion in his journal entries for 30 or 31 Oct. 1822, Box 13, Folder 82.

"*What, however . . . I owed him*" Alexander Hamilton, "Vindicating Address to the Public," Box 25, Folder 143.

164   *His man of business, Syme* 26 Nov. 1822, Box 13, Folder 82.

"*in order . . . friends*" 28 Nov. 1822, Box 13, Folder 82.

"*little wretch . . . not at all!*" 2 Dec. 1822, Box 13, Folder 82.

*John Mackintosh* The controversies, which quickly became personal attacks, can be followed in the series of pamphlets published by John Mackintosh and James Moir in 1822 and 1823.

"*endeavored . . . James Hamilton Junior*" JH to AH, Edinburgh, 20 Feb. 1823, Box 1, Folder 7.

"*I fairly own . . . kept*" JH to AH, Edinburgh, 10 Feb. 1823, Box 1, Folder 7.

"*is so far removed . . . Hospital*" JH to AH, Edinburgh, 20 Feb. 1823, Box 1, Folder 7.

"*In short . . . office*" 10 Feb. 1823, Box 13, Folder 83.

165   "*I have gained . . . £200 or £300*" 3 Sept. 1822, Box 13, Folder 82.

*He made every effort* 4 Sept. 1822, Box 13, Folder 82.

"*an affecting leave of her*" 7 Sept. 1822, Box 13, Folder 82.

"*sweet Lady Portsmouth . . . forget me*" 14 Sept. 1822, Box 13, Folder 82.

"*betray . . . visibly tend*" The Fine Gentleman's Etiquette, p. 7; Chesterfield, *Letters*.

"*had discovered . . . other sex*" EN, 2:23.

*her own husband* 13 Dec. 1822, Box 13, Folder 82.

*mere Miss Hanson* 4 March 1823, Box 13, Folder 83.

"*cottages . . . dinners*" Ferrier, *Marriage*, p. 125.

"*seulement des Bourgeoise*" 2 Jan. 1809, Box 12, Folder 75.

166   "*bourgeois that nobody knows*" Fine Gentleman's Etiquette, p. 7. On the social distance between aristocratic patients and their physicians, see Digby, pp. 177–178.

"*Mild . . . sound policy*" 5 Feb. 1823, Box 13, Folder 83.

"*have done with her for ever*" 8 Dec. 1823, Box 13, Folder 83.

"*I . . . wished-for point*" 5 Feb. 1823, Box 13, Folder 83.

*the beautiful Lady Kintore* 9 Sept. 1822, Box 13, Folder 82.

"*whim . . . acceded*" Emmeline Hawkins to AH, 21 March 1823, Box 1, Folder 9.

"*I am hurried . . . it will be*" 2 Sept. 1822, Box 13, Folder 82.

*his second visit* 22, 25 Sept., 2–5 Oct. 1822, Box 13, Folder 82.

"*O Deo! que divina prazer*" 10 Oct. 1822, Box 13, Folder 82.

"*a secundo vez*" 13 Oct. 1822, Box 13, Folder 82.

*stars recurred* 22, 31 Oct. 1822, Box 13, Folder 82.

"*What an exquisite . . . symmetry!*" 20 Dec. 1827, Box 14, Folder 85.

"*Oh! what a matchless leg*" 30 Sept. 1830, Box 16, Folder 90.

"*then . . . ¾ hour*" 22 Oct. 1830, Box 16, Folder 90.

*place his hand* 7 Feb. 1829, Box 14, Folder 86.

"*swelling . . . blushing timidity*" 2 Oct. 1828, Box 14, Folder 85.

*without trembling with emotion* 13 Sept. 1829, Box 15, Folder 87.

167  *pressed his hand* 7 Oct. 1829, Box 15, Folder 87.

"*Oh . . . were mine*" 23 Dec. 1822, Box 13, Folder 82.

"*I call on Louisa . . . poor Louisa!!!*" 24 Dec. 1822, Box 13, Folder 82.

"*my beloved Daddy*" Emmeline Hawkins to AH, dated 6 Jan. 1822 but really 1823, Box 1, Folder 9.

*Louisa would get a separation* 11 Feb. 1823, 6, 10 March 1823, Box 13, Folder 83.

"*relieves me from difficulties*" 9 March 1823, Box 13, Folder 83.

"*divine . . . such goodness*" 5 Nov. 1822, Box 13, Folder 82.

"*What noble . . . resource left*" 28 May 1823, Box 13, Folder 83.

"*character of Turk . . . harem*" Elizabeth Fowler (a companion of the Hawkins sisters) to AH, Burnside, 18 March 1823, Box 2, Folder 11.

"*genius for* matrimony" Emmeline Hawkins to AH, 24 Aug. 1823, Box 1, Folder 9.

"*I grow horribly qualmish . . . his*" Emmeline Hawkins to AH, 11 Dec. 1823, Box 1, Folder 9.

168  "*the generality . . . in return*" Emmeline Hawkins to AH, 24 Aug. 1823, Box 1, Folder 9.

"*the delightful* thrill . . . *far away*" Emmeline Hawkins to AH, 16 Nov. 1822, Box 1, Folder 9.

"*in some degree . . . trio*" Emmeline Hawkins to AH, dated 6 Jan. 1822 but really 1823, Box 1, Folder 9.

"*eternal constancy*" 6 March 1823, Box 13, Folder 83.

"*into Catherine's hands . . . of the matter*" 5 Feb. 1823, Box 13, Folder 83.

"*Catherine . . . good fortune!*" 18 March 1823, Box 13, Folder 83.

"*I told you . . . drive her*" Emmeline Hawkins to AH, 21 March 1823, Box 1, Folder 9.

169  "*for . . . owing to me*" 23 March 1823, Box 13, Folder 83.

"*is in the family way . . . practical affection*" 28 Oct. 1823, Box 13, Folder 83.

*a phrase with its own echoes EN*, 3:21–20.

"*all is so far well . . . idade!!*" 18 Nov. 1823, Box 13, Folder 83.

"*Is it possible . . . contempt*" Lady Kintore to AH, 9 Feb. 1824, Box 2, Folder 11.

"*to preserve . . . dignity*" Emmeline Hawkins to AH, 26 Dec. 1823, Box 1, Folder 9.

"*he cannot receive . . . refuses to give*" Emmeline Hawkins to AH, 11 Dec. 1823, Box 1, Folder 9.

170  "*unhappy concluding sentence*" Lady Kintore to AH, 9 Feb. 1824, Box 2, Folder 11.

"*For my part . . . man*" Emmeline Hawkins to AH, 11 Dec. 1823, Box 1, Folder 9.

"*Need I say . . . those I love*" Emmeline Hawkins to AH, Edinburgh, Nov. 1822, Box 1, Folder 9.

"*her sisters . . . to a physician*" Emmeline Hawkins to AH, Edinburgh, 26 Dec. 1823, Box 1, Folder 9.

"*and . . . bearing down of the womb*" Emmeline Hawkins to AH, Edinburgh, 6 Jan. 1822, Box 1, Folder 9.

171  "*that Lord Kintore . . . next infant*" Emmeline Hawkins to AH, Edinburgh, 26 Dec. 1823, Box 1, Folder 9.

"*occasioned . . . Dr Alexander Hamilton!!!*" 15 Dec. 1823, Box 13, Folder 83.

"*our character . . . worship you?*" Emmeline Hawkins to AH, Edinburgh, 2 Dec. 1823, Box 1, Folder 9.

"*nothing else . . . in Edinburgh!!!*" 17 Dec. 1823, Box 13, Folder 83.

"*The story . . . predecessors*" Marchioness of Stafford to C. Kirkpatrick Sharpe, Richmond, 11 Feb. 1824, in Sharpe, 2:285. The references to Lady K. and Lord K. are not explained in the letters, but the timing is precisely right for the Kintore scandal.

"*Never Oh! never . . . torture*" 15 Dec. 1823, Box 13, Folder 83.

"*my heart . . . I am become*" 27 Dec. 1823, Box 13, Folder 83.

"*I begin . . . same with me*" 15 Dec. 1823, Box 13, Folder 83.

"*Woe be to them . . . ruin them here*" 3 April 1824, Box 13, Folder 83.

"*with indignation for writing the letter*" 25 March 1824, Box 13, Folder 83.

"*dear Mrs Hamilton*" Louisa Kintore to AH, 3 and 9 Feb. 1824, Box 1, Folder 9.

172 "*Dr. H. . . . improper*" Louisa Kintore to AH, 9 Feb. 1824, Box 1, Folder 9.

"*such selfish . . . destruction to me*" 25 March 1824, Box 13, Folder 83.

"*annual allowance*" 22 Jan. 1824, Box 13, Folder 83.

"*I again . . . for many years*" 3 Jan. 1823, Box 13, Folder 83.

"*dissuades me . . . funds*" 21 March 1823, Box 13, Folder 83.

*another loan obtained from Syme* The documents relating to the purchase of the house are Scottish Record Office, RS27/1432FF14QR-144R, RS27/995FF126V-141R, RS27/2646FF75R-77R.

"*a castle of a house*" 11 June 1829, Box 14, Folder 86.

"*irritated . . . content myself*" 4 Feb. 1824, Box 13, Folder 83.

"*& . . . my great rival . . . contempt*" 25 March 1824, Box 13, Folder 83.

173 "*as I requested . . . my mind*" 27 March 1824, Box 13, Folder 83.

"*incautiously tells me . . . remuneration from her*" 16 April 1824, Box 13, Folder 83.

"*no longer brook . . . forever*" 21 April 1824, Box 13, Folder 83.

"Bellissima e Divina Creature" Notes dated 8 July 1824, inserted into Somnia notebook, 1828, Box 16, Folder 90; 28 July 1829, Box 14, Folder 86.

"*the deepest affliction . . . name*" 1 Jan. 1824, Box 13, Folder 83.

"*Scoundrel!*" 29 Dec. 1823, Box 13, Folder 83.

"*the revival . . . James Hamilton Junior*" Alexander Hamilton, "Vindicating Address to the Public," Box 25, Folder 143.

"*hurts & irritates . . . uncle*" 16 Jan. 1824, Box 13, Folder 83.

"*loan of £624 . . . kindness to me*" 26 Jan. 1824, Box 13, Folder 83.

"*For, a child . . . public opinion*" 11 Feb. 1828, Box 14, Folder 85.

"*All future . . . his ruin also*" 29 Jan. 1824, Box 13, Folder 83.

174 "*arrived . . . unlooked-for change*" 23 Dec. 1824, Box 13, Folder 83.

"*principal part . . . complaints*" Medical Ledger, 1818–1831, note on inside cover, Box 5, Folder 39.

"*the most talented physician . . . gentleman*" 9 Jan. 1829, Box 14, Folder 86.

"*told me . . . plunged in despair*" 1 Jan. 1824, Box 13, Folder 83.

"*Ah! . . . lodgings*" 11 Jan. 1824, Box 13, Folder 83.

*on Ludlow's arrival* Account with Mr. Ludlow, 1823, Box 4, Folder 30.

*Ludlow did accompany him* For example, see 19 May 1824, Box 13, Folder 83.

"*her brother . . . change!!*" 7 March 1824, Box 13, Folder 83.

175 "*flattered . . . abstruse and laborious*" John Hanson to AH, London, 18 Mar 1824, Box 1, Folder 8.

"*full of fears . . . eight years past*" Newton Hanson to AH, London, 20 March 1824, Box 1, Folder 8.

*pay £140 per year* John Hanson to AH, 1 May 1824, Box 1, Folder 8.

"*I hope soon . . . I shall do*" 1 April 1824, Box 13, Folder 83.

*suggested that Lesassier* 30 April 1824, Box 13, Folder 83.

"*money-lender . . . him*" 7 May 1824, Box 13, Folder 83.

*rate was high* That is, £500 less interest paid in advance. 29 May 1824, Box 13, Folder 83.

"*the great question . . . two years*" 7 May 1824, Box 13, Folder 83.

*he wrote to James McGrigor* Note on letter from JM to AH, London, 22 April 1824, Box 1, Folder 13.

176 "*so that . . . family*" 19 June 1824, Box 13, Folder 83.

"*the little mysterious girl*" 19 May 1824, Box 13, Folder 83.

"*Mary Ann . . . dream*" 12 June 1824, Box 13, Folder 83.

"*her love . . . attention*" 5 June 1824, Box 13, Folder 83.

*they quarreled* 14 June 1824, 4 July 1824, Box 13, Folder 83.

"*expressing . . . produce an explosion*" 16 July 1824, Box 13, Folder 83.

"*violent quarrel . . . taking fire*" 22 June 1824, Box 13, Folder 83.

177   "*How . . . difficult to know*" 18 June 1824, Box 13, Folder 83.

"*irrevocable will . . . practice for ever!*" 27 Oct. 1824, Box 13, Folder 83.

*Lady Portsmouth . . . promised* 4 July 1824, Box 13, Folder 83.

"*In the singular friendship . . . every thing*" 6 July 1824, Box 13, Folder 83.

"*I may . . . would have done*" 8 July 1824, Box 13, Folder 83.

"*tie her down to live with us*" 21 July 1824, Box 13, Folder 83.

"*What a life . . . useless a woman*" 7 Sept. 1824, Box 13, Folder 83.

"*that ill-fated Lady . . . familiar with*" 26 Aug. 1827, Box 14, Folder 85.

"*It is really . . . thoroughly miserable*" 16 Sept. 1824, Box 13, Folder 83.

*leaving Pierre* 25 Nov. 1824, Box 13, Folder 83.

*perhaps the entire £1,200* 13 May 1828, Box 14, Folder 85.

*Lady Portsmouth demanded* 14 Dec. 1824, Box 13, Folder 83.

*Lesassier retaliated* 16 Dec. 1824, Box 13, Folder 83.

178   "*telling the Doctor . . . pay him with*" Copy of letter from AH to Thomas Syme, probably never sent, 19 May 1825, Box 1, Folder 8.

"*again & again . . . concealment*" 27 May 1825, Box 14, Folder 84.

"*harm . . . unutterable joy*" 13 June 1825, Box 14, Folder 84.

*diamond pin* 11 June 1824, Box 13, Folder 83.

*eventually paid by John Hanson* 28–29 July 1828, Box 14, Folder 85; 16, 22 Oct. 1829, Box 15, Folder 87.

"*scurrilous . . . from her*" 8 Jan. 1825, Box 14, Folder 84.

"*Oh! Hamilton . . . virtues in him*'" Newton Hanson to AH, 14 April 1825, Box 1, Folder 8.

179   "*It does appear . . . guidance*" John Hanson to AH, 4 May 1825, Box 1, Folder 8.

*Newton Hanson made a point* JM to AH, 3 May 1825, and AH to JM, 7 May 1825, Box 1, Folder 13.

"*a plaintive story . . . far & wide*" 21 May 1825, Box 14, Folder 84.

*He had become so notorious* 29 April 1824, Box 13, Folder 83.

*Mrs. Joanna Home . . . street* 16 April 1828, Box 14, Folder 85.

"*I owe . . . No one!*" 1 Nov. 1824, Box 13, Folder 83.

"*it strikes me . . . future peace of mind!*" 10 Sept. 1825, Box 14, Folder 84.

## Chapter 12. Compare What I *Might* Have Been with What I *Am*

180   "*One thing . . . take place*" 16 Feb. 1824, Box 13, Folder 83.

"*the closing scene . . . circumstances!*" 28 July 1826, Box 14, Folder 84.

"*Shocked . . . I am reduced!!*" 5 Aug. 1826, Box 14, Folder 84; for crises of masculinity associated with financial failure, see Ditz.

"*Sir . . . can I do?*" James Kemp?, 4 July 1829, Invoices and Receipts, Box 5, Folder 35.

181   "*he felt . . . people of Edinburgh*" 5 May 1827, Box 14, Folder 85. Lesassier was finally able to negotiate an agreement through his solicitor, 29 June 1827.

"*I am . . . poverty as this!*" 18 Aug. 1826, Box 14, Folder 84.

"*My father . . . rapid fortunes*" 26 Sept. 1826, Box 14, Folder 84.

*Isabella Hodgeson* 16 Nov. 1823, Box 13, Folder 83.

"*Poor old lady . . . family*" 7 Sept. 1826, 14 Nov. 1826, Box 14, Folder 84.

*he was not invited* 14–15 Nov. 1826, Box 14, Folder 84.

*The death of his hated grandmother* 11–17 June 1827, Box 14, Folder 85.

182   "*how shall I . . . event*" 11 June 1827, Box 14, Folder 85.

"*Nothing . . . Edinburgh can bestow!*" 5 Nov. 1826, Box 14, Folder 84.

"*abruptly . . . eternal annihilation*" 21 Dec. 1824, Box 13, Folder 83.

*pension would be forfeited* 16 June 1826, Box 14, Folder 84.

"*to examine . . . part*" 21 Dec. 1824, Box 13, Folder 83.

"*The fact is . . . Secretary at Wars*" 15 July 1826, Box 14, Folder 84.

"*Most likely . . . disease*" 21 Dec. 1824, Box 13, Folder 83.

"*Still fearing . . . feeling*" 16 July 1826, Box 14, Folder 84.

183   "*under such glaring . . . insignificance*" 3 Dec. 1825, Box 14, Folder 84.

*William Fergusson* 19 Sept. 1827, Box 14, Folder 85.

*"who is clearing . . . very much"* 23 Dec. 1824, Box 13, Folder 83.

*"is not a polished . . . gain £100 a year"* 3 Dec. 1825, Box 14, Folder 84.

*"to a factory . . . £100 a year"* 4 May 1825, Box 14, Folder 84.

*"Now that I . . . forgotten"* 28 June 1825, Box 14, Folder 84. Notes for the midwifery lectures make up over four thousand pages and fill Boxes 16–23, Folders 92–131.

184   *"too palpable a plagiarism"* Lecture 8, Box 19, Folder 109. Lesassier was referring only to the section on the different types of labor, but in fact most of his lectures follow his notes of James Hamilton's lectures word for word, with some additions from his reading and own cases.

*"old and tried friend Ella"* 1 Nov. 1826, Box 14, Folder 84.

*"At last . . . suspense"* Ella Anderton to AH, Manchester, 5 July 1826, Box 1, Folder 2.

*"We have . . . business"* Ella Anderton to AH, Manchester, Dec. 1826, Box 1, Folder 2.

*"And I am . . . twenty years"* 1 Nov. 1826, Box 14, Folder 84.

*"an odious climate . . . illiberal place"* 4 May 1825, Box 14, Folder 84.

*"must begin . . . lodgings"* 6 June 1825, Box 14, Folder 84.

*"the circle . . . dread"* 4 May 1825, Box 14, Folder 84.

*"in consequence . . . in the place"* 29 Aug. 1825, Box 14, Folder 84.

*"again degenerate . . . intoxication"* 1 Nov. 1826, Box 14, Folder 84.

*"high words . . . thither again"* 3 Nov. 1826, Box 14, Folder 84.

*"that if I went . . . thoughts of Manchester"* 16 Nov. 1826, Box 14, Folder 84.

*"the moral certainty . . . away to Liverpool"* 17 Oct. 1826, Box 14, Folder 84.

185   *"professing . . . leave Edinburgh"* 24 Aug. 1826, Box 14, Folder 84.

*"Force nothing, . . . judicious head"* 28 Aug. 1827, Box 14, Folder 85.

*"grasped any floating straw"* 12 July 1826, Box 14, Folder 84.

*"poor credulous fool"* 8 April 1825, Box 14, Folder 84.

*"From all this . . . next spring"* See the list of psalms inserted into journal, also 17 April 1825, Box 14, Folder 84.

*He kept track* The classic statement of the issues involved in modern analysis of pre-Freudian dreams is Dodds, especially chapter 4, "Dream-Pattern and Culture-Pattern," pp. 102–134. The belief in dreams foretelling the future was common enough among well-to-do Scots for Ferrier to poke fun at it in *Marriage.*

*Dreams of his hanging* 5, 9 Oct. 1825, Box 14, Folder 84.

*dreams of a funeral* 9, 11 Oct. 1825, Box 14, Folder 84.

*"that the little Doctor . . . street"* 4 Jan. 1825, Box 14, Folder 84.

*"The fact is . . . despairing of it"* 6 Jan. 1825, Box 14, Folder 84.

*"As to . . . contempt they deserve"* 10 April 1825, Box 14, Folder 84.

186   *"Quand tu . . . abstiens-toi"* Inside front cover, Autobiographical Reminiscences 1827, Box 14, Folder 85.

*it is divine providence* Devlin, pp. 6–57, makes the point repeatedly that peasants' attitudes toward God, Christ, and saints was not orthodox piety, but rather stemmed from self-interest, with prayers directed toward helping them and hurting their enemies. Lesassier's attitudes were very similar.

*"Catherine's mother . . . poor me!!"* 10 Nov. 1825, Box 14, Folder 84.

*"& surely . . . hold out"* 1 Feb. 1826, Box 14, Folder 84.

*He sold his carriage* 25 May 1825, Box 14, Folder 84.

*"for alas! . . . creditor!!"* 1 March 1826, Box 14, Folder 84; 13 April 1827, Box 14, Folder 85.

*The new trustees* 20 Aug. 1826, Box 14, Folder 84; 6 Nov. 1827, Box 14, Folder 85.

*depositing his jewels* 31 Jan. 1826, 4 Feb. 1826, Box 14, Folder 84.

*"to prevent me . . . lying beside me"* 16 Nov. 1827, Box 14, Folder 85.

*He deposited his plate* 8 Sept. 1826, Box 14, Folder 84.

*"having engaged . . . disgraceful extremity"* 21 May 1827, Box 14, Folder 85.

*These financial makeshifts* See Hufton, chs. 3 and 4, "An Economy of Makeshifts"; Fissell.

*"many families of consequence here"* 29 Aug. 1828, Box 14, Folder 85. For a literary example of this, see Márquez, p. 154.

187   *"were all blanks! . . . money!"* 3 June 1825, Box 14, Folder 84.

*she offered him a loan* 5–11 June 1826, Box 14, Folder 84.

*"one of the most . . . quarter"* 5 Jan. 1826, Box 14, Folder 84.

*"had a design on her purse"* 17 Sept. 1827, Box 14, Folder 85.

*£700 loan on her house* 31 Jan. 1827, Box 14, Folder 85; "Note of Expense of Bond and Disposition in Security by Miss Campbell to Mr. John Cassie," 25 Jan. 1827, Invoices and Receipts, Box 5, Folder 38.

*£400 loan* 15–22 June 1829, Box 14, Folder 86.

*"Besides plate . . . taken ill"* 26 Feb. 1826, Box 14, Folder 84.

*"secure . . . fortune"* 22 July 1826, Box 14, Folder 84.

*"that Mary . . . connection with me!"* 9 Oct. 1826, Box 14, Folder 84.

*"no attempt . . . affection"* 23 Nov. 1826, Box 14, Folder 84.

*legacy of £50* 15 Nov. 1827, Box 14, Folder 85.

*Lady Portsmouth* 23, 25 Jan. 1826, Box 14, Folder 84. See Chapter 11.

*"by apparent neglect"* 25 Jan. 1826, Box 14, Folder 84; 2 March 1827, Box 14, Folder 85.

*"every motive . . . please her"* 2 March 1827, 30 April 1827, Box 14, Folder 85; 31 May 1829, Box 14, Folder 86.

*"whatever she should be able to spare"* 9 Dec. 1828, Box 14, Folder 85.

188   *"her natural pusillanimity"* 2 Oct., 13, 22 Nov. 1826, Box 14, Folder 84.

*"When I . . . future"* 29 Nov. 1826, Box 14, Folder 84.

*"what could . . . old maid!"* July 1827, Box 14, Folder 85.

*"Yet . . . making of me"* 7 Jan. 1830, Box 15, Folder 88.

*"once more . . . transitory life"* 1 July 1829, Box 14, Folder 86.

*"after . . . years of cold neglect"* 16 Feb, 2, 8 Nov. 1825, Box 14, Folder 84.

*"within the space . . . £400 a year"* 27 Sept. 1827, Box 14, Folder 85.

*New acquaintances* 6 Nov. 1825, Box 14, Folder 84.

*"absurdly . . . Lady Kintore"* 17 April 1827, Box 14, Folder 85; 11 Aug. 1829, Box 15, Folder 87.

*"A physician . . . character"* 19 April 1827, Box 14, Folder 85.

*"After all . . . road to eminence"* 17 March 1827, Box 14, Folder 85.

*"it would sink . . . this house"* 6 Sept. 1827, Box 14, Folder 85.

*"splendid mansion"* 22 Nov. 1827, Box 14, Folder 85.

*six vases for evergreens* 27 Jan. 1828, Agenda 1828, Box 14, Folder 85.

*"to metamorphose . . . brass-grate"* 17, 24 Sept. 1827, Box 14, Folder 85.

189   *French chairs* 9 July 1828, Box 14, Folder 85.

*"a superb set . . . guineas"* 28 April, 17 May 1828, Box 14, Folder 85.

*"perhaps 25 shillings . . . play upon"* 19, 22, 23 May 1828, Box 14, Folder 85.

*"a beautiful large set . . . ivory ones"* 2 Oct. 1830, Box 16, Folder 90.

*"I doubt . . . met with"* 22 May 1828, Box 14, Folder 85.

*"a new silk cloak . . . squirrel"* 8 Nov. 1827, Box 14, Folder 85.

*"never before . . . general notice"* 23 Nov. 1827, 25 Aug. 1828, Box 14, Folder 85.

*"to shew . . . contemptuously moving"* 22 Nov. 1827, Box 14, Folder 85.

*Monsieur de Rochepaliere* 5 May 1828, Box 14, Folder 85. Despite numerous efforts, Lesassier was unable to find any evidence for Pierre's claims, though this did not prevent him from believing them. There is no external evidence—nothing outside of Lesassier's journals—for any of them.

*"exceedingly . . . actual title"* 4 July 1827, Box 14, Folder 85.

*Marquis de Lafayette* 1828–30, Box 2, Folder 12.

*"notwithstanding . . . I am descended"* 4 July 1827, Box 14, Folder 85.

*"I should certainly . . . their heads"* 16 Nov, also 10, 12 Nov. 1829, Box 15, Folder 87.

*"satisfy . . . friends here"* 4 July 1827, Box 14, Folder 85.

*"to remind our guests of my title"* 27 May 1830, Box 15, Folder 88.

*"it has produced . . . deference & respect"* 10, 13 April 1830, Box 15, Folder 88.

*"peace at home . . . married state"* 11 May 1828, Box 14, Folder 85; 19 July 1829, Box 14, Folder 86.

*"dejected . . . during my quarrels with Catherine"* 11 Dec. 1829, Box 15, Folder 87.

190   *"usual stroll"* 31 Jan. 1828, Box 14, Folder 85.

"*idle, but laughing & enjoying our remarks*" 21 Dec. 1830, Box 16, Folder 90.

"*reading and conversing*" 21 Oct. 1827, Box 14, Folder 85.

"*some hot negus together*" 8 May 1828, Box 14, Folder 85.

*tarts and cookies* 18 Sept. 1827, Box 14, Folder 85; 14 Jan. 1829, Box 14, Folder 86.

"*aggravated . . . forgive myself*" 12 Jan. 1824, Box 13, Folder 83.

"*Oh! what man . . . existence!*" 17 March 1829, Box 14, Folder 86.

*Catherine . . . wanting to read in bed* 2 March 1830, Box 15, Folder 88.

"*I do not know . . . ought to do*" 19 Aug. 1826, Box 14, Folder 84.

"*this low . . . disgrace of mine*" 17 Nov. 1830, Box 16, Folder 90.

"*as to ever writing to any lady again!!*" 15 Dec. 1823, Box 13, Folder 83.

*Mrs. Ramsay* 24–30 March 1828, Box 14, Folder 85.

*Mrs. Scott* 7 July 1828, Box 14, Folder 85.

*Catharine Hill* 11 June through 28 Nov. 1828, Box 14, Folder 85.

*Euphemia Maugham* 20 Oct. 1828, 10 Nov. 1828, Box 14, Folder 85.

*Margaret Wallace* 2–16 Oct. 1828, Box 14, Folder 85.

*Catherine Johnson* 1–10 Aug. 1830, Box 16, Folder 90.

*Isabella Ross* 15–30 Sept. 1830, Box 16, Folder 90.

*ugly, but with my eyes* 9 Sept. 1829, Box 15, Folder 87.

*May and Mary* 17 Nov. 1827, Box 14, Folder 85.

*Margaret* 6–7 May 1829, Box 14, Folder 86.

191    "*Self-reproach . . . disagreeable one*" 29 Sept. 1828, Box 14, Folder 85.

*Acquiring women* If it is true that Victorian masculinity required men to redirect their sexual energy into their professions, Lesassier reminds us how radical an effort that could be. See Roper and Tosh; Mangan and Walvin.

"*This is my birth-day . . . myself*" 12 Sept. 1827, Box 14, Folder 85.

"*incomparably . . . thick hair*" 1 Jan. 1828, Box 14, Folder 85.

"*a triumph . . . over age*" 3 Sept. 1828, Box 14, Folder 85.

"*shrinking trembling . . . unsuspecting affection*" 8 Sept. 1829, Box 15, Folder 87.

"*libidinous, gray-haired, old, goat*" 13 May 1830, Box 15, Folder 88.

*is it astonishing . . . child?* 14 Sept. 1829, Box 15, Folder 87.

"*excessively depressed*" 15 Sept. 1828, Box 14, Folder 85.

"*embrace*" 8 Oct. 1828, Box 14, Folder 85.

"*At times . . . my life*" 11 Oct. 1828, Box 14, Folder 85.

*Who could imagine . . .* 7, 16 Oct. 1828, Box 14, Folder 85.

*It was foolish* 16 Oct. 1828, Box 14, Folder 85.

192    "*so languid . . . folly, & error!*" 7 March 1825, Box 14, Folder 84.

"*the very individuals*" 20 Feb. 1826, Box 14, Folder 84.

"*ignorant upstart . . . Dr Beilby*" 7 March 1826, Box 14, Folder 84.

"*who had not . . . what I am*" 20 Feb. 1826, Box 14, Folder 84.

*he gathered together* I have been unable to determine precisely when the cases were collected in their present form. Though most appear to have been written between 1819 and 1822, the last one is dated 26 March 1825. It seems reasonable to assume that he began writing them as a record of his unusual cases in 1819, set them aside during the eventful period 1823–1824, then edited and added to them in 1825, when preparing his own set of lectures. Several have headings indicating where they might fit in a course, such as "Laborious labor Order 2d. Deficiency of space. Application of the short forceps." 12 Feb. 1822, Select Cases in Midwifery from my own practice, 1819–1825, Box 23, Folder 131.

*Elephant Man* Treves, *The Elephant Man and Other Reminiscences*, pp. 1–37; Howell and Ford; Pomerance. The varying presentations of the case, starting with Treves's, are analyzed in Graham and Oehlschlaeger.

*Silas Weir Mitchell* Mitchell; Sacks, *The Man Who Mistook His Wife for a Hat*.

*the case history* On case histories, see Lawrence, *Charitable Knowledge*, pp. 215–249.

193    *Susan Ferrier's Dr. Redgill* Dr. Redgill was portrayed as "vulgar, selfish, and *gourmand*," a man "who, for the sake of good living" installed himself in the household of his aristocratic patron. Ferrier, *Marriage*, p. 234.

"*without stirring . . . refreshment*" 11 May, Select Cases in Midwifery from my own practice, 1819–1825, Box 23, Folder 131.

*only once in the histories* The remarkable series of case histories described in Catherine Schrader's memoirs has much in common with Lesassier's. Though Schrader was well aware of her abilities, however, she is not so much the hero of the story as the Lord's able assistant.

"*could learn . . . patient*" Oct. 1819, Select Cases in Midwifery from my own practice, 1819–1825, Box 23, Folder 131.

"*a vague account . . . labor*" 11 May, Select Cases in Midwifery from my own practice, 1819–1825, Box 23, Folder 131.

"*near abandoning . . . resources*" 21 July 1820, Select Cases in Midwifery from my own practice, 1819–1825, Box 23, Folder 131.

"*On Friday . . . doing well*" 20 Aug, Select Cases in Midwifery from my own practice, 1819–1825, Box 23, Folder 131.

194   "*case of turning . . . impatient*" 21 July 1821, Select Cases in Midwifery from my own practice, 1819–1825, Box 23, Folder 131.

195   "*sent for to a poor woman*" 16 March 1828, Box 14, Folder 85.

"*happily snatched . . . trouble*" 17 March 1828, Box 14, Folder 85.

*his father died* 24 Jan. 1829, Box 14, Folder 86.

*He made wrong diagnoses* 11 Jan. 1827, Box 14, Folder 85.

*appeared . . . while tipsy* 8 Aug. 1827, Box 14, Folder 85.

*stole books* 1 Sept. 1828, Box 14, Folder 85.

"*pecuniary embarrassments . . . wretchedness*" 19 Aug. 1826, Box 14, Folder 84.

"*How could I . . . countrymen*" 26? Jan. 1829, Box 14, Folder 86.

"*nothing whatever . . . money*" 1 Feb. 1829, Box 14, Folder 86.

"*correct & consistent conduct*" 23 Feb. 1830, Box 15, Folder 88.

*His financial agent* 23–9 July 1827, Box 14, Folder 85.

"*Never did I hear . . . with the evil one*" 28 July 1827, Box 14, Folder 85.

"*darling house*" 1 Oct. 1827, Box 14, Folder 85.

196   "*Thus I lose . . . £12 a year!*" 1 July 1830, Box 16, Folder 90.

"*gliding away . . . hour-glass!*" 16 May 1830, Box 15, Folder 88.

*newly built suburbs* 31 May 1830, Box 15, Folder 88.

"*provoking assurance*" 15 June 1830, Box 15, Folder 88.

"*large, frosted, vase-shaped glass-globe[s]*" 10–16 April 1829, Box 14, Folder 86.

"*41–3/4 hours*" 14 July 1830, Box 16, Folder 90.

"*at his dinner-table . . . frock coats*" 16 Aug. 1830, Box 16, Folder 90.

"*stroll to High Street . . . expecting William IV*" 29 June 1830, Box 15, Folder 88.

"*What a professional finale!*" 5 Oct., 23 Dec. 1830, Box 16, Folder 90.

"*Insane proposal! . . . asylum*" 17 Aug. 1830, Box 16, Folder 90.

"*for which, I have any true respect*" 28 Aug. 1828, Box 14, Folder 85.

"*Oh! that I may be called on full pay*" 21 July 1830, Box 16, Folder 90.

"*Thinks I . . . proper turn*" 22 Nov. 1830, Box 16, Folder 90.

"*I am standing . . . commutation*" 2–11 Sept. 1830, Somnia [Dream notebook], Box 16, Folder 91.

197   *57 Northumberland Street* Gray's Edinburgh Directory, 1832–1851.

"*All the books . . . trunk-cover*" Loose note, 24 March 1831, Box 15, Folder 89. Presumably Lesassier took the 1831 journal with him when he left.

Epilogue. One Series of Hardships and Privations

198   *resided there* Divorce proceedings between Catherine Jane Crokatt and Alexander Hamilton, Scottish Record Office CS46/76/1836.

*Catherine had decided to learn guitar* 13, 20, 21 Sept. 1830, Box 16, Folder 90.

"*great object . . . first opportunity*" 17 Aug. 1826, Box 14, Folder 84.

"*patience . . . let her beware!*" 22 July 1826, Box 14, Folder 84.

"*gave himself up . . . native female*" Divorce proceedings between Catherine Jane Crokatt and Alexander Hamilton, Scottish Record Office CS46/76/1836.

*"faithful Christian girl Ignatia"* Alexander Hamilton, 31 May 1842, Wills and Inventories, Scottish Record Office SC70/1/62 pp. 315–319.

*whom he kept . . . "against him"* Divorce proceedings between Catherine Jane Crokatt and Alexander Hamilton, Scottish Record Office CS46/76/1836.

*"solemnly pledged"* Decreet of Aliment, Catherine Jane Crokatt against Alexander Hamilton, 8 July 1836, Scottish Record Office CS45/46/August 1836.

*Gibson spoke* Divorce proceedings between Catherine Jane Crokatt and Alexander Hamilton, Scottish Record Office CS46/76/1836. Sarah Hazlitt's journal provides a detailed description of the divorce process as well as a charming account of her travels.

199   *one more suit* Decreet of Aliment, Catherine Jane Crokatt against Alexander Hamilton, 8 July 1836, Scottish Record Office CS45/46/August 1836.

*Anna Maria Ignatia Hamilton* Alexander Hamilton, 31 May 1842, Wills and Inventories, Scottish Record Office SC70/1/62 pp 315–319.

*an inglorious war* See Kaye; Norris; Waller.

*claimant's own desire* Kaye, 1:415.

*"rest in a noble orchard . . . surpassing description"* Kennedy, 1:226–227.

200   *"instead of the fancied party . . . cattle to feed on"* Letter printed in *United Service Journal* (Nov. 1839): 420–421; see Kaye, 1:420–436.

*"the effect . . . perfect control"* 29 Jan. 1824, Box 13, Folder 83.

*"again day after day . . . stones"* Kaye, 1:422.

*"as men looked . . . they had become"* Kaye, 1:424.

*"heartily sick . . . expedition"* Letter printed in *United Service Journal* (Nov. 1839): 420–421.

*"the way . . . plunderers around them"* Kaye, 1:422.

*Surgeon Smith* Kennedy 2:50–51.

*trying to secure a legacy* 1 Aug. 1829, Box 14, Folder 86.

201   *"Oh! . . . done by me!"* 3 July 1829, Box 14, Folder 86.

*would have rescued* 7 Jan. 1830, Box 15, Folder 88.

*his estate . . . £700* Alexander Hamilton, 31 May 1842, Wills and Inventories, Scottish Record Office SC70/1/62 pp 315–319.

*sale of the magnificent house* Either would suppose that Catherine's money remained invested in the house, only one of many options. Scottish Record Office R527/2646FF 75R-77

*"alleged of him . . . bed room"* 12 Aug. 1829, Box 15, Folder 87.

*small medical school* Mackintosh, *Prize Examinations*.

*Edward Milligan* 19 Dec. 1829, Box 15, Folder 87.

*John Thatcher* 16 May 1829, Box 14, Folder 86.

*"Dr. Hamilton . . . have done"* MSS 1806, James Young Simpson Papers, Royal College of Surgeons.

*earliest uses of chloroform* Edinburgh Royal Maternity Hospital, #1, Indoor case-book, Edin 1844–71, James Young Simpson Papers, Royal College of Physicians. The case was Elizabeth Mackay, 22 Nov. 1847, delivered by J. Y. Simpson.

# BIBLIOGRAPHY

Manuscript Collections

Bard Papers. New York Academy of Medicine Library, New York.
Hamilton, Alexander Lesassier. Royal College of Physicians, Edinburgh.
Hewson Papers. American Philosophical Society Library, Philadelphia.
Longman Papers. University of Reading Library, Reading.
McGrigor, Sir James. Aberdeen Medico-Chirurgical Society, Foresterhill Centre, Aberdeen.
Minute Books. Royal College of Surgeons, Edinburgh.
Simpson, James Young. Royal College of Physicians, Edinburgh.
Simpson, James Young. Royal College of Surgeons, Edinburgh.
Additional manuscripts in the Scottish Record Office, Edinburgh, are cited in the notes.

Selected Printed Sources

Alcock, Thomas. "An Essay on the Education and Duties of the General Practitioner in Medicine and Surgery." *Transaction of the Association of Apothecaries and Surgeon-Apothecaries* 1 (1823): 1–95.
Altick, Richard. *The English Common Reader: A Social History of the Mass Reading Public, 1800–1900.* Chicago: University of Chicago Press, 1957.
Armstrong, Nancy. *Desire and Domestic Fiction: A Political History of the Novel.* New York: Oxford University Press, 1987.
Austen, Jane. *Jane Austen's Letters to Her Sister Cassandra and Others.* Ed. R. W. Chapman. Oxford: Clarendon Press, 1932.
——. "Love and Friendship," in *Minor Works.* London: Oxford University Press, 1969.
——. *Mansfield Park.* London: Oxford University Press, 1966.
——. *Northanger Abbey.* London: J. M. Dent, 1922.
——. *Pride and Prejudice.* London: Oxford University Press, 1970.
Baggerman, Arianne. "The Cultural Universe of a Dutch Child: Otto van Eck and His Literature." *Eighteenth Century Studies* 31.1 (1997): 129–134.
Barbier, Carl Paul. *William Gilpin: His Drawings, Teaching, and Theory of the Picturesque.* Oxford: Clarendon Press, 1963.
Barker-Benfield, G. J. *The Culture of Sensibility: Sex and Society in Eighteenth-Century Britain.* Chicago: University of Chicago Press, 1992.
Barrell, John, ed. *Painting and the Politics of Culture: New Essays on British Art, 1700–1850.* New York: Oxford University Press, 1992.
Baxandall, Michael. *Patterns of Intention: On the Historical Explanation of Pictures.* New Haven: Yale University Press, 1989.
Bell, Whitfield. "Philadelphia Medical Students in Europe, 1750–1800." *Pennsylvania Magazine of History and Biography* 67 (1943):1–22.
Bernbaum, Ernest. *The Drama of Sensibility: A Sketch of the History of English Sentimental Comedy and Domestic Tragedy, 1696–1780.* Boston: Ginn and Company, 1915.
Blakiston, John. *Twelve Years' Military Adventures in Three Quarters of the Globe.* 2 vols. London: H. Colburn, 1840.
Blanco, Richard L. *Wellington's Surgeon-General: Sir James McGrigor.* Durham, N.C.: Duke University Press, 1974.
Blaxland, Gregory. *The Middlesex Regiment (Duke of Cambridge's Own) (The 57th and 77th of Foot).* London: Leo Cooper, 1977.

Boswell, James. *Boswell's Column: Being His Seventy Contributions to the London Magazine under the pseudonym The Hypochondriack*. Ed. Margery Bailey. London: William Kimber, 1951.

Bourdieu, Pierre, and Passeron, Jean-Claude. *Reproduction in Education, Society and Culture*. London: Sage, 1977.

Boutflower, Charles. *The Journal of an Army Surgeon during the Peninsular War*. Manchester: Refuge Printing Department, 1912.

Brereton, J. M. *A History of the Royal Regiment of Wales (24th/41st Foot) and Its Predecessors, 1689–1939*. Cardiff: Published by the Regiment, 1989.

Brockbank, E. M. A. *A Centenary History of the Manchester Medical Society with Biographical Notices of its First President, Secretaries and Honorary Librarian*. Manchester: Sherratt and Hughes, 1934.

Bronson, Bertrand Harris. *The Traditional Tunes of the Child Ballads*. 4 vols. Princeton: Princeton University Press, 1972.

Brown, Joseph. *A Defence of Revealed Religion, Comprising a Vindication of the Miracles of the Old and New Testaments from the Attacks of Rationalists and Infidels*. London, 1851.

———. *Memories of the Past, and Thoughts on the Present, Age*. London: Longman, Green, Longman, Roberts, & Green, 1863.

Brown, William. "Mr. Brown on Surgical Apprenticeships." *Edinburgh Medical and Surgical Journal* 26 (1826): 83.

Brownstein, Rachel. *Becoming a Heroine: Reading About Women in Novels*. New York: Penguin, 1984.

Bruce, Anthony. *The Purchase System in the British Army, 1660–1871*. London: Royal Historical Society, 1980.

Bruce, A. P. C. *An Annotated Bibliography of the British Army, 1660–1914*. New York: Garland, 1975.

*Bulletins of the Campaign*. London, 1793–1815.

Bunbury, Thomas. *Reminiscences of a Veteran*. 3 vols. London: Charles J. Skeete, 1861.

Butler, Marilyn. *Romantics, Rebels and Reactionaries: English Literature and Its Background, 1760–1830*. New York: Oxford University Press, 1982.

———. "Satire and Images of the Self in the Romantic Period: The Long Tradition of Hazlitt's *Liber Amoris*." In G. A Rosso and Daniel P. Watkins, eds., *Spirits of Fire. English Romantic Writers and Contemporary Historical Methods*, 153–169. Rutherford, Madison, Teaneck, N.J.: Fairleigh Dickinson Press, 1990.

Cannon, Richard. *Historical Record of the Forty-Second; or, The Royal Highland Regiment of Foot*. London: Parker, Furnival, and Parker, 1845.

Cantlie, Neil. *A History of the Army Medical Department*. 2 vols. London: Churchill Livingstone, 1974.

Caracciolo, Peter L., ed. *The Arabian Nights in English Literature*. New York: St. Martin's Press, 1988.

Carlyle, Thomas. *The Collected Letters of Thomas and Jane Welsh Carlyle*. Ed. Charles Richard Sanders, Kenneth J. Fielding, and Clyde de L. Ryals. Durham, N.C.: Duke University Press, 1970–1995.

Chamberlaine, William. *Tirocinium Medicum; or, A Dissertation on the Duties of Youth Apprenticed to the Medical Profession*. London: Sherwood, Neely & Jones, 1812.

Chambers, Charles. "The Bombardment of Copenhagen, 1807—Journal of Surgeon Charles Chambers of H. M. Fireship Prometheus." In W. G. Perrin, ed., *The Naval Miscellany*, 3:367–466. London: Navy Records Society, 1928.

Chatterton, Thomas. *The Complete Works of Thomas Chatterton: A Bicentenary Edition*. 2 vols. Oxford: Clarendon Press, 1971.

Chesterfield, Lord. *Letters to his Son Philip Stanhope*. 2 vols. London, 1774.

*Colleccão das ordens do dia*. Lisbon: Antonio Nuñes dos Santos, 1809-[1823].

Colley, Linda. *Britons: Forging the Nation, 1707–1857*. New Haven: Yale University Press, 1992.

*Compilação das ordens do dia, do quartel general do exercito portuguez, 1810–1815*. 6 vols. Lisbon, 1815.

Cope, Zachary. *The Royal College of Surgeons: A History*. London: Anthony Blond, 1959.

Costello, Edward. *Edward Costello. The Peninsular and Waterloo Campaigns*. London: Longmans, Green, 1967.

Cullen, Peter. "Peter Cullen's Journal." In H.G. Thursfield, ed., *Five Naval Journals, 1789–1817*, 41–119 London: Navy Records Society, 1951.

[Cumberland, Richard]. *Henry*. 4 vols. London, 1795.

Davidoff, Leonore, and Catherine Hall. *Family Fortunes: Men and Women of the English Middle Class, 1750–1850*. Chicago: University of Chicago Press, 1987.

Davidson, Cathy. *Revolution and the Word: The Rise of the Novel in America*. New York: Oxford University Press, 1986.

Davidson, Cathy, ed. *Reading in America: Literature and Social History*. Baltimore: Johns Hopkins University Press, 1989.

*Death's a Friend*. London, 1788.

Decius. Letter to the *Royal Military Chronicle or British Officer's Monthly Register and Mentor* 5 (1811): 369.

Devlin, Judith. *The Superstitious Mind: French Peasants and the Supernatural in the Nineteenth Century*. New Haven: Yale University Press, 1987.

Dierks, Konstantin. "Letter Writing, Masculinity, and American Men of Science, 1750–1800." *Pennsylvania History* 65 (1998): 165–196.

Digby, Anne. *Making a Medical Living*. Cambridge: Cambridge University Press, 1994.

Ditz, Toby L. "Shipwrecked; or, Masculinity Imperiled: Mercantile Representations of Failure and the Gendered Self in Eighteenth-Century Philadelphia." *Journal of American History* 81 (1994): 51–80.

Dodds, E. R. *The Greeks and the Irrational*. Berkeley: University of California Press, 1956.

Dowling, Colette. *The Cinderella Complex: Women's Hidden Fear of Independence*. New York: HarperCollins, 1994.

Drinkwater, John. *A History of the Siege of Gibraltar, 1779–1783*. London: John Murray, 1844.

Dugaw, Dianne. *Warrior Women and Popular Balladry, 1650–1850*. Cambridge: Cambridge University Press, 1989.

Duncan, Andrew. "The English Apothecaries' Act." *Edinburgh Medical and Surgical Journal* 25 (1826): 414.

Edgeworth, Richard Lovell. *Essays on Professional Education*. London: J. Johnson, 1812.

Edwards, Owen Dudley. *Burke & Hare*. Edinburgh: Mercat Press, 1993.

Eliot, George. *Middlemarch*. New York: Penguin Books, 1985)

Elwood, Willis, and A. Félicité Tuxford. *Some Manchester Doctors: A Biographical Collection to Mark the 150th Anniversary of the Manchester Medical Society, 1834–1984*. Manchester: Manchester University Press, 1984.

*Encyclopedia Britannica*. 3 vols. Edinburgh: A. Bell and C. MacFarquhar, 1771; reprint edition, n.d.

Erly, John. *Dissertatio Inauguralis de Respiratione*. Edinburgh, 1818.

*Evidence, Oral and Documentary: Taken and received by the commissioners appointed by His Majesty George IV, July 23rd, 1826; and reappointed by his Majesty William IV, October 12, 1830, for visiting the Universities of Scotland*. 4 vols. London: H. M. Stationery Office, 1837.

Ferguson, Adam. *The Correspondence of Adam Ferguson*. 2 vols. London: William Pickering, 1995, 1:64.

Fergusson, William. *Notes and Recollections of a Professional Life*. Ed. James Fergusson. London: Longman, 1846.

Ferrier, Susan. *Inheritance*. London: Eveleigh Nash & Grayson, 1929.

——. *Marriage*. New York: Oxford University Press, 1986.

——. *Memoir and Correspondence of Susan Ferrier 1782–1854*. Ed. John A. Doyle. New York: AMS Press, Inc., 1970.

Fielding, Henry. *Tom Jones*. New York: Modern Library, 1950.

*The Fine Gentleman's Etiquette; or, Lord Chesterfield's Advice to His Son, Versified. By a Lady*. London: T. Davies, 1776.

Fissell, Mary. *Patients, Power, and the Poor in Eighteenth-Century Bristol*. New York: Cambridge University Press, 1991.

Fletcher, Anthony. *Gender, Sex and Subordination in England, 1500–1800*. New Haven: Yale University Press, 1995.

Forster, Robert, and Orest Ranum, eds. *Medicine and Society in France: Selections from the Annales ESC*. Baltimore: Johns Hopkins University Press, 1980.

Foucault, Michel. *The Birth of the Clinic: An Archeology of Medical Perception*. Trans. A. M. Sheridan Smith. New York: Pantheon Books, 1975.

Friedson, Eliot. *Profession of Medicine: A Study of the Sociology of Applied Knowledge*. New York: Harper & Row, 1970.

Fussell, Paul, ed. *The Norton Book of Travel*. New York: W. W. Norton, 1987.

Garnett, Thomas. *Observations on a Tour through the Highlands and Part of the Western Isles of Scotland*. 2 vols. London: 1800.

Gates, David. *The Spanish Ulcer: A History of the Peninsular War*. New York: W. W. Norton, 1986.

Giao, Manoel R. F. "British Surgeons in the Portuguese Army during the Peninsular War." *Journal of the Royal Army Medical Corps* 61 (1934): 298–303.

Gilpin, William. *Observations on the Highlands of Scotland*. Richmond, England: Richmond Publishing, 1973.

——. *Observations on the Mountains and Lakes of Cumberland and Westmorland*. Richmond, England: Richmond Publishing, 1973.

——. *Three Essays: On Picturesque Beauty; on Picturesque Travel; and on Sketching Landscape*. London: R. Blamire, 1794.

Gleig, George Robert. *Chelsea Pensioners*. London: H. Colburn, 1829.

Glover, Michael. *The Peninsular War, 1807–1814: A Concise Military History*. Newton Abbot, England: David & Charles, 1974.

Goldsmith, Oliver. *The Vicar of Wakefield and Other Writings*. Ed. Frank W. Hilles. New York: Modern Library, 1955.

Graham, Peter W., and Fritz H. Oehlschlaeger. *Articulating the Elephant Man*. Baltimore: Johns Hopkins University Press, 1992.

Grant, Anne. *Memoir and Correspondence of Mrs. Grant of Laggan*. 3 vols. London: Longman, Brown, Green, and Longmans, 1845.

*Gray's Edinburgh Directory*. 1832–1851.

Great Britain. *General Orders, 1809–1813*. 5 vols. London: 1811–1814.

Gunn, James. "The Memoirs of Private James Gunn." *Journal of the Society for Army Historical Research* 69 (Summer 1971): 90–120.

Guthrie, George James. *Commentaries on the Surgery of the War in Portugal, Spain, France, and the Netherlands*. London: Henry Renshaw, 1853.

——. *Treatise on Gun-Shot Wounds*. London: Burgess and Hill, 1827.

Halliday, Andrew. *Observations on the Present State of the Portuguese Army*. London: John Murray, 1811.

[Hamilton, Alexander Lesassier]. *Edward Neville; or, The Memoirs of an Orphan*. 4 vols. London: Longman, Hurst, Rees, Orme, and Brown, 1823.

Hamlyn, Hilda M. "Eighteenth-Century Circulating Libraries in England." *The Library*, 5th ser., 1 (1947): 197–222.

Hanawalt, Barbara. *Growing Up in Medieval London: The Experience of Childhood in History*. New York: Oxford University Press, 1993.

Hans, Nicholas. *New Trends in Education in the Eighteenth Century*. London, 1951.

Haydon, Benjamin Robert. *The Diary of Benjamin Robert Haydon*. Ed. Willard Bissell Pope. 5 vols. Cambridge, Mass.: Harvard University Press, 1960–1963.

Hazlitt, Sarah, and William Hazlitt. *The Journals of Sarah and William Hazlitt, 1822–1831*. Ed. Willard Hallam Bonner. *University of Buffalo Studies* 24.3 (1959).

Hazlitt, William. *The Complete Works of William Hazlitt in Twenty-One Volumes*. Ed. P. P. Howe. London: J. M. Dent, 1931.

Henderson, Bill. *Rotten Reviews: A Literary Companion*. New York: Pushcart Press, 1986.

Hennen, John. *Principles of Military Surgery*. London: John Wilson, 1829.

Henry, Walter. *Surgeon Henry's Trifles. Events of a Military Life*, ed. P. Hayward. London: Chatto and Windus, 1970.

Hodge, Jane Aiken. "Jane Austen and Her Publishers." In John Halperin, ed., *Jane Austen: Bicentenary Essays*, 75–85. Cambridge: Cambridge University Press, 1975.

Holland, Dorothy C., and Margaret A. Eisenhart. *Educated in Romance: Women, Achievement, and College Culture*. Chicago: University of Chicago Press, 1990.

Holmes, Geoffrey. *Augustan England: Profession, State, and Society*. London: G. Allen and Unwin, 1982.

Holmes, Richard. *Dr. Johnson and Mr. Savage.* New York: Random House, 1995.

Howell, Michael, and Peter Ford. *The True History of the Elephant Man.* Middlesex, England: Penguin Books, 1980.

Hufton, Olwen. *The Poor of Eighteenth-Century France, 1750–1789.* Oxford: Clarendon Press, 1974.

Inchbald, Elizabeth, ed. *British Theatre.* 11 vols. London: Longman, Hurst, Rees, and Orme, 1807.

"Instructions to Regimental Surgeons for Regulating the Concerns of the Sick, and of the hospital." September 1803. Reprinted in *Journal of the Army Medical Corps* 60 (1933): 141–149, 222–28.

Jacyna, L.S. *Philosophic Whigs: Medicine, Science, and Citizenship in Edinburgh, 1789–1848.* London: Routledge, 1994.

James, John Haddy. *Surgeon James's Journal, 1815.* Ed. Jane Vansittart. London: Cassell, [1964].

Jewson, Nicholas. "Medical Knowledge and the Patronage System in Eighteenth-Century England." *Sociology* 8 (1974): 369–385.

Johnston, William. *Commissioned Officers in the Medical Services of the British Army, 1660–1960.* 2 vols. London: Wellcome Historical Medical Library, 1968.

Jordan, F. W. *Life of Joseph Jordan, Surgeon, and an Account of the Rise and Progress of Medical Schools in Manchester, with Some Particulars of the Life of Dr. Edward Stephens.* London: Sherratt and Hughes, 1904.

Kaufman, Paul. *Borrowings from the Bristol Library, 1773–1784: A Unique Record of Reading Vogues.* Charlottesville: Bibliographical Society of the University of Virginia, 1960.

——. *Libraries and Their Users: Collected Papers in Library History.* London: Library Association, 1969.

Kay, Richard. *The Diary of Richard Kay, 1716–51, of Baldingstone, Near Bury: A Lancashire Doctor.* Ed. W. Brockbank and F. Kenworthy. Manchester: Printed for the Chetham Society, 1968.

Kaye, John William. *History of the War in Afghanistan.* 3 vols. London: Wm. H. Allen, 1878.

Keegan, John. *The Mask of Command.* Middlesex, England: Penguin Books, 1988.

Kelly, Lionel, ed. *Tobias Smollett: The Critical Heritage.* New York: Routledge and Kegan Paul, 1987.

Kempthorne, G. A. "The Army Medical Services at Home and Abroad, 1803–1808." *Journal of the Royal Army Medical Corps* 61 (1933): 144–146, 223–232.

——. "The Army Medical Services 1816–1825." *Journal of the Royal Army Medical Corps* 60 (1933): 299–310.

——. "The Medical Department of Wellington's Army, 1809–1814." *Journal of the Royal Army Medical Corps* 54 (1930): 65–220.

——. "The Walcheren Expedition and the Reform of the Medical Board, 1809." *Journal of the Royal Army Medical Corps,* 62 (1934): 133–138.

Kennedy, Richard Hartley. *Narrative of the Campaign of the Army of the Indus, in Sind and Kaubool, in 1838–9.* 2 vols. London: Richard Bentley, 1840.

Kenner, Hugh. *The Counterfeiters: An Historical Comedy.* Bloomington: Indiana University Press, 1968.

Kenney, James. "Sweethearts and Wives." In Thomas Hailes Lacy, ed., *Lacy's Acting Edition of Plays, Dramas, Farces, and Extravaganzas.* London: Thomas Hailes Lacy, n.d.

Kirkpatrick Sharpe, Charles. *Letters from and to Charles Kirkpatrick Sharpe, Esq.* Ed. Alexander Allardyce. 2 vols. Edinburgh: William Blackwood and Sons, 1888.

Kleinman, Arthur. *The Illness Narratives: Suffering, Healing, and the Human Condition.* New York: Basic Books, 1988.

Knapp, Lewis Mansfield. *Tobias Smollett, Doctor of Men and Manners.* Princeton: Princeton University Press, 1949.

Larpent, F. S. *The Private Journal of F. S. Larpent, Esq.* Ed. George Larpent. London: Richard Bentley, 1853.

Lawrence, Susan. *Charitable Knowledge: Hospital Pupils and Practitioners in Eighteenth-Century London.* Cambridge: Cambridge University Press, 1996.

——. "'Desirous of Improvements in Medicine': Pupils and Practitioners in the Medical Societies at Guy's and St Bartholomew's Hospital, 1795–1815." *Bulletin of the History of Medicine* 62 (1988): 171–192.

Lennox, Charlotte. *The Female Quixote.* New York: Oxford University Press, 1991.

"Letters from the Lower Deck, 1794–1811." In H. G. Thursfield, ed., *Five Naval Journals 1789–1817*, 351–376. London: Navy Records Society, 1951.

Lindemann, Mary. "Professional? Sisters? Rivals? Midwives in Braunschweig, 1750–1800." In Marland, pp. 176–191.

Long, Charles Edward. *A Reply to the Misrepresentations and Aspersions on the Military Reputation of the Late Lieut.-Gen. R. B. Long*. London: James Ridgway, 1832.

Long, Robert Ballard. *Peninsular Cavalry General (1811–13). The Correspondence of Lieutenant-General Robert Ballard Long*. Ed. T.H. McGuffie. London: George G. Harrap, 1951.

Lucas, James. *A Candid Inquiry into the Education, Qualifications, and Offices of a Surgeon-Apothecary*. Bath, England: S. Hazard, 1800.

MacDonagh, Oliver. *Jane Austen: Real and Imagined Worlds*. New Haven: Yale University Press, 1991.

MacFarlane, Alan. *Marriage and Love in England: Modes of Reproduction, 1300–1840*. Oxford: Basil Blackwell, 1986.

Mackintosh, John. *Prize Examinations of the Practice of Physic and Midwifery Classes at the Argyll Square School of Medicine*. Edinburgh: H. & J. Pillans, 1835.

——. *Reply to a Pamphlet, Entitled Notes on Dr. Mackintosh's Treatise on Puerperal Fever, by Mr. Moir, Surgeon*. Edinburgh, 1822.

——. *To the Members of the Medical Profession*. Edinburgh, 1823.

——. *A Treatise on the Disease Termed Puerperal Fever*. Edinburgh: William Blackwood, 1822.

MacLagan, David. *Disputatio medica inauguralis, quaedam de sanitate tuenda complectans*. Edinburgh, 1805.

——. *A Probationary Surgical Essay on Tetanus, Chiefly as Occurring after Wounds*. Edinburgh, 1816.

Macleod, Jay. *Ain't No Makin' It: Aspirations and Attainment in a Low-Income Neighborhood*. Boulder, Colo.: Westview Press, 1995.

Mangan, J. A., and James Walvin, eds. *Manliness and Morality: Middle-Class Masculinity in Britain and America, 1800–1940*. Manchester: Manchester University Press, 1987.

Marland, Hilary, ed. *The Art of Midwifery: Early Modern Midwives in Europe*. London: Routledge, 1993.

Márquez, Gabriel García. *Love in the Time of Cholera*. New York: Penguin Books, 1988.

Martins de Carvalho, Francisco Augusto. *Noticia historica do Regimento de Infantaria no. 9*. Coimbra, 1878.

Matthews, William. *British Diaries: An Annotated Bibliography of British Diaries Written between 1442 and 1942*. Berkeley: University of California Press, 1950.

Mayo, Robert D. *The English Novel in the Magazines, 1740–1815*. Evanston, Ill.: Northwestern University Press, 1962.

McGrigor, Sir James. *The Autobiography and Services of Sir James McGrigor, Bart., Late Director-General of the Army Medical Department*. London: Longman, Green, Longman, and Roberts, 1861.

——. *Sketch of the Medical History of the British Armies in the Peninsula of Spain and Portugal*. London, 1816.

McKeon, Michael. *The Origins of the English Novel, 1600–1740*. Baltimore: Johns Hopkins University Press, 1987.

McMicking, Neil. *Officers of the Black Watch*. Perth: Thomas Hunter & Sons, [1937].

Melville, Herman. *Pierre; or, The Ambiguities*. New York: Hendricks House, Farrar Straus, 1949.

Meyerstein, E. H. W. *A Life of Thomas Chatterton*. New York: Charles Scribner's Sons, 1930.

Michasiw, Kim Ian. "Nine Revisionist Theses on the Picturesque." *Representations* 38 (Spring 1992): 76–100.

Mitchell, Silas Weir. *Gunshot Wounds, and Other Injuries of Nerves*. Philadelphia: J. B. Lippincott, 1864.

Mitterauer, Michael, and Reinhard Sieder. *The European Family: Patriarchy to Partnership from the Middle Ages to the Present*. Chicago: University of Chicago Press, 1982.

Moir, James. *Notes on Dr. Macintosh's Treatise on the Puerperal Fever*. Edinburgh: Murray & Mitchell, 1822.

——. *Postscript to Mr. Moir's Notes on Dr Macintosh's Treatise on Puerperal Fever*. Edinburgh, 1822.

Moretti, Franco. *Signs Taken for Wonders: Essays in the Sociology of Literary Forms*. Trans. Susan Fischer, David Forgacs and David Miller. New York: Verso, 1983.

——. *The Way of the World: The Bildungsroman in European Culture.* London: Verso, 1987.

Mumford, Alfred A. *The Manchester Grammar School, 1515–1915: A Regional Study of the Advancement of Learning in Manchester Since the Reformation.* London: Longmans, Green, 1919.

Murray, Hugh. *History of British India.* London: Thomas Nelson, 1850.

Murray, Sarah. *A Companion and Useful Guide to the Beauties of Scotland, and the Hebrides, to the Lakes of Westmoreland, Cumberland, and Lancashire.* 2 vols. London, 1810.

Napier, W. F. P. *History of the War in the Peninsula and in the South of France, from the 1807 to the year 1814.* 3 vols. Kansas City, Mo.: Hudson Kimberly, 1904.

Norris, J. A. *The First Afghan War, 1838–1842.* Cambridge: Cambridge University Press, 1967.

*O investigador portuguez em Inglaterra; ou, Jornal literario, politico, &c.* London, 1811–1819.

O'Brian, Patrick. *The Far Side of the World.* New York: W. W. Norton, 1992.

O'Keefe, John. *The Plays of John O'Keefe.* Ed. Frederick Link. 4 vols. New York: Garland, 1981.

Oman, Charles. *A History of the Peninsular War.* 8 vols. Oxford: Clarendon Press, 1902–1930.

——. *Wellington's Army, 1809–1814.* London: Greenhill Books, 1986.

Ozment, Steven. *Three Behaim Boys. Growing Up in Early Modern Germany.* New Haven: Yale University Press, 1990.

Pakenham, Edward. *Pakenham Letters, 1800–1815.* [London]: John and Edward Bumpus, 1914.

Parkinson, James. *The Hospital Pupil; or Observations Addressed to the Parents of Youths Intended for the Profession of Medicine and Surgery.* London: Sherwood, Neely, and Jones, 1817.

Pascal, Roy. *Design and Truth in Autobiography.* Cambridge: Harvard University Press, 1960.

Paterson, James. *Kay's Edinburgh Portraits.* London: Hamilton, Adams, 1885.

Pelling, Margaret. "Medical Practice in Early Modern England: Trade or Profession." In Wilfred Prest, ed., *The Professions in Early Modern England.* London: Routledge, 1987.

Pomerance, Bernard. *Elephant Man: A Play.* New York: Grove Press, 1979.

Pool, Daniel. *What Jane Austen Ate and Charles Dickens Knew.* New York: Touchstone, 1994.

Porter, Dorothy, and Roy Porter. *Patient's Progress. Doctors and Doctoring in Eighteenth-Century England.* Stanford, Calif.: Stanford University Press, 1989.

Porter, Roy. *Health for Sale: Quackery in England, 1660–1850.* Manchester: Manchester University Press, 1989.

——. "The Patient's View: Doing Medical History from Below." *Theory and Society* 14 (1985): 175–198.

——. "A Touch of Danger: The Man-Midwife as Sexual Predator." In G. S. Rousseau and R. Porter, eds., *Sexual Underworlds of the Enlightenment,* 206–232. Manchester: Manchester University Press, 1988.

Porter, Roy, and Leslie Hall. *The Facts of Life: The Creation of Sexual Knowledge in Britain, 1650–1950.* New Haven: Yale University Press, 1995.

Preston, John. *The Created Self: The Reader's Role in Eighteenth-Century Fiction.* New York: Barnes and Noble, 1970.

Radford, Jean, ed. *The Progress of Romance: The Politics of Popular Fiction.* New York: Routledge and Kegan Paul, 1986.

Radway, Janice A. *Reading the Romance: Women, Patriarchy, and Popular Literature.* Chapel Hill: University of North Carolina Press, 1984.

Ramsay, Matthew. *Professional and Popular Medicine in France, 1770–1830: The Social World of Medical Practice.* Cambridge: Cambridge University Press, 1988.

Raoul, Valerie. *The French Fictional Journal: Fictional Narcissism and Narcissistic Fiction.* Toronto: University of Toronto Press, 1980.

Reeve, Clara. *Progress of Romance.* 1785. Reprint, New York: Facsimile Text Society, 1930.

*Reginald Dalton.* Edinburgh: Blackwood, 1823.

Reichard, Hans Ottokar. *Guide d'Espagne et du Portugal, 1793.* Paris: Les Editions de la Courtille, 1971.

*Relação das especies bibliographicas e iconographicas relativas á revolução franceze e imperio (1789–1815) indicando as que podem ser admittidas nas exposições biblio-historico-iconographicas que devem celebrar-se na Bibliotheca Nacional de Lisboa e No Museu de Artilharia para commemoração centenaria da Guerra Peninsular.* Lisbon, 1909.

Review of *Edward Neville.* In *Monthly Review,* ser. 2, 103 (January-April 1824): 106.

Review of *Matilda; a Tale for the Day.* In *Monthly Review,* ser. 2, 107 (May-August 1825):435–444.

Review of *Reginald Dalton*. In *Monthly Review*, ser. 2, 103 (January-April 1824): 199–208.

Riasanovsky, Nicholas V. *The Emergence of Romanticism*. New York: Oxford University Press, 1992.

Richardson, Alan. *Literature, Education, and Romanticism: Reading as Social Practice, 1780–1832*. Cambridge: Cambridge University Press, 1994.

Richardson, Robert G. *Larrey: Surgeon to Napoleon's Imperial Guard*. London: John Murray, 1974.

Richter, David. *The Progress of Romance: Literary Historiography and the Gothic Novel*. Columbus: Ohio State University Press, 1996.

Rivers, Isabel, ed. *Books and Their Readers in Eighteenth-Century England*. Leicester: Leicester University Press, 1982.

Robinson, Henry Crabb. *Henry Crabb Robinson on Books and their Writers*. Ed. Edith J. Morley. 3 vols. London: J. M. Dent, 1938.

——. *The London Theatre, 1811–1866: Selections from the Diary of Henry Crabb Robinson*. Ed. Eluned Brown. London: Society for Theatre Research, 1966.

Roper, Michael, and John Tosh, eds. *Manful Assertions: Masculinities in Britain Since 1800*. London: Routledge, 1991.

Rosner, Lisa. *Medical Education in the Age of Improvement: Edinburgh Students and Apprentices 1760–1828*. Edinburgh: Edinburgh University Press, 1991.

*Royal Military Calendar, or Army Service and Commission Book*. 5 vols. Facsimile of 3rd edition, London, 1820.

*Royal Military Chronicle or British Officer's Monthly Register and Mentor*, 1811–1814.

Sacks, Oliver. *A Leg to Stand On*. New York: Harper & Row Publishers, 1982.

——. *Awakenings*. New York: Harper Perennial, 1990.

——. *The Man Who Mistook His Wife for a Hat and Other Clinical Tales*. New York: Summit Books, 1985.

Schrader, Catherine Geertruida. *"Mother and Child Were Saved": The Memoirs (1693–1740) of the Frisian Midwife Catharina Schrader*. Trans. Hilary Marland. Amsterdam: Rodopi, 1987.

Scott, Walter. *Lives of the Novelists*. London: J. M. Dent, 1928.

Seavey, Ormond. *Becoming Benjamin Franklin: The Autobiography and the Life*. University Park: Pennsylvania State University Press, 1988.

Sharpe, Charles Kirkpatrick. *Letters from and to Charles Kirkpatrick Sharpe, Esq*. Ed. Alexander Allardyce. 2 vols. Edinburgh: William Blackwood and Sons, 1888.

Shelley, Mary. *The Journals of Mary Shelley*. Ed. Paula R. Feldman and Diana Scott-Kilvert. 2 vols. Oxford: Clarendon Press, 1987.

——. *The Letters of Mary Wollstonecraft Shelley*. Ed. Betty T. Bennett. 3 vols. Baltimore: Johns Hopkins University Press, 1988.

Sherrod, Drury. "The Bonds of Men: Problems and Possibilities in Close Male Relationships." In Harry Brod, *The Making of Masculinities. The New Men's Studies*. Boston: Allen & Unwin, 1987.

Smet, John Francis. "Extracts from Journals of John Francis Smet, Surgeon, 8th Hussars, 1815–1824." *Journal of the Society for Army Historical Research* 29 (1951): 172–178.

Smith, Adam. *The Theory of Moral Sentiments*. Indianapolis: Liberty Classics, 1976.

Smith, Jeremiah Finch. *The Admission Register of the Manchester School, with Some Notice of the More Distinguished Scholars*. 3 vols. Manchester: Printed for the Chetham Society, 1868.

Smollett, Tobias. *Letters of Tobias Smollett, M.D*. Ed. Edward S. Noyes. Cambridge, Mass.: Harvard University Press, 1926.

Spacks, Patricia Meyer. *Imagining A Self: Autobiography and Novel in Eighteenth-Century England*. Cambridge: Harvard University Press, 1976.

Speer, T. C. *Thoughts on the Present Character and Constitution of the Medical Profession*. Cambridge: J. Smith, 1823.

Spring, David. "Interpreters of Jane Austen's Social World. Literary Critics and Historians." In Janet Todd, ed., *Jane Austen: New Perspectives*, 53–72. New York: Holmes & Meier, 1983.

Stanhope, Philip Henry, 5th Earl. *Notes of Conversations with the Duke of Wellington, 1831–1851*. Oxford: Oxford University Press, 1938.

Starr, Paul. *The Social Transformation of American Medicine: The Rise of a Sovereign Profession and the Making of a Vast Industry*. New York: Basic Books, 1992.

Staves, Susan. *Married Women's Separate Property in England, 1660–1835*. Cambridge, Mass.: Harvard University Press, 1990.

Stearns, Peter N. *Be a Man! Males in Modern Society*. New York: Holmes & Meier, 1979.

Stevenson, Robert Louis. *David Balfour*. New York: Charles Scribner's Sons, 1922.

Stone, Lawrence. *The Family, Sex, and Marriage in England, 1500–1800*, abridged ed. New York: Harper & Row, 1979.

Sussman, Herbert. *Victorian Masculinities: Manhood and Masculine Poetics in Early Victorian Literature and Art*. Cambridge: Cambridge University Press, 1995.

[Taplin, William]. *The Aesculapian Labyrinth Explored; or, Medical Mystery Illustrated. A Series of Instructions to Young Physicians, Surgeons, Accoucheurs, Apothecaries, Druggists, and Practitioners of Every Denomination, in Town and Country*. Dublin: Zachariah Jackson, 1789.

*The Tatler; A Periodical Paper*. London, 1709–1711.

Templeman, William D. *The Life and Work of William Gilpin (1724–1804) Master of the Picturesque and Vicar of Boldre*. Urbana: University of Illinois Press, 1939.

Thursfield, H. G. *Five Naval Journals, 1789–1817*. London: Navy Records Society, 1951.

Tompkins, J. M. S. *The Polite Marriage*. Cambridge: Cambridge University Press, 1938.

——. *The Popular Novel in England*. Lincoln: University of Nebraska Press, 1962.

Treves, Frederick. *The Elephant Man and Other Reminiscences*. New York: Cassell, 1923.

*United Service Journal and Naval and Military Magazine*. London: H. Colburn, 1829–1841.

Vichness, Samuel E. "Marshal of Portugal: The Military Career of William Carr Beresford 1785–1814." Ph.D. diss., Florida State University, 1976.

Waller, John H. *Beyond the Khyber Pass: The Road to British Disaster in the First Afghan War*. New York: Random House, 1990.

Walsh, Thomas. *Journal of the Late Campaign in Egypt: Including Descriptions of That Country, and of Gibraltar, Minorca, Malta, Marmorice, and Macri*. London: T. Cadell and W. Davies, 1805. Reprint, Gregg International Publishers, 1972.

Ward, S. P. G. *Wellington's Headquarters: A Study of the Administrative Problems in the Peninsula, 1809–1814*. Oxford: Oxford University Press, 1957.

Warner, Michael. *The Letters of the Republic: Publication and the Public Sphere in Eighteenth-Century America*. Cambridge, Mass.: Harvard University Press, 1990.

Warre, William. *Letters from the Peninsular, 1808–1812*. Ed. Edmond Warre. London: John Murray, 1909.

Watson, Samuel J. "Flexible Gender Roles during the Market Revolution: Family, Friendship, Marriage, and Masculinity Among U.S. Army Officers, 1815–1846." *Journal of Social History* 29.1 (1995): 81–106.

Wellington, Arthur Wellesley, Duke of. *The Dispatches of Field Marshal the Duke of Wellington, during his various campaigns from 1799 to 1818*. Ed. John Gurwood. 12 vols. London: John Murray, 1837–1839.

——. *Selections from the Dispatches and General Orders of Field Marshal the Duke of Wellington*. Ed. John Gurwood. London: John Murray, 1841.

——. *Supplementary Dispatches, Correspondence, and Memoranda or Field Marshal Arthur Duke of Wellington, K.G.* Ed. 2nd Duke of Wellington. 11 vols. London: John Murray, 1858–1864. Reprint, New York: Kraus Reprint, 1973.

Willis, Paul. *Learning to Labor: How Working-Class Kids Get Working-Class Jobs*. New York: Columbia University Press, 1977.

Wollstonecraft, Mary. *Vindication of the Rights of Woman*. New York: W. W. Norton, 1988.

Woodford, Leonard W. "War & Peace—The Experiences of An Army Surgeon 1810–24." *Journal of the Society for Army Historical Research* 48 (1970): 43–58.

Woodforde, Dorothy Heighes, ed. *Woodforde Papers and Diaries*. London: Peter Davies, 1932.

Ziff, Larzer. *Writing in the New Nation: Prose, Print, and Politics in the Early United States*. New Haven: Yale University Press, 1991.

ACKNOWLEDGMENTS

All authors incur enormous debts in the course of completing a book, but the majority of my debts, like Lesassier's, are centered on Edinburgh. My deepest gratitude is to Joy Pitman, former archivist at the Library of the Royal College of Physicians of Edinburgh, who generously provided photocopies of most of Alexander Lesassier Hamilton's papers and also shared her own insights into his life and character. Without her, this book truly would not have been possible. Miss Ferguson and Iain Milne at the Library of the Royal College of Physicians of Edinburgh, Alison Stevenson and Ms. Smith at the Library of the Royal College of Surgeons of Edinburgh, Jo Currie at the Edinburgh University Library, and the staff of the Scottish Record Office were also helpful and generous with their time and attention. I would also like to thank Mr. A. Adam and the staff of the Aberdeen Medico-Chirurgical Society for help fulfilling a scholar's dream: complete access to their wealth of manuscripts and a ready supply of tea and biscuits.

Research and writing time for this book was generously supported by Distinguished Faculty Fellowship and Research and Professional Development grants from the Richard Stockton College of New Jersey.

The late Kitty and Sidney Michaelson provided me with a home in Edinburgh, and I deeply regret that they are no longer alive for me to present them with a copy of the book: I think they would have thoroughly enjoyed Lesassier's story in full after hearing so many anecdotes at dinner. I would also like to thank Gregg Michaelson and Rosa Michaelson, both for their friendly encouragement and for introducing me to the novels of Susan Ferrier. John and Elizabeth Grant were wonderfully hospitable and informative about Scotland, past and present. Jane Kellett helped me work out what life in Edinburgh's New Town must have been like for Lesassier and his household.

Finally, I would like to thank my family. Henry and Lillian Rosner, Mark Rosner and Abbee Goldstein, and Andy and Marianne Rosner have all listened to Lesassier stories with varying degrees of attention but unwavering support. John Theibault first suggested that Lesassier deserved a book of his own, and Alice and Monica Theibault are the best traveling companions a historian on a research trip could hope for. Thank you, one and all.

# INDEX

Adams, Mrs., 141
Afghan War, x, 199, 200
Aitchisson, Mr., 181
Albuera, 86
Allan, Isabella, 135, 138, 198
Anderson, Mr., 132
Anderton, Ella, 68–71, 93, 94, 127, 128, 153, 158, 165, 167, 184, 191
*Arabian Nights,* 13, 24
Army Medical Board, 33–37, 40, 46, 49, 52, 71, 92, 95, 96, 116, 127, 153, 154, 182, 197
assistant surgeon, 32–34, 45, 48, 52, 53, 76, 81, 84, 90, 95, 97, 106, 107, 109, 110, 113, 118–123, 155, 157, 223, 224
Astley's Equestrian Circus, 10
Atkinson, Dr., 59, 64
Austen, Jane, x, 3, 38, 141, 150; "Love and Friendship," 13; *Mansfield Park,* 7; *Northanger Abbey,* 13, 18, 58, 61; *Pride and Prejudice,* 4

Badajoz, 94
ballads, 91, 93, 94, 204, 219
Banner, Mr., 147, 148, 151
Banner, Mrs., 145–147
Barclay, John, 28
Baxandall, Michael, 17
Beilby, Dr., 162, 163, 172, 173, 192, 197
Bell, George, 26, 32, 38
Bento Garçao, Luiz, 117, 118, 120–122
Beresford, William Carr, 73, 87, 107, 110, 123
Berridale, Lord, 59, 175
Betty, 64, 138
Black, Joseph, 27
Blakiston, John, 108, 110
Blantyre, Lord, 74, 76, 85, 88–90, 97, 109, 117, 118
Bolton, Abraham, 45, 48–51, 73, 78, 85, 107
Boswell, James, x
Boutflower, Charles, 79, 85, 111
Brontë, Charlotte, 7
Brown, Joseph, 16, 51, 52, 79, 201
Burgos, 79, 101, 104, 105, 108, 112, 155
Burke and Hare scandal, 174, 201
Bussaco, 86, 110

Cabbell, Dr., 83, 84
Cairns, Mrs., 147
Campbell, Archibald, 26, 33, 135
Campbell, Mary, 26, 136, 139, 147, 161, 172, 173, 181, 187, 188, 195, 196, 200, 201
Campbell, Mrs. (great-aunt), 7, 26, 136, 173, 181, 187
Campbell, Mrs. Major, 56, 59, 61
Cantlie, Neil, 119, 128
case histories, 131–133, 144–146, 192–195, 238
Chatterton, Thomas, 12, 18
Chelsea Pensioners, 160
Chesterfield, Lord, 165
Cinderella Complex, 23
Ciudad Rodrigo, 94
Cleland, Mrs., 141
Cockburn, Mrs., 163
Coimbra, 76, 82–84, 87–90, 98
College of Surgeons of London, 33, 35–37, 52
Collier, Miss, 16, 18, 19
Collier, Mr., 14, 16, 18–21, 25, 27, 47
Collins, Ann, 8, 9, 22, 94, 157
consumer culture, x–10, 30, 50, 61–65, 67, 68, 70, 83, 85, 87, 95, 100, 106, 109, 126, 127, 141, 148–151, 157, 158, 161, 172, 177, 179, 187–189, 196
Costello, Edward, 80, 114
Courtney, staff surgeon, 42
Cullen, William, 27, 131, 144

Davidson, Captain, 54, 56
Dean, Ann, 19, 25, 60, 199
*Death's a Friend,* 30, 31, 135
Dent, William, 44
Dickens, Charles, 7, 208
Duizbeck, Colonel, 120
Duncan, Andrew, Jr., 15
Duncan, Andrew, Sr., 6, 15, 206
Dundas, David, 35–37, 52
Dunlop, Mrs., 134

Edinburgh University, 2, 3, 14, 16, 24–29, 32, 34, 37–39, 57, 87, 88, 97, 123, 127–133, 174, 175, 201

*Edward Neville*, 1, 4, 6–11, 13, 14, 16, 66, 99, 100, 154–160, 165, 167, 169, 192, 193, 203
Eeston, ensign, 64–66
Eighth brigade, 107, 108, 112, 119, 123–125
Elibank, Lady, 134, 163
Elibank, Lord, 134, 151, 163
Eliot, George, 8, 138, 193
Elkington, James, 78
Elvas, 78–82, 131, 218
Erly, John, 49, 74, 95–97, 130, 133

Ferguson, Adam, 206
Fergusson, William, 46, 48, 88, 96, 98, 107, 110, 111, 113, 183
Ferrier, Susan, 13, 18, 55, 147, 165, 193
Fielding, Henry, x, xi, 1, 18, 158
Flanagan, hospital mate, 42
Fletcher, Anthony, 138
Forbes, William, 54, 56
42nd regiment, 11, 48, 49, 52–54, 56, 57, 68, 72, 73, 76, 78, 80, 82, 83, 86, 88–90, 92, 94, 100–102, 104, 107, 116, 117, 128, 155, 182
Franck, Dr., 87, 89
Franklin, Benjamin, xii
Fraser, Captain, 50, 56
Fuentes d'Onoro, 88, 89, 97

Garcia Vaissa, Maria de, 47, 48
Garcias, Mathias, 111, 112, 115, 117, 120
Geddes, Mrs., 43, 46, 155
George IV, 196
Gibbon, Edmund, xii, 47
Gibson, John, ix, 198, 199
Gilpin, William, 58, 59, 208
Glasgow University, 15
Goldsmith, Oliver, 160
Grattan, William, 89
Gregory, James, 28
Gunn, James, 80, 101, 104–106, 128
Guthrie, George James, 79, 101, 102, 104, 122

Halliday, Andrew, 79, 88, 107, 110, 111
Hamilton, Alexander (professor of midwifery), 2, 8, 11
Hamilton, Alexander Lesassier. *See* Lesassier, Alexander
Hamilton, Catherine Jane Crokatt, ix, 136–140, 147, 150–152, 154, 162, 167, 168, 171, 172, 176–181, 185–187, 189, 190, 195, 197–199, 201
Hamilton, Catherine Reid, 2, 26, 29–31, 135, 136, 181, 182

Hamilton, Henry Parr, 29
Hamilton, James, 4, 5, 7–9, 11, 15, 20, 24–30, 32, 33, 38, 39, 41, 47, 53, 56, 57, 88, 95, 96, 107, 115, 127–129, 133–136, 142, 146, 148, 151–153, 162–164, 171, 173, 174, 176, 179, 180, 182, 184–186, 188, 201
Hamilton, John, 29–31
Hamilton, Joseph, 27
Hanson, John, 175, 176, 178
Hanson, Newton, 174–176, 178, 179, 182
Harrison, John, 34
Harrison, Miss, 60
Hastings Anderson, William, 162
Hastings Anderson, Mrs., 134, 163
Hawkins, Emmeline, 27, 166–173, 201
Hawkins, Isabella, 166–168, 171
Hawkins, James, 169, 170, 172
Hazlitt, Sarah, 239
Hazlitt, William, 8, 60
Hennen, John, 79, 89, 102, 103
Henry, 159
Henry, Walter, 76, 80, 102, 104
Hewit, Mr., 25, 26
Hill, Catherine, 190, 191, 196
Hodgeson, Isabella Hamilton, 4, 26, 29–32, 38, 40, 54, 62, 135–137, 140, 149, 154, 181, 199
Hodgeson, Thomas, 32, 154
Home, Joanna Stirling, 48, 49, 60, 98, 179
Hope, Thomas Charles, 28
hospital assistant, 46. *See also* hospital mate
hospital mate, 32–34, 36, 37, 39, 41, 42, 45–47, 50–53, 89, 97

Ignatia, 198, 201
Irwin, Alicia, 60–68, 138
Ivory, James, 198

Jenoway, Richard, ix, 17, 19, 20, 40, 59, 70, 150, 152, 172, 178, 184, 186, 196, 198
Joeburn, Mr., 42
Johnson, Catherine, 190
Jordan, Joseph, 19–22, 139, 183, 201
journals, x, xii, 2, 13, 25, 58, 79, 83, 93, 104, 139, 153, 161, 166–199, 202, 203

Kay, Mrs., 151
Keate, Thomas, 34, 49
Keegan, John, 77, 100
Kennedy, Richard, 199, 200
Kinnears bank, 178
Kintore, Lady Louisa, 164, 166–174, 178, 188, 190, 195, 201

Kintore, Lord, 167–171, 174
Kirkpatrick Sharpe, Charles, 171
Kitty, 51
Knight, Francis, 34, 35, 38, 39
Knox, Robert, 149, 174, 201

Lafayette, Marquis de, 189
Lane, John, 155
Larrey, Dominique Jean, 75
Lesassier, Alexander: apprenticeship, 14–22, 32, 34; birth, 2, 6; death, 200; divorce, ix, 198, 199; feelings toward James Hamilton, 28, 30, 32, 33, 39, 96, 127–130, 135, 141, 162, 163, 185; feelings toward Pierre Lesassier, 7, 14, 22, 23, 27, 53, 94, 184, 195; financial affairs, xi, 37, 40, 41, 50, 54, 56, 59, 93, 100, 109, 125–127, 129, 134, 136, 140, 149–152, 159–161, 163–168, 172, 174–181, 186–188, 195–197; inheritance, 11, 15, 25, 30, 41, 187; legally changes name to Hamilton, 129, 134; marriage, 136; M.D. degree, 131; medical practice, xi, 46, 55, 66, 73–75, 77, 79–81, 83–85, 88, 90, 100, 101, 103–105, 107, 109, 113–123, 125, 133, 134, 138, 141–148, 151, 152, 162, 163, 166, 174, 179, 182, 188, 190, 191, 194–196; noble birth, 2, 7, 189, 237; novel, 2, 7–11, 154–160, 167, 169, 193
Lesassier, Christina Smith Hamilton, 2–4, 6, 136, 206
Lesassier, Pierre, 2–4, 6, 8, 9, 10, 14, 15, 21–23, 28, 30, 32, 38, 53, 94, 149, 152–154, 157, 177, 178, 181, 182, 184–186, 189, 195
libraries, 47, 57, 59, 75, 159
Lindsay, William, 57, 71, 79, 94, 97
Lister, Joseph, 201
London medical schools, x, 14, 34, 37, 49
Long, Robert Ballard, 77, 86
Louis Philippe, 196
Ludlow, Henry, 174
Lying-In Hospital, 26, 128, 134, 138, 141–143, 164, 201

Macaulay, Thomas Babington, 208
Maccara, Major, 56
Mackintosh, John, 149, 164, 174, 201
MacLagan, David, 39, 87, 110, 123, 130, 133, 147
Macpherson, Alexander, 35, 37, 40, 45
Maitland, Fanny, 139, 176
Maitland, John, 139, 150, 186
Manchester Free School, 9
Manchester Infirmary, 20, 21, 34
Manoel, 83, 91, 116, 117, 127, 159
Marischal College, Aberdeen, 149
Marmont, August, 94, 99, 100

Massena, André, 83, 84, 87
*Matilda; a Tale of the Day*, 144–146
Maugham, Euphemia, 141, 190, 191, 196
McDermid, Mr., 52
McGrigor, James, 11, 55, 56, 79, 96–98, 104, 107, 109, 110, 112, 115, 116, 119, 120, 123, 132, 133, 153, 175, 179, 182, 183, 196
McKenzie, Christian, 138, 168, 198
McKenzie, Mr., 151
McLachlan, Alexander, 49, 95, 96
McLean, Daniel, 49, 78
McLeod, Swinton, 57, 80, 81, 83, 87, 88, 92, 196
McPherson, Donald, 71, 76, 78, 80, 82, 88
McPherson, Mrs., 151
medical cadetship, 38, 39, 87, 110, 123
medical practice, 16, 23, 77, 79, 80, 84, 89, 90, 101–105, 112–114, 130, 144, 151, 152, 183
Melville, Herman, 31
Meyerstein, E. H. W., 207
midwifery, 2, 5, 21, 25, 28, 43, 128, 129, 141–145, 151, 152, 161, 170, 172, 173, 192–195, 201, 203
Milligan, Edward, 148, 174, 201
Minto, Dr., 162, 163
Mitchell, Silas Weir, 192
Monro, Alexander secundus, 27
Monro, Alexander tertius, 28
Monroe, Catherine, 138
Moore, Sir John, 84
More, Helen, 138
Murray, Sir George, 84

Napoleon Bonaparte, 72, 73, 124, 105, 129
Nivelle, 119
novels, xii, 1, 13–15, 30, 31, 43, 55, 60, 61, 66, 70, 83, 96, 99, 135, 144, 146, 150, 154–160, 165, 167, 169, 180, 191–193, 208

O'Brian, Patrick, xii
O'Keefe, John, 10
Oman, Charles, 101, 106, 199
Orthez, 122, 123

Pakenham, Edward, 105
Pamplona, 108
Parkinson, James, 15
patronage, 39, 95, 96, 107, 127, 129, 132, 134, 148, 164, 172, 175, 179
Peninsular War, x, xi, 71–73, 84, 85, 87, 90, 94, 96, 97, 99, 100, 102, 105, 106, 108, 110, 119, 122, 124, 128, 199, 200
Pepys, Lucas, 34

Perston, David, 89
physician, army, 95, 96
picturesque, 57, 58, 77, 82, 83, 86, 88, 101, 111, 157, 181, 208, 215, 217
Pitman, Joy, ix
Portsmouth, Lady Mary Ann, 164–166, 169, 171, 174–178, 187
Power, Manley, 108, 109, 111, 112, 114, 116, 118, 120, 121, 123
professionalization, x, xi, 11, 12, 14, 15, 17, 22–24, 55–57, 75, 95, 97, 98, 104, 105, 107, 115, 122, 123, 126, 130–132, 134, 143, 144, 147, 148, 165, 174, 181, 185, 192

Ramsay, Mrs., 190, 196
Reed, Mr., 34
Reginald Dalton, 158
Rennie, Mrs., 147, 196
Richardson, Samuel, 1, 155
Rita, 90–93
Rochdale, 2, 6, 22, 23, 25, 30, 60, 126, 128, 133
Rochepaliere, Count de, 2, 189
Romilly, Captain, 43
Ross, Isabella, 190, 199
Royal College of Physicians of Edinburgh, ix, 202, 203
Royal College of Surgeons of Edinburgh, 2, 5, 37–39, 130, 133, 149
Ryan, hospital mate, 42, 43, 46, 155

Sacks, Oliver, 192, 229
St. Andrews University, 6, 95, 130
Salamanca, 94, 100, 101, 105, 108
Scott, Mrs., 190, 191
Scott, Walter, x
sensibility, 14, 18, 30, 144, 145
servants, 19, 25, 28, 42, 43, 47, 48, 64, 73, 83, 84, 91, 116, 117, 125, 127, 137, 138, 149, 150, 159, 168, 170, 176, 186, 190, 198, 199
Shapter, Dr., 32
Siddons, Mrs., 151
Simpson, James Young, 201, 229
Smith, Adam, 17
Smith, Anne, 138
Smith, Harry, 103
Smith, Surgeon, 200

Smollett, Tobias, 9, 159, 207
Souza, José Joaquin de, 109, 112, 120
staff surgeon, 75, 88, 89, 97, 98, 103, 106–111, 113–115, 119–121, 123
Stafford, Marchioness of, 171
Sterne, Laurence, 2
Stewart, Duncan, 57, 58, 99
Stirling, James, 48, 49, 53, 98, 99, 101, 109
Stubbs, Richmond Robert, 37
sublime, 43, 57, 59, 100, 101, 215
surgeon, regimental, 32–34, 46, 56, 75, 76, 95, 96, 110, 113, 120, 123, 126, 128
Sutton, Charles, 114–117, 120–122
Syme, James, 201
Syme, Thomas, 150, 151, 164, 172, 174, 178, 186, 197

Tait, Mrs., 141
Talavera, 72
Tegart, Deputy Inspector, 88, 98, 103, 107
Thatcher, John, 201
Thomson, John, 32, 38, 133, 201
Torres Vedras, 84
Toulouse, 123
Treves, Frederick, 192
Trinity College, Dublin, 3, 15, 70

vaccination, 113, 143
Veitch, Mrs., 141
Viana, 126, 127, 130, 133
Vitoria, 108, 112, 118

Walker, Anne, 139, 142, 161, 173, 178
Wallace, Margaret, 190, 191, 196, 204
Walsh, Thomas, 43, 45
Waterloo, 129, 133
Wellington, Duke of, 56, 72, 76, 77, 81, 84, 88, 96, 97, 99–101, 104–106, 108, 111, 114, 115, 117, 119, 217
White, Lieutenant, 87, 89, 90
Whitney, Phyllis, 156
William IV, 196
Williamson, Alicia, 191
Wollstonecraft, Mary, 55, 144
Wylde, John, 81
Wynn, William, 115